W9-DHF-791

Weak versus Strong Sustainability

To Ratinha

Weak versus Strong Sustainability

Exploring the Limits of Two Opposing
Paradigms

Eric Neumayer

London School of Economics and Political Science, London, UK

Edward Elgar
Cheltenham, UK • Northampton, MA, USA

Published by
Edward Elgar Publishing Limited
Glensanda House
Montpellier Parade
Cheltenham
Glos GL50 1UA
UK

Edward Elgar Publishing, Inc.
136 West Street
Suite 202
Northampton
Massachusetts 01060
USA

HD
75.6
. N48
1999

A catalogue record for this book
is available from the British Library

Library of Congress Cataloguing in Publication Data

Neumayer, Eric, 1970–
        Weak versus strong sustainability : exploring the limits of two
    opposing paradigms / Eric Neumayer.
        Includes bibliographical references.
        1. Sustainable development. 2. Economic development—
    Environmental aspects. 3. Neoclassical school of economics.
    I. Title.
    HD75.6.N49 1999
    338.9—dc21   99–15404
                                                                      CIP

ISBN 1 84064 060 X

Printed and bound in Great Britain by Bookcraft (Bath) Ltd.

Contents

Figures

Tables

Variables

A	Pollution abatement
AC	Average resource extraction costs
C	Consumption
	Cost function
D	Resource discoveries
E	Harvest of renewable resources
F	Production function
G	'Human induced' growth of renewable resources
GS	'Genuine saving'
H	Hotelling rent
	Hamiltonian
K	Stock of man-made capital
L	Labour
M	Stock of human capital
M_E	Share of energy in total production costs
N	Investment in human capital
P	Stock of pollution
	Price
R	Resource depletion
RC	Resource receipts
S	Stock of non-renewable resources
SI	Sustainable income
T	Time variable
U	Utility function
X	Stock of accumulated resource discoveries
Z	Stock of renewable resources
a	Natural growth function (renewable resources)
b	Natural restoration function (pollution)
c	Exponent in production function
d	Exponent in production function
e	Exponent in production function
f	Expenditure function for non-renewable resource extraction
g	Expenditure function for resource exploration
h	Expenditure function for renewable resource harvesting

i	Expenditure function for pollution abatement
j	Expenditure function for investment into human capital
k	Rate of 'resource augmenting' technical progress
m	Rate of Hicks-neutral technical progress
n	Reserves to production ratio
p	Exponent in production function
q	Exponent in production function
r	Rate of interest
	Discount rate
s	Exponent in production function
t	Time index
u	Average rate of consumption growth
v	Parameter
w	Parameter
z	Static reserve index
π	Profit
σ	Elasticity of substitution
α	Elasticity of output with respect to man-made capital
	Parameter
β	Elasticity of output with respect to non-renewable resources
	Parameter
γ	Conversion factor converting production into pollution units
λ	Shadow value of man-made capital
	General Lagrangian multiplier
μ	Shadow value of the stock of non-renewable resources
ω	Shadow cost of the stock of resource discoveries
ϕ	Shadow value of the stock of renewable resources
ψ	Shadow cost of the stock of pollution
ξ	Shadow value of the stock of human capital
ρ	Pure rate of time preference
η	Elasticity of the marginal utility of consumption
Γ	Lagrangian

Abbreviations and Acronyms

Abbreviations that are rather unfamiliar are explicated in the main text on their first appearance. Familiar abbreviations are used without further explanation throughout.

AIDS	Acquired Immune Deficiency Syndrome
AES	Allen partial Elasticity of Substitution
bn	billion (thousand million)
CES	Constant Elasticity of Substitution
CFC	Chlorofluorocarbons
CO_2	Carbon Dioxide
CSERGE	Centre for Social and Economic Research on the Global Environment
CV	Contingent Valuation
DICE	Dynamic Integrated Model of Climate and the Economy
DNA	Deoxyribonucleic Acid
DDT	Dichlorodiphenyltrichloroethane
EGrossS	Extended Gross Saving
EGS II	Extended Genuine Saving II
EGS II (El Serafy)	Extended Genuine Saving II as computed with the El Serafy method
EGS II (World Bank)	Extended Genuine Saving II as computed with the World Bank method
EKC	Environmental Kuznets Curve
ENetS	Extended Net Saving
FAO	Food and Agricultural Organisation
GEF	Global Environmental Facility
GPI	Genuine Progress Indicator
gNNP	green Net National Product
GDP	Gross Domestic Product
GNP	Gross National Product
GS	Genuine Saving
HDI	Human Development Index
IPCC	Intergovernmental Panel on Climate Change

ISEW	Index of Sustainable Economic Welfare
LDC	Less Developed Country
MRS	Marginal Rate of Substitution
NNP	Net National Product
NPP	Net Primary Productivity
NO_x	Nitrogen Oxides
OECD	Organisation for Economic Cooperation and Development
OPEC	Organisation of Petroleum Exporting Countries
R&D	Research and Development
SD	Sustainable Development
SI	Sustainable Income
SMS	Safe Minimum Standard
SO_x	Sulphur Oxides
SS	Strong Sustainability
UK	United Kingdom
UNDP	United Nations' Development Programme
UNEP	United Nations' Environment Programme
US	United States of America
WS	Weak Sustainability
WTA	Willingness-to-accept
WTP	Willingness-to-pay

Preface

In writing this book I have tried to ensure that it is open to a broad audience. Chapter 3 should be accessible for interested readers from all backgrounds who for the first time come across the issues of resource availability for sustained economic growth and the environmental consequences thereof. Equally, Chapter 4 examines the preservation of natural capital in a world of risk, uncertainty and ignorance without abstract mathematical modelling which makes economic reasoning so inaccessible for non-economics majors. Chapter 5 on measuring sustainability is more advanced, presents a more formal analysis and presupposes a more substantial economic education. Even so, however, the main lines of argument can be understood with only a minor economic background. I hope that I have written a book that is of use to everybody interested in the two opposing paradigms of weak and strong sustainability, be they economists or not.

Parts of earlier drafts have been presented at research seminars at various academic institutions and international academic conferences. The book has much benefited from discussions with the participants of these events as well as from talking to James Putzel (special thanks), Brian Barry, James K. Boyce, Lord Meghnad Desai, Mathias Hafner, Friedrich Hinterberger and Michael Jacobs. I would also like to thank David Pearce and Paul Ekins for many helpful comments. All remaining errors are mine as are all views expressed here. I thank Kirk Hamilton from the World Bank and several people from the US Bureau of Mines for providing material and data that would have been difficult to get hold of. I would also like to thank my parents, my sister and my friends in Germany who were there for me in times of despair.

Shorter and revised versions of various parts of the book have been previously published in journals: Section 2.4 in *Energy Policy* **27** (1), 33–43 (Neumayer 1999c), published by Elsevier Science; Chapter 4 in the *International Journal of Sustainable Development and World Ecology*, **5** (1), 27–42 (Neumayer 1998b), published by Parthenon Publishing; Section 3.3 in *Zeitschrift für Umweltpolitik und Umweltrecht*, **2/98**, 161–76 (Neumayer 1998a), published by Deutscher Fachverlag. Section 3.2 is forthcoming in *Journal of Economic Surveys* (Neumayer 1999g), published by Blackwell Publishers. Section 5.1.5 is forthcoming in *Environmental and Resource Economics* (Neumayer 1999f) and Section 5.1.6 is forthcoming in *Social*

Indicators Research (Neumayer 1999d), both published by Kluwer Academic.

Financial support from the German National Scholarship Foundation, the German Academic Exchange Service and the European Commission's DGXII Marie Curie Research Scheme is gratefully acknowledged.

London, June 1999.

Eric Neumayer
Lecturer in Environment & Development
London School of Economics and Political Science

1. Introduction and Overview

In recent years support for 'sustainable development' (henceforth: SD) has become very widespread. At the Rio summit in 1992 the vast majority of nation-states have formally committed themselves to SD in signing Agenda 21 (UNCED 1992). Especially since then, there has been hardly any politician, academic or businessperson who does not call for making development sustainable. In some sense this is not surprising: SD is like freedom or peace — that is, something to which no reasonable person would overtly object. Development always sounds good and that it has to be sustainable seems self-evident.

In this book two economic paradigms of SD — 'weak sustainability' and 'strong sustainability' — will be looked at with the objective of exploring their limits. 'Weak sustainability' (henceforth: WS) is based upon the work of two neoclassical economists: Robert Solow (1974a, 1974c, 1986, 1993a, 1993b), a Nobel Laureate, and John Hartwick (1977, 1978a, 1978b, 1990, 1993), a famous resource economist. WS can be interpreted as an extension to neoclassical welfare economics. It is based on the belief that what matters for future generations is only the total aggregate stock of 'man-made'[1] and 'natural' capital[2] (and possibly other forms of capital as well), but not natural capital as such. Loosely speaking, according to WS, it does not matter whether the current generation uses up non-renewable resources or dumps CO_2 in the atmosphere as long as enough machineries, roads and ports are built up in compensation. Because natural capital is regarded as being essentially substitutable in the production of consumption goods and as a direct provider of utility, I call WS the 'substitutability paradigm'.

In opposition to WS stands 'strong sustainability' (henceforth: SS). While WS is a relatively clear paradigm in that it builds upon a well-established core of neoclassical welfare economics, SS is not. It is more difficult to define SS and pin down its implications as many different scholars have contributed their own views on what SS should be. However, it is fair to say that the essence of SS is the belief that natural capital itself should be preserved for future generations in addition to the total aggregate capital stock. This is because natural capital is regarded as non-substitutable both in the production of consumption goods and as a more direct provider of utility. Hence, I call SS the 'non-substitutability paradigm'.

The objective of this book is to explore the limits of the two opposing paradigms of sustainability. In particular, it will assess whether either paradigm can provide a clear course of action and a measure[3] for whether sustainability is achieved or not. The book is an exercise in exploring the limits of what we can know about what sustainability requires. Its motivation stems from the fact that while reference to both paradigms is widespread in both the academic and non-academic literature on SD, a comprehensive analysis of the limits of WS and SS is missing.

The book is structured as follows: Chapter 2 discusses conceptual, ethical and paradigmatic issues of SD. The definitions, assumptions and the methodology of the analysis in the book are laid down. Then some arguments are presented which make SD plausible as an ethical choice. A kind of time-consistency problem of SD is discussed which results from the fact that the current generation can only commit itself, but not coming generations, to SD. Finally, two misunderstandings about what sustainability requires are corrected. It is shown that SD neither locks society into eternal poverty if it is poorly endowed at the start nor demands the choice of greatly inferior utility paths. These ethical issues of SD are dealt with before a distinction is made between WS and SS, because its arguments apply to both paradigms. It provides the foundation for the main analysis in later parts of the book.

Next in Chapter 2 the two opposing weak and strong paradigms of sustainability are characterised. It is shown that WS can be interpreted as an extension to neoclassical welfare economics with the additional requirement of keeping the value of total capital non-declining over time.[4] The implications of the substitutability assumptions are explained and 'genuine saving' (GS) is introduced as the theoretically correct measure for WS. As regards SS, two differing possible interpretations are given. One calls for keeping the value of natural capital in addition to the value of total capital non-declining. The other one calls for preserving the physical stocks of certain forms of natural capital. The implications of the non-substitutability assumption are explained and the 'sustainability gap' is introduced as a measure for SS.

Finally, Chapter 2 stresses the importance of the substitutability assumption using global warming as a case study. It is shown that the predominant critique against the neoclassical approach towards global warming with its recommendation for only minor emission abatement is misguided. This predominant critique is about lowering the rate of discount to be used. It is shown that the real disagreement must be over whether or not natural capital is substitutable. If one accepts the substitutability assumption, then calls for lowering the discount rate would lead to ethically dubious conclusions and to inconsistent and inefficient policy choices. Subsitutability is the issue, not discounting.

Chapter 3 analyses the validity of the basic assumptions of both paradigms. As mentioned, WS regards natural capital as being essentially substitutable both in the production of consumption goods and as a more direct provider of utility. SS, in contrast, regards natural capital as being essentially non-substitutable. Chapter 3 first examines existing theoretical and empirical evidence on the availability of natural resources for the production of consumption goods. Four propositions of resource optimism are stated and critically assessed. These propositions imply that a natural resource can either be substituted with another resource or man-made capital, or that the feedback mechanisms triggered by rising resource prices and technical progress will work to overcome any apparent constraint. Second, it discusses whether future generations can be compensated for long-term environmental degradation. It argues that an answer to this question must be speculative to some extent as we cannot know the preferences of future generations. It also argues that there are good reasons against both extreme positions. In other words, neither perfect substitutability nor perfect non-substitutability of natural capital as a provider of utility seems reasonable. As will be explained in Section 2.3.1, p. 23, WS tends to be rather optimistic about the environmental consequences of economic growth, however. Therefore it has to rely less on the assumption that natural capital is substitutable as a direct provider of utility. In other words, it has to rely less on the assumption that increased consumption opportunities can compensate future generations for the loss of natural capital in the form of long-term environmental degradation. Chapter 3 therefore analyses thirdly the link between economic growth and environmental degradation. The theoretical case both in favour of environmental optimism and environmental pessimism are put forward. However, since the likely environmental consequences of future economic growth cannot be solved theoretically, the existing empirical evidence on this question is examined as well.

In short, Chapter 3 comes to the conclusion that on strict terms neither paradigm of sustainability can be falsified. Science can therefore provide no reliable answer on which of the two paradigms of sustainability is 'correct'. As is so often the case for extra-paradigmatic disagreements, support for one paradigm or the other depends much on basic beliefs (here about possibilities of substitution and technical progress) which are non-falsifiable under scientific standards. A short discussion at the end of Chapter 3 shows that this conclusion does not depend on a restrictive theory of science.

The book offers an alternative explanation to that of Norton (1995) who argues that the debate between proponents of weak and strong sustainability cannot be resolved because there is no agreement on the scope of the true subject matter nor a consensually accepted methodology. Chapter 3 argues that it would still be impossible to unequivocally confirm or disconfirm either paradigm of sustainability, even if there was agreement on the subject matter and a consensually accepted methodology.

That, strictly speaking, both paradigms of sustainability are non-falsifiable implies that neither paradigm can be unambiguously supported by science. However, it does not imply of course that science cannot help in informing public policy choices with regard to the depletion of natural capital. Chapter 4 takes up the discussion where it ended in Chapter 3 and argues that a combination of the distinctive features of natural capital with the prevalence of risk, uncertainty and ignorance make a *persuasive* case for the preservation of certain forms of natural capital that provide basic life-support functions. It argues that, in principle, there are good reasons for the protection of global life-support resources such as biodiversity, the ozone layer and the global climate as well as the restriction of the accumulation of pollutants, unsustainable harvesting and soil erosion. Conversely, no explicit conservation policy for non-renewable resources used in the production of consumption goods seems warranted. In essence, therefore, Chapter 4 argues that science seems to support WS more with regard to the 'source' side of the economy and support SS more with regard to the 'sink' side of the economy.

However, it would be wrong to conclude that for the reasons put forward in Chapter 4 it can be inferred that the totality of the mentioned forms of natural capital providing basic life-support functions has to be preserved. This is because one has to distinguish between total and marginal values. While these forms of natural capital can be argued to be non-substitutable *in toto*, this does not mean that they cannot be substituted for to a certain extent at the margin. Economic valuation techniques can help to set these marginal decisions on rational grounds. However, it is often argued that because of uncertainty and ignorance and problems in valuing complex environmental resources cost–benefit analysis will be biased against natural capital. Three policy principles are discussed that are supposed to remove this bias: the precautionary principle, environmental bond systems and safe minimum standards. In one way or another they give more priority to preserving natural capital in the presence of uncertainty and ignorance.

Still, the question remains how much cost society should be willing to incur in order to preserve certain forms of natural capital. One option is to deliberately ignore opportunity costs. Given uncertainty and ignorance about the consequences of depleting natural capital one might choose to refrain from any marginal decisions and call for the preservation of the remaining totality of certain forms of natural capital. From this perspective, it is better to incur the definite and potentially large costs of preservation in order to prevent the uncertain, but potentially tremendous, costs of depletion. It is argued in Chapter 4, however, that following such a policy advice would be unreasonable. It would potentially impose substantial costs of preservation on the current generation and would most likely not be in the best interest of future generations either. Society has to face the fact that every policy decision for preserving natural capital implies an opportunity cost that has to be balanced somehow against the benefits of preservation.[5] Deliberately ignoring opportunity costs is tantamount to avoiding the often awkward decisions on how to spend scarce resources on which of several competing claims.

If, however, opportunity costs cannot be ignored, we are essentially back in the world of cost–benefit analysis and economic valuation. The only difference is that both the precautionary principle and safe minimum standards imply that the costs of preserving natural capital can exceed its estimated benefits by a certain factor. This is because of uncertainty and ignorance involved in the valuation of the benefits from preserving natural capital.

Science can help society in identifying certain forms of natural capital that provide basic life-support functions. But because of uncertainty and ignorance it cannot tell society exactly how far it can go with depleting natural capital without endangering the well-being of future generations. Equally, economic science can help society in providing information on the likely benefits and costs of preservation. But it cannot tell society how much present and certain costs relative to benefits it should be willing to incur in order to achieve future and uncertain benefits. That is, it cannot tell society how risk averse it should be with regard to the depletion of natural capital. The precautionary principle and safe minimum standards imply that preservation costs may exceed preservation benefits by a certain factor. Economic valuation techniques provide best available information on both benefits and costs. But to determine the factor by how much costs are allowed to exceed the benefits for preserving certain forms of natural capital is a political question, not a scientific one. In essence, this is the conclusion of Chapter 4.

One further thing economics can contribute is to help society in minimising the costs of preservation. Chapter 4 therefore also discusses a number of policy measures that (allegedly) minimise the costs of preservation, namely: the abolition of subsidies and the abatement of pollution that are both environmentally and economically harmful, the substitution of market-based for command-and-control instruments in environmental policy, the substitution of ecotaxes for taxes on labour and man-made capital, and the tightening of environmental regulation such that firms' competitiveness increases.

Chapter 5 assesses whether sustainability, as defined in this book, can be measured in practice. An optimal growth model is presented in order to show how 'genuine saving' (GS), the theoretically correct measure of WS, can be derived from so-called green net national product (gNNP). The model is set up for the case of a closed economy and the necessary amendments for the open economy case are discussed. Then a series of problems for practical measurements of GS are put forward. The most serious and comprehensive attempt to measure WS so far (World Bank 1997a) is critically assessed. Sensitivity analysis shows that the World Bank's conclusions about the dismal performance of many developing countries with respect to sustainability are largely reversed if the so-called 'El Serafy' method is used for resource accounting instead of the Bank's method. This method is argued to have some properties that render it more desirable for use in resource accounting. The examination then turns to the Index of Sustainable Economic Welfare (ISEW). Again, sensitivity analysis is employed to show that its conclusions about the dismal performance of all examined countries with respect to 'sustainable economic welfare' depend on a few, rather arbitrary, assumptions that lack a sound theoretical foundation.

Next, Chapter 5 turns to measuring SS. The analysis in Chapter 4 implies that the second interpretation of SS should be favoured over the first one: it is more sensible to preserve the physical stocks of certain forms of natural capital (to some extent). In contrast, keeping the aggregate total value of natural capital constant does not preclude the possibility that certain forms of natural capital that provide basic life-support functions are endangered or become irreversibly lost. In order to measure SS thus defined, one needs first of all sustainability standards for certain forms of capital. Environmental information systems and indicators can then provide data on whether the standards are fulfilled or not. Finally, one needs information about the costs of hypothetically reaching the standards in order to value monetarily the 'sustainability gap' between the standards and the economy's actual performance. As with WS, a number of problems with practical attempts to measure SS are put forward. In contrast to WS, however, no sensitivity analysis could be employed for empirical applications. The methodology for measuring SS is still in development and to the best of my knowledge there does not exist any comprehensive study yet that could be critically assessed. This will be left to future research.

Finally, Chapter 5 concludes that practical measures of SD have to be treated with a good deal of caution. As concerns measuring SS, one has to wait for some comprehensive applied studies in order to see how reliable they can be. As concerns WS, the indicative reliability of GS depends on a number of crucial assumptions and simplifications. The reliability can be increased in employing the El Serafy method for resource accounting and in maintaining efforts to provide more and better quality data and to include more variables. However, not all problems can easily be overcome and some are presumably simply unsolvable. Any practical measure of WS will always and by necessity be partial: it can only be measured what can be measured reasonably well. Other factors of sustainability that cannot be measured have to be left out. In practice therefore, there can never be such a thing as a completely reliable and comprehensive indicator of WS. One needs to be cautious therefore in interpreting the numbers that are generated — see the section on the World Bank (1997a) study and the concluding section to Chapter 5 where some policy implications for practical measures of WS are discussed.

More formal derivations of basic principles and results can be found in the accompanying appendices.

NOTES

1   A more neutral term from a gender perspective would be 'human-made' capital. To distinguish this form of capital more clearly from 'human' capital I shall refer to it as 'man-made' capital, however.
2   Capital is defined here broadly as a stock that provides current and future flows of service. For more detail see Section 2.1, p. 8.
3   Note that throughout the book I use the terms 'measure' and 'indicator' interchangeably.
4   Value of capital should be interpreted throughout the book in real terms in the sense that the value has to be adjusted for inflation.
5   The usage of the terms 'benefits' and 'costs' might at points be confusing to the reader. Whether something counts as a benefit or a cost depends on the reference point and on the perspective one takes. The benefits of preserving natural capital are the costs of depleting natural capital. Similarly, the benefits of depleting natural capital are the costs of preserving natural capital, where benefits and costs are to be interpreted inclusive of opportunity costs.

2. Conceptual, Ethical and Paradigmatic Issues of Sustainable Development

This chapter will lay the foundation for the main analysis in the following chapters. Section 2.1 defines the major terms used, describes the main simplifying assumptions and the methodology that will be employed. Section 2.2 discusses a few ethical issues of SD. It provides some justification for choosing SD, discusses a time-consistency problem of SD and resolves two misunderstandings about SD. Those readers who are most interested in WS versus SS itself might want to skip this section and go straight to Section 2.3, which introduces in more detail the two opposing paradigms. There it is explained what their major differences are with respect to the possibilities of substituting for natural capital and how one can measure whether sustainability is achieved. Section 2.4 provides a kind of case study on global warming in order to stress the importance of the substitutability assumption. It is argued that the conflict between those who demand drastic emission reductions and those who demand only minor reductions is often wrongly portrayed as a conflict about the right rate of discount. Instead, it is shown that discounting is not the real dividing issue, but substitutability of natural capital is. Again, those readers who are not particularly interested in global warming and who need not be convinced of the importance of the substitutability assumption might want to skip this section and go straight to the main analysis in Chapter 3.

2.1 DEFINITIONS, ASSUMPTIONS, METHODOLOGY

In this book the analysis is confined to two starkly differing *economic* paradigms of SD, namely weak and strong sustainability.[1] They are the most influential paradigms within debates and policy discussions about SD. For example, the World Bank, as the predominant institution in the international development business, supports WS (World Bank 1992).[2] On the other hand, SS has gained widespread support among many 'ecological economists', as well as among environmentally committed scientists from other disciplines and non-academic environmentalists (see, for example, the contributions to the journal *Ecological Economics*, published by the International Society for Ecological Economics).

Let us start with some definitions and assumptions. In some sense, SD is a vague concept — so much so that Pezzey (1992b) can present a whole gallery of differing definitions. Nevertheless, a definition most proponents of an *economic* concept of SD would be likely to accept is the following: development is defined here to be *sustainable if it does not decrease the capacity to provide non-declining per capita utility for infinity*.

For the analysis that follows, those items that form the capacity to provide utility are called capital. Capital is defined here broadly as a stock that provides current and future (potential) flows of service. Natural capital is then the totality of nature — resources, plants, species and ecosystems — that is capable of providing human beings with material and non-material flows of service.[3] Man-made capital is what has traditionally been subsumed under 'capital', that is factories, machineries, roads and so on. Human capital is knowledge and skill embodied in the human brain. For the main part of the analysis I shall only look at the first two forms of capital since those are the ones WS and SS concentrate on — human capital as well as any potentially further forms of capital are neglected until Chapter 5, p. 140, where it is assessed whether sustainability can be measured in practice. Note that I use the terms 'conserving capital' and 'preserving capital' interchangeably. The same applies to the terms 'utility' and 'welfare'.

To speak of 'nature' as natural capital is common in the literature on SD and should not pose any problem — not even to environmentalists who are critical of economic approaches towards the environment. If capital is simply defined as a stock that provides flows of service, why not regard nature as a capital stock that provides all kinds of environmental services?

Obviously the definition of SD used here is anthropocentric. Nature has value if and only if humans value nature. Humans might value nature for whatever reasons, however, and not merely because it contributes to the production of consumption goods or directly produces utility through environmental amenities. Humans might be ecocentric in their valuations and might very well value nature as such in attributing to it 'intrinsic' value (existence value). But it is still humans who determine the value. There is no value independent of human valuation in the definition of sustainability used here.

Note that SD is defined here as development that maintains the *capacity* to provide non-declining per capita utility for infinity. In other words, it is defined in terms of maintaining the capital that is necessary to provide non-declining future utility. It is not defined in terms of non-declining utility for infinity itself. Prominent environmental philosophers have similarly distinguished non-declining utility from non-declining opportunities (for example Page 1983, p. 53; Barry 1991, p. 262).

Note that my definition of SD is not utilitarian. That is, I do *not* embrace a definition of SD as '*maximised present-value* utility non-declining for infinity' which can be represented in compact form as:

$$SD = \arg\max \int_0^\infty U(t) \cdot e^{-\rho t} dt \text{ s.t. } dU/dt \geq 0 \ \forall t \tag{2.1}$$

where U is again (per capita) utility, ρ is the social discount rate and t a time index. I reject utilitarianism for my definition of SD for mainly two reasons: first because SD is defined here in terms of maintaining the capacity to provide non-declining future utility, not in utility terms itself (see the discussion above). Second, I reject utilitarianism because I regard it to be too restrictive an assumption. Utilitarianism leaves no space for free choice: utility *must* be shifted inter-temporally so as to maximise the discounted stream of utility over infinite time (subject to the non-decline constraint). *Voluntary* sacrifices of the current generation for the sake of future generations are not allowed according to this social decision rule: the sacrifice would either increase or decrease the discounted stream of utility; in the first case, the current generation *must* make the sacrifice, in the second case it is *forbidden* to do so.

On the other hand, utilitarianism has some advantages as well: the first is again tractability, which is one of the reasons why it is so commonly used in economics. The second is that present-value maximisation as the most common form of utilitarianism has some desirable ethical properties as well. If future generations are better off than the present one, then a positive discount rate can be reasonable in order to give more weight to the more present (and by presumption less well-off) generations. Discounting is not compelling, however. If it turns out that the appropriate discount rate should be zero, then the present-value maximisation will simply collapse into value maximisation. On the other hand, if the current generation was better off than future generations, a negative discount rate would be demanded by utilitarianism. The argument for the ethical desirability of discounting within a utilitarian framework is formalised in Appendix 2, p. 214, where the so-called Ramsey rule is derived from a dynamic optimisation model.

Clearly, my definition of SD does not give a complete social decision rule, since there are likely to be an almost infinite number of development paths that maintain the capacity to provide non-declining utility for infinity. It follows that there has to be some decision criterion, a social welfare function in the language of economists, to choose from different paths. The utilitarian criterion is to take that path of non-declining utility which maximises the

present (that is: the discounted) value. But an infinite number of other decision criteria exist the most prominent of which are listed in any textbook on
welfare economics — see, for example, Ng (1983). My definition of SD just
calls for 'maintaining the capacity to provide per capita utility non-declining
for infinity' whatever the complementary social decision criterion is. Note,
however, that I use a utilitarian framework at various places throughout the
book in analysing WS, because utilitarianism is usually embraced by proponents of WS (subject to the sustainability constraint). The same holds true for
Section 2.4, p. 29, where the importance of the substitutability assumption for
the case of global warming is stressed. This is because the analysis there focuses on the neoclassical approach towards global warming, as represented by
Nordhaus (1994), which is clearly utilitarian.

WS and SS have radically differing assumptions about which forms of
capital are necessary for providing non-declining utility. In order to highlight
this difference and to make the analysis in the book possible, I will assume for
simplicity that the utility of a representative individual can sufficiently be
described by a utility function of the following form

$$U = U(C,Z,P), \tag{2.2}$$

$$\partial U/\partial C, \ \partial U/\partial Z \ > 0, \ \partial U/\partial P < 0$$

where C is consumption, Z is the stock of renewable resources providing
environmental amenities and P is the stock of pollution. The first two components contribute positively to utility, hence their partial first derivatives are
positive. The last component, pollution, on the other hand, reduces utility,
hence its first derivative is negative. Note that I have split up natural capital
into the stock of renewable resources and the stock of pollution which, of
course, is a capital 'bad' rather than a capital good. I have done so to keep the
presentation consistent with later chapters. Nothing of substance would
change if we put Z and P together into one variable for natural capital (or
rather Z and some variable for the pollution-assimilative capacity of the environment).

Simplifying somewhat, WS holds that to achieve sustainability it is merely
necessary to preserve the value of the total aggregate stock of capital. Looking at the utility function in (2.2) it is clear that WS must assume that the
components in the utility function are substitutes. SS instead calls for preserving the natural capital stock itself as well. One of the reasons for this
additional requirement is that natural capital is regarded as non-substitutable
in providing utility. For more precise information on the difference between
WS and SS see Section 2.3, p. 22.

Why are the *stocks* of renewable resources and pollution included in the utility function rather than the resource and pollution *flow*? The reason is that if people have preferences for environmental quality, it makes sense to assume that they care about the whole stock of directly utility relevant renewable resources and pollution and not just incremental changes to the stock.[4] Why are *non-renewable* resources not included in the utility function? Because non-renewable resources are important for the production of consumption goods, but do (mostly) not produce any direct utility. Nobody derives direct utility from mineral and energy resources, but from renewable resources such as forests, wildlife and so on.[5] For the same reason, man-made capital is not included in the utility function: it does not provide any direct utility, but is a major input into the production of consumption goods.

Population growth is exogenous to the analysis. Whatever the size of the population, SD calls for maintaining the capacity to provide non-declining *per capita* utility. This requirement seems to be reasonable since the present generation is responsible for population growth. It can either reduce population growth or increase the capacity to provide utility to comply with the *per capita* requirement.[6] I concede that keeping population growth exogenous to the analysis is not satisfactory. But as Solow (1986, p. 149) has put it: 'The welfare economics of an endogenously changing population is altogether murky'.[7]

That the capacity to provide non-declining per capita utility should be maintained *for infinity* is more for convenience. Even the universe and hence humankind might come to an end in finite time, but since this end is beyond all human time understanding, it seems reasonable to circumscribe the distant end somewhat metaphorically as 'for infinity'. Doing so also ensures better mathematical tractability. What is actually meant with 'for infinity' is that development cannot be sustainable if it maintains the capacity to provide non-declining utility only temporarily and leads to a decline in this capacity after some finite time.

Speaking of the 'present' and 'future' generations is of course a fictitious simplification. Every day some people are born while others die so there is a permanent flow of people into and out of the present generation, while 'future' generations are not a given but are contingent on the 'present' generation's actions. One has to interpret the notions of 'present' and 'future' generations as ideal types in Max Weber's (1922) usage of the term. Therefore, they are not really existent but they help enormously in conceptualising and analysing academic problems.

The analysis of this book mainly looks at *inter*-generational as opposed to *intra*-generational distributional questions. That is, in effect, for most of the analysis I assume that either the *intra*-generational distribution is just or that it is otherwise taken care of. These are strong assumptions, of course, abstracting from existing inequities. Inter-generational fairness questions are at the centre of concern of most proponents of SD, but that is not a good reason to exclude intra-generational conflicts *per se.*[8] Heyes and Liston-Heyes (1995, p. 3) are presumably correct in arguing that 'it may be that those embroiled in the environmental sustainability debate have become so obsessed with intergenerational equity that intragenerational equity considerations have been swept under the rug'.

My justification is that I want to focus on inter-generational distributional questions here.[9] Ignoring to a large extent intra-generational distributional issues makes the analysis much easier. And again, this admittedly restrictive assumption ensures tractability, because then I can let different generations be represented by a representative agent of each generation. At certain points I shall loosen this assumption somewhat, however, and ask what consequences the unequal intra-generational income distribution has on the likelihood of achieving sustainability. This will be the case, for example, in Section 2.4, p. 29, on global warming and in Section 4.5, p. 123, on the opportunity costs of preserving natural capital.

The methodology I am using is that of the boundedly rational individual who attempts to maximise his or her utility. This methodology is usually called the economic paradigm although it is debatable whether there can be anything like *the* economic paradigm when economists themselves disagree about the specifics of 'their' paradigm (on this see, for example, Sen 1987 and Hausman 1992).

I want to put emphasis on the word *boundedly.* I am interested in real-world problems and I do not want to dispose of those problems by simply assuming them away. Hence I do not assume the presence of either perfect information, or perfect foresight, or boundless computational capacity. For a good case for this view on 'rationality', see Simon (1982).

The motivation for choosing the economic paradigm as methodology is not that I am convinced that it reflects actual human behaviour at all times and to all extent correctly. There is more to human life than being a rational utility maximiser. But there is no better alternative to the economic paradigm and especially so if one is looking for something tractable. The main reason for sticking to the economic methodology is a different one, however: I want to grant the paradigms of sustainability I am looking at the most favourable conditions, especially because of my primary interest in exploring their limits. Since I am looking at economic paradigms of sustainability, it seems only fair to analyse them according to their own standards. It is all too easy to dismiss a paradigm as pure nonsense from a perspective outside the discipline. I am taking WS and SS seriously as economic paradigms; but I can only do so by basing my analysis on the economic methodology.

In Section 2.2, I present some arguments why it is justifiable to pursue SD. After that, it will simply be assumed that the ethical decision to strive for SD as defined above has already been taken. I assume that policy makers act in accordance with the SD goal without pursuing any other interest that would contradict this aim. That is, they are credibly committed to SD. In terms of political economy this assumption is utterly naive, of course. It fits nicely into the analysis here, however, which is essentially about exploring the limits of the two paradigms of sustainability as if they were the central goal for policy makers.

What about consumer sovereignty? It is a central value for many econo-mists, but it can only refer to the sovereignty of the present generation's con-sumers since future generations are not present today and cannot reveal their preferences in today's markets. Of course, with overlapping generations and parents who are somewhat altruistic towards their offspring, there exists some protection for the welfare of future generations (Howarth and Norgaard 1993; Barro and Sala-i-Martin 1995, pp. 128–37). Indeed, depending on how ex-actly parents value the welfare of their offspring, SD might not clash with consumer sovereignty. But in general, there is no guarantee that private altru-ism will lead to sustainable or socially optimal outcomes both because this parental altruism might very well be of insufficient reach and because the welfare of future generations has to a certain extent the characteristics of a public good since what is beneficial for my own children often will be benefi-cial to others as well (Sen 1967).[10] Hence, consumer sovereignty could well conflict with SD. I assume here, however, that either consumers also act in accordance with the SD goal or — in case of conflict — that consumer sover-eignty is overridden by the policy makers. This leaves open the question why consumers should vote for policy makers who override their preferences, of course. However, I am assuming away any problems of political economy in order to focus on my central research questions which presuppose that society is committed to SD. In this sense, the danger of 'some tyranny of decision-making in the name of sustainability' (Pearce 1997b, p. 9) is excluded in my analysis *by assumption*.

In some instances I shall present models to prove a point or for reasons of analytical rigour. These will mainly be simple models and I shall always ex-plain the intuition behind the models presented. It is of great importance for me that I write clearly and concisely in a manner that is understandable not only by trained economists but also by everybody interested in SD with some basic knowledge of economics. The assessment is to a fairly large extent conceptual, but wherever possible empirical evidence to support conceptual reasoning is included and I undertake empirically oriented sensitivity analyses in Chapter 5 in assessing whether sustainability can be measured in practice.

2.2   THE ETHICS OF SUSTAINABLE DEVELOPMENT

Why is it that — past concern about the welfare of coming generations notwithstanding — scrutinising the consequences of economic activity on the
capacity for generating future utility has only recently become an explicit
academic enterprise? The answer is that it is only now that humankind itself
and its economic activity has reached a scale that is at least potentially big
enough to threaten the welfare prospects (if not the existence) of future generations. The exponential rise in human numbers and in human resource appropriation and environmental destruction especially over the last few decades is unprecedented in history (see WRI various years). Also, human activity has now reached a scale that is capable of generating new environmental
hazards. The greenhouse effect is an example which shows that the uncertainties mankind has to cope with have vastly increased (IPCC 1996a, 1996b).

But this fact alone is not enough to make a case for SD. Ethical principles
— and the aim to maintain the capacity to provide non-declining per capita
utility for ever is such a principle — never follow from facts alone. Hence this
section briefly discusses the ethics of SD before the following main Chapters
take the commitment to SD for granted. Section 2.2.1 presents arguments for
committing to SD. Section 2.2.2 discusses a kind of time-consistency problem
of SD, that is, the incentive problems that arise from the hazard that coming
generations deviate from SD. Section 2.2.3 resolves two misunderstandings
about what SD actually requires and clears the way for the main analysis in
later chapters.

2.2.1   Reasons for Committing to Sustainable Development

Before actually providing some arguments to derive SD as an ethical principle let us first make explicit what everybody understands intuitively: why is it
that the welfare of future generations cannot simply be left to their own care?
The answer is of course that their very existence and the conditions of their
existence are dependent on the present generation's actions. Future generations are 'downstream in time' so to speak and are therefore vulnerable to the
choices made 'upstream in time'. This vulnerability is exacerbated by the fact
that future generations almost by definition are not present in today's market
and political decisions, that they have no present voice or vote or market
power. However, the fundamental asymmetry between the present and the
future really goes both ways: everything the present does can affect the future,
nothing that the future does can affect the present any more. Harm that is
undertaken now cannot as such be undone in the future, but, equally, present
sacrifices for the benefit of the future cannot be compensated for by the future

because by that time the present generation will not be around. This fundamental asymmetry puts the present generation into a strong position of domi-
nance: it is an inter-temporal dictator, not (necessarily) by its own wish but
simply due to the fact that the flow of time is unidirectional and cannot be
reversed. A natural seductive question is then: why not exploit this unequal
position and maximise our own utility without any concern for the future?
'Après nous le déluge?' Indeed, why not?

A positive reply could be that since people have children this shows their
concern for the future. The problem with this argument is that not all people
have children, that some who do have them, treat them rather badly and that
while people might care about their own children and grandchildren and
great-grandchildren maybe, as soon as we consider the distant future things
have become already so remote that nobody could claim direct kinship rela-
tions any more. Immediate offspring concern does not reach as far as the
consequences of our economic activity do — global warming being a case in
point.

More generally, the positive argument does not answer the question *why*
we should care for the future. As I said, normative principles do not follow
from facts. So let us come up with a normative argument. Maybe we should
care for the future because it is right or just to do so. But not a lot has been
gained therewith, the question then being why concern for the future is right
or just.

One possible answer was given by Immanuel Kant's deontological moral
theory which found its most widely known expression in his categorical imperative: 'Act only according to that maxim by which you can at the same
time will that it should become a universal law' (Kant 1785, p. 51, my trans-
lation). Following this imperative, we should not only care for the future as
such, but even espouse the principle of maintaining the capacity to provide
non-declining future utility. This is because we could not wish that any other
principle should become a universal law since this would imply that we possibly would have been worse off due to decisions of others in the past, which
is not in our own interest.

However, the next question is then 'why should we follow the categorical
imperative?'. As with all moral principles, there can be no conclusive, definitive answer that could not be questioned for some reason or other. Nevertheless, a good argument for following the categorical imperative can be made
by applying the 'veil of ignorance' of John Rawls's (1972) Theory of Justice.[11] According to Rawls, moral principles are considered just or fair if they
could be chosen by a representative rational individual in an 'original position' behind a virtual veil of ignorance concerning his or her future position
both in time and space and his or her social position in society.[12] They are
considered fair precisely because, due to this ignorance, the representative

individual cannot construct principles that are directly designed to further his or her own advantage. What is important for our analysis here is that the representative individual would not know which generation he or she would belong to. Hence accepting the categorical imperative as a moral norm, and the principle of sustainability following therefrom, could be said to lie in the best self-interest of the individual: if I do not know which generation I shall belong to, then the categorical imperative and the principle that no generation is allowed to gain at the expense of future generations could be said to protect my interests best.

Note, however, that the imperative does not follow compellingly from the original position. If the representative individual behind the veil of ignorance exhibited strong risk preference he or she might be willing to accept a 'first come first serve' rule in which the first generations are allowed to improve their own lot at the expense of the welfare and, indeed, the existence of later generations. On the other hand, the acceptance of the categorical imperative does not depend on extreme risk averseness, as the 'maximin' or 'difference' principle does, which Rawls himself derived from his theory of the original position.[13] For more on the distinction between the principle of sustainability and the maximin principle see Section 2.2.3.1, p. 19.

To summarise, arguments derived from Kant's deontological moral philosophy and from a Rawlsian 'original position' point of view can make SD plausible as an ethical choice. Of course, many ethical issues have not been discussed here (such as Parfit's (1983) 'non-identity-problem'). But the book is in general not about moral philosophy. The limited purpose of this small section was to give a start-up motivation for committing to SD and to show that the principle of sustainability is not an implausible moral norm for intergenerational decision making.

2.2.2 The Time-consistency Problem of Sustainable Development

In this section a problem is highlighted that is rarely recognised in the literature on SD. The problem is as follows: assume that the present generation commits itself to SD, that is to maintain the capacity to provide non-declining per capita utility *into the indefinite future*. Obviously, it can only control the present, but not the indefinite future. It can make present sacrifices that it expects not to contradict SD, but it cannot force the next generation, and the next after the next and so on to commit themselves to SD. There is a time-consistency problem here: the present generation would like, but is unable to bind all coming generations to its own ethical choice for SD. Some future generation might well find it appropriate to deviate from SD or to abandon it completely. But this possibility has severe repercussions on the incentives for the current generation to opt for SD in the first instance: what is the point in making present sacrifices if the benefits of those sacrifices that were thought to benefit all future generations can be reaped by some single future generation that opts out from SD?

There is no easy solution to the fundamental time-consistency problem of SD. There exist two basic approaches to mitigate the problem, however. The first is to design sustainability policies such that an enduring commitment to SD by future generations is in their own self-interest. Suppose as an example that the current generation is undertaking enormous public investments into man-made and other forms of capital for the sake of future generations. For finance there are basically two possibilities: one is to raise taxes now; the other is incurring debts via issuing long-term bonds that have to be repaid in the future. To mitigate the time-consistency problem it would be in the interest of the current generation to finance its investments via debts that are to be repaid gradually over a long time period. Why? Because defaulting on debt is likely to be a self-defeating strategy for a coming generation that refuses to commit to SD, since defaulting on the 'sustainability debts' would raise the risk-premium and hence the interest payments for debts that this generation issues for its own selfish purposes as well.[14] It is as if the coming generation is locked into servicing the debt and therefore into sticking to a sustainability policy once undertaken by earlier generations. The disadvantage of this approach is that it might have enormous and possibly undesired inter-generational distributional consequences as well. If the investment is to be paid by long-term debts the burden to the current generation is likely to be less than if the investment is to be paid by a current increase in taxation.[15] This distributional side-effect can very well be desirable in some instances, however, since it forces the next generations to contribute to the costs of achieving SD. Another disadvantage of the first approach is that some future generation could undertake other steps that would endanger the goal of SD while at the same time serving the 'sustainability debts'. Therefore, the first approach does not give any guarantee to the current generation; it can mitigate, but cannot overcome, the time-consistency problem.

The second approach is to influence coming generations such that they regard their enduring commitment to SD as a decent and 'right' decision. Surely, the current generation cannot influence very distant generations directly, but it can influence the next generation through the education of the current children and adolescents. If each generation instructs its offspring to regard SD as a desirable goal then the problem of time consistency could be overcome. Admittedly, there is no guarantee that future generations will stick to SD, but the current generation might well be sufficiently convinced that they feel undeterred from incurring costs for the benefit of the future due to the still existing possibilities that their efforts will be frustrated by coming generations.

2.2.3 Two Misunderstandings about Sustainable Development Resolved

There are two main misunderstandings about SD that should be corrected right at the beginning of this analysis because if they represented valid claims then the justification for the book would be severely put into doubt.

2.2.3.1 'SD might lock society into eternal poverty'

The first one is that sticking to SD will lock society into eternal poverty if it is poorly endowed at the start. Solow (1974a) developed this argument when he examined how applying Rawls's (1972) maximin rule to the inter-generational problem of the optimal depletion of a given stock of a non-renewable resource and the accumulation of man-made capital would affect current and future utility. Richter (1994, p. 46) and Dasgupta (1994, p. 35) have raised similar concerns. I shall not reproduce Solow's model since his proposition is easy to understand intuitively. The argument is as follows:

1. The maximin-rule means that the utility of the worst-off generation has to be maximised.

2. It follows that utility has to be constant throughout time, that is, utility has to be equal for all generations. Why? Imagine otherwise: some generation has higher utility than other generations. But then the maximin criterion would call for shifting utility away from this generation to others who are worse off. The same applies vice versa if some generation has lower utility than other generations. Only, this time, utility has to be shifted towards this generation. Equilibrium is where all generations have equal utility. Hence utility has to be constant throughout time. (In Solow's model utility can be shifted to and from generations simply by allocating more or less of the available stock of the non-renewable resource to them.)

3. It follows that the initial generation cannot be asked for even the smallest sacrifice in the consumption of their share of the resource that would allow investment into man-made capital and an accumulation of this form of capital over time because that would make it worse off than future genera-tions. Hence if the initial situation is such that society is poor, humankind will be locked into poverty throughout time.[16] That is, the welfare proper-

ties of the maximin criterion depend very much on 'the mercy of the initial conditions' (Solow 1974a, p. 33).

If the argument was valid, then it would establish a huge rebuff for the SD case because society would be required to stick to constant utility when it might have had rising utility throughout time due to the accumulation of man-made capital if only some initial small sacrifice was made. It would be rather difficult then to do justice both to the present and to future generations. Fortunately, the argument is flawed and its supposed problem is similar to what Adelman (1990, p. 8) in another context referred to as the question of how many angels can dance on the point of a pin: a difficult non-problem.

There are two possible ways to show this. The rather pragmatic counter-argument says that we are presently in a situation no longer that is character-ised by an initial lack of wealth. That earlier generations have made sacrifices for us, we cannot change any more. It is futile to imagine how poor we would still be, had earlier generations already applied the maximin criterion. Now that we are no longer poor, applying the maximin criterion does not lock future generations into eternal poverty. Dasgupta and Heal (1979, p. 311) seem to endorse this argument for rich countries. But one of the problems with this line of thought is just that: it does not apply to poor countries and arguably most of the developing countries are still very poor by any measure. Another problem is that it still locks society into a constant utility time path although maybe from a higher initial level of utility.

Fortunately, the second counter-argument does not depend on the present generation being rich and refutes the supposition that sustainability locks society into a constant path of utility over time. It simply says that SD neither is equivalent to, nor implies the maximin criterion: SD is *not* calling for constant or equal utility, but for maintaining the capacity to provide non-declining utility. This might appear as a minor difference in the choice of words, but it produces a huge difference in its ethical prescriptions. For SD, properly interpreted, allows earlier generations to make *voluntary* sacrifices in order that coming generations can enjoy higher utility whereas the maximin criterion does not. In some sense this counter-argument turns the debate over SD from its head back to its feet. The 'locked into eternal poverty' argument sprang from concern over the present generation's utility, whereas SD was genuinely developed out of concern for the utility of future generations. No proponent of SD ever denied the present generation the right to make *voluntary* sacrifices for the future (nor, to be correct, did Solow do so explicitly; he was only exploring the consequences of applying the maximin criterion). SD rules out 'mortgaging the future', so to speak, but it does not rule out be-queathing a better world. On the other hand, nor does SD *require* to bequeath a *better* world. Barry's (1991, p. 267) claim that

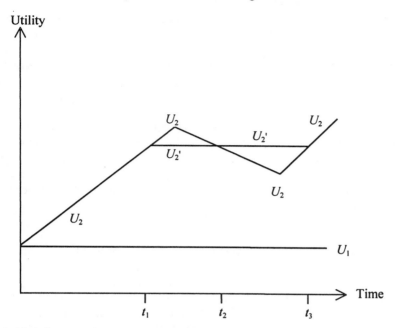

Figure 2.1 Non-declining versus constant utility

if one believes that successive generations made sacrifices in the (no doubt vague) expectation that each generation would pass on more than it inherited, this would constitute a prima facie case for saying that the present generation has a certain obligation to continue with this process

is not backed by the principle of sustainability. SD as defined here only calls for *maintaining* the capacity to provide non-declining future utility.

A different, and still unresolved question is whether the obligation to some future generation changes if an earlier generation deviated from the principle of sustainability. Does this generation have to compensate for the deviation of the past or does it simply have to maintain the now lower capacity to provide non-declining utility? Strictly speaking, sustainability would only require the latter, but compensation might be expected if the costs of doing so are low. There really is no general answer to this question, however.

2.2.3.2 'SD demands the choice of greatly inferior utility paths'

A similar argument as that under Section 2.2.3.1 holds that SD requires society to prefer very low constant utility paths to a persistently rising path that has a temporary very small decline in utility somewhere along the path. Remember from section 2.1, p. 8, that SD was not defined in direct utility terms, but in terms of maintaining the capacity to provide non-declining future welfare. Nonetheless, for the sake of refuting the argument, assume that a society committed to SD could directly choose a utility path over time and assume for simplicity that there are only two utility paths which society could choose from: U_1 provides constant utility forever, U_2 provides higher utility than U_1 everywhere, but with a temporary dip along the path. Look at Figure 2.1 which is taken from Pezzey (1995, p. 4) with amendments. The argument asserts that SD requires that U_2 is preferred over U_1. Beckerman (1994, p. 196) and Heyes and Liston-Heyes (1995, p. 3) therefore conclude that sticking to SD would force society to choose greatly inferior utility paths. Again, if the argument was valid it would present a huge rebuff against the case for SD. Fortunately, it is not valid.

The counter-argument runs as follows: if the economy is 'productive' in the sense that saving a share of current income for investment leads to a net increase in future utility (Pezzey 1995, p. 12), then the utility path with the temporary decline in utility can be modified into a path that is non-declining along the whole path by saving a certain amount before the decline is supposed to occur and then using those savings later on to prevent the decline. Referring to Figure 2.1, ensuring sustainability would mean starting 'extra-saving' from time t_1 to t_2 and to use these 'extra-savings' to prevent a decline in utility from time t_2 to t_3. That is, from t_1 to t_3 society deviates from U_2 to follow the utility path U'_2, after t_3 society returns to the original path U_2.

The assumption that the economy is 'productive' is not very restrictive, so applying SD does not force society to choose greatly inferior utility paths. What it does, however, is to require earlier generations to save more so that later generations do not have to experience a decline in utility. Hence, the earlier generations' utility does not rise as much if the sustainability constraint is binding as it would without the constraint. But, then again, this is what SD is all about.

2.3   WEAK VERSUS STRONG SUSTAINABILITY

In Section 2.1, p. 8, SD was defined as development that does not decrease the capacity to provide non-declining per capita utility for infinity. But what does that mean and how is it to be ensured? This, of course, is the point of divergence and it opens fundamental disagreements that are not to be confused with semantic disputations about the meaning of the term. SD is a 'contestable concept' (Jacobs 1995b, p. 4) in that there is real struggle over its interpretation in practice.

In this section the two paradigms of sustainability relevant for the analysis are presented. Their main difference derives from starkly contrasting assumptions about the substitutability of natural capital. Section 2.3.1 presents WS and Section 2.3.2 presents SS.

2.3.1   The Paradigm of Weak Sustainability

WS is often called 'Solow–Hartwick sustainability' (for example, by Gutes 1996, p. 150) because it is based on the work of Nobel Prize winner Robert Solow (1974a, 1974c, 1986, 1993a, 1993b) and John Hartwick (1977, 1978a, 1978b, 1990, 1993), himself a famous resource economist. WS requires keeping *total net investment*, suitably defined to encompass all relevant forms of capital, above or equal to zero. This requirement is best known as the so-called *Hartwick rule*.

Note that usually the relevant literature (for example, World Bank 1997a) speaks of savings rather than investment. This is misleading, if not simply wrong. What matters for sustainability is investment not saving, and saving is equal to investment only for the special case where there are no government expenditures. For a closed economy, if there are government expenditures and no taxes, then saving equals investment plus government expenditures; or, more realistically, if there are taxes as well, saving plus taxes equal investment plus government expenditures. Usually, saving is derived from dynamic optimisation models like the one in Section 5.1, p. 141, that do not include government expenditures. For these models saving equals investment. Having noted this, I shall speak mainly of saving instead of investment for the rest of this book in order to refer to the relevant literature.

Ignoring any other forms of capital for the moment, then, loosely speaking, the requirement to keep aggregate total net saving (investment) above or equal to zero is equivalent to keeping the *aggregate total value* of man-made capital *and* natural capital at least constant.[17] It means that natural capital can be safely run down as long as enough man-made capital is built up in exchange. In the words of Solow: 'Earlier generations are entitled to draw down the pool (optimally, of course!) so long as they add (optimally, of course!) to the stock of reproducible capital' (Solow 1974a, p. 41).

The policy recommendation of WS is clear-cut: obey the Hartwick rule in ensuring that total net investment is above or equal to zero. Again, the relevant literature often speaks of keeping 'genuine saving' (GS) non-negative, where the term 'genuine' was introduced by Hamilton (1994) to distinguish it from traditional net saving measures which included only depreciation of man-made capital. To monitor whether the economy follows the Hartwick rule, proponents of WS recommend changing the traditional national accounting system in order to construct a green net national product (gNNP) of which GS can be derived. The gNNP is properly constructed as follows:[18]

> Take traditional net national product (NNP) and augment it for investments in, and deduct deterioration of, natural capital (and possibly other forms of capital) measured at net marginal value to get gNNP. Then keep GS non-negative over time.

If investment in man-made capital is big enough, an explicit policy of sustainable development is not even necessary for then sustainability is guaranteed quasi-automatically.[19] If not, apply suitable measures (for example, a resource tax, saving subsidy or environmental regulation) to ensure non-negative GS (Mikesell 1994, p. 85).

Under which conditions does following the Hartwick rule ensure WS? It does so given that: first, the components in the utility function are substitutes for each other and, second, it holds true that

- resources are super-abundant;
- or the elasticity for substituting man-made capital for resources in the production function is equal to or greater than unity, even in the limit of extremely high output–resource ratios;
- or technical progress can overcome any resource constraint.

Because of these assumptions I call WS the 'substitutability paradigm'. Appendix 4, p. 222, provides a proof for the proposition that following the Hartwick rule ensures WS. Note that WS with its focus on GS is also defined in terms of maintaining the *capacity* to provide non-declining utility rather than in direct utility terms. However, given the very simple utility function for the representative consumer from Section 2.1, p. 8, Appendix 4 shows that keeping GS non-negative throughout leads to non-declining utility over time.

If there is technical progress that is not embodied in capital, then following the Hartwick rule is too 'conservative', in the sense that WS no longer requires at least constant value of the total capital but can be achieved with some decline in value of the total capital as well. In that case, following the Hartwick rule overshoots the sustainability goal in that the capacity to provide future utility is actually rising. But note that population growth is a force in the other direction. With a growing population (and no disembodied technical change), the *per capita* total value of capital must remain constant to maintain the capacity to provide non-declining *per capita* utility.

Quite clearly, given the assumptions about the availability of natural resources and possibilities for substitution for natural capital in the production of consumption goods, WS is a paradigm of resource optimism. As regards natural capital as a provider of direct utility, the reader might be uncomfortable with the proposition that the components in the utility function are substitutes for each other. It means that a rise in consumption (*C*) can compensate future generations for a decline in the stock of renewable resources (*Z*) or a rise in the pollution stock (*P*). It is important to note therefore, that WS holds that there are good reasons to presume that with rising *C* and hence rising incomes, *Z* will *eventually* rise as well or at least stay constant and *P* will fall or at least stay constant (see, for example, World Bank 1992). That is, WS holds that the environment is a superior good and that economic growth is therefore also good for the environment. Hence, proponents of WS are in favour of economic growth *either* because a rise in *C* can compensate for a decline in *Z* or a rise in *P* *or* because a rise in *C* will prevent a decline in *Z* and a rise in *P* since the environment is a superior good. Because the proponents of WS believe that, eventually, with rising incomes the state of the environment will improve as well, I call them environmental optimists.

Note that although WS is deeply rooted within neoclassical economic thinking in its belief in good prospects for the substitutability of natural capital, it is still conceptually different. What makes it different are two things: first is the willingness of its proponents to take natural capital both as an input into production and as a direct source of welfare seriously and include it into their models (compare Colby 1991). Second, WS differs from 'present-value maximisation', the reigning utilitarian paradigm of neoclassical welfare economics, in postulating the constraint that the capacity to provide non-declining utility must be maintained at any point in time.[20] More formally, WS in effect denies the validity of *potential* Pareto improvements in an inter-generational context and demands *actual* compensation if future generations would suffer from an action that benefits the current generation. That is, for inter-generational allocation decisions WS rules out the validity of the so-called Hicks–Kaldor test (Hicks 1939; Kaldor 1939) that is the common decision criterion in traditional welfare economics. Present-value maximisation and sustainability can strikingly conflict with each other. Appendix 1, p. 212, provides a stylised example showing that applying present-value maximisation as the decision criterion could even lead to the optimal (efficient) choice of a path that finally ends up in catastrophe, that is to zero utility and therefore to the extinction of humankind![21] I do not claim that this stylised example is particularly realistic, but it shows that, in principle, applying present-value maximisation can lead to utmost unsustainability. As Chichilnisky (1996) has shown, the clash between present-value maximisation and sustainability holds true even for less restrictive definitions of sustainability. Her definition only rules out dictatorship of the present and the future, that is, giving no weight to the distant future or no weight to the present, but does not rule out declining utility along the path. Not surprisingly, since present-value maximisation with any positive constant discount rate gives only infinitesimal small weight to the distant future it clashes with this definition of sustainability as well.

2.3.2   The Paradigm of Strong Sustainability

The distinction between WS and SS should presumably be credited to Pearce et al. (1989). David Pearce and his colleagues from the Centre for Social and Economic Research on the Global Environment (CSERGE) have also provided arguments for stronger versions of sustainability (for example, Pearce, Barbier and Markandya 1990, Turner and Pearce 1992). Others have contributed as well. To list just a few: Paul Ekins (1994), Michael Jacobs (1991), Clive Spash (1993, 1994), Herman Daly, one of the founders of the International Society for Ecological Economics, and Robert Costanza, co-founder and until 1997 the president of the Society (Daly 1991, 1992a, 1992b, 1994, 1995a, 1996; Daly and Costanza 1992). What makes it difficult to define SS is that these authors have at times quite differing views on what SS is and what it implies.[22] To give but one example: Herman Daly and Robert Goodland are very pessimistic about the environmental consequences of economic growth (Goodland and Daly 1992; Daly and Goodland 1994). Daly states that 'sustainable development ... necessarily means a radical shift from a growth economy and all it entails to a steady-state economy, certainly in the North, and eventually in the South as well' (Daly 1996, p. 31). David Pearce, on the other hand, insists that economic growth is an increase in net added value and is not logically bound to any degree of environmental degradation (personal communication). (On the link between economic growth and environmental degradation see Section 3.3.2, p. 76.)

At least some of the proponents of SS are quite pessimistic about natural resource availability and believe that past levels of resource depletion ('the onetime bonanza of fossil fuel consumption', Daly 1992b, p. 244) cannot be sustained into the future:

> Historically, in the 'empty world' economy, manmade capital was limiting and natural capital superabundant. We have now, due to demographic and economic growth, entered the era of the 'full world' economy, in which the roles are reversed. More and more it is remaining natural capital that now plays the role of limiting factor. (Daly 1995a, p. 50)

In spite of SS being more difficult to define than WS, it is fair to say that the essence of SS is that it regards natural capital as fundamentally non-substitutable through other forms of capital. I therefore call SS the 'non-substitutability paradigm'. There are two differing interpretations of SS in the literature. In one interpretation SS is the paradigm that calls for keeping *both* the *aggregate total value* of man-made capital *and* natural capital *and* the *total value of natural capital itself* at least constant. Thus SS encompasses WS, but also postulates an additional requirement that refers to natural capital, a sub-category of total capital. Note that SS in this interpretation does not demand the preservation of nature as it is. For example, SS does not require never using non-renewable resources such as coal, as Klepper and Stähler (1996, p. 2) erroneously suggest. It requires, however, reinvesting the receipts from coal mining into the development of renewable energy sources in order to keep the aggregate value of the total natural resource stock constant (Hohmeyer 1992). More generally, Barbier, Pearce and Markandya (1990) have suggested a depreciation compensation in the natural capital stock with adequate shadow projects.

In the other interpretation SS is not defined in value terms, but calls for the preservation of the *physical* stock of those forms of natural capital that are non-substitutable (so-called critical natural capital). If the flows from these resource stocks are used, their regenerative capacity must not be exceeded, so that their environmental function remains intact (Goodland 1995; Hueting and Reijnders 1998). Also note that this interpretation does not allow for any substitutability among different forms of 'critical' natural capital. Nor does it imply keeping nature as it is, however. Indeed, such a task would be impossible. But it calls for maintaining its functions intact. Hueting and Reijnders (1998, p. 145) give the example that 'the rate of erosion of topsoil may not exceed the rate of formation of such soil due to weathering'.

In Chapter 4 I shall argue that the second interpretation of SS is more reasonable. There I shall also discuss some reasons for justifying the assumption of non-substitutability. In short, the main suggested reason for non-substitutability is a combination of the following factors (see Turner and Pearce 1992, p. 7):

- We are largely uncertain and ignorant about the detrimental consequences of depleting natural capital.
- Natural capital loss often is irreversible.
- Some forms of natural capital provide basic life-support functions.
- Individuals are highly adverse to losses in natural capital. A stronger suggestion would be that individuals cannot be compensated for any environmental degradation via increased consumption opportunities (Spash 1993).

To distinguish SS clearly from the substitutability assumption of WS, it will be implied for the analysis in this book that SS holds that rising consumption cannot compensate future generations for environmental degradation, that is, it cannot substitute for a declining stock of directly utility-relevant renewable resources and a rising stock of pollution. Such a position is often derived from a normative rights-based theory of inter-generational justice. Sen (1982, p. 346), for example, argues that 'lasting pollution is a kind of calculable oppression of the future generation', which he regards as being similar in character to torture. Consequently, Sen (1982, p. 347) rejects the idea that future generations could be compensated for 'lasting pollution' via increased material welfare:

> Even if the future generation may be richer and may enjoy a higher welfare level, and even if its marginal utility from the consumption gain is accepted to be less than the marginal welfare loss of the present generation, this may still not be accepted to be decisive for rejecting the investment when the alternative implies long-term effects of environmental pollution.

Similarly, Barry (1991, p. 264) regards environmental pollution as not amenable to compensation by doing future generations some other good, as he makes clear in drawing the following analogy:

> We will all agree that doing harm is in general not cancelled out by doing good, and conversely that doing some good does not license one to do harm provided it does not exceed the amount of good. For example, if you paid for the realignments of a dangerous highway intersection and saved an average of two lives a year, that would not mean that you could shoot one motorist per year and simply reckon on coming out ahead.

Maybe the most elaborate and explicit argument for non-compensability was put forward in two articles by Spash (1993, 1994). He makes it very clear that in his view 'compensation does not licence society to pollute, provided the damages created are less than the amount of compensation' (Spash 1993, p. 127) and postulates an 'inviolable right of future generations to be free of intergenerational environmental damages'.

How to measure SS? The first interpretation of SS (non-declining value of the natural capital stock in addition to non-declining value of the total capital stock) would call for a kind of gNNP, which we encountered already in the last section on WS, with an additional constraint. The only difference is that not only must GS be non-negative, but also the value of the natural resource stock must be kept intact. The second interpretation of SS (preserving certain critical stocks of natural capital) would call first of all for a physical measure to indicate whether the stocks are maintained. In a further step, the gap between the actual stocks and the sustainability standards can be measured monetarily. Because Chapter 4 argues that the second interpretation of SS is more reasonable, Section 5.2, p. 191, looks only at measuring this 'sustainability gap'.

2.4 THE IMPORTANCE OF THE SUBSTITUTABILITY ASSUMPTION: THE CASE OF GLOBAL WARMING

In this section it will be stressed how important the assumption of substitutability is, using global warming as a case example. The best-known cost–benefit analysis of the expected consequences of global warming is Nordhaus (1991a), updated in Nordhaus (1994) and Nordhaus and Popp (1997). Nordhaus found that large-scale greenhouse gas abatement is unwarranted and that only minor policy measures should be undertaken that would not prevent a substantial increase in accumulated greenhouse gases in the atmosphere. These results had 'great policy influence, especially in the United States' (Cline 1992, p. 312) buttressing significantly the US resistance against any substantive global climate treaty at the Rio Conference in 1992. As I will show in this section, Nordhaus implicitly presupposes the validity of the assumptions of the paradigm of WS.

Most of Nordhaus's critics have concentrated on the issue of discounting and demanded that a lower discount rate should be applied for reasons of inter-generational fairness: being later in time should be no reason for counting less (for example, Broome 1992; Azar and Sterner 1996). However, it will be shown here that these criticisms first miss the point and second lead to ethically dubious conclusions and inconsistent and inefficient policy choices. The real disagreement is not about the right discount rate, but about whether consumption growth can compensate for environmental degradation caused by global warming or not. Discounting is not the issue, but substitutability is. Any call for aggressive emission abatement must therefore directly attack the substitutability assumption of neoclassical economics.

I select global warming as a case example because its features — current economic activity has large-scale long-term future consequences on both environmental amenities and the capacity to provide material goods — suggest it as an ideal object of study for questions of sustainability. The impacts of global warming will not be felt for another 50 years or so (Fankhauser and Tol 1996, p. 665). That is, global warming will impact upon future generations but mostly not upon the current one. Hence the benefits of abating greenhouse gas emissions will be enjoyed by future generations, while the costs of abating greenhouse emissions are borne by the current generation. Much of what will be said here could similarly be applied to other global long-term environmental problems, however, such as ozone layer depletion, biodiversity loss, and the problem of radioactivity caused by nuclear waste.

Discussing global warming is no easy task: the science and economics of global warming is complex (see IPCC 1996a, 1996b), there are numerous highly technical models for cost–benefit analysis (IPCC 1996b, pp. 374–96) and there is a vast and continually growing literature discussing the pros and cons of controlling CO_2 and other greenhouse gas emissions.[23] Quite clearly, I cannot and do not want to discuss all the details of this debate. I shall restrict my discussion to the cost-benefit analysis of the 'DICE–model' in Nordhaus (1994), the updated and expanded version of Nordhaus (1991a), because this is the best-known and best-documented study and is representative in many respects for other studies using similar models which are reviewed in Toth (1995). The model in Nordhaus (1994) is itself updated in Nordhaus and Popp (1997) which is 'basically a version of the DICE model that adds another dimension, that of different uncertain states of the world' (p. 3). All the fundamental objections that apply to Nordhaus (1994) are valid for Nordhaus and Popp (1997) as well.

2.4.1 The Neoclassical Approach towards Global Warming: the Nordhaus Models

Nordhaus's (1994) DICE–model — the Dynamic Integrated Model of Climate and the Economy — is a dynamic optimisation economic growth model based on Ramsey (1928) in which a social planner maximises the integrated sum of the utility of per capita consumption. Output is produced by a constant returns to scale Cobb–Douglas production function. Output production generates greenhouse emissions which lead to global warming which leads, in turn, to losses in output.[24] Nordhaus (1994, p. 94) suggests an optimal reduction rate of greenhouse gases in 2025 of 11.1 per cent of uncontrolled emissions and of 13.4 per cent in 2075.[25] Note that because uncontrolled emissions are expected to grow tremendously over time, Nordhaus's optimal policy recommendation does not call for any emission cuts relative to, say, the 1990 level, but for further and substantial increases in greenhouse gas emissions over time that are only slightly lower than uncontrolled emissions (see ibid., p. 87).

Nordhaus implicitly assumes the validity of the substitutability assumption which is the centre of the paradigm of WS. He does so in two closely related ways: first, all benefits and costs are meshed together and computed as shares of total output — regardless of whether they are connected to environmental amenities or consumption related. The only costs due to global warming are costs in the form of output losses.[26] This is valid only if future generations do not care about whether, say, the costs of global warming are connected to environmental amenities that provide them with direct utility or restrain their capacity to consume material goods. Second, Nordhaus presumes perfect substitutability in the way he discounts the future. His formula for discounting is the so-called Ramsey formula which is formally derived and discussed in Appendix 2, p. 214. The formula is as follows:

$$r = \rho + \eta(C) \cdot \frac{\dot{C}}{C} \qquad (2.3)$$

The social discount rate r should be equal to the sum of the pure rate of time preference ρ and the product of the elasticity of the marginal utility of consumption $\eta(C)$ and the per capita growth rate of consumption $\dot{C}/C$. If $\rho > 0$, this is called (pure) utility discounting. Nordhaus (ibid., p. 123) calls discounting because of $\eta(C)\dot{C}/C > 0$ 'growth discounting'.

Nordhaus sets the pure rate of time preference ρ equal to 3 per cent (Nordhaus 1994, p. 11). He assumes a logarithmic utility function for which $\eta(C)$ is equal to 1 (ibid., p. 11f.) and projects $\dot{C}/C$ to be about 3 per cent in the first few years, declining slowly in later decades (ibid., p. 125). Hence his overall discount rate is approximately 6 per cent.

Setting the pure rate of time preference equal to 3 per cent is highly controversial and Nordhaus's reasons as well as the criticism thereof will be discussed later on. The rate of pure time preference is of no particular relevance for our argument that Nordhaus implicitly assumes the validity of the substitutability paradigm, however. Setting $\eta(C)$ equal to 1 is somewhat arbitrary, but so is more or less any assumption about the algebraic form of the representative consumer's utility function from which the elasticity of the marginal utility of consumption follows. Instead of simply assuming a specific utility function, one can also try to infer values for $\eta(C)$ from actual consumption decisions. Pearce and Ulph (1995, p. 17) have reviewed studies that have done this and provide a best estimate for $\eta(C)$ of 0.8 with a lower bound of 0.7 and an upper bound of 1.5. Nordhaus's selection of $\eta(C) = 1$ appears to be acceptable therefore. The more problematic part is $\dot{C}/C$. Nordhaus estimates output to grow at about 3 per cent per annum in the first years with the growth rate gradually declining later on. This is a rather high estimate and others have come up with lower figures — see the discussion below. Naturally, predicting future growth rates is never easy and always reflects a best guess that can turn out to be vastly beside the point *ex post*. Remember that in the 1960s few, if any, would have predicted the downward trend in growth rates of many countries from the early 1970s onwards.

The specific value of $\dot{C}/C$ is not relevant for our discussion here, however. Whatever its value, the underlying assumption is perfect substitutability of natural capital. To see why, recall the ethical rationale for the inclusion of $\eta(C)\dot{C}/C$ in the Ramsey formula: given that $\eta(C)\dot{C}/C > 0$, the future should count less because it is then presumed to be *better off* due to the increase in consumption (weighted by the elasticity of the marginal utility of consumption). That is, future losses arising from global warming, for example, in the form of environmental amenities, are implicitly assumed to be perfectly compensable by increased consumption. Natural and other forms of capital are perfect substitutes.

One might think that if the current generation was committed to WS this would demand higher emission abatement than found by Nordhaus since he does not explicitly take WS as a side constraint to his cost–benefit analysis. This is not true, however. Solely judged from the requirements of WS it is most likely that no explicit abatement policy whatsoever is warranted! The reason is that if, as all estimates seem to agree upon, damages from unrestricted emissions are to be less than 10 per cent of GNP (IPCC 1996b, p. 218) by the middle of the next century and future generations are likely to be materially better off by much more than 10 per cent, then there is no need to combat global warming for reasons of sustainability — given the validity of the substitutability paradigm. Of course, the estimates about harm caused by global warming might be significantly wrong. Although its likelihood is very small, there is the possibility of a run-away climate catastrophe with dramatic damages if warming becomes extremely high (ibid., pp. 207f.). Alternatively, although not likely, the future economy might grow at only minimally positive rates or might even contract, as Woodward and Bishop (1995, p. 105) seem to fear. Then WS would call for some emission abatement. But currently best available estimates suggest that this is not the case. A society committed to WS might still undertake some emission abatement *in excess* of its duty to ensure WS or it might undertake some adaptation measures to protect certain items of cultural heritage such as Venice (Nordhaus 1991b, p. 51) But in general no active policy to combat global warming is demanded by WS.

One might wonder why Nordhaus without endorsing any sustainability constraint comes to the conclusion that some, albeit minor, emission abatement is warranted, while WS of itself warrants no abatement whatsoever. The answer is that Nordhaus endorses a utilitarian framework in which it can happen that even though the future is better off than the present, the current generation is still called upon to provide some additional sacrifices which make it still worse off in comparison to the future. This will be the case if the future benefits after discounting are higher than the present costs of sacrifice that bring the future benefits into effect. In this sense, Nordhaus's computations are more friendly to future generations than a mere commitment to WS would be.[27]

2.4.2 Critiques of the Nordhaus Models: Why Discounting is not the Issue

Many aspects of Nordhaus's methodology have been attacked. To give but a few examples:

- Ayres and Walter (1991) contend that Nordhaus's land prices and vulnerability coefficients are too low.
- Cline (1996) criticises Nordhaus's method of computing agricultural costs as biased towards producing low estimates.
- Ekins (1996a) suggests that taking into account beneficial side-effects of restricting CO_2 emissions such as reductions in SO_x and NO_x emissions (so-called secondary benefits), which Nordhaus ignores, would warrant much higher abatement.
- Howarth (1996) criticises Nordhaus for ignoring people's values for the protection of biodiversity and ecosystems and, more generally, for largely neglecting negative impacts of global warming on ecosystems.
- Tol (1994) suggests that intangible goods should directly enter the utility function rather than the production function.
- Price (1995) contends that Nordhaus overestimates the uptake of CO_2 emissions in the oceans.
- Chapman, Suri and Hall (1995) examine the consequences of a doubling of the CO_2 concentration in the atmosphere causing higher temperatures than expected by Nordhaus.

I cannot discuss these criticisms here for reasons of space. Rather I shall concentrate on the question of discounting on which most critics of Nordhaus have focused. Lowering the applied discount rate would drastically increase the warranted emission abatement as confirmed by studies of Fankhauser (1994) and Chapman, Suri and Hall (1995), because the distribution function of the net costs of global warming is heavily skewed towards the distant future.

Before examining the demand to use lower discount rates in detail, let us first look at why Nordhaus sets the pure rate of time preference equal to 3 per cent. He does so because he believes in economic efficiency and wants to set his discount rate equal to the real rate of return to investment which he takes to be about 6 per cent per annum Estimates of this rate, which is also called the opportunity cost of investment, vary, but they usually lie in the range of 4 per cent to 10 per cent per annum in developed countries (Nordhaus 1991a, p. 926). Manne and Richels (1995, p. 5) believe that 5 per cent represents a lower bound, Pearce (1993a, p. 60) thinks that 7 per cent comes close to the long-run average real rate of return, Cline (1992, p. 262) estimates it to be about 8 per cent. The World Bank usually does not accept any project with a rate of return of less than 10 per cent (Markandya and Pearce 1991, p. 140). So Nordhaus's estimate of 6 per cent represents a good, conservative guess of the real return. Now, efficiency requires that the government does not use a

discount rate different from the opportunity cost. Hence with $\eta(C)C/C$ to be estimated as 3 per cent, it can be inferred that society's pure rate of time preference must be 3 per cent because only then is the social discount rate equal to the opportunity cost of investment: 3 per cent + 3 per cent = 6 per cent.[28]

The reason why the government should not use a discount rate different from the opportunity cost of investment is that using a different, say lower, rate would channel scarce resources away from investments that provide the future with a higher real rate of return. This inefficiency can arise within the limits of a given public budget in that resources are channelled away from highly productive public investments in, say, primary education towards emission abatement with a lower real rate of return. It can also arise with an endogenously determined public budget in crowding out highly productive private investments for the sake of low-return public investments into emission abatement. No doubt, the reader will realise that this argument is valid only if the substitutability paradigm is valid.

Let us now turn to the critique to Nordhaus's approach towards discounting. Many economists and philosophers have since long demanded to set the pure rate of time preference equal to zero for reasons of inter-generational fairness: being later in time should as such be no reason for counting less (for example, Ramsey 1928; Pigou 1932; Rawls 1972; Broome 1992; Cline 1992; Azar and Sterner 1996). The main argument is that future generations are excluded from today's market and political decisions (for example, Broome 1992, p. 89f.). If future generations could reveal their preferences they would surely opt for higher investments for the benefit of the future, thus driving down the real rate of return on investment. Since we cannot know counterfactually what the real rate of return on investment would be if future generations were not excluded from today's market and political decisions, it can be said to be fair to set the pure rate of time preference equal to zero: being later in time should be no reason for counting less. Hence the discount rate would be down from 6 to 3 per cent.

But that is not the end of the story. Critics have also argued that Nordhaus's projection of C/C might be too high (Rabl 1996, p. 143). Cline (1992, pp. 284ff.), in remembrance of the dismal per capita growth performance of many developing countries in the 1980s, projects worldwide C/C to be about 1.5 per cent in the middle of the next century, 1 per cent by 2100 and 0.5 per cent by 2275 which would bring down the rate of discount to 0.5 to 1.5 per cent. Azar and Sterner (1996, pp. 177ff.) have further abandoned the assumption of a worldwide representative consumer and have examined the consequences of *intra*-generational unequal distribution. They argue as follows: if it is right to apply the Ramsey formula to future generations and ask what their marginal utility of rising consumption is, then it must also be right to ask for the marginal utility of the much poorer people in the present-day developing world. It was taken as a justification for discounting that future generations are expected to be better off in Ramsey's formula. For the same reason Azar and Sterner (ibid., p. 178) argue 'that a given ... cost which affects a poor person (in a poor country) *should be valued as a higher welfare cost than an equivalent cost affecting an average OECD citizen'*.

Because the costs of global warming are relatively higher in developing countries than in developed countries because of their greater vulnerability and their more restricted capacity for adaptation (IPCC 1996b, p. 218), adjusting C/C along the lines of Azar and Sterner (1996) substantially increases the level of abatement that is warranted by a cost–benefit analysis of global warming. The same holds true for reducing the pure rate of time preference (possibly to zero) or lowering estimates of C/C for the representative world consumer.

Although I have some sympathy for these criticisms I shall now argue that they first miss the point and second lead to inconsistent conclusions and inefficient choices. The two points are linked together. They miss the point because they do not attack the most problematic aspect of Nordhaus's approach, namely the substitutability assumption. They lead to inconsistent conclusions and inefficient choices because lowering the rate of discount is inconsistent with current savings behaviour and applying low discount rates only to global warming tempts public authorities to channel scarce resources in emission abatement that exhibits rates of return far inferior to alternative public investments in, say, public health care or education.

Take setting the pure rate of time preference equal to zero. The first thing to note is that such a proposal is inconsistent with current savings behaviour. Applying such a low rate of discount for policies to maximise social welfare would imply far more investment and would require a far higher savings rate than is actually prevalent in any existing country (IPCC 1996b, p. 133).[29] The second thing to note is that while it is true that future generations are not present in today's markets, the actual rate of discount used by the present generation does not violate the WS constraint *if* consumption is rising over time. If future generations were around and could reveal their preferences in today's markets, investment into man-made capital would be higher, the real rate of return to investment and hence the discount rate would be lower and consumption would rise *still faster* over time. But given the validity of perfect substitutability, there is no justification to lower the rate of discount for reasons of sustainability if non-declining utility can already be ensured by the actual rate of discount. The third thing to note, related to the last point, is that the proposal to lower the rate of discount is, somewhat surprisingly at first sight, contestable on ethical grounds as well. The reason is as follows: even

with a conservative estimate for $\dot{C}/C$ of 1.5 per cent, future generations will be almost 4.5 times better off 100 years from now. Even if the costs of global warming by that time were, say, 50 per cent of GNP, the future generation 100 years hence will still be 2.25 times better off than the present generation. If that is the case, then setting the pure rate of time preference equal to zero and forcing the current generation to make more sacrifices for emission abatement than with a pure rate of time preference of, say, 3 per cent is dubious for reasons of inter-generational fairness. As Lind (1995, p. 384) has put it:

> Can we justify current generations sacrificing 2–3 per cent of GWP [gross world product, E.N.] to increase the wealth of future generations who even after deduction for the high damage scenario are 2–15 times richer than the present generation? The answer is clearly no on the basis of intergenerational equity, which must weigh in favour of the current generation.

Ironically, given the validity of the substitutability paradigm, inter-generational fairness instead of calling for a zero pure rate of time preference would rather call for quite a high pure rate of time preference.

What about the argument of Azar and Sterner (1996)? Here things are somewhat different. If we discount future values because they accrue to richer people in the future then it is consistent to count values that accrue to the future *intra*-generational poor differently from those that accrue to the rich. With global warming, there will be winners and losers and it could be argued that the future beneficiaries of emission abatement are located mainly in some of the future developing countries whereas those who are likely to undertake the abatement investments are located mostly in the present developed countries. Furthermore it could be argued that due to this difference in location the future beneficiaries will not be better off (very much) than the current people asked to undertake sacrifices: even if the now poor will be, say, 4.5 times better off in 100 years they will not be much better off, if at all, than the currently rich. Hence it would follow that, given a zero pure rate of time preference, the discount rate should be equal to 0 per cent or only slightly above. It might even be negative!

Azar and Sterner's (ibid.) reasoning is consistent with the spirit of the Ramsey formula. But it still leads to inconsistent conclusions and inefficient choices. Their reasoning is inconsistent with the actual provision of aid from the current rich to the current poor which is of a rather limited magnitude.[30] As Schelling (1995, p. 397) has put it:

> It would be strange to forgo a per cent or two of GNP for 50 years for the benefit of Indians, Chinese, Indonesians and others who will be living 50 to 100 years from now — and probably much better off than today's Indians, Chinese, and Indonesians — and not a tenth of that amount to increase the consumption of contemporary Indians, Chinese, and Indonesians.

But such a policy would also be hugely inefficient, even if the current rich were ready to make large sacrifices for the sake of people living in developing countries either now or in the future. Given perfect substitutability, there are many much more attractive investment options from the viewpoint of the beneficiaries than investing in emission abatement. As Nordhaus (1991b, p. 57) notes, real rates of return to investment into education are extraordinarily high in poor countries: about 26 per cent for primary education, 16 per cent for secondary and 13 per cent for higher education. No doubt, poor people would be much better off if scarce resources were invested in these opportunities rather than in combating global warming. Given perfect substitutability, Schelling (1995, p. 401) is right in expecting that 'if offered a choice of immediate development assistance or equivalent investments in carbon abatement, potential aid recipients would elect for the immediate' — as would their future descendants if they had a voice.

2.4.3 The Real Issue: Substitutability of Natural Capital

The problem with all these propositions to lower the discount rate is that they do not attack the weakest point of Nordhaus's methodology, namely the assumption of perfect substitutability. Given this assumption, large-scale emission abatement is *either* ethically dubious because future generations are better off than the present generation anyway and inconsistent with the observed magnitude of current savings, *or* it is inconsistent with the behaviour of the currently rich towards the currently poor and imposes upon the poor inefficient investments whose financial resources they would rather use for different purposes if given a choice.

There have been some proposals in the literature to treat environmental costs and benefits differently from other values. One is the so-called Krutilla–Fisher approach. Krutilla and Fisher (1975) presume that environmental benefits are likely to increase *relative* to other benefits in the economy — for example because future richer people will appreciate relatively more environmental amenities if the income elasticity of environmental appreciation is bigger than one (the environment as a superior good). *De facto*, this increase in relative value means that environmental benefits are discounted at less than other values or maybe even not at all. If the relative importance of environmental benefits grew sufficiently strong, they could even count more than their nominal value so that, *de facto*, they would be 'discounted' at a negative rate. Krutilla and Fisher also presume that some of the benefits from environmental destruction are likely to depreciate over time. The developmental benefits from dam construction, for example, are likely to depreciate over time as superior technologies become available. *De facto*, this depreciation in relative value means that these benefits are discounted more heavily than other, especially environmental, values. Note the words *de facto*: formally, the same uniform discount rate is applied to all values, it is rather the values that appreciate or depreciate, respectively, before they are uniformly discounted to present-values.

That the relative value of environmental goods might be rising over time has found the approval of the leading economist experts on global warming — see IPCC (1996b, p. 130). Recently, Rabl (1996) has applied the Krutilla–Fisher rationale to global warming under the presumption that the environmental benefits of combating global warming are likely to rise over time. Similarly, but without recourse to the Krutilla–Fisher approach, Tol (1994) examines the effect of letting intangible goods whose value increases over time with per capita income enter the utility function. Not surprisingly, Rabl and Tol find that higher emission abatement is warranted than Nordhaus did.

The Krutilla–Fisher approach does not go a long way in departing from the substitutability paradigm, however. What it says is that environmental and other values are still perfectly substitutable for each other, if only their value has been appreciated or depreciated beforehand. The approach does not attack the heart of the substitutability paradigm therefore.

Not surprisingly, proponents of SS with their belief in the non-substitutability of natural capital represent the opposite extreme to Nordhaus's computations. While not every effect of global warming will be detrimental to natural capital, a consensus is emerging (see IPCC 1995, pp. 28–36) that it will lead to or at least can lead to

- a change in the species composition of forests with the possible loss of species and the disappearance of entire forestry types;
- an increase in the frequency and the range of pests, pathogens and fires;
- an increase in desertification;
- a disruption in mountain resources of food and fuel for indigenous people;
- an increase in the salinity of estuaries and freshwater aquifers;
- a disruption of saltwater marshes, mangrove ecosystems, coastal wetlands, coral reefs, coral atolls and river deltas due to, among others, increased coastal flooding;
- an increase of heat waves with damaging effects on ecosystems and human health;
- an increase in the potential transmission of infectious diseases like malaria and yellow fever.

In putting ecosystems under severe stress, global warming can therefore damage the capacity of natural capital

- to provide food, fibre, medicines and energy;
- to process and store carbon and other nutrients;
- to assimilate waste, purify water, and regulate water runoff;
- to control floods, soil degradation and beach erosion;
- to provide opportunities for recreation and tourism.

Given this list of potentially severe damages to natural capital due to global warming, it should come as no surprise that SS calls for aggressive policies to combat global warming since natural capital as such should be kept intact. While some warming might be unavoidable, SS would try to ensure that the future is harmed as little as possible, even if it is materially better off than the present. According to this view, global warming will degrade natural capital and since natural capital cannot be substituted for, global warming has to be prevented quite regardless of the costs of doing so. This position is shared by many environmentalists (see for example Leggett 1990) and it stands in marked contrast to Schelling's (1991, p. 221) belief that 'any disaster to developing countries from climate change will be essentially a disaster to their economic development'.

The real disagreement is about the validity of the substitutability assumption. The proponents of SS and the environmentalists regard the disturbance of the global atmospheric cycle as a harm to future generations that cannot be compensated for by higher consumption even if future generations are as much as 20 times materially better off.

2.5   CONCLUSION

This chapter has laid the foundations for the analysis of the coming chapters. In Section 2.1 SD was defined as development that does not decrease the capacity to provide non-declining per capita utility for infinity. Notably, SD was not defined in direct utility terms, but in terms of the capacity to provide utility. The relevant terms were explained and the economic paradigm was chosen as methodology because both WS and SS are essentially economic. In Section 2.1 it was merely assumed that the current generation is committed to SD, but in Section 2.2.1 some reasons based on Kant's deontological moral theory and Rawls's 'Theory of Justice' were provided for why such a commitment might be a reasonable choice. The commitment might suffer from a time-consistency problem, however, as argued in Section 2.2.2. No definite solution to this problem could be provided, but the argument was put forward that if each generation tries to convince the next generation through the education of its children that a commitment to sustainability is a 'just' thing to do, then there might be a chain of commitment such that the time-consistency problem can be mitigated, if not overcome.

In Section 2.2.3 two popular misunderstandings about SD were resolved. It was shown that SD does not lock society into eternal poverty if it is poor at the start of its commitment to sustainability because SD does not require constant utility throughout time. Hence sacrifices for the sake of future generations are anything but ruled out. It was also shown that SD does not demand the choice of greatly inferior utility paths if a temporary decline in utility along the path can be avoided via increased saving before the expected decline. Section 2.2.3 is important for the later analysis because if these claims about SD were true, a commitment to sustainability could hardly be seen as a defensible choice for society to make. Section 2.3 presented the two paradigms of sustainability. The essence of WS is its assumption that natural capital is substitutable. In contrast, the essence of SS is that it regards natural capital as non-substitutable. In order to highlight the importance of these differing assumptions Section 2.4 looked at the case of global warming. It was shown that the proper conflict between those who demand an aggressive abatement policy and those who call for only minor abatement efforts is about the substitutability of natural capital, not about the 'correct' rate of discount. The next chapter takes a closer look at the validity of these opposing assumptions with respect to the substitutability of natural capital.

NOTES

1 For a short overview of sustainable development views from other disciplines, see Heinen (1994).
2 That is not to say, of course, that everybody in the Bank supports WS. For a differing view of one of the leading economists in the Bank's Environment Department, see Serageldin (1996).
3 It follows that those items of nature that provide disutility to human beings do not count as natural *capital*. The most conspicuous examples are viruses and bacteria that cause diseases.
4 It has become increasingly common in the environmental economics literature to put the *stock* of natural capital into the utility function rather than the *flow* derived from the stock. See, for example, Bovenberg and Smulders (1995), Beltratti (1995), Tahvonen and Kuuluvainen (1993), and Barrett (1992).
5 Except for jewellery perhaps and even there it could be said that gold, silver, diamonds and so on are used to produce the consumption good jewellery and are therefore not directly contributing to utility.
6 The United Nations projects world population by 2050 to be between 11.2 billion (high variant) and 7.7 billion (low variant) (United Nations 1997). An active policy to reduce population growth can make the low variant outcome more likely (Robinson 1998).
7 For a discussion of some ideas concerning an 'optimal' size of population see, for example, Hammond (1988), Daily, Ehrlich and Ehrlich (1994), Broome (1996), and Dasgupta (1998).
8 Note, however, that the so-called Brundtland Report (World Commission on the Environment and Development 1987), which was quite influential in promoting the debate on sustainability, put emphasis on both inter- and intra-generational justice. From this report stems also the best-known non-academic definition of SD as development that 'satisfies the needs of the present without compromising the needs of the future' (Chapter 2, paragraph 1). Also, in 'Southern' debates about SD, the notion of intra-generational fairness features prominently (for example Guha 1989; Agarwal and Narain 1991).
9 In other writings I have put priority on questions of intra-generational fairness. See, for example, Neumayer (1999e).
10 A (pure) public good is characterised by two characteristics: first, non-rivalness in consumption and second, non-excludability. The former means that the consumption of a public good by any individual does not diminish the consumption possibilities for any other individuals. The second characteristic is more problematic. It means that nobody can be excluded from consuming the good. While this might sound rather innocuous, it has the negative consequence that in general there is no sufficient incentive for any private individual to produce the good. This is because since nobody can be excluded from consumption, nobody can be made to pay for the costs of providing the good either. But if the costs cannot be regained, the good will not be privately produced in the first instance. This is the reason why public goods are usually referred to as prime examples for the necessity of government intervention.
11 Rawls (1972, p. 140) himself claims that the notion of the veil of ignorance is already implicit in Kant's moral philosophy.

12   Rawls actually spoke of many individuals, but given his information assumptions the number of individuals can be reduced to one representative individual without loss of generality.

13   Note, however, that Rawls (1972, pp. 284ff.) did not apply his principle to inter-generational matters.

14   Strictly speaking this holds true only if interest rates on debt do not vary according to the purposes for which the debts were contracted.

15   Under certain rather strong assumptions there is no difference, however, in inter-temporal distributional consequences between taxation and debt (Ricardian equivalence), see Barro (1974).

16   This holds true as long as there is no *exogenous* technical progress, that is, technical progress that is independent of the accumulation of man-made capital which is the underlying assumption in Solow (1974a).

17   Strictly speaking, saving and investment measure the change in quantities at prevailing prices, whereas aggregate total value encompasses both quantity and price changes, that is, capital gains, at the same time (Hartwick 1994, p. 4). For a closed economy there are no aggregate capital gains and hence the two measures are equivalent. This is different for open economies where capital gains have to be taken into account (see the discussion of the open economy case in Section 5.1.3, p. 152).

18   For more detail, see Section 5.1.2, p. 142.

19   This is an important point to note. Statements such as 'sustainability is a very tough objective for industrial societies to meet' (Jacobs 1996, p. 8) are contingent on a different definition of sustainability than WS.

20   For an eloquent defence of traditional welfare economics, see Beckerman (1994).

21   Of course, much depends on the exact model specifications. But there are present-value maximisation models (for example, Dasgupta and Heal 1974 and Solow 1974a) with either sub-exponential or zero technical progress that lead to eventual catastrophe for *any* positive constant discount rate (Pezzey 1995, p. 11).

22   Also, while some like Herman Daly would regard themselves as proponents of SS, others like David Pearce would not like to be labelled as proponents of either WS or SS at all.

23   Throughout the book I concentrate mostly on CO_2 emissions since CO_2 has contributed over the last 20 years and is expected to contribute in the future 'about 60 per cent of the radiative forcing from the increase in the greenhouse effect' (Cline 1991, p. 906). The reader should always keep in mind, however, that an efficient strategy to combat global warming would have to take into account all greenhouse-relevant emissions.

24   For a quick overview of the model, see Nordhaus (1994, Chapter 2, pp. 7-21).

25   If uncertainty is also taken into account, then 'the optimal policy ... tends to raise control rates because of the asymmetry in the net damage function' (Nordhaus and Popp 1997, p. 10).

26   On page 10 of his book, Nordhaus (1994) assures the reader that, 'by consumption we mean a broad concept that includes not only traditional purchases of goods and services like food and shelter but also non-market items such as leisure, cultural amenities, and enjoyment of the environment'. This turns out to be an empty promise, however, since on the following pages consumption is used in its traditional sense of consumption of marketed goods and services.

27   Note, however, that WS should be regarded as traditional neoclassical welfare economics plus the *additional* requirement to maintain the capacity to provide non-declining welfare over time. In that respect, WS would come to the same conclusion as Nordhaus does.

28   Note the following caveat, however: observable real rates of return to investment might be high because the economy is non-optimally managed. In particular, major environmental externalities might not be optimally internalised. The social discount rate should take these externalities into account then. Hence the social discount rate would be lower than the private real rate of return to investment (Dasgupta, Barrett and Mäler 1996). See Appendix 3,

p. 218, for a derivation of the result that social discount rates are lower when environmental pollution is taken into account than when they are not.

29 My guess is that the advocates of setting the pure rate of time preference equal to zero if confronted with this argument would retort that policies to boost savings and investment should be undertaken to maximise social welfare.

30 Again, I would guess that Azar and Sterner (1996) would demand to raise this level of aid so as to maximise world social welfare, if only to remain consistent with their own approach.

3. Resources, the Environment and Economic Growth: Why Both Paradigms of Sustainability Are Non-falsifiable

This chapter discusses a natural question that comes to the reader's mind after having been confronted with the two paradigms of sustainability: if they have so starkly differing assumptions about the substitutability of natural capital, can there be a reliable answer as to which paradigm is 'correct'? If society is committed to SD, can science unambiguously endorse one of the two paradigms of sustainability? It will be argued here that both paradigms are non-falsifiable under scientific standards. Therefore there can be no unambiguous support for either WS or SS.

Section 3.1 puts the discussion into context in giving a brief history of resource and environmental concern. Section 3.2 looks at natural capital as an input into the production of consumption goods. It suggests that the resource optimism of WS can be expressed in four propositions and critically assesses each one of them. It looks at:

- Substitution of a resource with other resources.
- The role of prices in overcoming resource constraints.
- Substitution of natural resources with man-made capital.
- The role of technical progress in overcoming resource constraints.

Then, Section 3.3 turns to environmental degradation. Section 3.3.1 looks at the substitutability of natural capital as a direct provider of utility and examines whether future generations can be compensated for long-term environmental degradation with increased consumption opportunities. Section 3.3.2 analyses the environmental consequences of economic growth. It presents, first, the theoretical case for environmental optimism, afterwards the theoretical case for environmental pessimism. Since theory is shown to be unable to resolve the dispute, the empirical evidence is assessed. Section 3.4 concludes and explains why the main argument that both paradigms are non-falsifiable under scientific standards does not depend on a restrictive theory of science.

3.1 A SHORT HISTORY OF RESOURCE AND ENVIRONMENTAL CONCERN

Modern concern that limited availability of natural resources will constrain the possibilities for consumption growth or, for that matter, even non-declining consumption dates back at least to Malthus (1798). He was convinced that the limitedness of land put an absolute scarcity constraint on food consumption growth. While population rose at a geometric rate, the production of food could only be expanded at an arithmetic rate, Malthus thought. Hence, he believed that population could grow only until the minimum subsistence level of per capita food consumption was transgressed and had to decline sharply afterwards — only to grow and hit the absolute scarcity constraint afterwards again in an apparently endless vicious circle. Later on, Jevons (1865) warned against a running out of coal as an energy resource and expressed concern about detrimental consequences of rising coal extraction costs on economic growth and the competitiveness of British industry.

We know by now, of course, that both had been wrong: population grew tremendously in the 19th century and, even more than 130 years after Jevons's alarm, worldwide proven reserves of coal in 1996 would last for another 224 years at current consumption rates (British Petroleum 1997, p. 30). Moreover, coal is not seen as an essential resource any more. Malthus and Jevons committed mistakes other resource pessimists repeated later on. Malthus did not consider the power of technical progress and he was not aware of the fact that, as Ricardo (1817) first realised, land availability is more a question of relative as opposed to absolute scarcity, that is, land is a heterogeneous resource and it is possible to get the same amount of nutrition out of an ever lower quality acre by investing increasing inputs. Jevons, for his part, underestimated the scope for exploration and finding new reserves of coal and neglected the powerful possibilities of substituting other energy resources for coal. One has to keep in mind, however, that concern about the availability of natural resources was deeply rooted in mainstream economic thinking by that time and many classical economists, most notably Mill (1862) and Ricardo (1817), shared the belief that the economy had to stop growing sooner or later due to a resource constraint.[1] In those days economics had a reputation as a 'dismal' science (Barnett and Morse 1963, p. 2).

It was not before the so-called marginal revolution and the rise of neoclassical economics at the turn of the century, mainly due to Alfred Marshall, Léon Walras and Irving Fisher, that concern about resource availability vanished. In its leading macroeconomic metaphor, the income–expenditure cycle, the depletion of natural resources is non-existent in a seemingly endless circular exchange of labour which produces goods to receive income which is in turn exchanged for the produced goods. Reality seemed to buttress this new thinking: the economy kept on growing, especially in the 'golden years' after the Second World War and even if it did not, as in the Great Depression, the reasons were no longer sought in limited natural resources.

Concern about natural resource availability emerged again with the publication of the Club of Rome's 'Limits to Growth' report (Meadows et al. 1972). This concern became popular and widespread after the quadrupling of world oil prices, as OPEC first boycotted the US and the Netherlands for their support of Israel in the Yom Kippur War in 1973 and soon learned to exercise leverage over the OECD countries.[2] Meadows et al. prophesied that the exhaustion of essential mineral and energy resources would make economic growth infeasible some time in the next century. Therefore, a halt to economic growth and even an eventual economic contraction might be enforced through resource scarcity. Essentially the same message was echoed by the Global 2000 Report to the President of the US in 1980 (Barney 1980) and twenty years after their first report, Meadows et al. published an updated, but hardly revised restatement of their argument (Meadows et al. 1992).

Economists, contrary to the wider public, this time did not share the concern about resource availability. Only some 'outsiders', often regarded as eccentrics by the mainstream economist community, had sympathy with the report's motivation and goal, without overlooking the criticisms that could be raised against it (Daly 1992a, first published in 1977; Georgescu-Roegen 1971, 1975; Mishan 1974). In economic terms Meadows et al. were naive in extrapolating past trends without considering how technical progress and a change in relative prices can work to overcome apparent scarcity limits. This criticism was put forward vigorously in a fierce attack by neoclassical economists and other scientists who rejected the report(s) as pure nonsense (Beckerman 1972, 1974; Cole et al. 1973; Solow 1974b; Nordhaus 1973, 1992). For them the depletion of non-renewable resources had to be tackled with traditional economic instruments and had to be taken on board by neoclassical economics (Solow 1974a,c; Dasgupta and Heal 1974; Stiglitz 1974) — but limits to growth due to resource constraints were a non-problem.

For a long time environmental problems were rather regarded as temporary than enduring and were thus by most people not perceived as a fundamental problem of industrialisation and economic growth *per se*. This is true, for example, for the times when many people died due to air pollution (smog) in London at the beginning of this century. The public awakened to the detrimental side-effects of industrialisation and rapid economic growth in the early 1960s, when Carson (1962) expressed her fear about a 'silent spring' due to the death of birds being exposed to DDT. The book became very popular and so, albeit slowly, became the environmental movement popular (for an overview, see McCormick 1989). It was not before the ozone layer depletion, global warming, and biodiversity loss became big issues in the 1980s, however, that environmental degradation was perceived as a potential constraint to economic growth as such. Interest by that time shifted away from natural resource availability towards the environment as a medium for assimilating wastes (from 'source' to 'sink') (Pearce 1993b).

Indicative of this trend is that the second 'Club of Rome' report by Meadows et al. (1992) was much more concerned with environmental degradation than the first report (Meadows et al. 1972). Nevertheless, it seems fair to say that environmental pessimists believe that economic growth in the long run is constrained both by resource availability and by its detrimental effects on the environment. Again, mainstream economists, although expressing some concern about environmental pollution, do not believe in environmental limits to growth (Ravaioli 1995).

The following section starts with the 'source' side of the economy in analysing the availability of resources for the production of consumption goods. So far, the pessimists have been wrong in their predictions. But one thing is also clear: to conclude from the pessimists having been persistently wrong that there is no reason whatsoever to worry is tantamount to committing the same mistake the pessimists are often guilty of — that is the mistake of extrapolating past trends. The future is something inherently uncertain and it is humans' curse (or relief, if you like) not to know with certainty what the future will bring. The past can be a bad guide into the future when circumstances are changing. That the alarmists have regularly and mistakenly cried 'wolf!' does not imply that the woods are safe.

3.2   RESOURCE AVAILABILITY

First, let us have a look at natural capital as an input in the production of consumption goods. Just how scarce are natural resources and can they easily be substituted for by man-made capital or technical progress?[3] The resource optimism of WS can be summarised in four propositions (see the box on the next page).

If resource optimism is correct, then there is no need to worry about the depletion of natural resources: either the world will not be running out of a resource or it will not matter if it does since another resource or man-made capital will function as a substitute. It is the objective of this section to show that as regards the differing assumptions of WS and SS with respect to the substitutability of natural capital in the production of consumption goods, both paradigms are non-falsifiable under scientific standards.

> **A summary of resource optimism in four propositions**
>
> Resource optimism holds that if some resource A is becoming scarce in an economic sense[4] its price will rise, which triggers the following four mutually non-exclusive effects:
>
> a) Demand shifts away from resource A and another resource B becomes economical and substitutes for resource A.
> b) It becomes economical to explore and extract as well as recycle more of resource A. As a consequence, the price of resource A will decline again, thus signalling an ease in economic scarcity.
> c) Man-made capital will substitute for resource A.
> d) More effort is put into technical and scientific progress in order to reduce the necessary resource input per unit of output, thus easing any resource constraint. Also technical and scientific progress make resource extraction cheaper and thus the extraction of a resource's lower-quality ores economical. As a consequence prices will decline again, signalling an ease in economic scarcity.

3.2.1   Substitution With Other Resources

Let us first look at proposition (a) of resource optimism which essentially says that a resource B will substitute for resource A if the latter is running out. If the proposition is correct, then there is no need to worry about the depletion of resource A and since A could be any resource, there is no need to worry about the depletion of any resource at all. The point is that the depletion of a resource does not matter economically if it is or becomes unnecessary for production. It was this Beckerman (1972, p. 337) had in mind when he commented rather cynically on the first 'Limits to Growth' report from the Club of Rome:

> Why should it matter all that much whether we do run out of some raw materials? After all ... economic growth has managed to keep going up to now without any supplies at all of Beckermonium, a product named after my grandfather who failed to discover it in the nineteenth century.

Conversely, the existence of a resource does not matter economically as long as it is without an economic use. As Ray (1984, p. 75) observes:

> All materials used by industry were 'new' at some point in history; they have become 'resources' as a result of scientific and technological advance discov-

ering them and developing their use. Bauxite did not even have a name before it was discovered that it could be processed into a new metal: aluminium.

It is clear, that proposition (a) taken to its logical limit only applies to resources B that are quasi-undepletable, be they renewable or non-renewable. An example for the former is renewable energy from solar influx that will vanish some time in the very long run, but will provide its daily service for all plausible human time understanding. An example for the latter is cold fusion, which is based on a non-renewable resource and which might provide services some time in the future at reasonable costs without an immediate or even intermediate risk of running out. These two examples make clear that ultimately resource B must be something close to what economists call a 'backstop technology'. A backstop technology is a resource that can provide services at constant marginal costs in infinite amount (Dasgupta and Heal 1974). If such a resource exists, then the economy can be saved from doomsday for an indefinite time (Prell 1996).

Is a backstop technology possible? Strictly speaking, neither of our two examples is really a backstop technology, because the amount of services potentially provided, although very huge indeed, is still finite. Presumably, there cannot be any backstop technology in the strict sense, because the first law of thermodynamics (conservation of mass) states that energy cannot be created anew and because the second law of thermodynamics states that entropy in a closed system is monotonically increasing over time, that is, energy is used up and cannot be used over and over again (Söllner 1997, pp. 181, 183). For all human relevance the universe is a closed system. But note: it is the universe that is a closed system, not the earth itself which is an open system in the sense that it is getting a steady, constant, finite influx of energy from the sun. It is a closed system only in so far as it does not exchange matter with the outside. Georgescu-Roegen's (1975, p. 370) suggestion that every car built today implies 'fewer plowshares for some future generations, and implicitly, fewer future human beings, too' due to the laws of thermodynamics is *not* correct in a system that receives a steady, constant, finite influx of energy where it is not compelling that entropy permanently increases.[5]

Now, cold fusion may remain a natural scientist's dream for ever, but solar energy comes close to a backstop technology for energy resources — at least in principle: the solar energy influx exceeds current total world energy demand at about three orders of magnitude (Norgaard 1986, p. 326; Hohmeyer 1992, p. 10). Whether this vast energy influx can be used at reasonable economic costs is less clear, however. Lenssen and Flavin (1996, p. 772) optimistically suggest that, due to rapidly declining provision costs, solar and wind energy as well as geothermal technologies will become fully competitive to fossil energy resources in the near future. They believe that the current energy infrastructure which is based mainly on oil, gas and coal will gradually be replaced by an energy infrastructure based mainly on solar energy and other renewables and using hydrogen as the medium to transfer primary energy to final energy users. They project world primary energy use to rise by slightly less than 50 per cent from 1990 to 2050 and project about half of this energy demand to be provided by renewables in 2050 and more than 85 per cent in 2100 (ibid. 1996, p. 775). Boyle (1993) from the energy policy and research unit of Greenpeace International provides a similar optimistic view.

A different picture is painted by Trainer (1995) who represents the opposite, pessimistic view. He believes that the prospects of renewable resources providing sufficient energy at reasonable economic costs are vastly overestimated in neglecting difficulties of 'conversions, storage and supply' of renewable resources 'for high latitudes' (ibid., p. 1009). He suggests that if the world must depend on renewable energy resources only, then it 'must be based on materially simple lifestyles, a high level of local economic self-sufficiency, and a steady-state or zero-growth economy' (ibid., p. 1025).

Which of the two projections will be closer to *future* reality, we do not know. Projections are highly dependent on prophesying the *future* development of scientific and technical progress, the *future* growth of the economies, populations and world energy demand, and on predicting *future* changes in energy and environmental policies. Beyond the very immediate time span, these projections *necessarily* become closer and closer to sophisticated guesses and speculations lacking a sound and reliable scientific basis. Mistakes in past projections represent a case in point: many reports in the early 1970s overestimated the amount of nuclear power the world would be using in the mid-1990s by a factor of six, while leading studies in the early 1980s overestimated the cost of a barrel of oil by almost a factor of five (Lenssen and Flavin 1996, p. 770). These flawed estimates should remind us that our ability to project world energy supply and its composition, world energy demand and prices is very limited indeed in the intermediate and distant future.

So far we have dealt only with energy resources. Whether solar energy and other renewable energy resources can substitute for non-renewable non-energy resources is even less clear. Direct substitution possibilities might be low, but a backstop energy technology has another advantage as well: if it provides services at not too high costs it can boost the availability of other resources that can be extracted economically — at least if we assume that ever lower quality ores can be extracted with ever rising energy and other inputs and that the costs of extraction do not rise steeply and quickly towards infinity. It was this that Adelman (1990, p. 1) referred to in stating that 'the total mineral in the earth is an irrelevant non-binding constraint', for the question really is whether it will be possible or not to extract ever more resources from ever lower quality ores at reasonable economic costs. Energy is the one and only real limiting factor in the long run, because given enough energy there will always be enough natural non-energy resources extractable from the crust of the earth.

However, there does not seem to exist any serious study that has tried to compute the prospects of backstop technologies to substitute on a large scale for the depletion of non-energy resources in the long run or to facilitate the mining of resource ores of low concentration — which would be an overwhelming task and presumably therefore has not been attempted yet. What we have are more or less optimistic statements, but no comprehensive, detailed analysis — see, for example, Gordon et al. (1987), Scott and Pearse (1992), Beckerman (1995) or Goeller and Zucker (1984, p. 456) who assure the reader that they

> believe that, with a few exceptions, the world contains plentiful retrievable resources that can supply mankind with the necessary materials for the very long term, and that these resources can probably be extracted and converted to useful forms indefinitely with acceptable environmental consequences and within the boundaries of foreseeable economic constraints.

3.2.2   The Role of Prices in Overcoming Resource Constraints

Now let us look at proposition (b). It highlights more than any of the other four propositions the role resource prices play in overcoming resource constraints. Prices serve different functions in an economy, the most important being that they signal economic scarcity and that they act as a coordination mechanism pushing the economy towards efficiency and triggering technical progress. That the pessimists have persistently either ignored or downplayed the role that prices play in easing resource constraints, allowed a former economics professor of mine to make the ironic comment that the world has already run out of oil many times — apparently without any dramatic damage. It is naive, as Meadows et al. (1972) and many others have done, to compare current amounts of resource use with current proven reserves and simply extrapolate from the past that hence the resource will be depleted in x years. For the gradual depletion of a resource affects its price which affects supply and demand to which the economy adapts permanently. This dynamic process makes mockery out of simple-minded static computations of a resource's remaining life-time.

To highlight the role that prices play for resources let us introduce the famous Hotelling rule (Hotelling 1931). The rule says that, under some restrictive assumptions (on which more will be said later on), the resource rent (that is, the price of the resource for the marginal unit minus the marginal cost for extracting this unit) must in a perfectly competitive economy rise at a rate equal to the interest rate for a given stock of a non-renewable resource.[6] The resource rent can be interpreted as the net marginal profit for the resource extractor and is often called 'Hotelling rent'. The rule holds true, with some amendments, for renewable resources as well — see Appendix 2, p. 214. Because of their much higher importance as an input into production, the analysis here refers solely to non-renewable resources.[7]

The intuitive reason why the rule must hold in a context of rational utility-maximising agents is as follows: imagine otherwise, for example, that the resource rent rose at a rate lower than the interest rate. Then it would pay the resource owner to liquidate more of the resource, deposit his or her receipts in a bank and earn interest on his or her account — which gives him or her a higher net rate of return than leaving the resource in the ground since by assumption resource rents rise at a lower rate than the interest rate. It would pay to liquidate more of the resource up until marginal extraction costs rise so much that the resource owner is just indifferent between extracting a marginal resource unit and leaving this unit in the ground. It might be profitable to even liquidate the whole resource stock! Now imagine instead that the resource rent rose at a higher rate than the interest rate. Then it would pay the resource owner to leave more of the resource in the ground in order to extract it later on, thus getting a higher net rate of return than if he or she had extracted the resource right now and had put the receipts in a bank account. The deeper reason why the Hotelling rule must hold is that for the resource owner a stock of non-renewable resource is just another asset in his or her portfolio, so it has to earn an equal net rate of return as the other portfolio assets do. Hence equilibrium is where resource rent rises at a rate equal to the interest rate.

The following simple model derives the Hotelling rule:[8] A representative resource extracting firm maximises its profit π from a given resource stock S over an infinite time horizon. Since we assume perfect competition, the firm takes the price P as given. The problem of the firm is to

$$\underset{R}{Max}\ \pi = \int_{0}^{\infty} \{P(t)R(t) - C[R(t)]\} \cdot e^{-rt}\, dt \qquad (3.1)$$

$$\text{s.t. } \dot{S}(t) = -R(t) \qquad (3.2)$$

$$\text{and } \int_{0}^{\infty} R(t)dt = S(0) \qquad (3.3)$$

where t is a time index, P the price of the resource and R the quantity of resource extracted at each instant of time, and C the total cost of extraction. r is the interest rate that is exogenously given to the model and used by the firm to discount future profits to its present-value. That is, in equation (3.1) the firm chooses a suitable R that maximises the present (discounted) profit of the resource. Equation (3.2) is an equation of motion, where $S(t)$ is the total remaining stock of the resource at each instant of time and the dot indicates the derivative of S with respect to t. Equation (3.2) simply says that the resource stock decreases by the amount of extraction. Equation (3.3) is an integral constraint which says that the integrated sum of all resource depletion should be equal to the initial resource stock $S(0)$. In other words, as time reaches infinity the total stock should be exhausted which is demanded by efficiency: the firm would forgo profits if it did not use up its stock.

The problem is solved by forming the Lagrangian Γ and maximising with respect to R:

$$\underset{R}{Max}\ \Gamma = \int_{0}^{\infty}\{P(t)R(t) - C[R(t)]\}\cdot e^{-rt}\,d - \lambda R(t) \qquad (3.4)$$

where λ is the (constant) Lagrange-multiplier. Assume the cost function to be 'well behaved', that is, strictly convex, continuous and twice differentiable, so that $d^2C/dR^2 > 0$ and the necessary first-order condition is also sufficient for a maximum:

$$(P - \frac{dC}{dR}) = \lambda e^{rt} \qquad (3.5)$$

Define H to be the resource rent:

$$H \equiv (P - \frac{dC}{dR}) \qquad (3.6)$$

λ is constant for this so-called isoperimetric problem (Chiang 1992, pp. 139–43, 280–82). Differentiating (3.5) with respect to time and dividing the result by (3.5) leads to

$$\frac{\dot{H}}{H} = r \qquad (3.7)$$

that is, in the optimum the resource rent rises at the rate of interest (Hotelling rule). The basic result does not change if the firm maximises profits over a *finite* time period. Neither does the basic result depend on the firm being a price taker. If the firm is a price-setting monopolist, for example, it is marginal revenue minus marginal cost that rises at the interest rate and resource depletion is in general slower than under perfect competition (Pearce and Turner 1990, pp. 284–86). The form of market structure is of no further interest to the analysis here, however.

That the resource rent rises at the interest rate holds true more generally, however, only in a setting of certainty about, for example, the size of the resource stock, the date of exhaustion, the existence and marginal costs of a backstop technology and so on.[9] Deshmukh and Pliska (1985) show that the resource rent need not rise at the rate of interest if uncertainty is introduced. One important aspect is the exploration of new reserves. Pindyck (1978) is the seminal paper showing how prices (and resource rent) can fall over time as the exploration of new reserves increases the available resource stock.

To see this, look at the following very simple setting: assume that the marginal costs of resource extraction are constant and equal to zero. Before the discovery of new reserves the resource stock was of size S. The resource rent had to increase at the rate of interest (equation 3.7) and economic efficiency

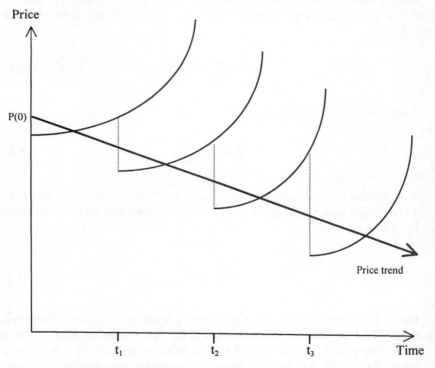

Figure 3.1 Price path with continuous unexpected resource discoveries

demands that the stock is fully exhausted at time $t = \infty$ (equation 3.3), so the price P_0 that was initially set at time $t = 0$ is specified as well (see Figure 3.1). As new reserves become known at time $t = t_1$, the available stock rises. The resource rent still has to rise at the interest rate and economic efficiency still requires that the resource stock is fully exhausted at time $t = \infty$. But the available resource stock has increased, so it follows that the price set at time $t = t_1$ after the discovery of new reserves must lie below the price at time $t = t_1$ just before the discovery. That is, the price at time $t = t_1$ falls down because of new discoveries. If new discoveries are frequent and large enough the overall trend in the resource rent can be downwards over time, as Figure 3.1 shows. Hence actual resource rents might not only fail to rise at the interest rate, but even fall over some time period if unexpected discoveries are made. Note that this does not contradict the Hotelling rule which demands resource rent to rise at the interest rate only for a *given* stock of resources, that is, excluding new formerly unknown resources. And ultimately, of course, the Hotelling rent and therefore the resource price have to rise again because the total resource stock in the earth is finite.

We have derived this qualification to the Hotelling rule in a particularly simple context and looked at unexpected discoveries in an otherwise static environment. But the main result holds true for more complicated contexts as well (see Hartwick and Olewiler 1986; Perman, Ma and McGilvray 1996, pp. 154–59): the resource rent is responsive to changes in the underlying economic scarcity of a resource which suggests resource rent to be a good indicator of economic scarcity. The resource rent reflects the opportunity cost of current resource extraction, that is, the trade-off between resource extraction now and resource extraction in the future. It is a measure of anticipated scarcity of the resource. Rising resource rents would indicate rising scarcity, whereas falling resource rents would indicate falling scarcity and no rise or fall would suggest no change in scarcity.

Unfortunately, resource rent is not directly observable and hence inherently difficult to measure. This is the reason why attempts to validate Hotelling's rule empirically have resulted in contradictory conclusions — see for example Miller and Upton (1985) versus Farrow (1985) and Halvorsen and Smith (1991) who reject the Hotelling hypothesis (for an overview, see Berck 1995). Swierzbinski and Mendelsohn (1989) explain the apparent contradictory results as follows: Miller and Upton (1985) demonstrate that stockholders use the Hotelling rule at each moment of time to forecast the value of their stocks. That time-trend tests of the Hotelling rule (for example, Farrow 1985 and Halvorsen and Smith 1991) have generally failed to support the rule is due to the fact that because of dynamic uncertainty and consistent updating in information the true mean rate of change in the resource price persistently deviates from the deterministic Hotelling rule. Because of that, it is hard to validate or reject the Hotelling rule. Mackellar and Vining (1989, pp. 522f.) even suggest that due to

> changing unit extraction costs, producers' price expectations, imperfect competition, exploration, inefficient capital markets, durability and recycling of the resource in question, and so on, virtually any path of real resource prices over the last century could be judged consistent with the theory [of Hotelling, E.N.].

Note, however, that what Farrow (1985) and Halvorsen and Smith (1991) really reject is not the Hotelling rule as such, which *must* hold in a context of rational utility maximisers, but the simplistic proposition that actual resource rent is rising at the interest rate. One has to keep in mind that the Hotelling rule as introduced above only holds for some rather restrictive assumptions. Hartwick and Hageman (1993, p. 222) have made this point clear:

> We can summarize Hotelling's rule this way: *if*, under quite restrictive assumptions regarding (a) mineral quality, (b) market uncertainty including stock size uncertainty, (c) agents' foresight, and (d) the functioning of futures markets, mineral stock owners are extracting at each date so as to maximize the discounted future profits from their mineral holding, *then* the rental earned on the marginal ton extracted will increase over time at the rate of interest. ... Failure to demonstrate that 'rent rises at the rate of interest' might reflect the invalidity of any one of the assumptions on which this prediction is based. What such failure does not imply, however, is that mineral stock owners are not maximizing discounted future profits (that is, the current market value of the mineral deposit).

Because of the difficulties in measuring resource rent, studies of resource scarcity have come up with two alternative indicators: unit extraction costs, that is, the value of factor inputs per unit of output of the resource-extracting industry, and relative resource prices, that is, the ratio of a resource price index to an overall price index.

The relative resource price indicator is closest to resource rent. It includes the current extraction cost plus the resource rent, that is, the opportunity cost of current extraction. Its rationale is that with approximately constant marginal current extraction costs the change in the overall resource price is a good proxy to the change in the unobservable resource rent, so that with rising resource scarcity the overall resource price would rise relative to a suitably defined overall price index. Its chief advantage is that it is easily observable: 'In today's closely integrated global marketplace, most natural resource commodities trade at a single, US dollar-denominated price' (Mackellar and Vining 1989, p. 525). The rationale for using unit extraction costs instead is that if resource extraction is a Ricardian process, that is, it starts from the high-quality ores and moves continually to the lower-quality ores, then one would expect unit extraction costs to rise with rising resource scarcity. In a competitive context it is reasonable to presume that resource extraction follows a Ricardian process for then 'the market serves as a sensing-selective mechanism, scanning all deposits to take the cheapest increment or tranche into production' (Adelman 1990, p. 3). Unit extraction costs are less easy to observe, at least in highly integrated resource industries because then it becomes difficult to isolate resource extraction costs proper from other costs such as transportation and processing costs (Mackellar and Vining 1989, p. 519).

The classical study of resource scarcity is Barnett and Morse (1963). It examined unit extraction costs for the period 1870–1957 for agricultural, mineral and forest resources in the United States finding a general downward trend with the exception of forestry. Barnett (1979) and Johnson, Bell and Bennett (1980) updated the original study to the 1970s coming to the same principal conclusions of falling unit extraction costs which they interpreted as a decline in resource scarcity.

At the beginning of the 1980s the studies undertaken by Slade (1982) and Hall and Hall (1984) shed some doubt on these findings. Slade (1982) examined relative resource prices for several mineral and energy resources finding evidence for 'U-shaped' price trends, that is, after prices had fallen over a substantial period of time, they were then starting to rise. Slade (ibid., p. 136) concluded that 'if scarcity is measured by relative prices, the evidence indicates that non-renewable natural-resource commodities are becoming scarce'. Similarly Hall and Hall (1984, p. 363) found evidence for 'measurable increasing scarcity of important natural resources' in studying both unit extraction costs and relative resource prices for energy and forestry products in the United States. Both studies claimed that part of the rise in oil prices in the 1970s was due to rising scarcity and not simply an artefact of the exercise of market power by OPEC (Slade 1982, p. 136; Hall and Hall 1984, p. 373). More recent studies have mostly failed to support these findings of rising scarcity.[10] Slade (1988, p. 200) herself admitted in a 1988 paper that there was no statistically significant upward trend in resource prices and in 1992 Slade (1992, p. 7) concluded that there is no evidence of an increase in unit extraction costs and that 'when we consider a century of data, the most striking feature is the decline in the relative price of the majority of mineral commodities'. A recent study by Uri and Boyd (1995) equally failed to find any increase in unit extraction costs or relative resource prices for several mineral resources.

Figure 3.2 shows the trend in the price index (based on constant prices with 1977–79 = 100) of a metals and minerals commodity bundle consisting of copper, tin, nickel, bauxite, aluminium, iron ore, manganese ore, lead, zinc and phosphate rock over the period 1960–94. Even without applying statistical tests it is apparent that there is no visually detectable general trend of prices rising over time. If anything, there is a downward trend in prices.

Can one conclude, therefore, that resources have not become more scarce in an economic sense over the past and will not become scarce in the future? There are two objections to doing so:

1. As pointed out, empirical studies do not measure resource rent, the theoretically correct indicator, but a surrogate indicator. Unfortunately, the forward-looking properties of the surrogate indicators are very poor. They can be very misleading, that is, suggesting the opposite of the true underlying scarcity trend. What is more, they can be contradictory: Brown and Field (1978) detected a rising trend in the relative resource price of lumber while at the same time the unit cost was falling. Why is it that the indicators can be very misleading and contradictory?

   Take unit extraction costs first. If the resource is becoming scarce, unit extraction costs will rise given that resource extraction follows a Ricardian process. However, improvements in the extraction technology countervail this effect and if technical change is sufficiently strong, unit extraction costs can *fall* in spite of *rising* future economic scarcity (Farzin 1995, p. 118). Unit extraction costs only measure the costs of extracting already discovered deposits but do not reflect the costs of future extraction (Fisher 1979, p. 257). It is a backward-, not forward-looking indicator. 'The unit cost measure does not warn us of impending physical exhaustion' (Brown and Field 1979, p. 219). This is no mere theoretical possibility:

Source: WRI (1987, Table 15.3, 1992–93, Table 15.4).

Figure 3.2 Metals and minerals price index (1977–79 = 100)

In the 19th century, technical progress steadily reduced unit extraction cost in the US lumber industry despite the fact that forest resources were disappearing at a rapid rate. The number of some whale species in the oceans has dwindled while superior hunting methods have steadily reduced unit extraction costs. (Mackellar and Vining 1989, p. 520)

Relative resource prices are in principle better suited to predict future resource scarcity, since expectations about the future should enter current prices. In the absence of a complete set of futures markets, however, relative resource prices also fail to reflect future scarcity accurately. That is, relative resource prices are only an imperfect forward-looking indicator. To give an example: Farrow (1995) suggests that the market did not anticipate the end of hunting of passenger pigeons which became extinct 'with hardly a ripple in its commercial price' (Brown and Field 1978, p. 241). More generally, often market prices do not or, rather, cannot take into account ecological thresholds and irreversibilities in depleting natural capital. Resource prices would be much higher if the environmental externalities were internalised. Equally, they cannot work for resources that are characterised by open access.

Since resource prices are supposed to function as a proxy for the unobservable resource rent, problems arise if the link between the price and the rent is rather weak. This will be the case if, for example, substitution among other factor inputs in the processing of the resource is high, because then the price will rise less than the rent. Similarly, if the raw resource (for example, bauxite) has a small share in the production costs of the final good (for example, aluminium), then the price for the final good will be much more influenced by changes in other factor prices than by the resource rent. Another major problem is the selection of an appropriate deflator or numeraire to transform nominal into real resource prices. As Hartwick and Olewiler (1986, pp. 148ff.) report from other studies, trends in resource prices can be quite divergent depending on which deflator — for example, index of factor inputs, index of intermediate goods, index of final goods and services — is used.

The most fundamental objection against using relative resource prices as an indicator for resource scarcity was provided by Norgaard (1990, 1991). His argument is as follows: in an ideal system of complete markets, including futures and options markets, relative resource prices should reflect present and future scarcity accurately. The problem is that this full set of markets is not existent and that therefore traders in natural resource markets have to form their own expectations about scarcity and the future price paths. Since these traders are boundedly rational utility maximisers with imperfect information and imperfect foresight, they might well be

badly informed about real resource scarcity. The same holds true if their
only concern is over the next 5–10 years, as Aage (1984, p. 108) suspects,
or the next 10–20 years, as Ray (1984, p. 76) suggests. But if that is the
case, then

> the cost and price paths their decisions generate are as likely to reflect their
> ignorance as reality. To control for whether or not allocators are informed,
> however, we would have to know whether resources are scarce. Since this is
> the original question, the exercise is logically impossible. (Norgaard 1990,
> pp. 19f.)

Inferring the real underlying scarcity trend from the time series of the
indicator is therefore flawed from the beginning. Norgaard (1991, p. 195)
suggests that the only thing one can really test is whether or not allocators
believe that a resource is scarce and not real scarcity.

2. Past trends cannot simply be extrapolated into the future (and most defi-
   nitely not into the far future). That the resource constraint is not binding
   yet, does not imply that it will not be so in due course. To give an example: the World Bank projects world output to rise at about 3.2 per cent per
   annum (World Bank 1992, p. 9), which means that it would already be
   about 3.5 times higher than present in 2030. It is not all that clear whether
   there are sufficient resources for such a tremendous growth of output. The
   point is that resource pessimists are concerned whether there will be
   enough resources to satisfy a demand that exceeds past levels of demand
   by orders of magnitude.

What about the prospects of recycling, that proposition (b) also refers to?
These prospects are limited as well. Strictly speaking, given a backstop energy technology, the second law of thermodynamics imposes no physical
constraint on the possibilities of recycling material. In principle, given an
unlimited supply of energy, all material could be recycled — a fact that follows directly from the first law of thermodynamics (conservation of mass)
and that was at first denied by Georgescu-Roegen, but later on accepted
(Georgescu-Roegen 1986, p. 11). However, there is an economic constraint
since, for many materials, the costs of recycling material are likely to become
prohibitively high as the recycling rate tends towards 100 per cent. Recycling
can ease a resource constraint for some time, but it cannot overcome it in the
end. For a detailed discussion of the physical principles governing the possibilities of recycling material, see Georgescu-Roegen (1986), Biancardi et al.
(1993, 1996), Khalil (1994), Kummel (1994), Mansson (1994), and Converse
(1996).

3.2.3   Substitution With Man-made Capital

Now let us turn to proposition (c). Evidently, proposition (a) cannot be a satisfactory solution, if there is no backstop technology that can substitute for all economically relevant resources and substituting them by renewable resources is either infeasible or would hugely overstretch their regenerative capacity.[11] Equally, proposition (b) cannot be a satisfactory solution if we take on a very long-run perspective, because in the end a non-renewable resource is just that: non-renewable and it will be depleted in some finite time.[12] The resource might still be substituted with man-made capital then.

But can man-made capital substitute for an ever diminishing resource stock? Daly (1994, p. 25) tries to refute the possibility of substituting man-made capital for natural capital (here: natural resources) with a general argument:

> One way to make an argument is to assume the opposite and show that it is absurd. If man-made capital were a near perfect substitute for natural capital, then natural capital would be a near perfect substitute for man-made capital. But if so, there would have been no reason to accumulate man-made capital in the first place, since we were endowed by nature with a near perfect substitute.

Daly's argument is incorrect, however. It says that if A is a near perfect substitute for B, then B must be a near perfect substitute for A. However, the conclusion does not follow from the premise. A might have some additional desirable properties that B does not have: for some production purposes A and B are almost near perfect substitutes with almost linear isoquants. But for other purposes, A has some desirable properties that B does not have. Hence, A can substitute for the totality of B, but not vice versa. Hence, there is reason to accumulate A and substitute for B.

Solow (1974a) and Dasgupta and Heal (1979) have proved that, in theory at least, man-made capital can substitute for an ever diminishing natural resource.[13] Dasgupta and Heal (1979) examine under which conditions a non-renewable resource is essential and when it is inessential, where an essential resource is defined as a resource for which 'feasible consumption must necessarily decline to zero in the long run' (p. 199). To make analysis possible they have to assume some sort of production function and they take the constant elasticity of substitution (CES) production function, which is the most prominent production function in economics, for reasons of simplicity. Since they assume that labour is constant, one can as well normalise it to one and suppress it and put only man-made capital K and resource input R as arguments into the function. Hence the constant elasticity of substitution refers to the elasticity of substitution between reproducible man-made capital and the non-renewable resource. Let us call this elasticity σ. The CES function can be represented as follows:

$$F(t) = \left\{ \alpha K(t)^{(\sigma-1)/\sigma} + \beta R(t)^{(\sigma-1)/\sigma} + (1-\alpha-\beta) \right\}^{\sigma/(\sigma-1)} \qquad (3.8)$$

where F is produced output and $\alpha, \beta > 0$, $\alpha+\beta < 1$, and

$$\sigma = \frac{d \ln\left(K/R\right)}{d \ln\left|MRS_{K,R}\right|} \Rightarrow \sigma \geq 0 .\text{[14]} \qquad (3.9)$$

where MRS is the marginal rate of substitution between K and R:

$$MRS_{K,R} = \frac{dK}{dR} = -\frac{\partial F/\partial R}{\partial F/\partial K} = \frac{P_R}{P_K} \qquad (3.10)$$

and P_K, P_R is the price of the man-made capital factor and resource factor price, respectively. The higher is σ, the better can resources be substituted by man-made capital. There are three cases to distinguish: first, $\sigma > 1$; second, $\sigma = 1$ and third, $\sigma < 1$.

The first case is trivial and therefore uninteresting. To see this, note that with $\sigma > 1$ all exponents become greater than zero and since resources enter the production function only in an additive way they are inessential. However, for the same reason it is possible to have $F(K,0) > 0$, that is, production without any input of resources, which contradicts the first law of thermodynamics. That something can be produced without any resource input is a physical impossibility. $\sigma > 1$ can therefore be dismissed.

The third case is uninteresting as well. Note that for this case the average product of the resource, F/R, is

$$F(t)/R(t) = \left\{ \alpha K(t)^{(\sigma-1)/\sigma} + \beta R(t)^{(\sigma-1)/\sigma} + (1-\alpha-\beta) \right\}^{\sigma/(\sigma-1)} \cdot R(t)^{-1} \quad (3.11)$$

or equivalently,

$$F(t)/R(t) = \left\{ \alpha \left(\frac{R(t)}{K(t)} \right)^{(1-\sigma)/\sigma} + \beta + (1-\alpha-\beta)R(t)^{(1-\sigma)/\sigma} \right\}^{\sigma/(\sigma-1)} \qquad (3.12)$$

and it is bounded above as the resource becomes depleted, because as $R \to 0$, F/R becomes

$$\lim_{R \to 0} {F(t)}/{R(t)} = \beta^{\sigma/(\sigma-1)} \tag{3.13}$$

With a finite resource stock and no technical progress, the boundedness of the average product F/R implies that total output is finite so that output must decline to zero as time goes to infinity. In the limit with $\sigma = 0$ the CES-function degenerates into a so-called Leontief production function of the form $F(K,R) = \min(vK, wR)$ with $v > 0$, $w > 0$, which means that all substitution possibilities are ruled out and we reached perfect complementarity (Varian 1992, p. 20).

In the second case, with $\sigma = 1$ the CES function is formally undefined but can be shown to collapse into a function that is known by economists as the Cobb–Douglas production function (Chiang 1984, pp. 428ff.). It takes the following form:

$$F(t) = K(t)^{\alpha} \cdot R(t)^{\beta} \tag{3.14}$$

It is apparent, that the resource is not trivially inessential since without resources ($R = 0$) no production is possible, that is, $F = 0$. However, dividing F by R and taking the partial derivative of F with respect to R shows that

$$ {F}/{R} = \frac{K^{\alpha}}{R^{(1-\beta)}} \quad \text{and} \quad \partial F / \partial R = \beta \left({F}/{R} \right), \tag{3.15}$$

so for $\sigma = 1$ both the average (F/R) and marginal product $\partial F / \partial R$ of the resource are unbounded and both F/R and $\partial F / \partial R \to \infty$ as $R \to 0$. This combination ensures that the case $\sigma = 1$ is non-trivial: it is not overtly clear whether the resource is essential or not. Dasgupta and Heal (1979, pp. 200–205) prove that it is not if $\alpha > \beta$, that is if the elasticity of output with respect to man-made capital is higher than the elasticity of output with respect to the nonrenewable resource. There is no direct intuition for this result beyond the mathematical necessity. However, since in a competitive economy these elasticities are equal to the share of total income going to the factors man-made capital and resources, respectively (Euler's theorem), Dasgupta and Heal (1979, p. 200) circumscribe the condition $\alpha > \beta$ with the condition that man-made capital is 'sufficiently important in production'. Solow (1974a, p. 39), Hartwick (1977, p. 974) and Dasgupta and Heal (1979, p. 205) suggest that man-made capital's share is as much as four times higher than the share of resources, so that resources are not essential for the Cobb–Douglas case.[15]

There are several objections that can be raised against being optimistic as a consequence of this analysis, however:

1. The first objection is that we do not know whether σ is greater than, equal to or smaller than 1. In one of the rare attempts to estimate elasticities of substitution for non-energy resources, Brown and Field (1979, p. 241) found high elasticities of substitution for steel, copper, pulp and paper through man-made capital and labour. Deadman and Turner (1988, p. 91) present qualitative evidence for low elasticities of substitution for beryllium, titanium and germanium. There are more econometric studies on the relationship between man-made capital and energy. Table 3.1 summarises the findings of several studies. It is important to note that the reported values are not the σ's as defined above, but so-called 'Allen partial elasticity of substitution' values, σ(AES), with

$$\sigma(AES) = \frac{\partial \ln K}{\partial \ln P_E} \Big/ M_E \qquad (3.16)$$

where P_E is the price of energy and M_E is the share of energy in total production costs. σ(AES) is not bounded below by zero and its values are not directly transferable into values of σ. However, negative values of σ(AES) signal complementarity between man-made capital and energy and the more negative is σ(AES) the higher is the complementarity. Vice versa for positive values of σ(AES) which signal substitutability (Allen 1938, p. 509).

Table 3.1 shows extreme variance in results ranging from complementarity to substitutability. There is much dispute about possible explanations for these 'notably contradictory' (Solow 1987, p. 605) findings, without a resolution — see Berndt and Field (1981) and Solow (1987). Some argue that time-series econometric studies are likely to find complementarity, whereas cross-section analyses are likely to find substitutability between energy and man-made capital (Griffin 1981, pp. 71–4). This is because relative factor price variations tend to be much more pronounced cross-sectionally than over time within one country. If these relative price differentials have been existent for a long time, cross-section studies are likely to find long-run equilibrium effects and in the long run we would always expect higher substitutability between factors than in the short run.

Looking at Table 3.1 shows, however, that some studies do not fit this explanation. At best, it can therefore only be part of the story. Another explanation offered by Berndt and Wood (1979, pp. 349f.) is that studies that find substitutability usually tend to include only three factors (labour, manmade capital and energy) in the production function, whereas studies that find complementarity include materials as a fourth factor. But, again, there are some studies using four inputs and still finding substitutability between capital and energy (for example, Turnovsky et al. 1982). A third reason for the differing results is given by Solow (1987) and Chichilnisky and Heal (1983). They develop models in which different countries can exhibit either substitutability or complementarity between energy and man-made capital in spite of having the same physical production function. These differences can occur because of differences in energy prices and differences in energy demand conditions. Overall, it has to be said that a satisfactory explanation for the variance in results from econometric studies has not been found yet and that we do not have a reliable answer on the question whether energy and man-made capital are substitutes or complements. Hence it is not possible to conclude that resources in reality are inessential.

Table 3.1 Estimates of the capital–energy Allen partial elasticity of substitution

σ(AES)	Sample	Type of data	Source
−1.39	US	1947–71 time-series	Hudson and Jorgenson (1974)
−3.22	US	1947–71 time-series	Berndt and Wood (1975)
1.07 / 1.03	US/9 OECD countries	1955–69 cross-section	Griffin and Gregory (1976)
1.22	7 OECD countries	1963–74 time-series	Özatalay et al. (1979)
−2.32	Netherlands	1950–76 time-series	Magnus (1979)
0.36–1.77	10 OECD countries	1963–73 time-series	Pindyck (1979)
−3.8	US	1971 cross-section	Field and Grebenstein (1980)
2.26	Australia	1946–75 time-series	Turnovsky et al. (1982)
−1.35	US	1971–76 cross-section	Prywes (1986)
2.17	Taiwan	1956–71 time-series	Chang (1994)

2. The second objection is that we cannot rule out the possibility that σ becomes smaller than 1 as more and more of the resource is used up. That is, σ is not constant over time, but itself a function of time, that is, $\sigma = \sigma(t)$. Dasgupta and Heal assume a CES production function for simplicity, but there is no reason to expect that in reality the elasticity of substitution between man-made capital and resources is constant over time. As Dasgupta and Heal (1979, p. 207) admit themselves, constancy might be a flawed assumption as the resource is run down and the ratio of man-made capital to resources becomes very high. Especially in that phase even assuming σ = 1 might contradict physical laws since it assumes that F/R and $\partial F/\partial R \to \infty$ as $R \to 0$, that is, the average product and the marginal product of the resource tend toward infinity as the resource stock tends to zero.

3. The third objection applies the same kind of argument to the share of man-made capital and the resource share of total income. There is no reason to expect that in reality those shares remain constant as the stock of resource tends toward depletion (Slade 1987, p. 351). That is, α and β are not constant over time, but themselves functions of time, that is, $\alpha = \alpha(t)$ and $\beta = \beta(t)$. Hence, even if σ was constantly equal to 1 throughout, the elasticity of output with respect to the resource $\beta(t)$ might supersede the elasticity of output with respect to man-made capital $\alpha(t)$ after which the resource will become essential.

4. The fourth objection is that the dichotomy of man-made capital versus resources is an artificial and flawed one since man-made capital consists partly of resources. Victor (1991) looks at the properties of a Cobb-Douglas production function if it is assumed that man-made capital is itself produced from man-made capital, resources and labour. Let the production function F be of the form[16]

$$F = K^c R^d L^e , \text{ with } c, d, e > 0 \text{ and } c + d + e = 1 \qquad (3.17)$$

Now let the production function for producing man-made capital goods be of the form

$$K = K^p R^q L^s , \text{ with } p, q, s > 0 \text{ and } p + q + s = 1 \qquad (3.18)$$

Solving (3.18) for K gives

$$K = R^{\left(\frac{q}{1-p}\right)} L^{\left(\frac{s}{1-p}\right)} \qquad (3.19)$$

Substituting (3.19) into (3.17) and re-arranging we arrive at

$$F = R^{\left(\frac{c \cdot q}{1-p}+d\right)} L^{\left(\frac{c \cdot s}{1-p}+e\right)} \tag{3.20}$$

It is obvious that man-made capital can no longer infinitely substitute for an ever declining resource stock. Of course, resources might still be substituted for by an ever increasing labour input; but in contrast to man-made capital, labour is not a factor that can be increased indefinitely since labour is supplied by human beings who, by the way, also consume natural resources. That is, in effect, given that resources are needed for the production of man-made capital goods, resources become essential for production even for the Cobb–Douglas case: man-made capital cannot infinitely substitute for vanishing resources.

Note, however, that just because substitution possibilities are restricted, this does not imply that R and K are complements as Daly (1995a, p. 51) erroneously suggests when he argues as follows:

> Manmade capital is itself a physical transformation of natural resources which are the flow yield from the stock of natural capital. Therefore, producing more of the alleged substitute (manmade capital), physically requires more of the very thing being substituted for (natural capital) — the defining condition of complementarity.

The first part of this argument is undoubtedly correct because it follows from the first law of thermodynamics (conservation of mass). The problem with the second part of the argument is, however, that the conclusion ('complementarity') does not follow from the correct observation. In economic terms perfect complementarity is defined as a limitational production function of the form $F[K(R), R] = \min (vK, wR)$, with $v > 0$, $w > 0$ being parameters and isoquants that look like rectangles. In words, increasing man-made capital input in the production process for output does not increase output if resource input is not increased at the same time. Daly (1995a, p. 55) accepts this definition. However, the simple fact that one input into the production of man-made capital is natural capital does not imply complementarity thus defined.

One can show this both for the case that the economy is on the production possibility frontier and for the case that it is not. Let us start with the latter case first: assume an economy with an endowment of 5 units of man-made capital and 10 units of resources. Assume for simplicity that each unit of capital together with 2 units of resources produces exactly 1 unit of the consumption good. Further assume that man-made capital and resources are perfect substitutes in the production of the consumption good, that is, instead of using 10 units of resources and 5 units of capital to produce 5 units of the consumption good, one could also use 10 additional units of capital to substitute for the resource. Assume, however, that the production of each capital good itself requires 0.5 units of natural resources. Now, produce 10 additional units of the capital good to substitute for the 10 units of resources in the production of the consumption good. Since the production of each unit of capital requires only 0.5 units of natural resources, total resource input has decreased by 5 units. These 5 units could be used to increase production. It follows that $K = K(R)$ does not imply that output cannot be increased without increasing resource input at the same time.

Of course, as soon as all resources have been substituted for in the production of the consumption good, then, in the absence of technical progress, there is no longer leeway for substitution since the resource requirement for the production of the capital good is presumed to be fixed. That is, with $K = K(R)$, it is not possible to increase production indefinitely while at the same time driving resource use down to zero. This is the case of the economy being on the production possibility frontier. By assumption all the available resources are in efficient use and output cannot be increased further. However, for this case as well Daly's argument is not correct: the pure fact that resources are needed for the production of man-made capital ($K = K(R)$), does not imply anything for the shape of the isoquants in the production function for the consumption good and therefore does not imply that $F[K(R), R] = \min (vK, wR)$. As Pearce (1997c, p. 296) points out, if Daly's argument was valid then all forms of capital would be complements to each other since all forms of capital embody to some extent other forms of capital as well. Daly's misrepresentation prompted Solow (1997, p. 267) to retort that 'one of his [Daly's, E.N.] lesser problems is that he does not understand what economists mean when they speak of complements and substitutes'.

3.2.4   The Role of Technical Progress in Overcoming Resource Constraints

Let us finally turn to proposition (d). Technical progress can be divided into what economists call 'resource-augmenting' technical progress and what I call 'augmenting-resource' technical progress for lack of a *terminus technicus*. Resource-augmenting technical progress increases the efficiency of resource use and means that ever more output can be produced from a given amount of resources or that for a given output ever less resource input is needed, respectively. 'Augmenting-resource' technical progress reduces resource extraction costs which means that lower-quality ores of a resource become economical to extract. This implies that the economically relevant resource stock *increases* although the total physical stock of a finite non-renewable resource cannot be increased, of course. It is this Baumol (1986) had in mind when he spoke misleadingly of 'the possibility of continuing expansion of finite resources'. Note that this conjecture does not contradict the laws of thermodynamics, as Young (1991) erroneously suggested.

In some sense technical progress is the strongest proposition of the resource optimists. Let us turn to resource-augmenting technical progress first. It is easy to show that if there is permanent resource-augmenting technical progress, that is, if a unit of output can be produced with ever declining resource inputs, then the resource is inessential even if substitution possibilities between man-made capital and resources are nil (Dasgupta and Heal 1979, p. 207). Assume, for example, that there is exponential resource-augmenting technical progress. The production function now looks like

$$F = F\left[K(t), R(t) \cdot e^{kt}\right] \qquad (3.21)$$

with k as the rate of technical progress. It is obvious that permanent resource-augmenting technical progress can compensate for an ever diminishing natural resource stock. The same holds true as Stiglitz (1974) proves for so-called Hicks-neutral technical progress, that is, technical progress that cannot be attributed to a production factor, given

- that the production function is Cobb–Douglas, that is, $\sigma = 1$,
- that m/β is sufficiently large, where m is the rate of Hicks-neutral technical progress and β is the income share of the resource, so that m/β can be loosely[17] interpreted as the rate of resource-augmenting technical progress (Toman, Pezzey and Krautkraemer 1995, p. 145).

However, whether permanent resource-augmenting technical progress is possible, especially in the limit as resource stocks go down, is unclear. Ayres and Miller (1980) and Gross and Veendorp (1990) suggest that assuming so contradicts the first law of thermodynamics (conservation of mass). There are likely to be limits to increasing efficiency. While it might be possible to reduce the required resource input per unit of output by a factor of, say, 10 or sometimes even 100, for most resources it is presumably technically not possible to increase efficiency by a factor of 1000 or more.

Unfortunately, it is rather difficult to measure resource-augmenting technical progress. Take energy use as an example. Often one finds figures of en-

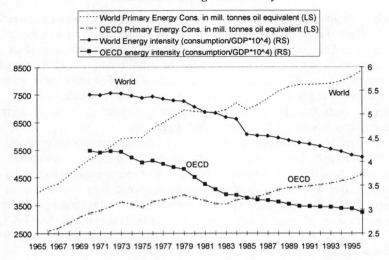

Sources: Primary Energy Input: British Petroleum (various years), GDP: World Bank (1991, 1995b) and IMF (1997).

Figure 3.3 Energy consumption and energy intensity

ergy intensity declining over time.[18] See Figure 3.3, which shows the time trend in energy intensity for the world and for OECD countries.

Energy intensity is the ratio of energy input expressed in physical terms to the value of economic output, usually GDP.[19] The problem with this measurement is that it does not directly measure changes in the technical energy efficiency of production which is what we are looking for when we want to measure resource-augmenting technical progress. A decline in the energy intensity of an economy can come about for a number of reasons other than technical progress itself, for example because of a change in the sectoral structure of the economy, because of substitution of labour or man-made capital for energy, because of a change in the energy input mix towards energy sources which can provide more useful work per unit of heat and so on (Patterson 1996; p. 381, Kaufmann 1992). Reliable evidence on this point is hard to get. Kaufmann (1992) claims that his more complex econometric testing approach refutes earlier evidence from simpler regression models, for example, Howarth (1991), which found technical progress to be a statistically significant and important contributor to the decline in energy intensity. Kaufmann (1992, p. 54), on the contrary, suggests 'that most of the changes are associated with shifts in the types of energies used and the types of goods and services consumed and produced'. Equally inconclusive is the situation for non-energy resources. Slade (1987, p. 351) cites evidence that suggests that technical progress has been resource saving in some sectors but resource using in others.

Another caveat in inferring conclusions from looking at resource-augmenting technical progress is that even if resource intensities are falling over time, *absolute* resource consumption may well rise if the rate of consumption growth is higher than the rate of resource-augmenting technical progress. Looking again at Figure 3.3 shows that while energy intensities have fallen over time both worldwide and for the OECD countries, consumption of primary energy has continuously risen due to tremendous population and output growth. Recent evidence even seems to suggest that resource intensity might revert to rise again at high levels of income. De Bruyn and Opschoor (1997, p. 266) found evidence for developed countries showing their aggregate consumption of materials, energy and transport 'again increasing faster than GDP' in the late 1980s and early 1990s after more than a decade of de-linking resource consumption from economic growth.

In fact, falling energy intensity and rising absolute energy consumption are even more closely related: resource-augmenting technical progress reduces the implicit price of energy, thus making production cheaper, boosting production and favouring the substitution of energy for other factors of production, which in return implies, *ceteris paribus*, an increased demand for energy (Brookes 1990, 1992). Khazzoom (1987) and Brookes (1990, 1992) believe that this 'rebound' effect will in most cases be strong enough to lead to a *net* increase in energy use. Howarth (1997, p. 8) has shown, however, that this conjecture will only hold true under the conditions that '(i) energy accounts for a large fraction of the total cost of energy services and (ii) the production of energy services constitutes a substantial fraction of economic activity'. He finds that neither of these conditions is empirically plausible.

Let us now turn to 'augmenting-resource' technical progress. Slade's (1982) and Berck and Roberts's (1996) models show how improvements in the resource-extraction technology can lead to a persistent downward trend in unit extraction costs and real resource prices over quite a long time span although the total resource stock becomes physically smaller.

Using the simple model we introduced in Section 3.2.2, p. 51, we can show how the resource price can fall over time given sufficient progress in resource-extraction technology. Assume that there is exponential technical progress at a constant rate k so that resource-extraction costs develop according to $C(t) = C(0) \cdot e^{-\kappa t}$ The new problem facing the competitive resource-extracting firm is to

$$\text{Max} \, \Gamma = \int_0^\infty \left[P(t)R(t) - R(t) \cdot C(0) \cdot e^{-kt} \right] \cdot e^{-rt} \, dt - \lambda R(t) \qquad (3.4')$$

which has the first-order condition:

$$P = \lambda e^{rt} + C(0) \cdot e^{-kt} \tag{3.5'}$$

Differentiating (3.5') with respect to time leads to (λ constant)

$$\dot{P} = r\lambda e^{rt} - kC(0) \cdot e^{-kt} \tag{3.6'}$$

Both terms on the right-hand side of (3.6') are positive. The second term is increasing in k (for $0 < k < 1$), hence (3.6') can become negative if k is sufficiently large: resource prices can fall if technical progress is sufficiently strong.

Technical progress can boost the economically relevant resource stock and ease the resource constraint over a significant time span. However, whether there will be and can be permanent and at best exponential technical progress is unclear, of course. That there has been enormous technical progress in the past is beyond doubt, but there is no assurance that there will also be permanent technical progress in the future. As Lecomber (1975, p. 45) has put it: 'The central feature of technical advance is indeed its uncertainty'. It all boils down to whether you believe strongly in technical progress or not. It is worth quoting Beckerman (1972, p. 338) at some length here:

> In fact, given the natural concentrations of the key metals in the Earth's crust as indicated by a large number of random samples the total natural occurrence of most metals in the top mile of the Earth's crust has been estimated to be about a million times as great as present known reserves. Since the latter amount to about a hundred years' supplies this means we have enough to last about one hundred million years. Even though it may be impossible at present to mine to a depth of one mile at every point in the Earth's crust, by the time we reach the year A.D. 100,000,000 I am sure we will think up something. If the idea that actual reserves might be a million times currently proved reserves seems unbelievable it should be borne in mind that existing proved reserves are probably about a million times as big as those known in the days of Pericles.

This is resource optimism in its purest form, but it is also pure speculation. We simply cannot rely on Beckerman's faith becoming true.

So far we have only looked at the 'source' side of the economy. Now we take a look at the 'sink' side of the economy and environmental degradation.[20] In reality, of course, there is no such strict dichotomy between both aspects since a renewable resource that becomes exhausted while using it up in production might have provided other environmental amenity functions for human beings as well. Or the mining of resources produces environmentally detrimental side-effects as is the case in extracting bauxite for the production of aluminium.

3.3 ENVIRONMENTAL DEGRADATION

First of all, we shall analyse whether future generations can be compensated for long-term environmental degradation via increased consumption. For behind the paradigm of WS stands the presumption that rising output can compensate future generations for a degraded environment, whereas SS as defined in Section 2.3.2, p. 26, denies this possibility.

3.3.1 Can Future Generations be Compensated for Long-Term Environmental Degradation?

The problem with assessing this question is that one has to rely to an enormous extent on speculation since we cannot know for sure how future generations will value consumed output relative to environmental services. It seems safe to assume that all individuals independent of the generation they belong to share the same basic needs and wants (such as water, food, shelter, fresh air, basic enjoyments). One might want to argue therefore that ever rising output cannot compensate for the extinction of all renewable resources and for ever rising pollution since this would most likely endanger the satisfaction of basic needs and wants. It does not follow, however, that all environmental damage has to be avoided and that consumption growth cannot compensate for environmental degradation to a certain extent. Barry (1991, p. 248) argues that while 'it is true that we do not know what the precise tastes of our remote descendants will be, they are unlikely to include a desire for skin cancer, soil erosion, or the inundation of all low-lying areas as a result of the melting of the ice-caps'. Whether this argument makes sense or not depends on what you mean by 'tastes'. Surely, nobody has a desire for skin cancer as such, but whether future generations will accept an increase in the rate of skin cancer or not might depend on what they get in exchange for it. Given the choice between no change at all and a society with hugely improved living standards and increased life expectancies but a somewhat higher chance of developing skin cancer at some age, I would not be too sure that future generations would prefer the former option to the latter. The point is that not imposing any harm on the future carries with it a tremendous opportunity cost. The world we live in is full of trade-offs and decisions on how to solve these trade-offs can sometimes be quite awkward. As we shall see in Section 4.5, p. 123, there are no easy answers on these questions. But, as will be argued in more detail there, ignoring the existence of fundamental trade-offs does not seem to be appropriate.

Ideally, one would want to ask future generations which harm they regard as not amenable to compensation. Since this is simply impossible, one could as a substitute try to find out which forms of harm to the environment the *current* generation regards as undesirable no matter what the cost of avoiding the harm. More formally, it would have to be investigated whether and to what extent individuals of the current generation exhibit something close to what economists call 'lexicographic preferences' with respect to the environment. Unfortunately, there is hardly any reliable evidence on this point as I shall show now.

It is often claimed that substantial minorities in contingent valuation (CV) studies respond in ways that can be interpreted as being consistent with lexicographic preferences with respect to wildlife and biodiversity protection: 24 per cent of the sample in Stevens et al. (1991), 23 per cent of the sample in Spash and Hanley (1995) and 14 per cent or 19 per cent (depending on the definition) in Hanley and Milne (1996). These studies do not really prove the existence of lexicographic preferences with respect to the environment, however, as a closer inspection makes clear. In Stevens et al. (1991, p 398), for example, the 24 per cent of the sample actually consist both of people who state that wildlife preservation is always more important to them than having more money *and* of people who state that more money is always more important to them than wildlife preservation. Also, their indicated preference is not challenged with a real test. In Spash and Hanley (1995) respondents are counted as exhibiting lexicographic-type preferences for biodiversity protection if they state that biodiversity should be protected irrespective of the costs and refuse to indicate a private willingness-to-pay for biodiversity protection. However, the respondents are not pushed hard with regard to the cost side of protection. Because of the hypothetical character of CV studies, it is all too easy and cheap for individuals to state that they want environmental preservation no matter what the cost. Lexicographic preferences cannot be inferred from these results as long as everything remains hypothetical and the respondents' indicated preferences are not exposed to the acid test of real sacrifices.[21]

In Hanley and Milne (1996, p. 260) respondents are confronted more elaborately with the cost side of preservation. While 99 per cent affirm that 'wildlife and landscape have the right to be protected', this response rate goes down to 49 per cent if protection 'costs jobs/money', down to 38 per cent if it costs 10 per cent of the respondent's income and ends up at 19 per cent if preservation cost was 25 per cent of the respondent's income. As can be seen, the preferences of individuals become 'less lexicographic' as costs increase. And, of course, for a really reliable test respondents would have to be willing to give up almost all their income to keep them just on this side of the bare existence minimum and they would have to do so in reality. Do we really believe that there are more than a few individuals who would go so far?

Be that as it may, even if one accepted that about one-fifth of the population exhibited lexicographic preferences with respect to wildlife, biodiversity and landscape protection as indicated by the mentioned studies, would it follow that one should regard environmental harm as non-compensable? The answer is no. First, it would have to be shown that lexicographic preferences are existent in more general terms for environmental amenities and not only for preserving species and landscapes. Do people want to preserve the current climate and reduce carbon dioxide emissions very drastically no matter what the cost? I doubt it. Second, the vast majority quite clearly does *not* exhibit lexicographic preferences, however measured. Their indicated preferences rather follow the usual trade-offs that conform with the substitutability assumption of WS. That only a minority exhibits behaviour that is compatible with lexicographic preferences is also confirmed by a contingent ranking study of Foster and Mourato (1997, p. 18) who find that 'only some 18 per cent of respondents answered *all* their ranking questions lexicographically'.

All these qualifications notwithstanding, SS is quite explicit in rejecting the possibility of compensation for long-term environmental degradation. It seems fair to say that it rejects compensability also for normative reasons. In other words, consumption growth *should* not be allowed to compensate for future environmental degradation. The proposition would therefore not be refuted by the fact that empirical evidence for existing lexicographic preferences is rather weak. However, if it is taken as a normative position the more important it then becomes to scrutinise how much opportunity costs both the present and future generations would have to bear in order to obey such a normative prescription. This is a question that will be taken up in more detail again in Section 4.5, p. 123, on the problem of opportunity cost of preserving natural capital.

In conclusion, the proposition of SS that natural capital should in principle be regarded as non-substitutable as a direct provider of utility and that therefore increased consumption cannot compensate for environmental degradation seems hard to defend if it is taken as a *positive* position and is non-refutable if it is taken as a *normative* position. On the other hand, presumably not many people will find the opposite extreme suggestion very attractive that rising consumption can always compensate coming generations for a deterioration in the environmental conditions. There is the possibility, however, that preferences will accommodate to a changing world. Individuals born into a world where, for example, 99 per cent of all species are lost might build up preferences such that they do not feel this as a great loss. Arguably, many people living in urban areas have already become used to encountering only a small number of animals and plants personally. The same holds potentially true for environmental pollution as well. The point is that preferences are determined partly by the changing outside world; they are not as solid and unchanging as the Rocky Mountains, as Becker and Stigler (1977, p. 76) suggest. Still more frightening is the emerging possibility of adapting individuals to a world empty of environmental amenities and full of pollution via genetic engineering.

However, it seems fair to say that proponents of WS sincerely believe that in the end economic growth will be rather beneficial and not harmful for the environment (World Bank 1992). The paradigm of WS would therefore not have to rely so much upon the substitutability assumption with respect to natural capital as a more direct provider of utility.

I shall take the conjecture that economic growth will improve environmental conditions as the main proposition of WS with respect to environmental degradation and call it 'environmental optimism'. It is therefore necessary now to analyse the link between economic growth and environmental degradation.

3.3.2   Economic Growth and Environmental Degradation

Before discussing in detail the theoretical arguments concerning the environmental consequences of economic growth and the available evidence which will fill the rest of this section, let us examine first why it is that the economic activity and especially economic growth pose a problem for the environment. The first law of thermodynamics, that is, the law of conservation of mass, implies that no material can be destroyed, it can only be transformed into other goods (bound to become waste some time), and into waste, pollution and so on. That is, if all other things are equal, then economic activity and the more so economic growth 'is inevitably an entropic process that increases the amount of unavailable (that is, dissipated or high entropy) resources at the expense of available (that is, ordered or low entropy) resources: the stock of wastes increases and environmental quality decreases'[22] (Smulders 1995, p. 165).

Of course, it is the WS-proponents' argument that all other things are *not* equal and we turn to this now in presenting the case for environmental optimism. After that, the opposite case of environmental pessimism is put forward and it is assessed whether empirical evidence is able to decide between the opposite claims.

3.3.2.1 The case for environmental optimism

There are several reasons suggesting that economic growth might be beneficial for the environment in spite of the first law of thermodynamics:

1. One that is often cited (for example Beckerman 1992a, 1992b; Baldwin 1995) is that demand for environmental quality is a superior good as economists call it, that is, a good with an income elasticity greater than one: as incomes grow environmental concern rises more than proportionally. Environmental protection rises more than proportionally with economic growth if demand for environmental quality is a superior good if the political system is responsive to the preferences of its people — and both theory (Olson 1993) and empirical evidence (Rueschemeyer, Stephens and Stephens 1991; Barro 1996) suggest that the political systems in high-income countries are more responsive to the preferences of its citizens than in poor countries. Given that past environmental destruction is not infinitely persistent and irreversible, the rising share of environmental protection in relation to total expenditure implies that environmental quality increases.

   A similar argument is that with rising incomes people become better educated and better able to express their desires and defend their interests. It becomes more difficult with rising incomes to externalise environmental costs upon others, because the latter are better able to fight this degradation of their welfare. Also, richer people are more likely to be aware of environmental hazards due to better education and information. Hence in rich countries more environmental costs are internalised than in poor countries implying that pollution in poor countries is higher (a similar line of argument is offered by Markandya and Perrings 1991, p. 4).

2. The second reason buttresses the first one in that it suggests that rich countries might not only have the higher demand for environmental protection, but also have the better means for satisfying this higher demand. If you are rich you can better afford spending money on the environment and you have the technical equipment for environmental protection. But it is more than that: rich countries also 'have the advanced social, legal and fiscal infrastructures that are essential to enforcing environmental regulations and promoting "green awareness"' (Baldwin 1995, p. 61).

3. The third reason is that with economic growth it becomes more likely that more modern capital is newly installed or replaces old capital and Grossman (1995, p. 21) claims that later vintage capital by and large tends to be less pollution intensive. Ausubel (1995) suggests that technical progress will vastly reduce the emission of CO_2 in the beginning and middle of the

21st century, thus drastically reducing any need to cut down emissions artificially by introducing taxes. There is some weak support for the claim that
later vintage capital is less pollution intensive which is confined to case
studies, however — see, for example, Wheeler and Martin (1992). Systematic evidence on this claim is still missing.

4. The fourth reason is that at higher levels of income the share of industry
goes down while the share of services goes up and it is often presumed that
services are less pollution-intensive than industrial manufacturing. Even
within industries the share of heavy-polluting manufacturing (like chemis-
try, steel and cement production) decreases in favour of less-polluting
high-tech manufacturing. For some weakly supporting evidence, see
Jänicke, Mönch and Binder (1992).

5. The fifth reason puts forward a similar, more fundamental argument: economic growth is not logically equivalent to rising output in material terms
but to rising output in value terms (Pezzey 1992a, p. 324). That is, economic growth means a rise in total net value. Resource depletion and environmental destruction as such are not objectives of economic activity,
rather they are 'unwanted' side-products of adding value to the inputs of
production. Where this value comes from and how pollution intensive it is
are logically separate questions from the growth in value. The economic
value per unit of pollution can rise or, inversely, the pollution intensity per
unit of economic value can fall.

The same argument applies to resource use and resource intensity which
would further buttress the optimists' view on resource availability in Section 3.2, p. 47. Note that this decoupling of economic value from resource
input and pollution can stem either from technical improvements or from
the changing pattern of output away from resource- and pollution-intensive
towards less-intensive goods. It can also stem from re-use of goods, recov-
ery and recycling of materials. There is 'no definite upper limit' on the
'service output of a given material' (Ayres 1997, p. 286).

6. The sixth reason takes a closer look at the environmental consequences of
poverty. As Beckerman (1992a, 1992b, 1993) and Barbier (1994a) observe, poor people are often locked into a trap in which poverty causes environmental degradation which causes poverty in return. That is: because
you are poor you are forced to exploit your environment, which in turn
makes you poorer, which in turn raises the pressure on the environment
and so on. As Markandya and Pearce (1988, p. 35) observe, the very high
time preference rates of poor people which is due to their poverty makes it
completely rational for them to destroy the resource their living is depend-

ent upon. Deforestation for the collection of fuelwood seems a good example for this conjecture. Beckerman (1992a, p. 482) concludes that 'in the end the best — and probably the only — way to attain a decent environment in most countries is to become rich'.

7. A seventh reason is that with rising incomes the pressure on the environment due to tremendous population growth goes down since population growth tends to go down. Figure 3.4 plots the average annual growth rates between 1990 and 1993 of almost all countries against their 1993 per capita income in current US dolars. There is a weak tendency for lower population growth rates being correlated with higher per capita incomes shown by the linear trend line.

3.3.2.2   The case for environmental pessimism
There are several objections to the proposition that economic growth might be beneficial to the environment, however:

1. The first objects to the presumption that the rich care more about the environment than the poor do (see, for example, Martinez-Alier 1995). The available systematic evidence on this point is far from conclusive (see Kriström and Riera 1996; Flores and Carson 1997). There is some casual evidence, however, suggesting that some societies with very low incomes place a high value on the conservation of species and amenities that are

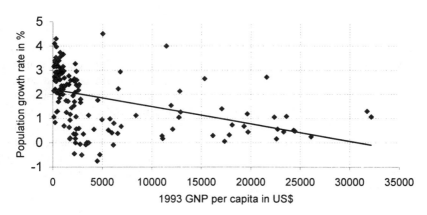

Source: World Bank (1995b).

Figure 3.4 Population growth rates and per capita income

often characterised by common property (Bromley 1989b; Kanbur 1992; Shafik and Bandyopadhyay 1992).

A similar argument is that although environmental concern might rise more than proportionally, rising incomes lead to an inflation in demands for all kinds of things. More and more goods and more and more new goods need to be produced to satisfy the rich consumer's desire which in itself means higher pressure on the environment. Poor people do not travel by plane very much and do not drive a Porsche.

2. The second objection is that while pollution per unit of output might decrease, total pollution might still increase if the rate of growth in output is higher than the rate of decrease in pollution per unit of output. As Lopez (1992, p. 154) observes for technical change, its effect on pollution is in principle ambiguous:

> Technical change has two effects: (i) it increases the efficiency of conventional factors of production, and (ii) it may generate biases toward more or toward less environment-intensive technologies. Insofar as (i) is effectively equivalent to conventional factor accumulation, its effect on the environment is negative. The effect of (ii) is to decrease environmental degradation if technical change is environment saving. Given that environmental control costs are a very small fraction of the total cost in developed countries, it is likely that the bulk of the R&D efforts by the private sector are still oriented more toward the development of conventional factors saving techniques rather than to environmental saving techniques. Hence, it is likely that the effect (i) of technical change dominates the effect (ii), implying that growth, even if generated by technical change only, will lead to increased pollution.

On the other hand, Cavendish and Anderson (1994, p. 774) cite evidence that 'in a large number of cases pollution per unit of output can be, and often historically has been, reduced by factors of 10, 100, and sometimes 1000 or more (depending on the case) once the process of substitution is complete'. But there are also limits to this trend of substitution — first physical limits, but second, and much more important, economic limits, because often the marginal costs of reducing pollution per unit of output is rising steeply as pollution is tending towards zero. Not everything that is physically possible in theory will ever be put into practice because doing so would be prohibitively costly.

3. A third objection is this: in so far as pollution is decreasing because the pattern of output is changing, there are limits as well. This time, however, the limits are not determined by technology or economic cost, but rather by people's preferences and social conventions. While it might be possible to

substitute recreational and cultural activities which tend to be rather low pollution intensive for the consumption of high pollution-intensive material goods, this substitution cannot go on for ever. As far as we can judge from people's revealed preferences, material goods are rather highly appreciated.

4. The fourth objection acknowledges that structural changes in the economy impact upon environmental quality. That does not work unambiguously in favour of the environment, however. At low levels, with rising incomes the share of agriculture goes down while the share of industry goes up with possibly detrimental effects on the environment, especially if not accompanied by a tighter environmental policy. Also, at low levels the share of heavy-polluting manufacturing (such as chemicals, steel and cement production, heavy engineering) is usually quite high.

5. The fifth objection suspects that one important reason why high-income countries could become cleaner was that they exported their most polluting industries to lower-income countries. In importing goods that are highly resource or pollution intensive but produced elsewhere, developed countries can make their environmental record look cleaner than it actually is if one took account of the international trade linkages and attributed resource use and environmental pollution to the final consuming country (Proops and Atkinson 1994; Atkinson and Hamilton 1996). Of course, when everybody wants to become rich, there are no poor countries to take on the dirty industries any more. Hence becoming 'cleaner' as a consequence of becoming rich is no longer possible. The available evidence for this argument is rather inconclusive. See Hettige, Lucas and Wheeler (1992a, 1992b) and Suri and Chapman (1998) for some weak support; see Leonard (1988), Tobey (1990), Grossman and Krueger (1993) and the contributions to Low (1992a) for contrary evidence. For an overview, see Levinson (1996).

6. The sixth objection contests that economic growth is a necessary and sufficient condition for reducing population growth.[23] It is argued that investing in female education and providing retirement insurance schemes are the best ways to reduce population growth. While these might correlate often with economic growth, the latter is neither necessary nor sufficient to achieve the goal: there are poor countries like Uruguay with an income of US$2640 and low population growth with an average annual growth rate of 0.59 per cent, there are rich countries like the United Arab Emirates with an income of US$21 610 and high population growth with an average annual growth rate of 2.71 per cent (data from World Bank 1995b). Quite

clearly, population growth is determined by many other factors beside the level of a country's income. This can also be seen in referring back to Figure 3.4: while there is a linear trend detectable, there is also considerable variance around the trend.

3.3.2.3 Empirical evidence

From theory no definite answer can therefore be found. Economic growth could be either good or bad for the environment. And quite clearly, the environmental consequences of economic growth is an empirical rather than a theoretical matter. What does the evidence tell us? Available econometric studies, some time-series, but mostly cross-sectional, paint a complex picture depending on which indicator for which aspect of environmental quality one chooses to focus on (Shafik and Bandyopadhyay 1992; Binswanger 1993; Panayotou 1993; Grossman and Krueger 1993, 1995; Grossman 1995; Cropper and Griffiths 1994; Shafik 1994; Selden and Song 1994; Holtz-Eakin and Selden 1995; Baldwin 1995). One has to be rather cautious in interpreting the generated results: first, the quality of data they rely on is very poor indeed; second, so far only very simple econometric techniques have been used; and, third, different studies have come up with different relationships for the same indicator depending on the modelling technique. Nevertheless it seems possible to come to the rather robust conclusion that there are three qualitative cases to distinguish (see the stylised graphs in Figure 3.5):

1. Indicators showing an unambiguous improvement as incomes rise. Examples would be access to clean water and adequate sanitation (stylised graph A).

2. Indicators showing a deterioration first until a certain level of income is reached after which an improvement takes place. That is, on a graph with the environmental quality on the ordinate and income on the abscissa the graph would show a U-curve. Often in the literature, however, the level of pollution is put on the ordinate so that the graph shows an inverted U-curve (stylised graph B). This curve is called an 'Environmental Kuznets Curve' (EKC) after Kuznets (1955) who hypothesised that income distribution would first become more unequal as development started off in a country and more equal later on. Examples would be the emission of suspended particulate matter, sulphur oxides, faecal coliforms, the quality of ambient air and the rate of (tropical) deforestation. This second case has gained the most attention for reasons we shall discuss further below.

3. Indicators showing an unambiguous deterioration in specific aspects of
   environmental quality as incomes rise (stylised graph C). Examples would
   be the generation of municipal waste and the emission of CO_2 per capita.
   Strictly speaking the data suggest that at very, very high levels of income
   there will be a turning point for CO_2 emissions so that it would follow an
   EKC rather than a continuously rising trend. But this level is much higher
   than any of the income levels of present countries (Holtz-Eakin and Selden
   1995). [24]

It follows that one has to look carefully at concrete environmental indicators to gauge the environmental consequences of economic growth. Hence no
general conclusions can be drawn from the existing evidence so far. Why are
there (at least) three different qualitative cases to distinguish? One possible
explanation for the observed variance is that those environmental aspects that
are most important in everyday life and that are rather difficult to externalise
on others improve already at quite low income levels, whereas those that can
easily be externalised on to others, as for example with CO_2 emissions,
worsen steadily with economic growth (Shafik 1994, p. 768). Another possible explanation is that some by-products of economic activity such as sulphur
and nitrogen oxides (SO_x and NO_x) can rather easily be eliminated — whereas

Environmental
Degradation

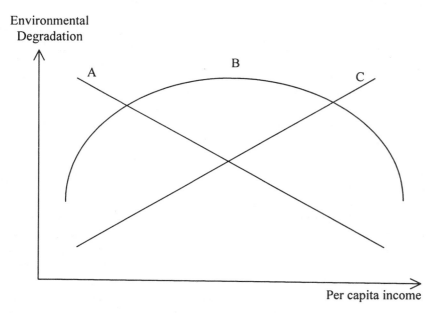

Per capita income

Figure 3.5 Environmental degradation and per capita income

central components of the economy, like CO_2 and solid waste, cannot easily be disposed of.

Unfortunately, the reduced-form econometric models that are commonly used in the EKC literature are not able to discriminate between the varying theoretical hypotheses we looked at above to explain the observed data. It is, for example, not possible to tell clearly which part of the effect came about via quasi-automatic changes during the course of development (for example, by substituting cleaner technologies for dirtier ones or by a change in the structure of the economy) or due to deliberate environmental policy efforts (Grossman and Krueger 1995, p. 372). However, there are other studies that have examined the causal factors for environmental change on a more disaggregated level. Selden, Forrest and Lockhart (1996), for example, have tried to decompose changes in US emissions of particulate matter, SO_x, NO_x, non-methane volatile organic compounds, carbon monoxide and lead over the time period 1970 to 1990 into a scale, composition of the economy and various technique effects. They found that the non-energy efficiency technique effect had the largest impact on the reduction of these emissions over time, both absolutely and per capita. What this finding tentatively suggests is that governmental regulation of emissions, that is, an induced policy response to growing environmental pollution, and emission abatement technology played a significant role in bringing about these improvements in environmental quality (ibid. p. 28).

This conclusion is supported by an international study of some developed countries for the International Energy Agency (IEA 1997). It finds that increases in economic activity and structural changes within the economy would have increased energy use dramatically if these effects had not been counteracted with improvements in the efficiency of energy use.[25] IEA (ibid.) suggests that energy policies have an important impact on the efficiency of energy use and supports its finding with the help of international comparisons. With respect to CO_2 emissions, IEA (ibid., pp. 254ff.) finds that fuel switches from oil to nuclear power and natural gas have played an important role in addition to efficiency improvements in bringing down the carbon intensity of output, if not absolute emissions.

Barrett and Graddy (1997) have tested the hypothesis that improvements in environmental quality partly come about via induced policy responses. They find that countries that exhibit high political and civil liberties tend to have lower air pollution[26] than countries with low liberties.[27] Barrett and Graddy (ibid., p. 2) suggest that 'a low-freedom country, with an income level near the peak of the inverted-U, can reduce its pollution at least as much by increasing its freedoms as it can by increasing its income per head'.

Torras and Boyce (1997) come to similar findings, using the same data as Barrett and Graddy (1997) on political and civil liberties. In addition, they find that increased literacy rates tend to reduce pollution levels.[28] Since they define higher political and civil liberties and increased literacy rates as constituting a more 'equitable power distribution', they conclude that 'a more equal distribution of power ... can positively affect environmental quality' (Torras and Boyce 1997, p. 26).[29]

What all these studies suggest is that environmental degradation is not a given and is not a simple function of the level of a country's income, even though of course many of these other explanatory variables like liberties and literacy rates tend to be highly correlated with income (see Barro 1996). Policy does matter and can influence environmental quality to a considerable extent.

An important caveat to keep in mind in interpreting the evidence and especially as concerns those indicators which appear to follow an EKC is the following: first, most less developed countries (LDCs) are just about to enter the level of income where many emissions are still rising and doing so rapidly. Second, the mentioned econometric studies often use indicators on a 'per capita' or 'per unit of output' basis, but total pollution can still rise in spite of falling pollution intensity with rapid output or population growth.

The turning point found after which pressure on the environment is supposed to diminish is usually slightly below or around US$(1985)5000 income per capita (Panayotou 1993; Shafik 1994; Grossman and Krueger 1993, 1995) or somewhat higher between US$(1985)8000 and 10 000 (Selden and Song 1994), depending on modelling strategy, sample size, definition of variables and the like. Even within single studies the range of turning points can be quite large, for example, from US$1900 for lead to US$11 600 for cadmium in Grossman and Krueger (1993). Average global per capita income in 1985 was about US$(1985)4360, with a median of US$(1985)2420, that is, with a distribution function heavily skewed toward zero (own computations from Penn World Table Version 5 (Summers and Heston 1991)). This large difference between the mean and the median of the world income distribution suggests that total global environmental pollution is likely to rise in the future even for those emissions that are suggested to fall again after still higher levels of income are reached. These projections open up the alarming possibility of *total* pollution rising tremendously with future economic growth in spite of diminishing pollution per unit of output or per capita.[30] As Ekins (1997, p. 824) has put it, the existing evidence shows 'a stark environmental prospect, unless past growth/environment relationships can be substantially changed'. Even Low (1992b), an economist at the World Bank and generally in favour of economic growth, admits that 'absolute toxic emission levels continue to rise worldwide' (p. 13) and that 'it remains to be seen at what point a cross over might occur, such that not only pollution intensity but also absolute pollution levels decrease with rising incomes' (p. 8).

For Baldwin (1995, p. 61) 'the nightmare scenario is that income growth in the poorest LDCs would stall at the point where they are in the high-emission stage, but not quite out of high-growth stage of their demographic transition'. Or even if it does not stall, it might be too late since environmental thresholds might have been exceeded and dramatic and possibly irreversible environmental deterioration will already have taken place. As Panayotou (1993, p. 1) observes, these thresholds are more likely to be relevant in today's low-income fast-growing countries where often 'tropical resources such as forests, fisheries and soils' exist which 'are known to be more fragile and less resilient than temperate resources'. The problem is that nobody knows where those thresholds are and attempts to measure them must rely on very crude assumptions that can easily be contested by opponents.

One cannot even rely on total pollution decreasing again once high enough levels of income are reached, since econometric evidence provides only correlations, but no reliable causal relationship. Cross-section econometric studies provide a picture of different countries being at different levels of income and exhibiting different environmental quality at a *given* moment of time. There is absolutely no guarantee that the environmental quality of a country that is *now* poor will be equal to the environmental quality of a country that is *now* rich *once* it has become rich itself. This is because external and internal conditions in low-income countries can be quite different from the external and internal conditions of countries with high incomes now at their time of development.

3.4   CONCLUSION

Chapter 3 has tried to assess the validity of the opposing claims of WS and SS with respect to the substitutability of natural capital. The conclusion that arises from the analysis is that both paradigms are non-falsifiable under scientific standards. Both rest on certain assumptions as well as hypotheses and claims about the (distant) future that are non-refutable. That does not mean, of course, that either paradigm is nonsensical. Both of them have some theoretical plausibility as well as empirical evidence in their support. But as neither paradigm can be refuted it does mean that science can give no unambiguous answer which paradigm of sustainability society should follow if it is committed to SD.

To see this tension between, on the one hand, the paradigms having some theoretical and empirical plausibility, and, on the other hand, science being unable to endorse either paradigm unambiguously due to their non-falsifiability, take the four propositions from resource optimism as an example. The power of resource optimism stems from the fact that not all four propositions need to hold true in isolation, but that any one of them or some combination thereof is already sufficient to save the economy from resource scarcity. Resource optimism is grounded in the belief that any natural resource can be substituted by another resource, *or* by man-made capital *or* by technical progress *or* by some combination thereof. The critical assessment of resource optimism in Section 3.2, p. 47, shed some doubt on all of the four propositions in examining them in isolation. But none of the propositions could actually be refuted, and the less so if they are seen together and their interactions are taken into account.

On the other hand, it was also shown that none of the propositions can be relied upon either. Each one of them ultimately rests on basic beliefs about future substitution possibilities or technical progress. As Lecomber (1975, p. 42) has written as long ago as 1975:

> Everything hinges on the rate of technical progress and possibilities of substitution. This is perhaps the main issue that separates resource optimists and resource pessimists. The optimist believes in the power of human inventiveness to solve whatever problems are thrown in its way, as apparently it has done in the past. The pessimist questions the success of these past technical solutions and fears that future problems may be more intractable.

What makes the resource optimism of WS non-refutable is that the optimism is only sound if *at any point of time in the future* at least one of the propositions will hold. The propositions of WS are surely logically conceivable, but whether they are possible in practice or even likely to occur, we do not know. The only thing we do know is that they are *not* certain.

The contest between WS and SS cannot be settled by theoretical inquiry. Nor can it be settled by empirical inquiry since such an inquiry would be dependent on information that is only 'forthcoming in the always receding future', where 'predictions ... are clouded by uncertainty regarding preferences, human ingenuity and existing resource availability' (Castle 1997, p. 305). The call for increased efforts into empirical studies on the potential for substitution of natural capital based on today's technologies, as expressed for example in Victor, Hanna and Kubursi (1995, p. 83), is understandable. As the analysis in this chapter has shown, there has been rather limited actual empirical research on the question of substitutability. But it would be a mistake to believe that such studies could solve the dispute between WS and SS. For as Victor, Hanna and Kubursi (ibid.) observe themselves the question of sustainability is not really one of short term substitution ... based on currently available technologies. Rather it is the potential for new, yet to be invented, technologies to substitute for natural capital. No one can reliably predict what new technologies will be developed, and whether the assumed degree of substitution implicit in weak sustainability will become reality.

This conclusion differs starkly from the apparent self-confidence with which proponents of both paradigms of sustainability advance their position and presume that their assumptions hold in reality. We actually know much less about the substitutability of natural capital in the production of consumption goods than the two paradigms of sustainability want to make us believe.

What is true for resource availability applies to the 'sink' side of the economy as well. It was argued that whether natural capital should be regarded as substitutable in the utility function is in principle a matter of speculation as we do not know the preferences of future generations. In as far as future preferences are endogenous and contingent on past levels of environmental degradation, the substitutability hypothesis might be a self-fulfilling prophecy. It was also argued that inferring information from the preferences of the current generation does not give an unambiguous picture either. The available evidence that supposedly shows that a substantial minority of individuals exhibit something close to lexicographic preferences with respect to natural capital is rather shaky. Also, the vast majority of individuals seem to exhibit preferences that are compatible with the substitutability assumption. It has to be said, however, that some proponents of SS at least see the non-substitutability of natural capital as a direct provider of utility more normatively than positively. They frame the issue as one of an inviolable right of future generations to be free from long-term environmental degradation. On this normative aspect of non-substitutability it will be argued in more detail in Section 4.5, p. 123, that a policy that takes seriously the proposition that long-term environmental degradation is in principle not amenable to compensation would impose tremendous opportunity costs on the present and future generations that neither might be willing to incur. The right of future generations to be free from environmental degradation might turn out to be a major burden to them in the end.

The next sub-section in this chapter looked at the link between economic growth and the environment. This is because proponents of WS sincerely believe that in the long run the state of the environment improves with economic growth, so that they have to rely less on the assumption that natural capital is substitutable without limit in utility functions as well. The results that were found on resource optimism apply equally to the environmental optimism of WS. The proposition of WS that economic growth is good for the environment in the long run is logically conceivable, but we do not know whether it will be possible to realise and likely to occur. Ferguson et al. (1996, p. 28) rightly argue that the existing evidence 'cannot be used to justify a view that economic growth ... will automatically be good or bad for the environment. ... The nature of this relationship lies to a large extent in the hands of those responsible for environmental policy and its enforcement'.

There is nothing inevitable about environmental quality deteriorating at early stages of development. Panayotou's (1993, p. 14) claim that the existing evidence 'implies a certain inevitability of environmental degradation along a country's development path, especially during the take off process of industrialization' seems unfounded in its generality. At the least, as Grossman and Krueger (1995, p. 372) suggest, given the recent increase in environmental awareness and the still expanding development of new cleaner technologies it might be possible for countries with current low incomes to achieve environmental improvements at lower levels of income than has previously been the case. Equally, Grossman's claim that 'attention to environmental issues is a luxury good poor countries cannot afford' (quoted in Ferguson et al. 1996, p. 6) is his own normative statement that does not follow from the existing evidence.

On the other hand, there is nothing inevitable either about environmental quality improving at high levels of income. Panayotou (1993, p. 14) is again claiming too much when he says in quite general terms that economic growth is 'a powerful way for improving environmental quality in developing countries'. This is because one cannot rely on economic growth curing environmental ills sooner or later. Even Panayotou (ibid., p. 15) admits that following a development path along an environmental Kuznets-curve might be far from optimal because of high environmental damage costs, because it might be extremely costly to raise environmental quality *ex post* (that is, after deterioration has taken place), because of the potential existence of environmental thresholds and because at least some forms of environmental degradation damage human health and economic productivity and are, ironically, themselves impediments to faster economic growth. Hence, there might be a good case for policy makers to prevent environmental degradation at any stage of development.

One has to presume therefore that no general conclusions on the relationship between economic growth and the environment can be drawn. As Common (1995a, p. 103) has put it: 'Definitive "scientific" answers to these questions [of the relationship between economic growth and environmental quality, E.N.] are impossible. They are essentially matters of informed judgement'. We simply do not know whether environmental optimism or pessimism is warranted. While there appear to be some cases historically where improvements in environmental quality coincided with higher incomes, one cannot rely on economic growth curing environmental ills. Economic growth on its own does not seem to be a viable prescription for the solution of environmental problems. A group of distinguished scholars from both economics and ecology came to a similar conclusion in their 'consensus' paper on 'Economic Growth, Carrying Capacity, and the Environment' (Arrow et al. 1995). In the end, whether one thinks economic growth will be beneficial or harmful to the environment in the long run remains a matter of belief.

Note that the conclusion that both paradigms are non-falsifiable and are therefore not amenable to a definite solution on scientific terms does not depend on a restrictive theory of science. I do not claim that paradigms can easily be refuted by falsification nor do I claim that only falsifiable propositions are scientific, as 'naive' or 'dogmatic' falsificationism would assert (compare Lakatos 1978, pp. 9ff.). Lakatos (ibid., p. 16) and Feyerabend (1975, p. 6; 1988, p. 38) are right in arguing that some of the most admired scientific theories are non-falsifiable. I merely argue that because both paradigms are non-falsifiable, there can be no definite scientific answer as to which of the two paradigms is 'correct'.

One might object along the lines of Popper's methodological falsificationism that even if strictly speaking some theories cannot be disproved by facts they might still become rejected by agreement of the scientific community (see Lakatos 1978, pp. 22ff.). But that does not help either. For as Kuhn (1962) has convincingly shown, the existence of two opposing paradigms makes a common agreement on which paradigm is 'correct' almost impossible:

> When paradigms enter, as they must, into a debate about paradigm choice, their role is necessarily circular. Each group uses its own paradigm to argue in that paradigm's defense. ... Yet, whatever its force, the status of the circular argument is only that of persuasion. It cannot be made logically or even probabilistically compelling .... The premises and values shared by the two parties to a debate over paradigms are not sufficiently extensive for that. (Kuhn 1962, p. 94)

It is as if the two groups saw 'different things when they look from the same point in the same direction' (ibid., p. 150). As we have seen, this disagreement is typical for the two opposing paradigms of WS and SS and their supporters.

By the same token, taking on a 'sophisticated falsificationist' approach (Lakatos 1978, pp. 31ff.) does not help either, because there simply is no scientific answer on which paradigm has 'corroborated excess empirical content' (ibid., p. 31) or 'explanatory surplus' (Gillies 1993, p. 215) over the other. Both of them have some theoretical plausibility and some empirical evidence in favour as well as against them.

Also, as Norton (1995, p. 125) observes, a paradigm that is accused of 'insufficient reach' (or insufficient corroborated empirical content in the language of Lakatos) can always answer 'by denying that some phenomena ... are "real"' and argue that they are 'actually bogus entities that are the ontological fallout, the theoretical dross, of failed paradigms'. Norton (1995) argues that it is characteristic for extra-paradigmatic disagreements (as the one between WS and SS) that there is agreement neither on basic principles nor on the scope of the true subject matter of the discipline or a consensually accepted methodology. Hence, he concludes, these extra-paradigmatic disagreements are not amenable to confirmation or refutation. Also, he suggests, the basic principles of WS and SS are too abstract to be directly supportable, or refutable, by empirical evidence.

Norton's argument conforms with my own conclusion. Note, however, that my conclusion was derived from a rather different line of thought than Norton's. The main argument here is that even if there was agreement on the scope of the true subject matter and a consensually accepted methodology, it would still be impossible to confirm or disconfirm either paradigm. That is, even for somebody standing outside both paradigms and trying as hard as possible to come to an unprejudiced conclusion, it would still be impossible to decide which paradigm is 'correct'.

The argument put forward here therefore provides a better answer than Norton's to the puzzling fact, observed by Tilton (1996, p. 92), that as concerns resource availability 'given the many opportunities participants have had to exchange ideas and views, one would expect to find some common core of accepted findings, some general consensus, emerging to which most if not all scholars subscribed'. But one does not find it. Tilton (ibid.) rightly stresses how desirable a resolution of the conflict would be:

> [T]he competing paradigms not only promote contrasting outlooks on the future of humanity, they may influence that future to the extent their proponents are successful in promoting their particular policy prescriptions. This makes the continuing debate between the concerned and unconcerned troubling. The anticipated exploitation of exhaustible resources either does or does not pose a significant threat to sustainable development. Which it is, is important. The policy recommendations of one group cannot be right unless those of the other are wrong.

But if the analysis here is correct, then Tilton's (ibid., p. 96) hope that the 'search for an appropriate and common paradigm' can be 'a first and essential step' to resolve the 'long-standing differences' between resource optimists and pessimists will not and, indeed, cannot be fulfilled.

One problem with the two paradigms of sustainability is that they are quite general in their claims about substitutability of natural capital and allow little distinction for specific cases. They put their arguments forward as generally applicable, apodictic, obvious *a priori* truths rather than as specifically applicable and empirically contingent claims. Pearce (1997c, p. 296) is right in saying that it is incorrect 'to caricature the issue as one of total substitutability' versus total non-substitutability. As I argue in the next chapter, the *likelihood* of whether natural capital can be substituted or not crucially depends on which form of natural capital one is looking at and cannot be answered in general terms (for a similar conclusion, see Mikesell (1995)). There I reconsider the importance of natural capital and I argue that if we take an explicit look at the distinctive features of natural capital in a world of risk, uncertainty and ignorance, then, indeed, a *persuasive* case can be made that the preservation of some specific forms of natural capital is a necessary requirement for sustainability. This holds especially true for those forms of natural capital that provide basic life-support functions for mankind.

NOTES

1 For more detail on this, see Barbier (1989, Chapter 1).
2 However, the rise in oil prices was clearly linked to the exercise of market power by OPEC and not to dramatically rising natural resource scarcity, although there is some evidence that prices had started rising before 1973 (Slade 1982, p. 136). In 1986 world oil prices, which had risen again in 1979 due to the first Gulf war between Iraq and Iran, fell to their pre-1973 level in real terms where, essentially, they have stayed ever since (British Petroleum 1997, p. 14). For a history of world oil prices see Adelman (1995).
3 Throughout the book technical progress is to be interpreted broadly as encompassing everything from the *invention* of a new technique to *innovation* and *diffusion*, that is, to the widespread incorporation of this technique into production processes.
4 Some natural resources are scarce in this world in a physical sense. If they have no productive use, nobody cares about this scarcity, however. Scarcity in an economic sense I define to be excess demand for the resource at a given price.
5 Of course, Georgescu-Roegen was not so naive as to overlook the fact that the earth is not a closed system. He merely claimed that using solar energy needs more non-solar energy input than is gained in energy eventually (Georgescu-Roegen 1986, p. 23). While this might be true for the present, there is absolutely no reason to expect that this has to be true in the future as well.
6 In a perfectly competitive economy, the interest rate is equal to the marginal product of man-made capital (Dasgupta and Heal 1979, p. 296).
7 In units of weight the German industry, for example, uses 50 times more non-renewable than renewable resources for production (Bringezu and Schütz 1996).
8 It is a partial equilibrium model and used here because it makes understanding the Hotelling rule easier than the formally better suited, but less easy to understand, general equilibrium model that is presented in Appendix 2, p. 214.

9   It also holds for uncertainty if agents form rational expectations and there is a complete set of contingent forward markets. Neither is very realistic. See Graham-Tomasi, Runge and Hyde (1986). On a more elaborate examination of risk, uncertainty and ignorance see Section 4.2, p. 98.

10   A recent study of Moazzami and Anderson (1994) finds empirical support for Slade's (1982) 'U-shaped' price trend hypothesis, however.

11   For Germany, for example, Bringezu and Schütz (1996) estimate that the ratio of non-renewable to renewable resource intake is 50:1 measured in weight. It also has to be taken into account that the growing of renewable resources has its ecological price in the form of fertiliser and pesticide use as well as soil erosion.

12   Although if we take on an even longer time perspective, fossil fuels will become renewed again, albeit at such a slow rate that this renewal is of no plausible relevance to humankind.

13   An important assumption is that there is no depreciation of man-made capital. As Dasgupta and Heal (1979, p. 226) indicate, the basic results would go through as well with capital depreciation as long as capital depreciates at less than an exponential rate. Note also that technical progress which Dasgupta and Heal exclude could counteract exponential capital depreciation. On this, see the discussion of technical progress in Section 3.2.4, p. 68.

14   Note that σ is bounded below by zero. With $\sigma = 0$, capital and resources are already perfect complements. A negative elasticity of substitution ($\sigma < 0$) is not possible. Formally, since both K and R are positive numbers and the absolute value of the MRS between K and R is always positive, σ can never be negative.

15   Slade (1987, p. 351) reports values that suggest that man-made capital's share and the resources' share are approximately equal. However, this is a misunderstanding. Berndt and Wood (1975), on which Slade based her values, included intermediate goods in the production function. Those intermediate goods do not fall from heaven and presumably the share of man-made capital in those intermediate goods is higher than the share of resources, so that the ultimate share of man-made capital is still considerably higher than that of resources, thus reconciling the reported values with those of Solow (1974a), Hartwick (1977) and Dasgupta and Heal (1979).

16   Note that here labour is not assumed to be constant and therefore enters the production function explicitly.

17   'Loosely' because formally it is not possible for the Cobb–Douglas production function to distinguish pure capital- from resource-augmenting technical progress.

18   Energy intensity generally falls also cross-sectionally with rising incomes. There is an important caveat, however. To compare energy intensity cross-sectionally, the GDP of each country has to be converted from the local currency into a common denominator, usually into US$. Until recently, it was common to use official exchange rates. Now, however, the United Nations and the International Monetary Fund pay more attention to the purchasing power of currencies and have published GDP figures measured in purchasing power parity. According to Khatib (1995, Table 1, p. 728) GDP in purchasing power parity is reasonably close to GDP as conventionally measured in the OECD countries. For developing, and Eastern European countries as well as countries of the former Soviet Union, however, GDP is often 200 per cent or even more higher if expressed in purchasing power parity than conventionally reported. China's GDP, for example, rises from US$415 to 2257 billion. Not surprisingly, Khatib finds that the energy intensity in developing countries drops significantly when GDP is calculated in purchasing power parity. The same is to be expected for resource intensities other than energy.

19   This is the most often used measure for energy intensity. For other, more contested concepts of measuring energy efficiency, see Patterson (1996).

20   Environmental degradation here means a decrease in the stock of (directly utility-relevant) renewable resources or an increase in the stock of pollution.

21   Smith and Mansfield (1998, p. 209) claim that the findings of their CV study show that 'there are no significant differences between people's choices with real and hypothetical offers'. Test persons in one group were asked what their willingness-to-accept for taking part in an opinion survey is that researchers at Duke University 'are considering establishing',

whereas another group was asked for their WTA for taking part in a survey that researchers at Duke University 'are establishing' and that would therefore take place for certain. However, since all respondents in the hypothetical case took part in a real survey prior to being asked their WTA, it is most doubtful whether they actually perceived the future surveys as hypothetical. Also, the specific wording of the hypothetical case made it hard for respondents to see the difference between the *real* survey they were just finishing and the future *hypothetical* survey. Arguably, Smith and Mansfield's (1998) rather strong conclusion about no difference between real and hypothetical offers cannot really be inferred from their study.

22 Strictly speaking and as mentioned earlier on, this argument does not apply since the earth absorbs a steady, constant energy influx from outside exceeding the current total world energy demand at about three orders of magnitude (Norgaard 1986, p. 326; Hohmeyer 1992, p. 10). It does apply approximately, however, when most of this influx is — as at present — not used.

23 A more extreme position holds that people are the 'ultimate resource' (Simon 1996) and that population growth is not bad for the environment. This, however, is a minority position that is usually, but not always (see, for example, Boserup 1990), held by people who think that economic growth is the best way to protect the environment (see, for example, Simon 1990, 1996).

24 Analysis by Dijkgraaf and Vollebergh (1998, p. 2) suggests, however, that an EKC for CO_2 emissions might be an artefact of the pooling of data in cross-section econometric analysis since 'time-series estimations per country reveal significant differences between countries. Not only do countries differ with respect to the height of the turning point (from increasing to decreasing emissions), but countries differ also with respect to the curvature of the Income–Emission Relation. Some countries show a clear EKC, but others have stabilizing patterns or even a linear Income–Emission Relation'.

25 In addition to overall indicators, IEA (1997) also provides most interesting disaggregated indicators for different economic sectors, including households.

26 For water pollution the impact of political and civil liberties is statistically insignificant.

27 Data on political and civil liberties are based on an index published by Freedom House (Finn 1996). Political liberties reflect the existence and fairness of elections, the existence of a real opposition and so on. Civil liberties reflect individual civil rights of free speech, demonstration, organisational freedom and the extent of the freedom of the press.

28 Torras and Boyce (1997, p. 21) find that, contrary to their expectation, higher income inequality sometimes tends to improve environmental quality. They reject their own findings on grounds of the 'questionable quality of the income-distribution data'. Somewhat astonishingly and inconsistently, however, they advocate a 'more equitable income distribution' for environmental reasons later on in their paper (p. 26).

29 For a more elaborate theoretical argument along these lines, see Boyce (1994).

30 I do not undertake any quantitative projections here for mainly two reasons. First, what we are really interested in here are qualitative results. Second, projections depend on forecasting future trends in economic and population growth, technological progress and so on and are therefore likely to be quite volatile and prone to mistakes. For some extrapolating of past trends into the future, see Selden and Song (1994, pp. 156–61) and Stern, Common and Barbier (1996, pp. 1157ff.).

4. Preserving Natural Capital in a World of Risk, Uncertainty and Ignorance

In the last chapter it was shown that both paradigms are non-falsifiable and that science cannot endorse fully and umambiguously either paradigm. That science cannot provide a clear answer on which paradigm of sustainability to follow is an important result. But the question still open is this: if society is faced with risk, uncertainty and ignorance about the consequences of running down natural capital, which forms, how much and at what cost should it preserve natural capital? This is the major topic of this chapter.

It has been mentioned already that both paradigms do have some evidence in their favour. The first aim of this chapter is to indicate which forms of natural capital are more *likely* to be non-substitutable than others and are therefore in need of preservation. Note the emphasis on 'likely': from the analysis in Chapter 3 it follows that the best we can hope for is to make a *persuasive* case for the importance of the preservation of natural capital. The major objective of this chapter lies somewhere else, however. It tries to explore the difficulties in finding the extent to which these forms of capital need to be preserved and how much cost should be incurred for preservation.

Section 4.1 starts out by highlighting distinctive features of some forms of natural capital. There are two aspects — basic life-support function and irreversibility of destruction — that distinguish some forms of natural from any other form of capital. Section 4.2 discusses in more depth what has hitherto been dealt with rather implicitly: that the real world is plagued by the absence of perfect information and certainty and characterised by risk, uncertainty and ignorance instead. Section 4.3 brings the first two threads together and states which forms of natural capital should be preserved. It argues that the protection of global life-support resources such as biodiversity, the ozone layer and the global climate as well as the restriction of the accumulation of pollutants and of unsustainable harvesting and soil erosion appear to be sound insurance policies for achieving sustainability. In contrast, no explicit conservation policy for natural resources used in production seems necessary. The latter holds true, if less clearly, for food resources as well. In essence therefore, Section 4.3 argues that available evidence supports WS more strongly with respect to the 'source' side of the economy, but supports SS more strongly with respect to the 'sink' side of the economy.

The next question is how, to what extent and for how much cost should certain forms of natural capital be preserved? Section 4.4 argues that while the total value of certain forms of natural capital can indeed be very large as some studies have aspired to show, this value is almost irrelevant for real policy choices as they are not about total preservation versus total destruction, but about marginal changes. Economic valuation techniques provide information about the relative costs and benefits of marginal preservation choices. However, because of problems in valuing environmental resources such as biodiversity and because of the uncertainties involved about system complexities, thresholds and so on it is often argued that a simple cost–benefit analysis tends to underestimate the value of marginal losses in natural capital and will lead to 'too much' depletion of it.

Section 4.4 therefore also discusses three policy principles that are supposed to rectify this bias against natural capital in coping with risk, uncertainty and ignorance, namely the precautionary principle, an environmental bond system and the concept of safe minimum standards (SMSs). All three principles function as a kind of insurance policy against the uncertain, but potentially very large, costs of running down natural capital. These principles are not clear, however, on the question of how large the costs of preservation are allowed to become. SMS have been either interpreted as providing a safe minimum standard regardless of the costs of preservation or subjected to the costs of preservation not being 'too high'. In the latter interpretation the SMS is basically a modified cost–benefit rule with the further qualification that the costs of preservation can exceed its benefits by a certain factor.

Section 4.5 discusses the problem of opportunity cost. It first critically assesses the option of ignoring opportunity costs in preserving natural capital and argues against such a position. It then looks at the second option and argues that the most fundamental question cannot be answered by science, but has to be left to society and its political decision-making procedures. This most fundamental question is how much, that is, by which factor, the costs of preservation are allowed to exceed best available estimates of the benefits of preservation. It is argued that natural science can help in providing information about natural capital and the likely consequences of its depletion, that is, it can help in reducing uncertainty and ignorance. Economic science can help in providing best available information on the costs and benefits of preservation. But neither science can answer how much cost society should be willing to incur to insure itself against the uncertain negative consequences of natural capital loss.

There is one further thing that economic science can do for a society that is committed to SD. It can help to find ways of preserving natural capital at minimal cost. Section 4.6 analyses the following policy measures:

- the abolition of economically and environmentally harmful subsidies,
- the abatement of economically harmful pollution,
- the substitution of market-based for command-and-control instruments,
- the substitution of ecotaxes for labour and capital income taxes, and
- the so-called 'Porter hypothesis' that tighter environmental regulation may increase firms' productivity.

It argues that considerable and almost self-paying progress towards preserving natural capital could be achieved if some of these measures were applied as a priority. Section 4.7 concludes.

4.1 DISTINCTIVE FEATURES OF NATURAL CAPITAL

If one wants to establish a case for an explicit preservation of certain forms of natural capital, one must start by trying to show that there are some characteristics of these forms of natural capital that distinguish them from man-made capital and, indeed, from any other capital. In my view, there are two aspects that can justify such a distinction: the provision of basic life-support functions and irreversibility of destruction.

- Some forms of natural capital provide very basic and fundamental life-support functions that no other capital can provide (Barbier, Burgess and Folke 1994), that is, functions that make human life on earth possible. Ecosystems and the biodiversity they exhibit are multifunctional in a way and to an extent that is not shared by other capital (Ehrlich and Ehrlich 1992). They are the basis of all life, human and non-human: it is the world ecosystem that contains the economy, not the economy that contains the world ecosystem (Daly and Townsend 1993, p. 3). Mankind can exist and indeed has to a large extent existed in the past without major man-made or other forms of capital, but it cannot live without functioning ecosystems. The outstanding value of natural capital is not that we can use fossil fuel, for example, but that nature enables the very existence of human life: food, water, fresh air and a bearable climate. Ecosystems might cope with piece meal destruction for a long time, but if a certain threshold is exceeded, the whole system could break down.

There are 'limits to meta-resource depletion' (Ehrlich 1989). Other life-support resources that really are non-substitutable and whose destruction would often lead to catastrophes are the ozone layer and the bio-geochemical cycle of the atmosphere.

- Some forms of natural capital are unique in that they cannot be rebuilt once they have been destroyed. That is, destruction of some forms of natural capital is irreversible or at least quasi-irreversible.[1] In general this is not the case for other forms of capital. Man-made capital can always be reconstructed if it has been destroyed. Reconstruction is costly, of course, and it may take some time, but at least it is possible in principle.[2] An example for irreversible natural capital loss is the destruction of biodiversity: it is impossible to bring an extinct species back to life.[3] Examples for quasi-irreversibility are the destruction of the ozone layer and global warming: both the ozone layer and the climate may regenerate to their former state if allowed to do so, but it takes 'too much time' (from a human perspective) to wait for the natural regeneration (Gowdy and McDaniel 1995). The consumption of 'non-renewable' resources is another example of quasi-irreversibility.

While these distinctive features might make a *qualitative* case for the preservation of natural capital, it does not give a precise answer on exactly which forms of natural capital should be preserved and especially not an answer to what extent. That some forms of natural capital provide basic life-support functions in their totality and can therefore not be depleted down to zero, does not mean that they cannot be degraded to some extent. In other words, it does not mean that if some part of them is lost, mankind loses their life-support function. Before going over to these aspects, however, we take a closer look at the implications of the notorious absence of perfect information and certainty for our analysis.

4.2 RISK, UNCERTAINTY AND IGNORANCE

If we are aware of the distinctive features of natural capital, why cannot we simply target all those forms of natural capital that provide basic life-support functions and would be irreversibly lost after destruction for preservation? If we lived in a world of certainty, there would not be any problem. But unfortunately there is widespread risk, uncertainty and ignorance in the world we live in. Ignorance here means more than risk and more than uncertainty, two notions that are well known in economics.[4] Let us discuss all three in the order of descending closeness to certainty.

Risk

Risk refers to a situation where the set of all possible states of the world, the probability distribution over the set of possible states and the resulting pay-offs can be objectively known. Buying a lottery ticket is a good example of engaging in a risky action, because the odds of winning can be objectively known as can the costs of buying the ticket and the value of potential prizes — hence the expected gain or loss can be computed without any remaining doubt.

In order to cope with risk, economists have included so-called option values in their traditional cost–benefit analyses.[5] In the environmental context, option value is the expected value of refraining from an action that leads with some given probability to irreversible environmental destruction in order to keep the option open of using the environmental resource in the future. Option value can thus be interpreted as a kind of risk premium: it lowers the net benefit of the considered action; it reflects an additional opportunity cost and the 'price' someone is ready to pay in order to keep open the option of future use of the environmental resource. The more risk averse the individual is, the higher will be the option value. On the other hand, if the individual is risk preferring, he or she will be more inclined to take the action and risk the irreversible environmental destruction.

Note that we are typically not confronted with a situation of risk when we try to judge the validity of running down natural capital because in most cases we do not know either the probability distribution of all possible states or the potential outcomes resulting from the different states of the world. What is worse: often we do not even know the complete set, that is, we are ignorant of the total number of possible states of the world.

Also note that even a situation of risk poses fundamental problems for any attempt to ensure sustainability. Consider a situation in which there is a 99 per cent chance of winning a big gain, but a 1 per cent probability of incurring a tremendous loss. Further assume that both gains and losses affect at least partially coming generations as well. Should society engage in or refrain from this risky action? There is no obvious answer. A possible solution could be to refrain from any risky action since the present is committed to maintaining the capacity to provide non-declining utility into the future and engaging in the action risks a tremendous loss and hence a decline in utility, even if the probability for this drastic loss is rather small. But is this solution plausible? Presumably not, because refraining from *any* action that risks a net loss brings with it an (opportunity) cost both to the current and the future generations.

The fundamental problem is this: in a risky world, ensuring sustainability with certainty can — if at all possible — only be achieved at high costs and if those costs are deemed too high to be acceptable, then sustainability can at best mean ensuring expected sustainability.

Economists would resort to inferring the risk preference or risk aversion from the present generation in order to compute the expected utility of the risky action. The decision criterion would be to engage in the action if the expected utility is positive and to refrain from the action if the expected utility is negative.

Of course, if there is a whole range of risky actions at a given time or over a bounded time interval, then due to the law of large numbers unlucky outcomes become compensated by lucky outcomes and a net gain equal to the expected overall value of a whole set of risky actions results. But things are different when potential losses, however unlikely, imply irreversible *and* catastrophic outcomes that cannot be compensated for. An obvious answer would be to refrain from actions that imply such outcomes, however unlikely they might be. But what to do if the outcomes themselves are not known with certainty? Here we have left the context of risk already, so we move on to uncertainty.

Uncertainty
Uncertainty refers to a situation where the probability distribution over a set of possible states of the world and the resulting payoffs cannot be known objectively, but individuals have subjective beliefs about the distribution and the payoffs.[6] Those beliefs can be updated (and in many cases improved) over time, that is, they are not static as in the context of risk, but dynamic.

Option values can be used in a context of uncertainty as well, except that this time it is the *subjectively* expected value that counts. Additionally, economists have included so-called quasi-option values in their traditional cost–benefit analyses to cope with uncertainty. In the environmental context, quasi-option value is the value of delaying an irreversible environmental destruction in order to acquire improved information and to make a better informed future decision.[7] For quasi-option values to make sense, we have to *expect* either that future information will tend to favour environmental preservation for given preferences or that the preference for environmental resources will increase over time. Only then is there a positive value, otherwise there would be a cost in keeping the environmental option open (Beltratti, Chichilnisky and Heal 1998; Chichilnisky and Heal 1993[8]). Note that quasi-option value, contrary to option value, does not depend on the valuer being risk averse; even a risk-loving valuer can exhibit a positive quasi-option value for preserving an environmental resource.

Taking option and quasi-option values into account changes the costs and benefits of a considered activity. As an example, see Albers, Fisher and Hanemann (1996) who argue convincingly from both a theoretical analysis and a case study of tropical forest management in Thailand that environmental destruction would be less if foresighted resource managers fully took into account option and quasi-option values.[9]

Uncertainty comes rather close to our present state of knowledge about many rather novel and complex, but most pressing environmental problems such as global warming. We know something about the effects of dumping greenhouse gases in the atmosphere, we know something about the climatic consequences, we can imagine different states of the world following and we have some idea about the probability distribution over these different states of the world. Our knowledge about climate change is still rather poor, however.[10] As Gottinger (1995, p. 51) has put it: 'Uncertainty dominates every aspect of the greenhouse gas issue'.

One obvious strategy to combat uncertainty is to invest in research in order to gain better information over the set of possible states, their payoffs and the probability distribution over the set of states. Note, however, that for cases of uncertainty in general and for global warming in particular it is not possible to convert a setting of uncertainty into a situation of mere risk. In most cases some doubt about the correctness of beliefs remains, either because the objective values cannot be known in principle, or because the costs of getting the correct values are 'too high' from an information costs perspective, where 'too high' means a region where the marginal costs of information gathering are higher than the marginal benefits. Also, as Faucheux and Froger (1995) observe, the adjustment of subjective beliefs presupposes a stationary stochastic environment which is not given if human action leads to irreversible destructions. Additionally, quite often there is no time to adjust since the stakes appear to be high and a decision is thought to be urgent (ibid.).

Thompson, Warburton and Hatley (1986) provide a nice example of the difficulties of gaining improved information in demonstrating how armies of experts have failed to solve the question whether the rate of fuelwood consumption in the Himalayas is in excess of the rate at which the forest grows:

> the expert estimates of these two rates vary by such enormous factors that we simply cannot say whether the spiral, if it exists, is upward or downward. There is something severely wrong with the Himalayas but we cannot tell what it is. The traditional response — a call for more research — has not worked. (Thompson, Warburton and Hatley 1986, p. 1)

Ignorance

Ignorance refers to a situation where we have no idea whatsoever about the set of possible states of the world, about the probability distribution over the set and about the resulting payoffs.[11] A weaker definition would allow for subjective beliefs where those beliefs are largely arbitrary, however, and lack a sound scientific foundation.

It seems fair to say that our knowledge about the extent and the likely consequences of biodiversity[12] destruction resembles more a situation of ignorance than of uncertainty. Estimates from UNEP of the number of existing species vary between five and thirty million (Wilson 1988, p. 5) of which about 1.4 million are named by biologists (Brown et al. 1994, p. 4). Even our knowledge about most of the named species is only rudimentary (Norton 1986). Estimates of the expected loss of species over the next 25 years vary between 2 and 25 per cent (Schuh 1995) and we are arguably miles away from knowing anything about the loss in value terms of this destruction of biodiversity. Especially, by their very nature, one cannot know the value of still undiscovered species that become extinct. As Norton (1986, p. 203) rightly argues, 'it is an understatement to refer to this level of ignorance as mere "uncertainty"'.

We are — almost necessarily — so ignorant of the complex interlinkages within ecosystems that we cannot, and could never, know the value of many single species or the whole of biodiversity to any reasonable extent of precision. Randall (1991, p. 64) suggests that there is a 'positive probability that literally any species, known or unknown, will eventually prove useful'. While possibly true, this probability might be vanishingly small or the species could be economically almost irrelevant. Furthermore, as Randall himself (ibid., p. 65) as well as Ehrenfeld (1986, p. 213) observe, whether future genetic engineering will drastically increase or reduce the value of biodiversity is completely unclear.[13]

Climate change is another example of ignorance. We have introduced it under the heading of uncertainty above, but IPCC (1996b, p. 161) rightly claims that 'when dealing with many of the effects of climate change, ignorance is perhaps a more appropriate concept than uncertainty'. The lesson is that often environmental problems have aspects of both uncertainty and ignorance.

Also, ignorance has in the past been quite common for environmental problems: DDT and CFCs were both thought to be benign for the environment before their detrimental effect was discovered (Bodansky 1991, p. 43). And ignorance is arguably a pretty good description of the quality of our knowledge about the consequences of human activity on the state of the environment in the long run.

4.3   WHICH FORMS OF NATURAL CAPITAL SHOULD BE PRESERVED?

The combination of risk, uncertainty and ignorance with the distinctive characteristics of natural capital (basic life-support functions and irreversibility of destruction) has ambiguous effects on the case for preserving natural capital: on the one hand, it provides a justification to be cautious about running down natural capital; on the other hand, it makes it difficult to say which forms of natural capital should be preserved and to what extent. Some forms carry more of the distinctive features than others, some are more prone to uncertainty and ignorance than others. It is therefore necessary to go one step beyond this abstract notion 'natural capital' and to distinguish which forms appear more and which forms appear less in need of explicit preservation. Or as Page (1997, p. 592) has put it: 'we need to identify the key components of the resource base, the things that are essential to sustainability'.

Biodiversity
We first take a closer look at the most basic form of natural capital: ecosystems and their biodiversity. The current biodiversity on earth is the result of billions of years of evolution. It contains valuable information and provides insurance value (Swanson 1997, Chapter 4). With respect to the first aspect, the more biodiversity there is, the wider is the set of options for biological activity. The more biodiversity there is, the more likely it is for the bio-industry to find the necessary information for curing illnesses, developing high-yield and robust agricultural crops and so on. With respect to the insurance value the argument that the more biodiversity there is the better equally applies. It is a well-established fact in ecology that ecosystems are characterised by highly non-linear, discontinuous and discrete changes in their ecological 'resilience', that is, in their ability to 'recover from and thus absorb' (Barbier, Burgess and Folke 1994, p. 17) external and internal shocks. Although certain so-called keystone species play a role in maintaining diversity, the stability of ecosystems ultimately depends on the extent of its resilience and not so much on the stability of individual components (Turner 1995). The complexity of ecosystems is still poorly understood and not easy to understand anyway. 'Ecosystems do not have single equilibria with functions controlled to remain near it. Rather, destabilising forces far from equilibria, multiple equilibria and the absence of equilibria define functionally different states' (Holling 1995, p. 49). Due to this fact, an ecosystem might be able to cope with piecemeal destruction for quite a long time, but it can break down unexpectedly fast after some (often unknown) threshold has been transgressed (Perrings and Pearce 1994) and it loses its self-organising capacity. In some

sense, every small-scale destruction increases the likelihood of unravelling the whole ecosystem (Randall 1991, p. 65). While not undisputed (see Perrings, Folke and Mäler 1992), there is a large body of evidence from ecological studies suggesting that 'resilience increases with system complexity, and complexity can be measured by biological diversity. In that way, the more diversity there is, the more resilience there is and hence the more sustainable the system is' (Pearce 1994b, p. 148).

Ceteris paribus therefore, the more biodiversity there is, the higher is its evolutionary potential and the bigger is the opportunity set open to future generations (Perrings 1994). Hence, there is a good case for preventing biodiversity loss. On the other hand, this does not imply that if we do not preserve the totality of ecosystems and their biodiversity, we shall lose their basic life-support functions and make human life on earth impossible. Losing some of the existing biodiversity would mean losing some of its informational and some of its insurance value in exchange for the benefits of depletion, but it would not mean that human life is at risk. Presumably we could survive without the 20 per cent of species that Myers (1993, p. 75) fears will be lost by 2020 or the 50 per cent or more by the end of the next century. Maybe we could even do without as much as 90 per cent of all living species. As far as I am aware, there does not exist any reliable estimate of where the disaster point is. However, for the same reason one needs to be cautious about the destruction of ecosystems and the depletion of biodiversity. Because depletion is a discontinuous process, because there exist thresholds and because of the unpredictability of the dynamic process of losses in biological diversity it is hard to establish a safe margin within which no major catastrophic consequences have to be feared (Perrings and Opschoor 1994). Perrings, Folke and Mäler (1992, p. 202) summarise this point very clearly:

> What can be said is that there must exist levels of biodiversity loss which cannot be sustained by human society without inducing catastrophic change/fundamental reorganization. A major task for *future* research is to fix the boundaries for sustainable levels of biodiversity and ecological services with greater precision than has been possible in the past, and to explicitly state the time and space scales we choose to work with [my emphasis, E.N.].

Finally, let us turn to why it is that much biodiversity is in danger of becoming depleted if no explicit effort for their protection were undertaken. Policy makers who act in the best interest of the country they represent will allocate the nation's limited resources to those activities that promise the highest net rate of return. That is, they will maximise the profits from a portfolio of different national assets. From this perspective, natural capital and hence biodiversity are but one asset in the portfolio, that is, they must compete with other assets for allocation of resources that are necessary for sustenance (Swanson 1994). Because of our uncertainty and ignorance about the real value of biodiversity, natural capital is often (rightly or wrongly) thought of as not being worth conserving and is hence converted into another form of asset that promises to generate a higher net rate of return. Thus, for example, forests are logged and converted into agricultural or grazing land or industrialised. Note that the extinction of species is only rarely the consequence of an intended attempt to (over-)exploit the species, but far more often the rather unintended side-consequence of transforming natural capital into another asset.[14] Actually, that is one of the reasons why we are uncertain about the exact extent of biodiversity loss.

One might want to object that biodiversity loss is often a consequence of failing to define explicit property rights and that biodiversity destruction is, hence, a consequence of open access and not a consequence of a deliberate national policy to maximise the profits of its national portfolio. While it has been known since Hardin (1968)[15] that open access provides powerful incentives for over-exploitation, this argument does not contradict our more general conclusion. As Swanson (1994, p. 814) rightly argues 'it is more likely that open access regimes are caused by decisions not to invest' in biodiversity, than a direct cause for biodiversity loss. That is, ill-defined property rights follow from the country's decision not to protect biodiversity and not vice versa. Things are somewhat different with the extinction of maritime resources where until recently the oceans have been, and still are to a large extent, outside the 200-mile coastal zones and are characterised by open access where no authority exists to allocate and enforce property rights.

Global Environmental Resources

There is also, more generally, a good case for protecting the 'global environmental system' (Clark 1995, p. 146) such as the global climate and the ozone layer. Both are fundamental life-support resources whose destruction would endanger the welfare, if not the existence, of coming generations. Note, however, that, similarly to the loss of ecosystems and species dealt with above, the empirical evidence does not imply that the biogeochemical cycle of the atmosphere will be destroyed with modest global warming. Best available science suggests that this will almost certainly not be the case for a doubling of CO_2 in the atmosphere (IPCC 1996a).

Older estimates of damage due to a doubling of CO_2 range between 1 and 2.5 per cent of GDP (IPCC 1996b, p. 203). More recent studies which better take into account sectors that might benefit from warming (such as citrus cropping and summer recreational activities) and the possibilities for efficient adaptive behaviour to reduce potential damages come to smaller estimates.

Indeed, they do not exclude the possibility that modest global warming might be beneficial — even for those countries that earlier studies expected to be damaged by warming (see Mendelsohn and Neumann 1999). On the other hand, to not endanger the biogeochemical cycle of the atmosphere, precautionary action should be undertaken to prevent large and unpredictable changes in the global climate. Since we do not know exactly beyond which concentration of CO_2 and other greenhouse gases these changes will occur we should make sure that our emissions stay well below the limit that best available science suggests to be the critical level.

As Chichilnisky and Heal (1993, p. 80) observe, none of the major early attempts to calculate the costs and benefits of greenhouse gas abatement such as Cline (1992), Manne and Richels (1992) and Nordhaus (1991a) has included option values. 'As uncertainty looms large in any projections regarding global warming, the extent of the underestimate [of the net benefits of greenhouse gas abatement, E.N.] could be important' (Chichilnisky and Heal 1993, p. 80). This is confirmed by later studies such as Nordhaus (1994) and Manne and Richels (1995) as well as Welsch (1995) and Eismont and Welsch (1996) who have adopted Dobbs's (1991) model of uncertainty for calculating optimal greenhouse gas emission trajectories.[16]

Contrary to what one might think there is most likely no quasi-option value as opposed to an option value in reducing greenhouse gas emissions now. Such a quasi-option value would only exist if it turned out at some future time that one wished to 'negatively emit', that is: subtract greenhouse gases from the atmosphere. Only then would current emissions be really irreversible and current emission reduction would exhibit a quasi-option value. This is rather unlikely, however, for even if one finds out in the future that there has been over-emission of greenhouse gases in the past, this would only call for a drastic reduction in future emissions, but most likely not for 'negative emissions'. Actually, quasi-option value may point in the opposite direction, if investment in greenhouse gas abatement capital is irreversible, that is, does not depreciate sufficiently quickly. For then there is a quasi-option value of waiting with the instalment of abatement capital until it turns out that it is actually necessary. There is a quasi-option value in 'learn now and act later if necessary' as opposed to 'act now and learn later'. On these aspects see Manne and Richels (1991), Kolstad (1996), and Ulph and Ulph (1997).

Whether uncertainty about the future warrants *immediate* substantive greenhouse gas reductions is therefore contested. An alternative strategy to investing in abatement capital now is to invest heavily in scientific research in order to resolve some of the uncertainty as soon as possible and then decide on abatement. The integrated cost–benefit analysis of Manne and Richels (1995) suggests that if uncertainty can be drastically reduced within the next decade or so, this would be the efficient strategy. Their point is strengthened by the fact that emission abatement is likely to be cheaper, *ceteris paribus*, in the future if technology exogenously develops towards more efficient energy use over time.

The case for waiting has to be balanced against the fact that the development of new technologies is often not exogenous, but endogenous and path dependent. That is, often there is no technological development without hard economic incentives. It might therefore be optimal to act now and build up pressure to develop and install low-emission technologies so that they are existent if it turns out in the future that they are needed (Grubb 1997). Also, early development ensures that low-emission capital and technology can be phased in over time which is much cheaper than an abrupt substitution of existing capital and technology. Ingham and Ulph (1991) and Ingham, Maw and Ulph (1991) provide evidence from a sophisticated vintage model of energy demand in which older capital is continuously replaced by new capital. They show that it can be quite costly to reach a specific emission reduction target by a certain time if action is delayed. The reason is that waiting brings with it the cost that in the meantime capital is installed that is not apt for emission reduction and is costly to replace once it has been installed.

Accumulating Toxic Pollutants
A good case can also be made for not letting emissions, especially highly toxic and health-damaging pollutants, accumulate in the environment. The aim should be to not let emissions exceed 'critical loads' after which the capacity of the receiving media to dissipate and diffuse emissions would be

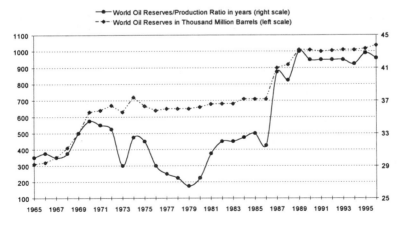

Source: British Petroleum (various years).

Figure 4.1 World oil reserves

damaged. Not following this rule would mean that the stock of pollution is continuously rising over time which is likely to endanger the sustainability goal.

Also ruled out would be the use of nuclear power with its highly damaging by-products on all stages of the nuclear cycle and its accumulating highly toxic nuclear waste radiating for tens of thousands of years. This is especially because nuclear waste cannot be disposed of but only more or less safely stored — a permanent burden to future generations. Following this prescription would also rule out the increased use of nuclear power for reducing CO_2 emissions in the atmosphere.

Natural Resources for Production
One might wonder why so little has been said about resources for production. The reason is that in a context of risk, uncertainty and ignorance it seems likely that the distinctive features of natural capital are especially relevant when it comes to the global environmental system and accumulating toxic pollutants as opposed to the global resource system. Property rights over energy and mineral resources are much better defined and the global environmental system, unlike the global resource system, lacks an 'automatic self-correcting feedback loop' (Clark 1995, p. 146) and especially lacks a functioning price system. Also, the prospects for technical progress appear to be strongest with respect to energy and mineral resources.

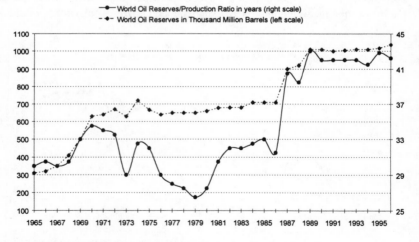

Source: British Petroleum (various years).

Figure 4.2 Word natural gas reserves

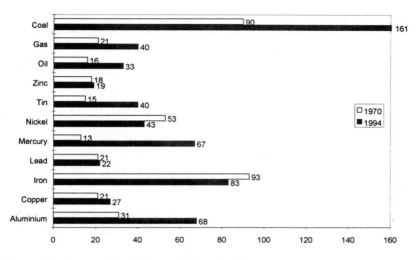

Sources: Meadows et al. (1972), WRI (1996-97), British Petroleum (various years).

Figure 4.3 Exponential reserve index for major resources

In Section 3.2, p. 47, we have seen how substitution and technical progress can interact powerfully to overcome natural resource constraint. There are good reasons to *presume* therefore that the global resource system will be much better taken care of through existing institutions than the global environmental system. It is the waste-absorbing function of the environment that is most under threat and least protected. That is not to say, that resource availability might never pose a problem, but the frequent falsification of alarms about immediate resource exhaustion presents a case in point.

The world economy has so far at least exhibited a most remarkable capability to overcome resource constraints via substitution and technical improvements. Reserves of both energy and non-energy resources have by and large persistently been rising over time. Figures 4.1 and 4.2 show the trend in world oil and gas reserves, respectively, together with their static reserves index, that is the current reserves to current production ratio in years. For both oil and gas both absolute reserves and the static reserves to production ratio are much higher than in 1965 (oil) or 1970 (gas), respectively. Figure 4.3 presents the exponential reserve index for major energy and non-energy resources in 1970 and 1992, respectively. The exponential reserve index states how long current reserves would last if future consumption were to *grow* at current rates of growth.[17] It shows that even the exponential reserve index has increased over the last 25 years in most cases or has decreased only slightly. Surely, there is no guarantee that this fortunate trend will continue into the future, especially as output and possibly resource input might be growing very fast, as the group of nearly industrialised countries becomes larger and larger and continues to catch up with the high-income countries. But the available evidence so far seems to strongly support the substitutability assumption of WS with respect to natural capital as a production input.

Food Resources
What about food resources? This is a topic where environmental pessimists believe that the limits to growth are close. The classic paper, written by a group of ecologists and often referred to in debates about sustainability — for example, by Myers (1993, p. 75), Rees and Wackernagel (1994, p. 383), Daly (1996, p. 57), and Dasgupta (1997, p. 6) — is Vitousek et al. (1986). They suggest that already almost 40 per cent of the terrestrial net primary productivity (NPP) of the earth is currently absorbed, dominated or destroyed by human activity. 'NPP provides the basis for maintenance, growth, and reproduction of all heterotrophs (consumers and decomposers); it is the total food resource on Earth' (ibid., p. 368). Because human appropriation of NPP cannot increase beyond 100 per cent, Vitousek et al. (1986) believe that substantial growth in food production is impossible. That is, if not the limits to eco-

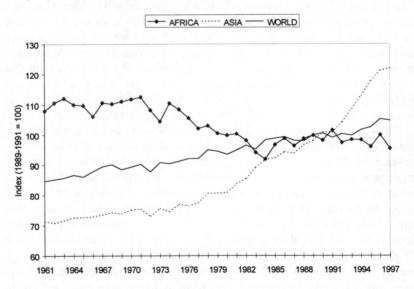

Source: FAO's online statistical database (http://apps.fao.org/).

Figure 4.4 Development of per capita food production

nomic growth, then at least the limits to population growth are close according to this view. It is highly contested, however. Beckerman (1995, p. 52) attacks Vitousek et al.'s computations as being completely meaningless: 'It simply means that a lot of the photosynthetic product that had previously been produced was of no use to us. It was, in effect, wasted. Now there is less of it. So what?'.

To feed more people there are basically two strategies. One is extensification: it is estimated that the amount of land usable for growing crops is three times larger than current usage (Preston 1996, p. 96). Alternatively, land could be used more intensively. In Europe, for example, usage of cropland fell by one-quarter and the total forested area grew by 30 per cent in spite of increased food production (ibid., p. 99). In India enormous gains in cereal production were made through the introduction of modern varieties and the so-called Green Revolution (Lipton 1989). Figure 4.4 shows the trend in per capita world food production alongside production in Africa and Asia. Of course, given the high aggregation of the index and the usually rather poor quality of the underlying data, the indices should be treated with care.

None the less, the figures reveal that while food production has caught up with growing world population and has even increased in per capita terms in Asia over the last thirty years or so, it has dramatically declined in Africa.[18] What this suggests is that the availability of food is more a problem of intra-generational, and as Smil (1994, p. 257) further claims even intra-national, distribution than a question of inter-generational sustainability. This finding is supported by those who have studied the political economy of famines and hunger (Drèze and Sen 1989; Drèze, Sen and Hussain 1995).

However, where there are clear signs of over-harvesting, soil erosion, land degradation and salinisation of irrigated fields, a good case can be made to enforce 'sustainable' harvesting, that is harvesting within the limits of natural regeneration, and to maintain soil fertility. The same applies to the protection of drinking water reservoirs. The availability of food and clean water is most basic to ensure the capacity to provide non-declining future welfare and where there are clear signs that danger to food and drinking water security is imminent, conservational steps should be undertaken.

Nature as such does not seem to impose limits on increasing food production to feed many more people. Waggoner (1994, p. 1) in a Task Force Report for the American Council for Agricultural Science and Technology comes to the conclusion that 'the global totals of sun on land, CO_2 in the air, fertilizer, and even water could produce far more food than ten billion [people, E.N.] need'. For other cautiously optimistic views on the availability of food for a human population rising up to ten or twelve billion people, see Ruttan (1991), Bongaarts (1994), Smil (1994) and Dyson (1996).

Summary

In summary, uncertainty and ignorance together with the distinctive features of natural capital make a persuasive case:

- for preventing large-scale biodiversity losses and the protection of ecosystems,
- for preserving global environmental life-support resources such as the global climate and the ozone layer,
- for limiting the accumulation of toxic pollutants and
- for restricting over-harvesting and soil erosion.

The case is strengthened by the fact that examples abound of negative interlinkages between environmental problems: deforestation often worsens loss of topsoil and land degradation and contributes to global warming; acid rain not only kills forests but also contaminates freshwater sources; ozone depletion contributes to global warming and some of the substitutes for CFCs have high global warming potentials. In contrast, there seems to be much less reason for being concerned about natural capital as a provider of resource input for production and food. What these results imply, is that the existing empirical evidence appears to support the non-substitutability assumption of SS more strongly with respect to the role natural capital plays in absorbing pollution and providing direct utility, whereas support is strong for the substitutability assumption of WS with respect to natural capital as a resource input.

Note, however, that for the case that SS seems to be supported by the empirical evidence, it strongly favours the second of the two interpretations SS was given in Section 2.3.2, p. 26. That is, from an SS perspective one would want to keep the physical stocks of certain forms of natural capital intact (to what extent will be discussed later on). In contrast, keeping the value of natural capital constant is not a reasonable conclusion from the evidence as it would not preclude that certain forms of natural capital that provide basic life-support functions are endangered or become irreversibly lost. The complete destruction of the ozone layer and the large-scale disruption of the biogeochemical cycle of the atmosphere cannot be compensated for even if other forms of *natural* capital are built up instead. An increase in the number of whales cannot substitute for a bigger hole in the ozone layer, for example. One could of course argue that the depletion value of life-support resources is very large or almost infinite so that it is impossible to keep the value of natural capital constant while running down these resources. Consequently, the two interpretations of SS would coincide in their policy conclusions. However, it seems more reasonable to target specific forms of natural capital directly if they are regarded as non-substitutable rather than rely on the hope that keeping the value natural capital non-declining will achieve their preservation indirectly.

Now we turn to the question to what extent preservation should take place and at what cost. So far, we have just made a case for the qualitative preservation of certain forms of natural capital in that it was argued that they cannot be completely destroyed. But that does not automatically imply that they have to be preserved in their remaining totality. Often in the literature on SS there is some confusion about total versus marginal values and opportunity costs are often implicitly or explicitly ignored. The next two sections deal with these issues.

4.4 TOTAL VERSUS MARGINAL VALUES AND POLICY PRINCIPLES TO COPE WITH RISK, UNCERTAINTY AND IGNORANCE

Some scholars stress the total value that natural capital, and especially natural ecosystems and the biodiversity they exhibit, have for human beings. Norton (1986, p. 205), for example, argues that this total value is virtually infinite:

> The value of biodiversity is the value of everything there is. It is the summed value of all the GNPs of all countries from now until the end of the world. If biodiversity is reduced sufficiently, and we do not know the disaster point, there will no longer be any conscious beings. With them go all value — economic and otherwise.

More recently, Costanza et al. (1997) have provided what they regard as a conservative estimate of the total value of the world's ecosystems. They suggest that this value lies in the range of US$16–54 trillion as a minimum estimate. For comparison, Costanza et al. indicate global GNP to be about US$18 trillion per year, so the estimated value of the world's ecosystems is very large indeed. Also note that in Costanza et al. the values for specific items whose magnitude they regard as likely to be infinite have been deliberately truncated to make them finite and to provide a lower bound estimate of the 'real' value.

The specific valuation approach taken in the study of Costanza et al. has been much criticised for methodological reasons (see the contributions in a special symposium published in *Ecological Economics*, **25** (1), 1998). However, for our purposes here these criticisms are of no major relevance. This is because the major problem with the study of Costanza et al. is not methodological and it does not matter much whether the numbers they come up with are approximately correct or not. Instead, the major point is that estimates of the *total* value of natural capital, or more concretely ecosystems, are virtually useless for practical preservation policy choices. The choices at hand are not between a complete destruction of ecosystems and a complete preservation of the remaining ecosystems. The real choices are always about discrete or marginal changes.

To give an example: if Brazil has to decide about clearing a certain part of its territory from tropical rainforests in order to convert it into an industrial development area, Costanza et al.'s estimates are of no help because the decision is not about destroying the totality of ecosystems. What the Brazilian government would need to know are the concrete costs and benefits of destruction. It would need to know what biodiversity there is and would have to establish the value of the biodiversity that is destroyed in converting the tropical rainforest into an industrial site. Economic valuation methods like the travel cost method, hedonic pricing and contingent valuation have been tremendously improved over the last two decades (for an overview, see for example, Freeman (1993), Barbier (1994b), Pethig (1994) and Georgiou et al. (1997); with special reference to biodiversity, see Brown et al. (1994)). In addition to the use-values for environmental resources, including the option and quasi-option values that have already been introduced in Section 4.2, p. 98, economic valuation techniques now also try to measure so-called non-use values like existence and bequest values. Existence value is the value individuals place on an item for its pure existence without intending to use it. Bequest value is the value individuals assign to an item for the purpose of bequeathing it to future generations. The objective is to measure the full value of the item being measured, as far as possible.

However, the vast amount of literature that has been generated on developing economic valuation techniques and their empirical application is equalled by a similarly vast amount of literature disputing the validity and reliability of economic valuation (for an overview see, for example, Hanley and Spash (1993), Common, Blamey and Norton (1993), Vatn and Bromley (1994), Hausman (1993), Diamond and Hausman (1994) and the references cited therein). Furthermore, the dynamic, complex and non-linear character of ecosystems makes valuation of ecosystems and biodiversity very difficult. Because of uncertainty and ignorance about the full extent of biodiversity loss due to a development project and its 'real' value, one could argue that a cost–benefit analysis is always likely to underestimate the value of lost biodiversity and will therefore lead to 'too much' depletion of natural capital. This will especially be true if the basic life-support value of ecosystems is hard to measure. The same holds true for the so-called 'primary value' of ecosystems which Gren et al. (1994, p. 56) define as the 'value of the ecosystem's self-organizing capacity'. Also, for every marginal decision it is hard to justify that the human lot is dependent on preserving this particular species or eco-system. On the other hand, with this kind of reasoning we may slowly and unconsciously slip beyond the threshold — initiating a vicious circle of large-scale ecosystem breakdown where biodiversity losses trigger the next losses in a domino fashion.

As an alternative to a simple cost–benefit analysis it is therefore often pro-posed to apply some policy principles that give more preference to preserva-tion in coping with uncertainty and ignorance. There exist at least three policy principles, namely the precautionary principle, an environmental bond system and the concept of safe minimum standards. These will now be assessed and it will be asked whether they can offer a way out of the valuation problem.[19]

4.4.1 The Precautionary Principle

The most basic principle to cope with risk, uncertainty and ignorance is the so-called 'precautionary principle'. O'Riordan (1993) and O'Riordan and Jordan (1995) list a whole range of (rather confusing) core elements of the precautionary principle, but there are two elements that are arguably the most important ones. First, *preventive* measures should be undertaken before there are *definite* scientific results 'proving' that protection of the environment is necessary. The motivation is to avoid regretting environmental inaction after unacceptable irreversible environmental destruction has already taken place. As environmentalists emphasise: it is better to be vaguely right in time than precisely right too late. One good example is global warming where a group of world scientists, among them more than 50 Nobel Laureates, have called for reductions of greenhouse gas emissions because 'there is only one respon-sible choice — to act now' (World Scientists 1997). Second and related to the first point, the burden of proof should shift to those who believe that an eco-nomic activity has only negligible detrimental consequences on the environ-ment. That is, the new default position should favour environmental preserva-tion, whereas current practice still favours economic activity over environ-mental preservation. The precautionary principle can thus be interpreted as an insurance scheme against uncertain future environmental catastrophes.

Several scholars from the Wuppertal Institute for Climate, Environment and Energy and from the World Resources Institute have derived from the precautionary principle a call for reducing material inputs by a factor of 10 over the long run (for example, Hinterberger, Luks and Schmidt-Bleek 1997; Hinterberger and Welfens 1996; Adriaanse et al. 1997). They argue that our knowledge about environmental externalities is so severely restricted that it is best to reduce material inputs without major discrimination across the board.

They also believe that most environmental problems are not caused by toxicity, but by the sheer scale of material input.

The precautionary principle was first integrated into official policy statements in the 1970s in former Western Germany in the form of the so-called *Vorsorgeprinzip* (Boehmer-Christiansen 1994). It soon found its way into virtually every official document on the environment and appeared in countless international environmental treaties (Cameron and Wade-Grey 1995). Some of this seeming 'success' of the precautionary principle was due to the fact that very often its application was merely rhetorical and did not change anything substantial. As Bodansky (1991) observes, part of the reason for this might be due to the fact that the precautionary principle is not able to give a clear answer on when it should be applied, that is, what are acceptable and unacceptable environmental dangers, at what costs it should be applied and what types of precautionary actions should be undertaken?

Two other policy measures that are often derived from the precautionary principle are supposed to be more apt for operationalising. One is an environmental bond system, the other is the concept of safe minimum standards.

4.4.2   An Environmental Bond System

The introduction of an environmental bond system was proposed by Perrings (1989), Costanza and Perrings (1990), Costanza and Cowell (1992) and Costanza (1994). Under this system any firm that wants to undertake a project that brings about some potential future risk is obliged to post an environmental bond at a governmental environmental agency that equals the expected — and, in the case of uncertainty or ignorance, best-guessed — future potential environmental damage. The firm can reduce the value of the bond by investing in research that shows convincingly that the potential damage is lower than the value demanded by the governmental agency, either in advance or after the initial posting of the bond in which case the firm would get some money back. That is, the value of the bond changes over time as the expected future potential damage changes. The bond is to be paid back in total either if the activity causing the potential damage ceases to exist and no damage is expected to be caused in the future or if, with continuing activity, it turns out that the fear of potential damage was unfounded. Interest from the bond should not be given back to the posting firm, according to the proposal, but invested in publicly financed research on the potential of future damages. Not returning the interest to the bondholder amounts to an implicit tax on the firm — a fact which the proponents of an environmental bond system do not explicate.

Environmental bond systems suppo&edly have advantages in coping with
risk, uncertainty and ignorance as summarised by Perrings (1989, p. 102):

> (1) it would register the value placed by the environmental authority on allow-
> ing an innovative activity to proceed without further research; (2) it would pro-
> vide an incentive to innovating firms to research the future effects of their own
> activities; (3) since the bond would yield interest income it would generate
> public research funds in direct proportion to the public concern about the future
> effects of innovative activities; (4) it would determine the timing of an innova-
> tive activity; (5) it would encourage sufficient advance experimental research to
> eliminate, so far as is possible in an uncertain world, catastrophic but unsur-
> prising conjectured outcomes; and (6) it would insure society against their re-
> ducible residuum of conjectured but unsurprising losses.

There are also some problems with environmental bond systems. One is
that they create moral hazard both on the side of the government agency and
on the side of the posting firm. The former has an incentive to 'hold up' the
posting firm, the latter has an incentive to overpollute if it is, due to asymmet-
ric information, able to realise that the damages of its actions exceed the value
of the bond as argued by Shogren, Herriges and Govindasamy (1993). As
they point out, there are so many unsolved problems with bonds that they are
even rarely used in labour markets where the conditions for their application
are much better. While representing an interesting idea, it seems likely therefore that environmental bond systems will not play a prominent role in policies to protect the environment in the near future (for a similar conclusion, see
Torsello and Vercelli 1998).

4.4.3   Safe Minimum Standards (SMSs)

Propositions to introduce safe minimum standards (SMSs) date back to
Ciriacy-Wantrup (1952) and were originally reserved for issues of species
preservation and biodiversity protection. Recently, however, the notion of
SMSs has been used increasingly for other environmental topics as well.
IPCC (1996b, p. 159), for example, speaks of an 'affordable safe minimum
standard' for the reduction of greenhouse gases. For reasons of space, I shall
only look at SMSs for the protection of species in this section, however.

SMSs call for granting a species some minimally viable standard. As
originally introduced by Ciriacy-Wantrup (1952), no explicit qualification
was made with respect to an upper limit of preservation costs. Later on, however, SMSs were interpreted as calling for imposing a safe standard, as long
as the economic costs of doing so are not 'unacceptably high'. Note that the
costs of protection are net of (expected) preservation benefits, where in the

case of uncertainty and ignorance some best guess of the size of benefits has to be made.

The concept of SMSs has been officially embraced by UNEP's Global Biodiversity Programme (Crowards 1996, p. 16). The Endangered Species Act in the US has many characteristics of an SMS (Castle and Berrens 1993, p. 122). It has been described as the 'most ambitious piece of species-protection legislation ever enacted by a single nation' (Ando 1998, p. 7). The US Fish and Wildlife Service has considerable leeway to intrude into property rights and impose conservation of endangered species on private agents. Economic actions that threaten the existence of endangered species are only allowed if 'the benefits of such action clearly outweigh the benefits of alternative courses of action consistent with conserving the species on its critical habitat' (US Congress 1978, p. 49).

SMSs have originally been intended for the protection of single species. However, it has now been recognised that the major threat for species derives more from a general destruction of habitats than from direct exploitation. Consequently, it was acknowledged that only the sustainable management of habitat areas is able to ensure the long-term survival of species (Barbier, Burgess and Folke 1994, pp. 60 and 62). Also, due to the complexity of ecosystems and our ignorance about their capacity for resilience as described above, it is increasingly recognised that a sustainable management that safeguards ecological thresholds must be flexible and cannot apply fixed rules like a fixed maximum (seemingly) sustainable yield (Holling 1995, p. 49). Strictly speaking, for many species there are 'no definite ecological–biological safe minimum standards' (Hohl and Tisdell 1993, p. 177) at all. Hence, SMSs by now tend more and more to mean the establishing of a viable standard for whole ecosystems where the standard is set well above some supposed minimum level. Protecting ecosystems is also a rather difficult and most likely an expensive task since misguided human manipulation of natural environments that reduces the resilience of ecosystems has to be avoided (Holling 1995). It is far from clear whether sustainable management of ecosystems is feasible and how it could be carried out (Carpenter 1994). Human protection of species might run counter to natural forces displacing one species by another emerging species which might or might not be good for ecosystem stability (d'Arge 1994).

There have been some attempts in the literature to base SMS on a solid theoretical foundation by deriving it from a game-theoretic decision model (see Bishop 1978, 1979; Smith and Krutilla 1979).[20] Ready and Bishop (1991) modelled a so-called insurance game where the 'minimax decision criterion' led to preferring preservation over extinction (as a consequence of economic 'development') as long as the expected loss following from extinction is higher than the expected net benefit of development.

To see this, look at the following insurance game (Table 4.1). Note that the games I construct are different from Ready and Bishop's (1991) games. I use gain matrices instead of loss matrices. Hence I use the maximin criterion, which selects the maximum of the minimum gains, instead of the minimax criterion, which selects the minimum of the maximum losses.[21] Let SMS be the strategy to protect a species via a safe minimum standard. Let EXT be the strategy not to protect the species and hand over the inhabited area to economic development in the course of which the species becomes extinct. Let the state DISEASE and NO DISEASE mean two possible states of the world: either a disease which causes human suffering breaks out or it does not break out. If it breaks out it can be cured with certainty by using the species, but not if the species is extinct. Let C be the cost to society due to the outbreak of the disease if it cannot be cured, that is, if the species became extinct in the past. Let B be the benefits to society due to handing over the area to development net of any development costs and further assume that the absolute value of C is bigger than B; that is, the potential costs due to the disease are bigger than the benefits from development.

Table 4.1 Payoff matrix for the insurance game

	DISEASE	NO DISEASE	Min Gain
SMS	0	0	0
EXT	B – C	B	B – C (< 0)

Table 4.1 provides the payoff matrix for this insurance game for each strategy/state of the world combination. The baseline is arbitrarily chosen as a situation where there is no disease and no development in the relevant area so far.

Let us proceed clockwise starting from the upper-left corner. If society chooses SMS, then no matter what happens its payoff will be 0, for there will be no development and the disease will be cured if the state of the world is DISEASE or the disease does not break out anyway if the state of the world is NO DISEASE, so nothing has changed relative to the baseline. If society chooses EXT and the state of the world is NO DISEASE, that is, preserving the species would have been useless anyway, then the payoff is B. If instead the state of the world turns out to be DISEASE, that is using the species would have cured the disease in future time if it had not become extinct, then the payoff is B – C which is negative since we assumed C > B.

Let us now compute the minimum gains to society for each strategy. In choosing SMS, society gets 0 in any case, so the minimum gain is 0. In choosing EXT, society gets B in case the disease does not break out, but it gets B – C (< 0) if it breaks out, so the minimum gain is B – C. The maximin criterion reflects extreme risk aversion by choosing that strategy that makes the deciding agent best off *in case the most unfavourable* state of the world occurs. Applying the maximin-criterion therefore requires adopting that strategy which *maximises* the *minimum* gain — therefore its name. Since 0 > (B – C), the optimal choice is to preserve the species in order to cure the disease if by chance it breaks out and to forgo the benefits from development, however low this chance might be. Preservation is the optimal choice as long as the costs of the SMS, that is, the direct cost of protecting the species, that were not included yet are not 'too high' — where 'too high' in this simple game can be computed as higher than C – B.

However, as Ready and Bishop (1991) have shown, this conclusion is highly reliant on the exact specification of the underlying game. In the insurance game it is assumed that a catastrophe, say a disease, has some probability of arising in the future and that preserving the species will cure the disease with certainty. By contrast, if one assumes that it is not the outbreak of the disease that is uncertain, but whether preserving the species will or will not cure the certain disease then the underlying game becomes a so-called lottery game. Arguably, the lottery game is the more realistic set-up and conforms with the argument of many environmentalists that biodiversity should be protected because it might bring about a cure for a disease that has been incurable so far (think of AIDS or cancer). The problem now is that the maximin criterion in the lottery game invariably opts for extinction and development as the preferred choice. 'Thus, a seemingly innocuous modification of the motivation of the problem has completely reversed the conclusion.' (ibid., p. 311).

To see this, look at the following lottery game. Let the strategies of the game and B and C be defined as before; only this time the states of the world are different. Let the state CURE and NO CURE mean two possible states of the world: either the certain disease can be cured or it cannot be cured. Table 4.2 provides the payoff matrix for this lottery game for each strategy/state of the world combination. The baseline is arbitrarily chosen as a situation where there is no cure for the existing disease and no development in the relevant area so far.

Table 4.2 Payoff matrix for the lottery game

	CURE	NO CURE	Min Gain
SMS	C	0	0
EXT	B	B	B

Let us proceed clockwise starting from the upper-left corner. If society chooses SMS and the state of the world is CURE, then society gets the payoff C (a gain) relative to the baseline. If instead the state of the world turns out to be NO CURE, then the payoff to society choosing SMS will be 0 since nothing has changed. If society chooses EXT and the state of the world is NO CURE, that is, preserving the species would have been useless anyway, then the payoff is B. If instead the state of the world turns out to be CURE, that is, using the species would have cured the disease in future time if it had not become extinct, then the payoff is B again since development is the only thing that has changed relative to the baseline.

Let us now compute the minimum gain to society for each strategy. In choosing SMS society gets either the gain of C or 0, so the minimum gain is 0. In choosing EXT society gets B in any case, so the minimum gain is B. Applying the maximin criterion requires taking that strategy which maximises the minimum gain. Since $B > 0$, the optimal choice is to extinguish the species in order to get the development benefits for sure and to forgo the possibility of curing the disease.

The preference for preservation given that the expected loss from extinction is higher than the expected net benefit from development is restored in the lottery game if one applies the so-called 'minimax *regret* decision criterion' (developed independently by Loomes and Sugden (1982) and Bell (1982)) instead of the maximin criterion. According to this criterion the decision is influenced by a desire to avoid post-decision regret, that is, regretting the negative actual consequences of an action that appeared to be the correct one given the information about expected future outcomes at the time of decision.

To see this, let us now compute the maximum regret to society for each strategy. Table 4.3 provides the regret matrix derived from the payoff-matrix of the lottery game in Table 4.2 for each strategy/state of the world combination.

Table 4.3 Regret matrix for the lottery game

	CURE	NO CURE	Max Regret
SMS	0	B	B
EXT	$C - B$	0	$C - B$

If the state of the world turns out to be CURE, then in choosing SMS society gets C and in choosing EXT society gets B. Since $C > B$ by assumption, the regret in choosing SMS is 0 and the regret in choosing EXT is $C - B$. If the state of the world turns out to be NO CURE, then in choosing SMS society gets 0 and in choosing EXT society gets B. Since B > 0, the regret in choosing EXT is 0 and the regret in choosing SMS is B − 0 = B. Hence the maximum regret in choosing SMS is max(0, B) = B and the maximum regret in choosing EXT is max(C − B, 0) = C − B. Applying the regret decision criterion requires taking the strategy which minimises the maximum regret. If C is at least twice as large as B, then it will be true that B < C − B and the optimal choice is again to preserve the species in order to prevent the regret of not being able to cure the disease in the case that the disease turns out to be curable.

However, whether public policy decisions should be based on regret is rather dubious, hence Hohl and Tisdell's (1993, p. 177) conclusion is correct that there is 'currently no solid theoretical foundation for the use of SMS'. What is worse: both the insurance and the lottery games can only cope with situations of risk, not with situations of uncertainty or even ignorance which as argued above are the more relevant ones. The reason is that for applying game theory at least the possible states of the world and the possible strategies have to be known.

The more general problem is that there is no widely accepted theory of choice under uncertainty and ignorance. This should come as no surprise since it is in the very nature of uncertainty and ignorance that they are not easily amenable to axiomatic analysis.[22] Dasgupta, Barrett and Mäler (1996, p. 2) are right in claiming that 'we do not have a theory, normative or otherwise, that would cover long-term environmental uncertainties in a satisfactory way'. Individuals taking actual decisions tend to violate substantial principles of rationality when faced with risk and uncertainty, especially in contexts with low probability (see Machina 1987; Pearce 1994b; Zeckhauser and Viscusi 1995). Equally, they tend to underestimate actual risks from everyday life, but overestimate actual risks from large-scale extraordinary disasters (Royal Society 1992, Section 5.3). As Zeckhauser and Viscusi (1995, p. 631) point out, decisions in these contexts reveal the limits of human rationality and are generally not overcome by providing better information. Note, however, that the often found aversion against risks of commissions rather than omission, against risks involving involuntary exposure, lack of personal experience and difficulty in imagining risk exposure that characterise many large-scale but small probability risks are not irrational in themselves, as Zeckhauser and Viscusi (1995) seem to suggest, even when their actual incidence is overestimated.

The absence of a well-specified game-theoretic foundation does not imply that SMS should not be applied by a society that is committed to sustainability but faced with uncertainty and ignorance. What it does say, however, is that there is no rigorous theory of choice that would justify SMS and that we have to discuss in more detail now how much cost should be incurred for applying SMS. In the next section the more general problem of the opportunity cost of environmental preservation and the implications for preservation, which has so far always been present in the background, will be addressed more directly.

4.5 HOW MUCH PRESERVATION? THE PROBLEM OF OPPORTUNITY COST

All choices exclude potential alternative choices and therefore incur opportunity costs. Let us start by having a look at the costs of preserving the remaining biodiversity on earth. The first thing to note is that the protection costs are likely to be high even in terms of direct management costs due to the complexity of safeguarding the resilience of an ecosystem. Agenda 21 estimates the total expenditure needs for global biodiversity protection to be in the range of $8–80 bn per annum (Panayotou, 1997, p. 220). Although such figures should always be treated with care, they give some tentative hint on the magnitude of costs for biodiversity protection. The main costs arise in terms of indirect costs, however, due to blocking economic development in a large part of a nation's area. Perrings's (1994, p. 93) fear that protecting the current biodiversity 'may very well condemn future generations to progressive impoverishment, especially in the light of the continuing expansion of the global human population' might be overdrawn. But the dilemma of full biodiversity protection is that there are *definite, present, real* costs for *uncertain, future* and perhaps *intangible* benefits in applying SMS. Also, the actual protector will not be able to reap all of the potential future benefits because some of the benefits are positive externalities to other people in other countries, that is, the protection of biodiversity has to some extent the characteristics of a global public good. Consequently, there are powerful incentives to free ride on others' effort for biodiversity protection. Since every potential protector has the incentive to free ride, none of them might have sufficient impetus to protect biodiversity.

Note that the dilemma that the opportunity costs are definite, present and real whereas the benefits of preservation are uncertain, future and intangible is not exclusive to biodiversity protection. It applies equally to many other environmental issues, most notably global warming. There are basically two possible answers to this dilemma. One is a deliberate decision to incur the opportunity cost for the sake of ensuring the benefits of being safe on preservation. This is the SMS as originally introduced by Ciriacy-Wantrup: safe minimum standards are established independent of the costs.[23] Because many of the costs of biodiversity depletion are rather speculative, but potentially very high, and because we do not know how much biodiversity is needed to keep up its basic life-support functions, one could decide to refrain from marginal decisions at all and opt for preserving the totality of remaining biodiversity disregarding the costs of preservation.

Another justification for total preservation would be if one regards biodiversity as non-substitutable with respect to providing direct utility for future generations. Similarly, with respect to environmental pollution, Spash (1993, p. 127) postulates an 'inviolable right of future generations to be free of intergenerational environmental damages', which would imply that 'the current generation would be obliged to identify all activities causing long-term damages and ban them *regardless of the cost*' (ibid., p. 128, my emphasis). Still more generally, Costanza (1994, p. 394) calls for preserving the complete stock of natural capital without qualification as regards the opportunity costs of preservation:

> While a lower stock of natural capital may be sustainable, given our uncertainty and the dire consequences of guessing wrong, it is best to at least provisionally assume that we are at or below the range of sustainable stock levels and allow no further decline in natural capital. This 'constancy of total natural capital' rule can thus be seen as a prudent minimum condition for assuring sustainability, to be abandoned only when solid evidence to the contrary can be offered.

The other possibility is to allow opportunity costs to influence the decision and to explicitly limit the costs society is willing to incur for biodiversity protection and pollution prevention. This is the SMS as it became interpreted over time with the qualification that costs must not be 'too high'. We shall now analyse each possibility and start with the first option of deliberately ignoring opportunity costs.

The first thing to note is that taking to its extreme the proposition that long-term environmental damage has to be avoided at any cost would lead to tremendous consequences on how modern society is organised. The energy sector, the chemical, pharmaceutical, biotechnological and mining industry, the car manufacturers, even the computer and electronics industry — they all have one thing in common: they all produce more or less lasting pollution as a side-effect, if only in the form of carbon dioxide emissions. The point is that while environmental policy together with technical progress can make modern industrial society more or less harmful to the environment in the long run, it will certainly not be possible to maintain our current modes of production and living without inflicting some harm upon future generations.

The problem with the proposition that long-term environmental degradation has to be avoided at any cost is that there is a virtual infinity of actions of the present generation which affect the future and often the same action will have both beneficial and harmful aspects. The verdict that any action that inflicts some harm on coming generations is unjustified and cannot be compensated for calls for a virtual standstill in economic actions of the present generation. Radical environmentalists might be happy with such a scenario — but future generations will presumably be less fond of it, if such a tremendous opportunity cost is imposed on them.

What is true for avoiding environmental pollution, is equally true for the protection of biodiversity regardless of the cost. It is worth quoting Beckerman (1994, pp. 194f.) at some length here:

> Given the acute poverty and environmental degradation in which a large part of the world's population live, one could not justify using up vast resources in an attempt to preserve from extinction, say, every one of the several million species of beetles that exist. For the cost of such a task would be partly, if not wholly, resources that could otherwise have been devoted to more urgent environmental concerns, such as increasing access to clean drinking water or sanitation in the Third World.

Jacobs (1995c, p. 63) claims that in practice we are not faced with many choices of the 'preserve some obscure species' versus 'improve basic health care' type, but at least they cannot be ruled out in principle. While we might not want to preserve every beetle as such, we might well want to preserve the totality of remaining tropical rainforests where the vast majority of beetles resides if we can ignore opportunity cost. Hence there will remain many cases where fundamental ethical conflicts arise. These ethical conflicts are exacerbated by the fact that the vast majority of the world's biological diversity exists in only a few nation-states that belong to the poorest of the world, with the notable exception of Australia (Swanson 1994, p. 806). Ignoring opportunity cost is tantamount to a refusal to solve this ethical conflict. One could decide for this option, but I would claim that a society committed to SD would be ill advised to do so.

Also, if the argument that biological diversity is non-substitutable as a direct provider of utility was valid, one would expect to find very high values for the benefits of biodiversity protection in valuation studies. This expectation would hold even if one accepts the argument that valuation is problematic because of uncertainty, ignorance, thresholds and non-linear dynamic processes and even if one allows for the possibility that the current generation might not value biodiversity as much as future generations potentially do. However, if the non-substitutability argument was correct and the valued benefits very high, why ignore opportunity costs then and not rely on a comparison of costs and benefits?

Let us turn to the second option now. If opportunity costs are allowed to influence the decision to what extent certain forms of natural capital should be preserved, how do we know what the maximum costs are society should be willing to incur? Here the first thing to note is that if costs of preservation are allowed to enter the decision making, we are essentially back to economic valuation techniques and cost–benefit analysis. The only substantial difference is that the precautionary principle and SMS would function like a constraint that the benefits of an action destroying an environmental asset must not only be higher than its costs, but higher than its costs by a certain factor. Conversely, an environmental resource should be preserved not only as long as the estimated benefits of preservation are higher than the costs of preservation, but until the costs exceed the benefits by a certain factor. Note that the exact magnitude of this factor could vary according to the degree of uncertainty involved and the stakes at hand.

Stevens et al. (1991, p. 399) claim that since we do not know which particular species are worth protecting, applying the SMS with its focus on the costs of preventing species extinction is superior to cost–benefit analysis since it can do without making estimates of the potential benefits of protecting a specific species. But Stevens et al.'s (1991) claim is not correct if opportunity costs are allowed to enter the decision-making process, because then benefits and costs still have to be balanced against each other and the benefits of protection have to be estimated.

Natural science can help a society that opts for precautionary action and the establishment of SMS subject to costs not being 'unacceptably large' in improving information about environmental resources and the likely consequences of depletion. Similarly, economic science can help society in improving valuation techniques and providing best available information on costs and benefits. As some studies have shown, the clash between preserving biodiversity and economic development is sometimes an artificial one because biodiversity could generate economic use and non-use values above the opportunity costs of biodiversity protection (Brown et al. 1994; Pearce 1997a).[24] The problem usually is a combination of lack of information about these values, lack of markets for wildlife products and lack of appropriate mechanisms (institutions) to capture at least parts of these values for those who would otherwise have an interest in the destruction of biodiversity and would oppose biodiversity conservation (Swanson 1997).

To overcome this problem, increased efforts should be undertaken for biodiversity valuation studies to provide at least some rough idea of the value of biodiversity. Even if there are many problems with economic valuation techniques, especially in valuing non-use values, it is better to have some idea of the value, in order to put some weight against the net benefits of environmental destruction. The resistance of many environmentalists against 'putting a price tag on the environment' is counterproductive as long as they cannot demonstrate that there is a better way (other than ignoring opportunity costs) to protect the environment against the vested interests behind, and the economic logic of, actions leading to environmental destruction. When natural capital is underpriced or not priced at all, social and economic decisions will be biased against the preservation of natural capital. This will be true at all stages, beginning from research and development and extending to final consumption and production decisions.

Second, and maybe more importantly, where possible markets should be created, property rights specified, and the capture mechanisms should be improved. That is, measures should be undertaken to transform hypothetical demand for biodiversity protection into effective demand. Doing so would include

- developing ecotourism (Ramsamy 1994; Filion, Foley and Jacquemot 1994) and raising visitor prices to natural parks to profit-maximising levels;
- tacking back outright bans on the utilisation of wildlife products (for example, for elephant ivory or for wood from tropical forests) in order to stimulate its economic use — if remaining regulatory policies can ensure that this economic use is sustainable. Where sustainable use cannot be ensured via regulation and an outright ban seems necessary, the losers of the ban should be compensated to take away their incentive to thwart the conservation policy (Pearce 1997a, p. 8);
- strengthening existing, but rudimentary mechanisms to transfer money for biodiversity conservation from the 'North' to the 'South'. This could encompass, for example, a financial strengthening of UNEP's Biodiversity Programme and the Global Environmental Facility (GEF) (Pearce 1995), the creation of markets for transferable development rights (Panayotou 1994), governmental support for private 'debt-for-nature swaps' or even governmental participation therein (for an introductory overview, see Deacon and Murphy 1997) and 'joint implementation' programmes (for an introductory overview, see Pearce 1994a).

As Panayotou (1997, p. 229) points out, Costa Rica is a promising model example since it receives several million dollars from US pharmaceutical companies for (potentially) using the country's biodiversity in developing new medicines. According to Panayotou (ibid.), Costa Rica also earns hundreds of millions of dollars from scientific research and ecotourism.

In conclusion, there now exists a large literature on the ecology and economics of biodiversity and both sciences are permanently improving over time (for an overview, see www.orst.edu/dept/ag_resrc_econ/biodiv, a bibliography online on the internet, and Perrings, Folke and Mäler (1992)). However, and this is an important point, there is no science that can tell society how risk averse it should be with respect to depletion. For public policy decisions, it is up to society and its political decision-making procedures to decide by *how much* the costs of preservation can exceed the best available evidence on the benefits of preservation. Neither the precautionary principle nor the SMS can define what 'too high costs' are. This question is fundamentally a political one, not a scientific one.

Another thing that science, especially economics, can do is to identify ways to preserve natural capital at least cost. It is this question the next section focuses on.

4.6   LEAST-COST MEASURES FOR PRESERVING NATURAL CAPITAL

Given that preservation is costly, a society committed to SD would be well advised to use measures first that achieve preservation at low, or even negative, economic costs. Let us discuss some of the potential measures that have been proposed by various scholars.

4.6.1 Abolishing Environmentally and Economically Harmful Subsidies

What can be said rather unambiguously is that measures that both protect the environment and improve economic efficiency should be undertaken and can be expected to receive support from both paradigms of sustainability. In many instances governments have introduced subsidies, failed to establish and protect property rights, and invited rent-seeking behaviour leading to both environmental destruction and to growth-retarding distortions in the economy. Abandoning these practices, it is claimed, would be good for the environment in dramatically easing the pressure on the remaining ecosystems and be good for economic activity at the same time. These are the World Bank's (1992) famous 'win win situations'. They indeed open the way for a 'free lunch': society can have both a better environment and higher economic activity at no, or even negative, net cost. To give an example: countries that are characterised by the failure to establish and protect property rights and to guarantee the rule of the law are not only likely to have low investment into long-term assets especially from abroad, but also tend to have high deforestation rates as Deacon (1994) has shown.

The prospect for these 'win win situations', especially as concerns subsidies, is, at least in principle and theory, higher than one might expect. For example, world-wide over-fishing is estimated to be subsidised by about US$54 bn yearly (FAZ 1997). Roodman (1996, p. 6) estimates environmentally damaging and economically distorting subsidies for water use, energy use, and agriculture to be at least US$500 bn. Panayotou (1997, p. 217) states an upper estimation of US$1000 bn. The latter figure comes close to 5 per cent of world GNP!

Note, however, that often behind these subsidies stand vested political interests, as for example with the European Union's Common Agricultural Policy, which means that they are difficult to abolish (see Roodman 1996, pp. 52–6, for more detail). The abolition of these subsidies would come at negative economic costs, but at high political costs and would create immense distributional conflicts.

Sometimes there are also good reasons for the subsidies, for example, when they function to provide the poor with essential means for their living. Here, abolishing the subsidies has to go hand in hand with a compensation for the poor via other means, if one wants to protect them from a further decline in their standard of living. Finally, there are some cases, as in agricultural subsidies in Northern developed countries, where the environmental impact of abolishing the subsidies and liberating agricultural trade are ambiguous because trade liberalisation would make agriculture less intensive in the North, but more intensive in fertiliser and pesticide use in the South (Lutz 1992). All these caveats and qualifications notwithstanding, the reported figures give a rough idea of what could be done to make some progress towards sustainability.

4.6.2 Abating Economically Harmful Pollution

In many countries there are also likely to be many cases where environmental pollution directly harms economic productivity, either via damaging production inputs or via undermining the health of the labourers. Systematic evidence on this question is scarce, but many case studies have shown that often some level of environmental protection is self-financing because it leads to higher economic productivity (see, for example, World Bank 1992, Ch. 2, pp. 44–63).[25] Of course, policy makers have to intervene in order to get the situation changed since environmental pollution is most often the consequence of some economic agent externalising environmental costs and who is therefore not likely to abate emissions on his own just because this would be in the social interest.

4.6.3 Substituting Market-based for Command-and-control Instruments

Another possibility for enhancing sustainability while at the same time limiting the negative consequences on economic activity is using market-based instruments like emission taxes and tradable permits for environmental protection instead of the still much more widely used command-and-control instruments. Unfortunately, economists in the past have been over-optimistic about the advantages of market-based instruments and have often overlooked administrative and political economy problems with applying taxes and permits (see Common 1989; Hanley, Hallett and Moffatt 1990; Hahn 1990; Hahn and Axtell 1995; Stavins 1995, 1998). Indeed, the static efficiency advantages have often been exaggerated by comparing a theoretical ideal of market-based instruments with real-world examples of command-and-control instruments (Stavins 1996).

However, the static advantages are of minor interest in a sustainability context. What is more relevant here is the dynamic advantage of market-based instruments.[26] Both taxes and tradable permits are *dynamically efficient* in that they induce firms not only to reduce resource consumption or pollution emission to the warranted level but to explore and develop new and even less pollution- or resource-intensive technologies in order to pay less taxes or earn additional revenues via selling permits.[27] Command-and-control instruments, whether demanding a specific environmental performance or prescribing a certain technical standard, are *dynamically inefficient* because over-compliance would not save money for the firm and developing new technologies risks inducing the environmental authority to tighten the standard without the firm being able to reap the benefits of its improvement.

In Chapter 3, p. 44, we have seen that technical progress plays an important, if not the most important, role in overcoming resource constraints and in mitigating the pollution side-effects of economic activity — so from a sustainability point of view market-based instruments with their built-in dynamic efficiency have clear advantages over command-and-control instruments. There has been some increase in the use of market-based instruments in OECD countries over the last decade or so, but their extent remains modest and they have rather supplemented than replaced command-and-control instruments (Pearson 1995, p. 357). The OECD is encouraging its member states to make greater use of market-based instruments for environmental policy (OECD 1997). More research should go into the question of what the political economy problems in applying market-based instruments are and how they could be overcome. This recommendation gains additional justification when, as is not recognised widely yet, the positive effects on sustainability of replacing existing command-and-control instruments with taxes or permits are also taken into account. Note that I do not propose to substitute market-based instruments for command-and-control instruments in each and every instance. Which type of instrument is better to use is highly context specific. Rather, the point is that even given that market-based instruments are not always better, they are still much less used than they should be.

4.6.4 Changing the Tax Base of the Economy?

Taxes and permits, if initially sold to firms and not 'grandfathered', also raise revenues for the public authority. No wonder then that economists have come up with the idea of using market-based instruments also to raise public revenues in order to reduce other distortive taxes — going as far as proposing a grand-design change in the base of the tax system of a country away from taxing labour or capital income towards taxing resource and energy input and pollution emission. Some proponents of SS are strong supporters of such a proposition (Daly and Costanza 1992, p. 45).

There would be ample space for such large-scale changes since it is estimated that roughly 50 per cent of all state revenue in EU countries comes from taxes that are directly or indirectly levied on labour whereas less than 10 per cent comes from ecotaxes, that is, taxes on natural resource use and pollution taxes (Tindale and Holtham 1996, p. 64). Figures for other OECD countries are similar (McCoy 1996, p. 211). So far, only Norway and Sweden and, to a lesser extent, Denmark, Finland and the Netherlands have undertaken some preliminary steps in the direction of deriving state revenue from ecotaxes rather than other taxes.[28]

Substituting ecotaxes for taxes on labour and capital income has also gained some wider support among economists in recent years as a 'no regret' policy to combat global warming, because it is believed that raising taxes on CO_2 emissions and compensating fully with reductions in other distortive taxes will be good for both the climate and the economy, especially for fostering employment (Pearce 1991; Greer 1995; Jaeger 1995).[29] This is the so-called 'double-dividend hypothesis'.

If the hypothesis was true, this would be excellent from an environmental point of view. This is because the benefits from environmental protection are often uncertain, as argued in earlier sections of this chapter, in contrast to the direct costs of doing so. The optimal internalisation of environmental externalities via Pigouvian[30] taxes as presented in the neat little diagrams of environmental economics textbooks is very often virtually impossible in reality. If the double-dividend hypothesis was true, many more measures to protect the environment could be justified since it would not be necessary any more to know the exact magnitude of the environmental benefits. It would be enough to know that the environmental benefits are positive, however big, since due to the double-dividend environmental protection will come at no or even negative net economic costs.

Also, many environmentally harmful emissions cannot be measured because of the sheer number of emission sources or because measurement is prohibitively expensive. It would then be sufficient to tax inputs such as energy and resources which are much easier to monitor than pollution emissions. Doing so makes sense as long as the link between energy or resource input and pollution is sufficiently strong. Referring back to CO_2 emissions, it would be sufficient to tax different energy inputs approximately according to their carbon content rather than trying to measure CO_2 emissions exactly at the 'end of the pipe'. In short, the double-dividend hypothesis seems to open the way for a much bigger 'free lunch' than the abolition of environmentally and economically harmful subsidies. But does it really hold?

Prima facie the hypothesis appears to be convincing: substituting the taxation of 'bads' such as pollution for the taxation of 'goods' such as labour and capital while keeping the overall tax burden of an economy the same should enhance economic activity rather than reduce it. On closer inspection, however, economists using highly complex general equilibrium models have contested this view. The point is that a tax on energy input, for example, raises the costs of production and leads to higher prices. Thus the energy tax lowers the real wage and in the end amounts to an implicit tax on labour (tax interaction effect). This implicit tax has to be set higher than the direct tax on labour, however, because a successful environmental tax erodes its own base if the addressed firms partially reduce energy input or use less polluting inputs (erosion effect). Thus, substituting ecotaxes for labour taxes cannot but exacerbate existing distortions in the economy (Bovenberg and Mooij 1995; Bovenberg and Goulder 1995).

Considering capital as a second factor of production and capital income taxation has ambiguous effects: on the one hand, using revenues from environmental taxation to reduce capital taxes which are generally presumed to be highly distortive can under certain, fairly restrictive conditions lead to a double-dividend (Goulder 1994, pp. 12ff.). On the other hand, it has to be taken into account that CO_2 abatement policies tend to shift the costs of abatement towards capital since the energy sector is relatively capital intensive, thus exacerbating existing distortions in the taxation of capital income (Parry, Williams and Goulder 1997, p. 21). Given that capital is relatively mobile internationally and is therefore likely to be overtaxed in actual as compared to an optimal taxation system, the introduction of ecotaxes can produce a double-dividend if it leads to a net decrease of the tax burden on capital (Mooij and Bovenberg 1998). Taking into account yet another factor of production (for example, land) results in similar conclusions: a double-dividend is possible if the tax burden can be shifted towards the fixed factor which has to be an important production factor but must not be a good substitute for the polluting inputs (Bovenberg and van der Ploeg 1998). Given that fixed factors are more important in the short run than in the long run, we would also expect the prospects for a double-dividend to be rather low in the long run.

The effects on employment depend largely on whether the implicit fall in relative labour costs due to decreasing the taxes on labour income will be fully compensated by higher real wages or not. If they are, then no beneficial effects on employment are to be expected (Carraro, Galeotti and Gallo 1996; Koskela, Schöb and Sinn 1998). Taking more explicitly into account that labour markets are highly distorted relative to a market equilibrium makes reductions in unemployment more likely (Schneider 1997; Kirchgässner, Müller and Savioz 1998).

Other economists have insisted that a double-dividend is much more likely to hold. They have based their arguments more on logical reasoning than theoretical modelling, however, which weakens their case since the effects of taxation are usually so difficult to assess that they can only be captured in complex general equilibrium models. Jaeger (1995) argues that taxing pollution should be regarded as broadening the tax base of the economy via taxing a hitherto untaxed 'commodity'. Since it is a standard result in public economics that second-best taxation is the less distortive the wider is the tax base, one should expect the overall welfare burden due to taxation to decline and thus the double-dividend hypothesis to hold. Similarly, Ekins (1996b, p. 158) argues that the environmental externality should be considered as distorting other markets as well through market-interaction effects. Internalising this externality via a pollution tax should make other markets *less* distorted rather than exacerbating existing distortions since the distortion due to the environmental externality is abolished. A similar argument is put forward by an OECD document on 'Environmental taxes and green tax reform' which expects a limited, but positive contribution from a tax reform towards lowering unemployment (OECD 1997, pp. 9ff.).

The debate on the double-divided is unlikely to be resolved over the next decade or so. It might actually never be resolved since the conclusions are highly dependent on the modelling approach and every model can be contested for not including important aspects whose inclusion would alter the model results. It seems fair to say, however, that the double-dividend hypothesis has not yet been proved so far and that the relationship between the environment and the economy is more likely to remain one of a fundamental trade-off. That does not mean that environmental protection should not be undertaken, but that it has to be justified more for its environmental benefits alone rather than for its alleged additional beneficial effect on the general economy. In other words, environmental protection is not a free lunch.

Totally uncontroversial, however, is the fact that the economic costs of environmental protection will be lower (but still positive) if the revenue is used to reduce other distortive taxes rather than increasing the overall tax burden of the economy or returning the taxes to consumers via lump-sum transfers. Creating revenues that can be used to reduce other distortive taxes also represents an advantage of market-based instruments over command-and-control instruments *in addition to* the advantages already presented in the last subsection.

The numerically-solved general equilibrium model of Parry, Williams and Goulder (1997, p. 3) suggests that using command-and-control instruments instead of revenue-neutral market-based instruments could make a 5 per cent reduction in CO_2 emissions up to seven times and a 15 per cent reduction up to three times more costly. The initial marginal costs for command-and-control instruments is estimated to be approximately $25 per ton of carbon as compared to $0 per ton of carbon with revenue-neutral market-based instruments. This has powerful policy implications for whether or not to combat global warming, because, often, marginal benefits of carbon abatement are estimated to be below $25 per ton of carbon (Fankhauser and Tol 1996).[31] Hence traditional cost–benefit analysis would caution against any CO_2 emissions reduction if this reduction will be achieved via command-and-control as opposed to revenue-neutral market-based instruments.

4.6.5 Tighter Regulations for Increasing Productivity?

Equally contested as the call for a large-scale change in the tax base of an economy is the proposition put forward by Porter and van der Linde (1995) (the so-called 'Porter hypothesis') that there are many cases in which tightening environmental regulations would at the same time increase firms' economic profitability, that is, cases in which tighter environmental standards come at no economic costs or even with economic benefits.[32] The idea is that tighter regulation, if properly designed, would trigger firms to innovate and thus to become more productive. A famous example is that of 3M: when regulations for hazardous waste disposal tightened, the company realised that a new technique in producing adhesives enabled 3M to reduce hazardous waste by 10 tons per year at almost no cost and saving more than $200 000 annually (Porter and van der Linde 1995, p. 102).

Economists have not found the Porter hypothesis very convincing for two reasons (see Palmer and Simpson 1993; Oates, Palmer and Portney 1993; Palmer, Oates and Portney 1995). First, the Porter hypothesis assumes that firms are forgoing opportunities to increase their profitability, that is, they are working inefficiently. They need a government to tell them how to improve their productivity, so to speak. But if firms are under competitive pressure and work inefficiently, then they will be outcompeted by their more efficient rivals, which implies that the forgoing of profitable opportunities can at most be a transitory and marginal phenomenon. Second, even if those opportunities existed and were not seized by private firms, for example, due to market imperfections, it is still doubtful whether the government can know any better and is able to design environmental regulation such that firms' profits increase. If the Porter hypothesis was true, then why do we see firms lobbying against environmental protection instead of lobbying for tighter environmental regulation? Porter and van der Linde (1995) cite dozens of examples which allegedly buttress their case.[33] But 'examplerism' is no substitute for systematic empirical evidence and Jaffe, Peterson and Stavins (1995) in a survey of the existing evidence did not find any systematic support for the Porter hypothesis.

That is not to say that all firms, and even less so consumers who are not faced with constant competitive pressure, are always operating efficiently. If that was the case, how could we explain the existence of business consulting? One area where it has been shown that opportunities for environmental protection exist that are not widely exploited and could save money at the same time is energy conservation — both within firms and private households (Jochem and Gruber 1990; Jaffe and Stavins 1994; Jackson 1995). The reasons for this failure are presumably a mixture of lack of information and awareness, lack of technical expertise and lack of strong incentives because of the low share of energy costs among total expenditure. Here, policy makers could help to overcome these obstacles via inducing electric utilities to provide information and expertise and to 'sell' energy efficiency improvements. Thus some cheap if not costless steps towards environmental protection could be made.

One must beware not to overestimate the prospects for these costless opportunities, however. The claim that 20 per cent and more of CO_2 emissions in industrialised countries can be cut at no economic costs due to energy conservation measures — a claim which is often found in so-called bottom-up engineering studies of the costs of CO_2 emissions abatement (IPCC 1996b, pp. 303–43) — is rather dubious because it neglects the many informal transaction costs that prevent firms and consumers alike from seizing these self-paying opportunities. That something is costless in theoretical Nirvana does not mean that it will be costless in the actual world in which we live. It seems fair to say, therefore, that while there are some unexploited options and informed policy makers can help to realise these options, it is nevertheless true that substantial environmental protection will be costly.

4.7   CONCLUSION

In this chapter, I have shown that the combination of the distinctive features of natural capital with risk, uncertainty and ignorance suggest the conclusion that there are good reasons for the non-substitutability of specific forms of natural capital. I have demonstrated that a persuasive case can be made for preserving biodiversity and global environmental life-support resources such as the ozone layer and the global climate, for limiting the accumulation of toxic pollutants and for preventing unsustainable harvesting and soil erosion. In contrast, no explicit preservation policy seems necessary for natural resources used for the production of consumption goods and, if less so, for food resources. Essentially, while both paradigms are non-falsifiable (see Chapter 3), empirical evidence seems to support stronger WS with respect to the 'source' side and SS with respect to the 'sink' side of the economy.

However, identifying the forms of natural capital for preservation does not give exact boundaries on how much should be preserved. Just because something is non-substitutable *in toto*, does not imply that it is not substitutable to some extent at the margin. There is often a confusion between total and marginal values in the literature and it was argued that the estimation of total values is virtually irrelevant for real policy choices, which are about discrete, not total, changes. Valuation techniques and cost–benefit analysis are the tools that economics offers to deal with marginal choices.

I have argued that there are basically two options in dealing with the difficult question of how much preservation should take place in the presence of uncertainty and ignorance. One is suspicious of cost–benefit analysis and presumes that economic valuation techniques will not elicit the 'real' value of changes in natural capital. From this perspective, it is better to refrain from marginal decisions because of uncertainty and ignorance and to opt for the preservation of the totality of the remaining stocks of certain forms of natural capital independent of the cost. Potentially large, but still finite, present and real costs are incurred in order to prevent uncertain and future, but potentially virtually infinite, costs of natural capital depletion.

The other option is to apply valuation techniques in order to get best available estimates on the costs and benefits of preservation, but to allow the costs of preservation to exceed the benefits by a certain factor. Such a position can be derived from policy principles such as the precautionary principle and SMS that function as a kind of insurance policy against the potentially detrimental consequences of natural capital loss. This position would call for maintaining efforts to improve natural science knowledge about natural capital and the consequences of depletion and to improve both valuation techniques and capture mechanisms to make the hypothetical benefits of preservation real to the preserver.

Which option to take? I have argued in favour of the latter option and against ignoring opportunity cost. I readily admit that the latter option does not provide complete insurance against the non-achievement of sustainability and catastrophic outcomes. If we take the latter option, there is always the possibility of an *ex post* surprise, that is, the danger that we run down too much natural capital in spite of our *ex ante* expectation that this depletion of natural capital would not endanger sustainability. On the other hand, with the first option of preserving natural capital independent of the costs there is also the clear danger of significantly reducing other opportunities for current and future generations. Beckerman and Pasek (1997, p. 72) are correct in suggesting that it might be better ethically justified to spend scarce resources on health or education rather than on the preservation of natural capital: 'It is difficult to see in what way the environment is in some moral class of its own'. The point is that to ignore opportunity costs is to 'solve' these often awkward trade-off decisions in avoiding them or running away from them.

If one goes for the second option, then it has to be decided by which factor, possibly differentiated for differing forms of natural capital, the costs are allowed to exceed the benefits of preservation. It was argued that this is not a scientific question, but a political one that has to be decided by society's political decision-making procedures. What science can do is to keep providing better information about the potential consequences of the decline in certain forms of natural capital and to provide better and better estimates of benefits and costs of marginal choices. But it cannot tell society how much it should allow the costs of preservation to exceed the benefits.

Another thing that economics can do is to help achieve certain preservation targets at minimal cost. Indeed, this is one of the classical objectives of economics. I have therefore highlighted some measures that could be undertaken without major, if any, real economic costs. Realising these measures would mean establishing and protecting property rights, abolishing environmentally and economically harmful subsidies, abating economically harmful pollution, substituting market-based for command-and-control instruments, using the revenues from environmental taxation such that their economic costs are minimised and helping to overcome obstacles for realising self-paying energy efficiency improvements. These measures could be designed such that they are specifically targeted at preserving the indicated forms of natural capital. Putting these measures into practice would also mean rolling back substantially the current destruction of all kinds of natural capital.

The next chapter does not question the validity of either paradigm as the last two chapters have done. It also does not enquire to what extent and at what cost certain forms of capital should be preserved as this chapter has done. The next chapter instead takes each paradigm for granted in the relevant sections they are dealt with and asks whether they can be measured in practice.

NOTES

1   Note that reversibility need not be technically or physically impossible. It is sufficient that reversing a destruction is theoretically possible, but only at prohibitively high costs.
2   Admittedly, this is not true for unique historical buildings which provide non-material value, but certainly for man-made capital used in production.
3   At least so far. There are now efforts to store the DNA of threatened species artificially. One day, genetic engineering might bring 'extinct' species back to life if their DNA has been stored beforehand.
4   There is no consensus on the use of these terms in the literature. Often risk and uncertainty are used interchangeably. What I call uncertainty is often referred to as 'hard uncertainty' or 'Knightean uncertainty' after Knight (1921).
5   Weisbrod (1964) first introduced the concept of option value.
6   Another term often used for uncertainty is ambiguity (Dobbs 1991).
7   The seminal work on quasi-option values is Arrow and Fisher (1974).
8   Note that the authors speak of option values but mean quasi-option values in the usage of the terms here.
9   Whether option and quasi-option values can be accurately measured is the object of a fierce debate. On this, see Turner (1995), Gren et al. (1994), Cummings and Harrison (1995).
10 For a comprehensive summary of the state of the art, see Cline (1991, 1992) and IPCC (1995, 1996a).
11 Another term for ignorance used by O'Riordan and Jordan (1995, p. 10) is indeterminacy.
12 The term biodiversity is used throughout the book in a rather broad sense encompassing genetic, species and ecosystem diversity.
13 For the case that biodiversity will always remain a highly valuable information input into agriculture and pharmaceuticals, see Swanson (1996).
14 Notable exceptions being the whales and some highly valued species such as elephants, rhinoceroses and tigers.
15 Note his confusion of open access with common property.
16 Note, however, that Eismont and Welsch also suggest that a large number of individuals exhibit uncertainty preference rather than aversion, implying that the optimal abatement is lower than usually calculated. I doubt whether their presumption about the uncertainty preference of individuals is correct. In any case, it should be kept in mind that *if* (in accordance with our general assumption) the current generation credibly commits itself to sustainability, *then* it is likely to become relatively more uncertainty averse.
17 The exponential reserve index is computed as $\ln(uz + 1)/u$, where u is the average rate of consumption growth and z is the static reserve index (see Meadows et al. 1972, p. 68). For 1970, I have computed the average annual growth rate over the time period 1965–70 and for 1994 the average annual growth rate over the time period 1985–94 in order to average out coincidental annual fluctuations in consumption growth in the years for which the exponential reserve index is computed.
18 For trends in other world regions and for trends in cereal output, see Dyson (1994).
19 Note that, for reasons of space, the following discussion is limited mostly to biodiversity protection and global warming.
20 To speak of a game-theoretic decision model is actually misleading since the term 'game theory' is reserved for strategic *interactions* between two or more players. In the 'games'

that follow, the first player is 'society' and the second 'player' is nature which is not strate-gically interacting, but setting different states of the world. Strictly speaking, nature is therefore no player in the game theoretic sense and we should talk of decision theory rather than game theory. I use the term 'game theory' nevertheless to relate to the relevant litera-ture.

21 Both concepts are equivalent. In my view, the way I set up the games allows for much better understanding.

22 For a survey of the issues discussed and of competing theories see, for example, Page and MacLean (1983), Machina (1987, 1989), Kelsey and Quiggin (1992).

23 It must be said, however, that Ciriacy-Wantrup did not subject SMS to the qualification that costs must not be 'too high', he always argued that the costs of preservation, if properly undertaken, would be relatively small (see Ciriacy-Wantrup (1952, 1971)).

24 Pearce (1997d, p. 12), however, concludes from a survey of existing studies that in many cases the value of preserving tropical forests, where the vast majority of biodiversity re-sides, 'may well be insufficient to justify the prevention of deforestation and the planting of new forests'.

25 Similarly, as Repetto et al. (1997, p. 50) observe, the claim that environmental protection measures severely restrict productivity growth often ignores the significant economic and environmental costs that are generated by pollution at all stages of the production cycle.

26 For a theoretical and empirical analysis of these dynamic advantages, see Jaffe and Stavins (1995).

27 The incentive is less for tradable permits than for taxes because the application of less pollutive technologies drives down the equilibrium price for the permits and therefore the gains from applying a cleaner technology. This adverse effect can be overcome if the issu-ing governmental agency is willing to buy back permits at the initial market price (Parry 1998).

28 For an overview of ecotaxation in OECD countries, see Barde (1996) and OECD (1997, pp. 52–4). For developing countries I am not aware of any figures, but it seems that there as well opportunities for changing the tax base of the economy exist.

29 Note that this reveals a strikingly different interpretation of 'no regret' than the one en-countered in Section 4.4.1, p. 115, on the precautionary principle. There, it meant the pre-vention of regret over unforeseen environmental disasters, here it means the prevention of regret over incurring economic costs for environmental protection measures that, *ex post*, might turn out to have been unnecessary for achieving sustainability.

30 The tax is named in honour of Pigou (1932) who first developed the idea of internalising environmental externalities via taxes to reach a social optimum.

31 Often these estimates only provide a lower bound estimate of marginal benefits in ignoring the potential for dynamically rising and self-reinforcing costs caused by global warming and in ignoring the so-called secondary benefits from the reduction in other pollutants like sulphur dioxide, nitrogen oxides and particulates that would come along as an inevitable side-effect from the reduction of fossil fuel use which is one of the major ways to cut down CO_2 emissions (on this, see Ekins 1995, 1996a, and Burtraw and Toman 1997).

32 The hypothesis does not discriminate between market-based and command-and-control instruments.

33 Boyd (1998) provides examples for the opposite case that firms are not overlooking oppor-tunities for increasing profits in pollution prevention.

5. Can Sustainability be Measured?

In this chapter, I shall discuss whether sustainability can be measured in practice. Section 5.1 is concerned with WS. Section 5.1.1 describes the Hartwick rule and Section 5.1.2 derives genuine saving (GS), the theoretically correct measure of WS, from a model of so-called green net national product (gNNP). A gNNP is constructed for a closed economy and the necessary amendments for an open economy context are discussed in Section 5.1.3. A number of problems with measuring WS in practice are put forward in Section 5.1.4. The examination then turns to two attempts to measure WS: the World Bank (1997a) study in Section 5.1.5 and the Index of Sustainable Economic Welfare (ISEW) in Section 5.1.6. It is argued that the dismal conclusions of World Bank (1997a) about the unsustainability of developing countries crucially depend on its method for resource accounting. It is shown using sensitivity analysis that these conclusions are largely reversed if another method for resource accounting is employed. As regards the ISEW, it is argued that it has severe flaws since it lacks a sound theoretical foundation and its results depend on a few arbitrary assumptions. In sensitivity analyses it is shown that the dismal results of ISEW studies about decreasing 'sustainable economic welfare' of almost all countries for which an ISEW has been computed are reversed if key variables are changed and more realistic assumptions taken.

Section 5.2 is concerned with SS. It explains how to arrive at a monetary measure of the so-called 'sustainability gap'. First, sustainability standards have to be determined (Section 5.2.1). Then the gap between the standards and the economy's actual performance have to be measured in physical terms (Section 5.2.2). Lastly, the sustainability gap can be given a monetary value in measuring the necessary costs for achieving the standards (Section 5.2.3). The final Section 5.2.4 discusses a number of problems with a monetary valuation of the 'sustainability gap'. As the methodology for measuring SS is still in development, no comprehensive empirical study exists that could be assessed.

Section 5.3 concludes and states to what extent and subject to which qualifications the actual measures of SD dealt with in earlier sections can be regarded as reliable indicators and are useful in guiding policy choices. It argues that practical measures of SD have to be treated with great caution because of the many problems that were listed in Sections 5.1.4 and 5.2.4.

5.1 WEAK SUSTAINABILITY: MEASURING GENUINE SAVING (GS)

5.1.1 The Hartwick rule

What should a society committed to WS do? One answer to this question is the so-called Hartwick rule. Hartwick showed that

- *if* there is no disembodied technical progress and
- *if* there are no unanticipated future shocks,

then keeping GS *along the optimal path* above or equal to zero is a necessary, but not sufficient condition for ensuring WS.[1] The original analysis assumed a constant population. With a growing population *per capita* GS must be above or equal to zero.

Hartwick (1977) proved the rule for one consumption good and one non-renewable resource for the Cobb–Douglas production function, Hartwick (1978a) proved the rule for the more general CES production function and Hartwick (1978b) extended the analysis to renewable resources. Dixit, Hammond and Hoel (1980) proved the rule in a more general context, allowing for many types of consumption goods, heterogeneous capital goods and an endogenous labour supply. Becker (1982) was the first to prove the rule with environmental services as an explicit component of the utility function. Withagen (1996) proved the rule in a general optimal control context that is also applied here further below. All these papers implicitly assumed a closed economy without any trade in resources and commodities. Asheim (1986, 1994b), Hartwick (1994) and Sefton and Weale (1996) modified the rule for open economies.

Why is it that following the Hartwick rule is only a necessary, not a sufficient condition for ensuring sustainability? The answer is that following the rule must be feasible in the first instance. Because as time goes to infinity non-renewable resources will become exhausted, it must be feasible either to substitute without limit renewable resources or man-made capital for non-renewable resources, or to augment without limit the non-renewable resource via technical progress. Additionally, it must be true that directly utility-relevant environmental assets are improving over time. Alternatively, it must be possible to compensate for a deterioration in these directly utility-relevant environmental assets by an increase in consumption; and it must be true that any conceivable deterioration in environmental assets is reasonably far away from any threshold whose transgressing would cause potential catastrophic damage. That is, obeying the Hartwick rule is only sufficient for ensuring WS if the assumptions of WS with regard to the substitutability of natural capital in both production and utility functions are valid, where the latter can be replaced with the optimistic beliefs about the environmental consequences of economic growth.

In order to show what keeping GS above or equal to zero means when other forms of capital than man-made capital are included, I now derive a gNNP from a model of optimal growth. First, a closed economy is assumed, in Section 5.1.3 the analysis is extended to the context of an open economy.

5.1.2   GS in a Closed Economy: A Model of Optimal Growth

To see how a gNNP is properly constructed and a GS measure properly derived, let us look at the following optimal growth model which is an extended and modified version of the model in Hartwick (1990, 1993). Note that there is neither disembodied technical progress nor population growth in this model. Also note that there are no unanticipated future shocks.[2] It is as if all information about the future was available in the present.[3] It is assumed that the production technology exhibits constant returns to scale and that perfect competition prevails.

In addition to the man-made capital of traditional growth models we also include natural capital and human capital. We subdivide natural capital into the stock of non-renewable resources, the renewable resource stock and the stock of pollution, which, of course, is a capital 'bad' rather than a capital good. We are particularly interested in the dynamic changes of the capital stocks. We assume the following dynamics (let a dot above a variable represent the derivative of the variable with respect to time):

- $\dot{S}$, the change in the stock of non-renewable resources, is equal to resource discoveries D minus resource depletion R: $\dot{S} = D - R$.
- $\dot{X}$, the change in the stock of accumulated discoveries of non-renewable resources, is equal to current discoveries D: $\dot{X} = D$.
- $\dot{Z}$, the change in the stock of renewable resources, is equal to its natural growth $a(Z)$ plus 'human-induced' growth G minus resource harvest E: $\dot{Z} = a(Z) + G - E$.
- $\dot{P}$, the change in the stock of pollution, is equal to $\gamma F(.)$, pollution caused by production, minus natural restoration $b(P)$ minus abatement A: $\dot{P} = \gamma F(.) - b(P) - A$.

Note that γ is a 'conversion factor' converting production into pollution units.[4]

- $\dot{M}$, the change in the stock of human capital, is equal to investment into human capital N: $\dot{M} = N$. Note that for simplicity human capital is treated as if there was no depreciation of its stock over time; that is, knowledge is neither forgotten nor does it become obsolete.[5]
- Finally, $\dot{K}$, the change in the stock of man-made capital, is defined as a residual and is equal to total output $F(.)$ minus consumption C and other expenditures which consist of expenditures $f(.)$ for mining non-renewable resources, expenditures $g(.)$ for exploring and discovering non-renewable resources, expenditures $h(.)$ for harvesting renewable resources, pollution-abatement expenditures $i(.)$ and finally investment expenditures $j(.)$ into human capital:

$$\dot{K} = F(K, L, R, E, P, M) - C - f(R, S) - g(D, X) - h(E, Z) - i(A) - j(N).$$

Note that $\dot{K}$ is *net* investment into man-made capital. That is, $\dot{K}$ is defined such that depreciation of man-made capital is already netted out.

The arguments of the production function $F(.)$, the growth functions and the expenditure functions together with the signs of their partial derivatives are motivated as follows (let subscripts denote derivatives):

- $F(K,L,R,E,P,M)$: production $F(.)$ depends on the input of man-made capital K, labour L which for simplicity is assumed to be exogenously given as a constant,[6] renewable resources R, non-renewable resources E, but also on P, the *stock* of pollution, for example, the stock of CO_2 or SO_x in the atmosphere. Note that usually it is not the flow of pollution that matters for production, but the accumulated stock. Additionally, production depends on the human capital *stock*. All partial derivatives are positive except for F_P which is negative.
- $f(R,S)$: it is reasonable to assume that the cost of non-renewable resource extraction $f(.)$ increases with the amount of resources extracted ($f_R > 0$) and decreases with the (remaining) stock of non-renewable resources ($f_S < 0$), that is, the smaller is the stock the more expensive is resource extraction.
- $g(D,X)$: it is reasonable to assume that the cost of resource exploration $g(.)$ increases with the amount of resources explored ($g_D > 0$). It also increases with the accumulated stock of discoveries ($g_X > 0$) because the easy to find resource deposits are discovered first, so that it becomes more difficult and hence more expensive to find later deposits.
- $h(E,Z)$: analogous to $f(.)$, only this time for renewable resources.
- $a(Z)$: it is common to assume that renewable resources follow a logistic growth path, in which the growth rate rises with the resource stock initially

($a_Z > 0$ for $Z < Z'$), but falls eventually after the stock has reached a certain size Z' ($a_Z < 0$ for $Z > Z'$).

- $b(P)$: natural restoration is negatively affected by a rising stock of pollution, that is, $b_P < 0$.
- $i(A)$: the cost of abatement $i(A)$ rises with the amount of abatement, hence $i_A > 0$.
- $j(N)$: the cost of building up human capital $j(N)$ rises with the amount of investment into human capital, hence $j_N > 0$.

To complete the model we introduce the very simple utility function for the 'representative consumer' from equation (2.2) in Section 2.1, p. 8. Assume that the problem of the social planner is to maximise

$$\int_0^\infty U(C,Z,P) \cdot e^{-\rho t} dt , \qquad (5.1)$$

that is the discounted utility integrated over infinite time. Remember that C is consumption, Z the stock of renewable resources, and P the stock of pollution. ρ is society's pure rate of time preference which is set exogenously to the model and which indicates by how much society discounts utility in the future for the pure reason of being later in time. Note that the pure rate of time preference could be set to zero, as indeed many authors demand for reasons of inter-generational fairness: being later in time should be no reason for counting less (for example, Ramsey 1928; Pigou 1932; Rawls 1972; Broome 1992; Cline 1992; Azar and Sterner 1996). Note as well, however, that within our framework setting the pure rate of time preference equal to zero is not a necessary condition for sustainability. Intuitively, this is the case because sustainability, that is, maintaining the capacity to provide non-declining utility, is secured via a side constraint to the maximisation exercise: GS has to be non-negative. Formally, for any pure rate of time preference there exists an optimal path along which GS as defined later in the text will be equal to or bigger than zero. See further below.

Hartwick (1990) included the *flow* of resource harvest and the pollution *flow* into the utility function. In contrast, I include the renewable resource *stock* and the *stock* of pollution into the utility function. If consumers have preferences for environmental quality, it is more reasonable to assume that they care about the whole stock of directly utility-relevant renewable resources and pollution and not just incremental changes to the stock.

The so-called current-value Hamiltonian for this maximisation problem is then given by

$$H = U(C,Z,P) + \lambda[F(.) - C - f(R,S) - g(D,X) - h(E,Z) - i(A) - j(N)]$$

$$+ \mu[D - R] + \omega[D] + \varphi[a(Z) + G - E] + \psi[\gamma F(.) - b(P) - A] + \xi[N] \quad (5.2)$$

where all the variables are defined as above and are evaluated at time t ($0 \le t \le \infty$) and where all time indices have been suppressed for ease of exposition. The λ, μ, ω, ϕ, ψ, ξ are utility-denominated co-state variables or dynamic Lagrange multipliers (shadow prices) for the state variables: $\lambda > 0$ is the shadow value of man-made capital K, that is the marginal value in utility terms of expanding K by one unit, $\mu > 0$ is the shadow value of the stock of non-renewable resources S, $\omega < 0$ is the shadow cost of the stock of resource discoveries X which is negative because X negatively impacts upon the costs of resource exploration, $\phi > 0$ is the shadow value of the stock of renewable resources Z, $\psi < 0$ is the shadow cost of the stock of pollution P and $\xi > 0$ is the shadow value of the stock of human capital M. K, S, X, Z, P and M are the state variables of the model.

The terms in square brackets represent the changes in capital stocks as explained above and represent the constraints of the maximisation problem. For simplicity, assume all functions to be 'well behaved' and continuously twice differentiable, so that the necessary first-order conditions for maximisation are also sufficient. Further assume that an optimal solution exists (on existence conditions, see Toman 1985). The control variables of the model are C, R, D, E, A and N. The dynamics of the model are given by the canonical equations for optimisation:[7]

i. First-order conditions for maximisation (maximum principle):

$$\frac{\partial H}{\partial C} = 0 \quad \Rightarrow \quad U_C = \lambda \quad\quad\quad (5.i.1)$$

$$\frac{\partial H}{\partial R} = 0 \quad \Rightarrow \quad \lambda[F_R - f_R] + \psi\gamma F_R = \mu \quad\quad\quad (5.i.2)$$

$$\frac{\partial H}{\partial D} = 0 \quad \Rightarrow \quad \lambda g_D - \omega = \mu \quad\quad\quad (5.i.3)$$

$$\frac{\partial H}{\partial E} = 0 \quad \Rightarrow \quad \lambda[F_E - h_E] + \psi\gamma F_E = \varphi \quad\quad\quad (5.i.4)$$

$$\frac{\partial H}{\partial A} = 0 \quad \Rightarrow \quad -\lambda i_A = \psi \quad\quad\quad (5.i.5)$$

$$\frac{\partial H}{\partial N} = 0 \quad \Rightarrow \quad \lambda j_N = \xi \quad\quad\quad (5.i.6)$$

ii. Dynamic first-order conditions

$$\dot\lambda = \rho\lambda - \frac{\partial H}{\partial K} \quad \Rightarrow \quad \dot\lambda = \rho\lambda - \lambda F_K - \psi\gamma F_K \tag{5.ii.1}$$

$$\dot\mu = \rho\mu - \frac{\partial H}{\partial S} \quad \Rightarrow \quad \dot\mu = \rho\mu + \lambda f_S \tag{5.ii.2}$$

$$\dot\omega = \rho\omega - \frac{\partial H}{\partial X} \quad \Rightarrow \quad \dot\omega = \rho\omega + \lambda g_X \tag{5.ii.3}$$

$$\dot\varphi = \rho\varphi - \frac{\partial H}{\partial Z} \quad \Rightarrow \quad \dot\varphi = \rho\varphi + \lambda h_Z - \varphi a_Z - U_Z \tag{5.ii.4}$$

$$\dot\psi = \rho\psi - \frac{\partial H}{\partial P} \quad \Rightarrow \quad \dot\psi = \rho\psi - \lambda F_P - \varphi(\gamma F_P - b_P) - U_P \tag{5.ii.5}$$

$$\dot\xi = \rho\xi - \frac{\partial H}{\partial M} \quad \Rightarrow \quad \dot\xi = \rho\xi - \lambda F_M - \psi\gamma F_M \tag{5.ii.6}$$

iii. Equations of motion[8]

$$\frac{\partial H}{\partial\lambda} = \dot K \quad \Rightarrow \quad \dot K = F(.) - C - f(R,S) - g(D,X) - h(E,Z) - i(A) - j(N) \tag{5.iii.1}$$

$$\frac{\partial H}{\partial\mu} = \dot S \quad \Rightarrow \quad \dot S = D - R \tag{5.iii.2}$$

$$\frac{\partial H}{\partial\omega} = \dot X \quad \Rightarrow \quad \dot X = D \tag{5.iii.3}$$

$$\frac{\partial H}{\partial\varphi} = \dot Z \quad \Rightarrow \quad \dot Z = a(Z) + G - E \tag{5.iii.4}$$

$$\frac{\partial H}{\partial\psi} = \dot P \quad \Rightarrow \quad \dot P = \gamma F(.) - b(P) - A \tag{5.iii.5}$$

$$\frac{\partial H}{\partial\xi} = \dot M \quad \Rightarrow \quad \dot M = N \tag{5.iii.6}$$

Equations (5.i.1) to (5.i.6) are of primary interest to us. Plugging (5.i.1) into (5.i.2)–(5.i.5), plugging (5.i.5) into (5.i.2) and (5.i.4), plugging (5.i.2) into (5.i.3) and rearranging terms we arrive at the current value Hamiltonian H^* along an optimal path

$$H^* = U + \lambda\big(F(.) - C - f(.) - g(.) - h(.) - i(.) - j(.)\big)$$

$$-\lambda(F_R - f_R - i_A\cdot\gamma F_R)\cdot R + \lambda g_D D$$

$$+\lambda(F_E - h_E - i_A\cdot\gamma F_E)(a(Z) + G - E)$$

$$-\lambda\, i_A(\gamma F(.) - b(P) - A) + \lambda\, j_N\, N \tag{5.3}$$

Now, the Hamiltonian is measured in utils, so to convert into real terms we have to divide the equation by $\lambda = U_C$. Let us assume that the utility function $U(C,Z,P)$ can be linearly approximated by

$$U(C, Z, P) = U_C \cdot C + U_Z \cdot Z + U_P \cdot P \tag{5.4}$$

The linearisation is for convenience only and for ease of exposition. Pemberton and Ulph (1998) have shown that the sustainability interpretation that will be given to gNNP and GS further below does not depend on the linearisation. Now plug (5.iii.1), (5.iii.4), (5.iii.5) and (5.4) into (5.3). Then we finally arrive at the gNNP function H^*/U^*_C:

$$gNNP = \frac{H^*}{U^*_C} = C^* + \frac{U^*_Z}{U^*_C} \cdot Z^* + \frac{U^*_P}{U^*_C} \cdot P^* + \tag{5.5}$$

$$\underbrace{+\dot{K}^* - \left[F^*_R - f^*_R - i_A^*\gamma F^*_R\right]\cdot R^* + g^*_D \cdot D^* + \left[F^*_E - h^*_E - i_A^*\gamma F^*_E\right]\cdot \dot{Z}^* - i_A^* \cdot \dot{P}^* + j^*_N \cdot \dot{M}^*}_{Genuine\,Saving}$$

where the stars indicate that we are dealing with optimal values. Appendix 3 shows that optimal resource pricing according to Hotelling's rule is implied by the model since we are evaluating the current-value Hamiltonian along an optimal path. The same holds true for the so-called Ramsey rule — see Appendix 3, p. 218.

Equation (5.5) says that the traditional NNP measure, in so far as it does not reflect the corrections yet or does so only imperfectly, has to be amended by the following terms:

$$\frac{U_Z}{U_C} \cdot Z \quad (>0)$$

U_Z/U_C is the willingness of consumers to pay (WTP) for a marginal increase in the stock of renewable resources. It is equal to the marginal utility of the stock of renewable resources. Hence the whole term values the total stock of renewable resources at consumers' marginal WTP. The term has to be added to consumption because consumers value the environmental amenity they can derive from the stock of renewable resources.

$$\frac{U_P}{U_C} \cdot P \quad (<0)$$

U_P/U_C is the willingness of consumers to pay for a marginal decrease in the stock of pollution. It is equal to the marginal disutility of the pollution stock. Hence the whole term values the total pollution stock at consumers' marginal disutility of pollution. The term has to be added to consumption because consumers suffer a loss in utility by the existence of the pollution stock. The term is negative since U_P is negative.

Note that the last two terms are a consequence of the 'greening' of the national accounts and *not* of sustainability as such, because both terms would have to be included in a green GNP (that is, without netting out capital changes) as well. These terms are relevant only if one is looking as well for an indicator of total current welfare as the Index of Sustainable Economic Welfare (ISEW) does — see Section 5.1.6, p. 177. Proponents of measuring WS are usually only interested in the GS part of gNNP which reflects the total capacity to provide future utility and which consists of the following items:

$$\dot{K} \quad (>0 \text{ or } <0)$$

This term represents net investment in man-made capital, that is gross investment minus depreciation of man-made capital. Note that it is already included in traditional NNP.

$$[F_R - f_R - i_A \gamma F_R] \cdot R \quad (>0)$$

This term represents the depletion value of non-renewable resources which has to be *subtracted* from NNP. Resource depletion R is valued at the terms in brackets. These are the price for the resource F_R minus its marginal extraction cost f_R which together form the so-called Hotelling rent we encountered already in Section 3.2.2, p. 51.[9] $i_A \gamma F_R$ is the marginal pollution effect of extracting one unit of the non-renewable resource valued at marginal abatement costs — for example, emission of CO_2 by using non-renewable energy. Since the gNNP is derived along an optimal trajectory of the current-value Hamiltonian, marginal abatement costs are equal to marginal social costs which in turn are equal to an optimal 'Pigouvian' tax (Hamilton 1996, p. 19).[10] What has to be subtracted, therefore, are what economists call total Hotelling rents (price minus marginal cost times the depleted quantity), but the revenues from an optimal Pigouvian tax have to be added to NNP! Note that the latter is in principle in accordance with standard national accounting procedures since indirect taxes are counted as value added there (Hamilton 1994, p. 163).[11]

The last term in the brackets seems to be extremely counter-intuitive. The formula demands that *for a given amount of depletion* the deduction for non-renewable resource depletion is lower if, in addition, the resource causes pollution, that is, the exact opposite of what one might have expected! The reason is that the existence of pollution makes the resource stock in the ground less valuable in comparison to a situation without resource use causing pollution. Hence the inter-temporal costs of using the resource now instead of preserving it for coming generations are less than without pollution. Note, however, that the total deduction term for the depletion of non-renewable resources need *not* be smaller because the amount of depletion will in general not be the same in an economy where resources cause pollution as in an economy without resource use causing pollution. If one changes the structure of the model, its optimal solution has to be calculated from the start resulting in a completely different time path of the endogenous variables.

Note that heterogeneous resource deposits of a resource (for example, differing quality deposits of oil with differing extraction costs) should be valued at individual deposit-type market prices and marginal extraction costs. For that reason, Hamilton (1994, p. 160) replaces $F_R - f_R$ (ignoring the pollution effect for a moment) with $\Sigma(F_{Ri} - f_{Ri})R_i$, that is, he values different deposit types separately and sums them up. Hamilton misses the point, however. Strictly speaking, the F_R and f_R terms are row vectors and the R term is a column vector, because there is more than one non-renewable resource in actual economies. Hence different deposit types can be taken care of by expanding the vectors. No change in notation is therefore needed and we can stick to our terminology.

Reich (1994) objects to taking depletion of existing resource stocks into account in arguing that human beings have never produced them and their stocks have never entered the national accounting system as an asset. Stahmer (1995, p. 103) argues in response that existing stocks should be regarded as a costless gift of nature. Hartwick and Hageman (1993, p. 229) argue that the *service flows* of resource stocks do enter the GNP, for example in the form of oil used in the economy. Hartwick and Hageman's argument misses the point, however. The goal of GS is to measure whether the capacity to provide future welfare is maintained or not. Where this capacity comes from, simply does not matter. As Repetto et al. (1989, p. 2) rightly argue, 'the value of an asset is not its investment cost, but the present-value of its income potential' in the future.

$g_D \cdot D$ (>0)

This term represents the value of discoveries of non-renewable resources which has to be added. New discoveries are valued at marginal discovery costs. This term is partly already included in standard national accounting where exploration expenditures are treated as investment (World Bank 1997a, p. 28).

$$\left[F_E - h_E - i_A \gamma F_E\right] \cdot \dot{Z} \left\{ \begin{matrix} > \\ < \end{matrix} \right\} 0 \quad \text{as} \quad \dot{Z} \left\{ \begin{matrix} > \\ < \end{matrix} \right\} 0$$

This term values the net change in the stock of renewable resources. Note that it is negative for a net decrease in the stock and positive vice versa. $i_A \gamma F_E$ is the marginal pollution effect of harvesting one unit of the renewable resource valued at marginal abatement costs — for example, emission of greenhouse gases by clearing rainforests. As with non-renewable resources, the value is calculated as the price for the resource minus its marginal harvesting cost *plus* an optimal Pigouvian tax times the amount of net stock change. Equally, if there is heterogeneity in quality of a renewable resource, individual market prices and marginal extraction costs should enter the correction term.

$$i_A \cdot \dot{P} \left\{ \begin{matrix} > \\ < \end{matrix} \right\} 0 \quad \text{as} \quad \dot{P} \left\{ \begin{matrix} > \\ < \end{matrix} \right\} 0$$

This term values the net change in the stock of pollution. The value is calculated as marginal abatement cost i_A times the amount of net change in the stock of pollution P. Note that marginal abatement costs are equal to marginal social costs which are in turn equal to an optimal Pigouvian tax. Again, the equality holds because gNNP is measured along an optimal path (Hamilton 1996, p. 19). The correction term is necessary because cumulative pollution *flows*, that is, a rising pollution *stock*, either decrease the assimilative capacity of the environment for future generations or have caused already environmental damage to future generations. The reverse holds true for a decreasing pollution stock. Parts of abatement expenditures are already netted out of national income as intermediate consumption.

Note as well that defensive expenditures for estimating environmental damage as suggested by, for example, Leipert (1989a), or maintenance costs as suggested by, for example, Bartelmus and van Tongeren (1993), or the necessary expenditures for reaching a 'sustainable' use of the environment as suggested by Hueting (1991) and Hueting and Bosch (1990) should *not* be included in GS. Things are different, however, with respect to measuring SS which is based on a different methodology — see Section 5.2, p. 191.

$$j_N \cdot \dot{M} \quad (>0)$$

This term values the increase in the human capital stock at its marginal investment cost. Educational expenditures on investment goods are already included in standard national accounting. World Bank (1997a) proposes to consider current educational expenditures, which make up more than 90 per cent of all educational expenditures (ibid., p. 34), as investment in human capital as well and not as consumption.

The underlying reason for all these corrections is that a degradation in one of the capital stocks reduces the capacity to provide future utility and hence gNNP must decrease to account for what economists call total 'user costs'. What is used up today is lost to the economy in the future. Vice versa, gNNP must increase if the capacity to provide future utility increases through a rise in one of the capital stocks. Note that, in principle, proponents of SS could espouse this form of measuring sustainability as well. They would simply suggest that because natural capital is nonsubstitutable its marginal productivity will be infinite as will be any depreciation allowance for natural capital. Hence development that draws down natural capital would be unsustainable.[12]

Pemberton and Ulph (1998, p. 4) show that gNNP can be interpreted as 'the maximum amount an economy can consume and keep welfare constant'. It could therefore be regarded as sustainable income or as Hicksian income, for it fulfils Hicks's (1946, p. 172) classical definition of income: 'We ought to define a man's income as the maximum value which he can consume during a week, and still expect to be as well off at the end of the week as he was at the beginning'. Note that for the model of gNNP employed here this interpretation is only correct if consumption is interpreted widely and includes the utility derived from the stock of renewable resources, $U_Z/U_C Z$, and the disutility derived from the stock of pollution, $U_Z/U_C P$.

How do our model results translate into a measure of WS now? Defining genuine saving *GS* as:

$$GS \equiv \dot{K} - \left[F_R - f_R - i_A \gamma F_R\right] \cdot R + g_D D + \left[F_E - h_E - i_A \gamma F_E\right] \cdot \dot{Z} - i_A \dot{P} + j_N \dot{M}$$

(5.6)

Then by Hartwick's rule (for a proof, see Appendix 4, p. 222):

$$GS \begin{Bmatrix} > \\ = \\ < \end{Bmatrix} 0 \Rightarrow \dot{U} \begin{Bmatrix} > \\ = \\ < \end{Bmatrix} 0$$

That is, *GS* is the proper measure of WS: WS is ensured as long as *GS* is bigger than or equal to zero for ever which means that utility does not decline for ever. If *GS* is negative, then the economy is on a weakly unsustainable path and something needs to be done to bring it back on a sustainable path if the objective is to achieve WS.

What could the government do to ensure WS if it is not quasi-automatically ensured, that is, if the economy happens to be on its 'optimal' path but violating the sustainability constraint? In our simple model there is no explicit public sector, but looking at the definition of GS can still answer the question: the government could increase net investment into man-made capital via lowering taxation of man-made capital or reducing government expenditures, for example; it could reduce resource extraction via taxing resource consumption; it could foster resource exploration via subsidising exploration activities; it could lower the stock of pollution via increasing pollution abatement; or it could step up investment in human capital. Note that doing any of these would imply an external shock to the economy so that the optimal path after the intervention would be different from the one before this external policy shock. After the policy shock the economy is again on an 'optimal' path given all parameters including the policy shock so that, this time, it is also on a sustainable path.

Devarajan and Weiner (1995, p. 4) have argued against deriving measures of sustainability from dynamic optimisation models. They have reasoned as follows:

> If the resource is being optimally managed, why worry? Since there is no way we can alter behavior that will lead to a higher welfare, there is little point in trying to adjust national accounts ... The assumption of optimal resource management is simply inconsistent with the phenomenon of environmental deterioration that provided the very motivation for adjustment.

This is confusing, however. The sustainability criterion imposes an *additional* constraint on the maximisation exercise. Given this constraint the economy will only be on its optimal path after the policy intervention (if that appears to be necessary to fulfil the sustainability requirement), not before. The government can alter behaviour which will lead to a higher welfare *given* the further constraint to ensure WS!

5.1.3   GS in an Open Economy

Note that the model implicitly assumes a closed economy: there is no trade in resources and commodities, there is no transboundary or global pollution. Asheim (1986, 1994b), Hartwick (1994) and Sefton and Weale (1996) modified the Hartwick rule for open economies trading with each other. Because the Hotelling rule must hold in the optimisation model, resource rent is assumed to rise at the interest rate.[13] With marginal extraction costs not falling at a rate higher than the interest rate, future resource prices will be higher than current ones, thus providing the resource exporter with improving terms of trade. Due to that, the exporter of natural resources can make a smaller correction to NNP in comparison to the closed economy and still ensure sustainability. The resource importer, on the other hand, faces a future deterioration in its terms of trade, so it must make a higher correction from NNP than would be the case in a closed economy. That is, it is the resource importer who must make an extra adjustment for the growing scarcity of the resource. Note that this analysis does not follow from any considerations of fairness, but solely from considerations of self-interest in the sense that each country strives to keep the value of its own capital stock at least constant.

If, for some reason, for example, unanticipated resource discoveries, future resource prices are declining, the prescriptions would be reversed, of course, and it would be up to the resource exporter to make a higher and up to the resource importer to make a lower correction from NNP than would be the case in a closed economy. Vincent, Panayotou and Hartwick (1997, p. 282) suspect that overly optimistic projections of future resource prices have been one reason for the poor economic performance of resource-rich in relation to resource-poor countries (for evidence on this performance, see Sachs and Warner 1995). Given a 'century-old decline in most resource prices', Vincent, Panayotou and Hartwick (1997, p. 282) suggest that 'underinvestment, not overinvestment, is the principal risk facing resource exporters'. That terms-of-trade effects must be taken into account implies that in an open economy context capital gains, that is changes in the value of capital due to changing prices, must not be excluded from the construction of gNNP as would be appropriate in a closed economy (Asheim 1994b, 1996).

Transboundary and global pollution present more difficult problems. According to the 'polluter-pays principle' it would be up to the country causing transboundary pollution to include the corresponding correction terms in its gNNP and GS. Presumably it was this Hamilton and Atkinson (1996, p. 678) had in mind when they reasoned that 'some portion of a given country's saving should, at least notionally, be set aside in order to compensate the recipients of the pollution emitted and transferred across international boundaries'.

On the other hand, if we realistically assume that sovereign nation-states are unwilling to compensate other nation-states, it might be more reasonable to stick to our presumption that each country should strive to keep the value of its own capital stock at least constant, independent of whether capital deterioration is caused within its own borders or beyond. According to this rule it would be up to the country receiving pollution to include the corresponding correction terms in its accounts or else to try to compensate the emitting country for pollution reductions.[14] One might regard this allocation rule as unfair, but it is not unusual that countries refuse to pay according to the 'polluter-pays principle' if they cause transboundary pollution. The big disadvantage of this allocation rule is that it provides incentives for countries to externalise their pollution on to other countries in order to increase their GS which is not the proper intention of sustainability.

With global pollution it is rather difficult to say who is the victim, and to what extent, and who is not. In dealing with problems like global warming it might be reasonable to demand that every country is accountable for its own current greenhouse-relevant emissions. This conclusion is not compelling, however, especially not if there is a history of emission accumulation. To give an example: developing countries are likely to resist being accountable for their full current emissions when it is the relatively much higher past emissions of the now developed countries that are mainly responsible for the *current stock* of greenhouse-relevant emissions (see, for example, Agarwal and Narain 1991). Along these lines, Neumayer (1999e) argues in defence of historical accountability for greenhouse gas emissions. Such a principle, however, is likely to be resisted by developed countries. Hence there is no straightforward allocation rule in this case.

The problem is that there has to be some international agreement on allocation rules. If not, double counting as well as no counting at all is likely to occur. It is rather questionable whether a world that is divided into sovereign nation-states will be able to agree on an unambiguous allocation rule. Note that if WS is taken seriously this is not a question of mere accounting. It really is about who is responsible for accumulating other forms of capital for environmental deterioration.

So far I have presented the *theory* of measuring WS. Now we turn to practical problems. After that, I shall assess practical attempts to provide a measure of WS in examining in detail the World Bank (1997a) study and the Index of Sustainable Economic Welfare (ISEW).

5.1.4 Practical Problems with Measuring GS

Providing a measure of GS in practice has to confront the following problems:

1. Asheim (1994a) and Pezzey and Withagen (1995) showed that starting to follow the Hartwick rule at some time does not imply WS. It remains true that given the assumptions under which the rule holds, following the Hartwick rule from the beginning up to infinity ensures WS, but not starting to

follow it at some date. Formally, the Hartwick rule requires that GS is kept above or equal to zero along the optimal path *at all instants of time*. If the economy has had negative GS in the past, then securing non-negative GS now no longer implies WS. The proof for this is quite tedious and will not be reproduced here, but the intuition of it is quite easy to understand: if society is not credibly committed to WS, then the economy is not managed in a sustainable manner and current relative prices are distorted. For example, prices for natural capital can well be too low. Hence, reinvesting the net receipts into other forms of capital does not ensure WS. If GS is *persistently* negative, it can be concluded that the economy is not on a sustainable path, but with zero savings or even with positive savings nothing definite can be said. So, strictly speaking, GS can only be a negative indicator for WS measuring unsustainability, not a positive indicator measuring whether sustainability is actually ensured. This restricts the policy usefulness of GS somewhat.

2. The theoretically correct gNNP is equal to the optimal solution of a dynamic optimisation model. That is, all value terms and all quantities have to be optimal since the economy is assumed to develop *along the optimal path*. It is a standard result in economics that optimality can be achieved as a perfect inter-temporal competitive equilibrium, that is, as an equilibrium of a decentralised economy with a complete set of property rights (that is, no externalities[15]) with competitive households and firms and a full set of forward markets where perfectly rational agents have perfect information and households take full account of the welfare of their actual or prospective descendants (Barro and Sala-i-Martin 1995, pp. 60–71). In reality none of these conditions hold. In reality, there is a state which raises income by distortionary taxes, externalities abound and are not internalised via an optimal Pigouvian tax, competition is severely restrained, there is nothing resembling a full set of forward markets, agents are boundedly rational with imperfect information and whether households take full account of the welfare of their descendants is open to debate. The world we live in is full of market failures — especially in an inter-temporal context encompassing future generations. As Aaheim and Nyborg (1995, p. 59) observe, the desire to green the national accounting system was driven by the presumption that natural resource use and environmental degradation are non-optimal. Simply assuming that there are no inefficiencies is therefore utterly unrealistic and is equivalent to solving the problem by assuming it away. The same holds true for assuming that existing distortions move in opposite directions and cancel each other out on average, which would wrongly suggest that existing prices and quantities can still be used as good approximations of the optimal values. Furthermore, efficient shadow

prices have to be established via valuation or estimation studies for many environmental services. This is because they do not carry prices yet either because of missing property rights or because the services are not priced in markets.

Contrary to what one might think, it does not even help trying to repair selected inefficiencies in isolation, for example by introducing more competition for firms. The theory of second best tells us that if there is more than one distortion in the economy, then correcting any subset of distortions in isolation does not mean that the resulting prices and quantities are necessarily any closer to the optimal values than before the exercise (Lipsey and Lancaster 1956). The reason is that any still existing distortion will work its way through the economy via general equilibrium effects. Hence what appeared to be an optimal correction of a distortion examined in isolation, might no longer be optimal taking into account the totality of other distortions. It follows that one has to treat GS as a measure of WS with caution. It is only a valid and reliable measure if one believes that the actual economy develops sufficiently close to its optimal path. If it does not, then the existing institutions and the prices and quantitites they generate may be significantly different from the optimal ones.

3. Even if the economy does not develop along its optimal path, Hamilton, Atkinson and Pearce (1997, p. 3) assert that *actual* values of GS point in the right direction at least. They argue that in an over-polluted state relative to the optimum, both the quantity of pollution and its shadow cost measured by marginal social pollution costs are higher than in the optimum. Hence GS will be lower in an over-polluted state than in the optimum. Hence moving from an over-polluted state towards the optimum provides the 'right' signal of increasing GS. The same holds true vice versa for an under-polluted state relative to the optimum (see also Hamilton and Atkinson (1996), where the argument is elaborated upon). In a partial equilibrium analysis the argument of Hamilton, Atkinson and Pearce (1997) is correct. But in dealing with questions of sustainability we are dealing with multiple markets and general equilibria to which the partial analysis results do not apply straightforwardly. There is hence no guarantee that moving to the (presumably unknown) optimum will provide the 'right' signals.

Even if we could safely ignore general equilibrium effects, *actual* values of GS are not guaranteed to point in the right direction for the accounting of resource depletion and resource harvest. In a state of overdepletion and over-harvest relative to the optimum the quantities are higher but the resource prices are likely to be lower than in the optimum. Because of quantities and prices deviating in the opposite direction from their optimal levels, it is unclear whether GS will be lower or higher in a state of over-depletion and over-harvest relative to the optimum. Hence increased GS cannot be trusted to provide the right signal of moving towards the optimal state. Analogous reasoning applies if we start from a state of under-depletion and under-harvest.[16]

4. Problems arise if one abandons the unrealistic assumption that there are no future unanticipated shocks. Future unanticipated shocks could be unexpected technical breakthroughs, unexpected resource discoveries, unexpected environmental destruction (as has been the case with global warming and the ozone layer depletion) and the like. If future shocks are not anticipated, as is arguably often the case, then the pre-shock prices are not representative for the post-shock prices and they do not adequately reflect economic scarcities. A regime change occurs and all prices and quantities have to be estimated again (Hartwick 1993, p. 195).

With unanticipated future shocks the interpretation of gNNP as sustainable income breaks down. The reason is quite simply that unanticipated future shocks by definition cannot be reflected in current prices and quantities. Note that unanticipated future shocks are different from risks. They are cases of uncertainty and ignorance as defined in Section 4.2, p. 98. That is, their probability distribution and contingent payoffs are not known in the present. Hung (1993) has shown that for cases of mere risk, NNP has to be augmented with the expected value of a future cost or benefit. Option and existence values (differentiated for each type of risk) have to be included and all prices are to be 'evaluated in terms of contingent (rationally anticipated) values' (ibid., p. 388).

This in itself is difficult enough. However, in most cases the probability distribution is presumably unknown, so that future costs or benefits are more or less unanticipated, which means, again, that a regime change occurs, and the computation procedure has to restart again.

As a special case of Hung's (1993) result, Vincent, Panayotou and Hartwick (1997) have shown how the investment rule for resource trading countries has to be augmented by the present-value of anticipated future terms-of-trade shifts, that is, the capital gain or loss on the resource stock due to the anticipation of changing future resource prices (see Section 5.1.3, p. 152, on GS in an open economy). However, it is not realistic to assume that changing future resource prices can be fully anticipated. One sufficient condition Vincent, Panayotou and Hartwick (1997, p. 277) cite — 'a complete set of futures markets' — is nowhere existent.

The difficulty of dealing with *unanticipated* as opposed to *anticipated* future shocks has prompted proponents of measuring GS to come up with suggestions concerning the treatment of rents accruing from the exploitation of resources that seem to be inconsistent with the underlying model from which GS is derived. Remember that our model of gNNP assumes efficient resource pricing according to Hotelling's rule, that is, the resource rent, and with approximately constant marginal costs the resource price as well, rises at the rate of interest.[17] Hamilton (1995, pp. 124ff.) correctly observes that historically resource prices have fallen instead of risen over time. The reason why reality seemingly clashes with theory is that the restrictive conditions under which Hotelling's rule holds true in theory are not fulfilled in reality. In the real world there is uncertainty and hence there are unanticipated shocks, so resource rent is not rising at the rate of interest, or better it is rising at the rate of interest only until an unanticipated shock emerges. The unanticipated shock will affect the magnitude of resource rent — it can be higher or lower than before the shock — after which it will rise again at the rate of interest until the next unanticipated shock occurs and so on.

Hamilton (ibid.) recognises that sticking to the assumption of resource rent and resource price rising smoothly and without interference at the rate of interest will distort his figures of GS. The theoretically correct and consistent way to deal with this problem would have been to stick to the assumption of efficient resource pricing which is implied by the optimal growth model underlying the construction of a gNNP and the measurement of GS, but to re-estimate GS for *every* unanticipated shock within the period of accounting. Hamilton instead proposes abandoning the assumption of efficient resource pricing so that GS does not have to be re-estimated for unanticipated shocks, which is understandable, given the practical impossibility of re-estimation. The problem with this proposition seems to be, however, that it is inconsistent with the method for resource accounting used. In Section 5.1.5.2, p. 164, it is argued that if one wants to abandon the assumption of efficient resource pricing for practical reasons, then it would be more consistent to also use a method for resource accounting like the El Serafy method that is not dependent on efficient resource pricing either.

5. A similar problem as discussed above arises if one abandons the unrealistic assumption that every determinant of the capacity to provide future welfare becomes embodied in one or the other form of capital. In the case of disembodiment gNNP cannot be simply regarded as sustainable income any more (Löfgren 1992; Aronsson and Löfgren 1993; Usher 1994). An example for disembodiment is autonomous or Hicks-neutral technical progress that is independent of the accumulation of man-made capital.[18] If these autonomous trends are correctly anticipated in the present then they can be interpreted as a positive or negative inter-temporal externality and can

therefore in principle be taken into account by augmenting gNNP with the current value of the externality (Aronsson and Löfgren 1993, 1995).

Weitzman and Löfgren (1997) have tried to estimate the upward correction for gNNP due to expected future technical progress. For the US they estimate that in 1987 sustainable income is about 40 per cent higher than gNNP and that the correction term for technical progress is almost an order of magnitude greater than all the other correction terms to derive gNNP from NNP taken together. Weitzman and Löfgren's (ibid.) result is not undisputed, however. Hamilton, Atkinson and Pearce (1997, p. 8) calculate an upward adjustment of only 3 per cent at maximum. Whereas Weitzman and Löfgren (1997) model technical progress as exogenous, Hamilton, Atkinson and Pearce (1997) use an endogenous R&D model of technical progress. However, as Pemberton and Ulph (1998) have shown, if techical progress is fully endogenous, then no correction term is warranted at all. The gNNP of an economy that develops along the optimal path includes already the amount of endogenous technical progress. The real point of divergence is therefore what fraction of technical progress should be regarded as exogenous. 'Depending on the view one takes, the correction factor could be anything from 0 to over 50 per cent' (ibid., p. 27).

If the estimate of Weitzman and Löfgren (1997) is approximately correct, this means, in effect, that any measurement of gNNP that ignores the role of technical progress is likely to vastly understate the sustainable income an economy can generate. Note, however, that as long as the contribution of technical progress towards sustainability is not changing over time, the correction factor for technical progress does not determine whether an economy is sustainable or not. This might appear paradoxical, but is to be explained as follows: anticipated future technical progress *raises* the *level* of utility an economy is able to generate over time. If this shifting factor is constant over time, technical progress does not rule out that because of negative GS the economy is losing its capacity to provide *this higher level* of sustainable income over time. The important message is that one has to distinguish between an effect on the *level* of gNNP and an effect on *changes* of gNNP from this new level, that is, GS. If technical progress is contributing more over time towards sustainability relative to the base year, then negative GS rates can be compatible with ensuring sustainability. If technical progress is contributing less over time towards sustainability relative to the base year, then zero GS rates are insufficient for ensuring sustainability and positive rates become necessary if society wants to prevent a decline *from this higher level* of sustainable income that was made possible by expected future technical progress.

6. There is no objective answer as to which components should be included in gNNP or GS and which should not. If one adds changes in natural and human capital to arrive at a 'green' NNP, why not also add changes in the 'social capital' of a society, as tentatively suggested by the World Bank (1997a), to arrive at a 'social' NNP? Putnam (1993) has convincingly shown how the legacy of different socio-institutional patterns can have tremendous consequences on the development of societies that are otherwise faced with similar conditions. Similarly, why not include 'cultural capital', as suggested by Berkes and Folke (1992, 1994), to arrive at a 'cultural' NNP? Berkes and Folke (1994, pp. 130f.) define cultural capital as

> people's views of the natural world and the universe, and the source of these values or cosmology; environmental philosophy, values, and ethics, including religion; and local and personal knowledge of the environment, including traditional ecological knowledge.

They rightly emphasise the importance of cultural capital thus defined on the capacity to provide future welfare. The problem is that the problems in valuing social or cultural capital, for example, are much more difficult to solve than the already difficult problems in valuing natural or human capital.

Depending on how the utility function is constructed and the constraints are set up, one gets a different set of numbers. That is, gNNP and GS are model dependent and vary depending on the particular model specification (Common 1993, p. 6f.). We could have included the *flow* of pollution instead of its *stock* into the utility and production functions of the above model. We could have let pollution impact negatively upon the natural growth of renewable resources as is the case with acid rain coming from SO_x emissions. We did not consider specifically deforestation which posits special problems of valuation due to the many interlinkages of deforestation with other environmental problems (see Hartwick 1992 and Hamilton 1997). Correction terms would have come out differently then, as would have their computed values.

The more interdependencies between resource extraction, pollution, production and direct utility effects one took into account, the more complicated would the model and the correction terms become. Estimates of GS will always be model dependent and will never be comprehensive in the sense that they capture every component of the capacity to provide utility and all interlinkages.

5.1.5   A Critique of the World Bank (1997a) Study

Several studies have been undertaken claiming to provide an admittedly crude measure of WS (for example, van Tongeren et al. 1993; Pearce and Atkinson 1993; Proops and Atkinson 1994; Hamilton and Atkinson 1996; World Bank 1997a). Pearce and Atkinson (1993) suggest that the US, Germany, Japan, Poland and the Czech Republic are weakly sustainable whereas most developing countries such as Burkina Faso, Papua New Guinea and Ethiopia are not. The World Bank (1997a) study suggests that the world taken together as well as the high-income countries are not weakly unsustainable due to high investments in man-made and human capital. It also suggests that most Sub-Saharan countries have had negative GS during the 1980s and 1990s, and most Middle East countries have had negative GS from the early 1970s onwards. Both regions would hence be detected as unsustainable.

I will now give a more detailed critique of the World Bank's (1997a) attempt to measure WS and to compute GS.[19] I shall show that the Bank's rather strong conclusions depend on a method for computing resource rents that is one of at least three competing ones. The so-called El Serafy method has some desirable properties suggesting it to be a better method to use. Sensitivity analyses using this method lead to opposite conclusions for both regions and indeed for most countries that appear unsustainable according to the World Bank (1997a). Let us have a closer look at the Bank's study first.

5.1.5.1   Structure of data and accounting methods in World Bank (1997a)

The data set underlying World Bank (1997a) consists of savings and accompanying data (World Bank 1997b). The structure of the set is described in detail in Appendix 5, p. 227. Of special interest here is what the Bank calls 'Extended Genuine Saving II' (EGS II): extended gross saving (that is, including education expenditures) minus depreciation of man-made capital minus resource rents from the depletion of natural resources minus damage caused by CO_2 emissions as a proxy for other air pollutants. Of all the data underlying World Bank (1997a) EGS II is closest to our definition of GS in equation (5.6), p. 151.[20] World Bank (ibid.) assigns all damage from CO_2 to the emitting country. As argued in Section 5.1.3, p. 152, on the open economy case, this allocation rule is not compelling. Damage from global warming is caused by the accumulated stock of CO_2 and other greenhouse gases. Developing countries could make a point in claiming that their incremental CO_2 emissions should count less than those from developed countries considering the already existing stock of CO_2 in the atmosphere mainly due to developed country emissions (see, for example, Agarwal and Narain 1991; Neumayer 1999e). Since damage from CO_2 emissions plays a negligible role in bringing

GS rates down below zero, I do not undertake sensitivity analyses for this correction term, however.

The years covered are 1970–94, for some countries only up to 1993. The data set includes 103 countries which are listed alphabetically in Appendix 6, p. 229, together with the number of years how often a country had negative EGS II rates out of the 25 possible years.[21] None of the former or current communist countries is included, presumably for lack of data with acceptable quality. Some of the very small countries are missing as well. The countries are grouped into regions and income groups as shown in Appendix 7, p. 231.

Appendix 8, p. 235, indicates the frequency of certain ranges of years for countries with negative EGS II rates. Forty-four countries never experienced negative EGS II rates throughout the period, including all high-income countries plus some lower- and low-income countries including Brazil, China, India, South Africa, Sri Lanka, Thailand and Turkey. Thirteen countries had one to three years with negative EGS II rates, including Argentina, Greece and Pakistan. Eight countries had four to six years with negative entries, including Egypt, Indonesia, Mexico, Peru and Myanmar. Thirteen countries had seven to ten years, including Chile, Côte d'Ivoire, Gambia and Syria. Twenty-four countries had more than ten years of negative EGS II rates which will be looked at in more detail below.

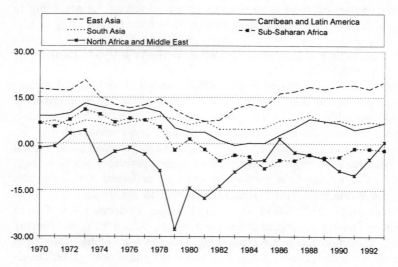

Source: Own computations from World Bank (1997b).

Figure 5.1 Extended Genuine Saving II rates for regions

Let us look at some aggregate figures now. The world taken together and the high-income countries in particular never have negative EGS II rates.[22] All of the other three income groups — upper-middle income, lower-middle income and low income group — experience a couple of years with negative rates, most notably the group of lower-middle income countries. The rates are only slightly negative, however, and they are not persistent in the sense that they become positive again in the early and mid-1980s and reach their former level in the early 1990s. The World Bank states that 'persistently negative rates of genuine saving must lead, eventually, to declining well-being' (World Bank 1997a, p. 28) and that 'where genuine saving is negative, it is a clear indicator of unsustainability' (World Bank 1995a, p. 53). It can be concluded therefore that at this level of aggregation no clear signs of unsustainability are apparent.

Figure 5.1 above shows EGS II rates for a selection of five different regions. The highest rates are achieved in East Asia where they usually fluctuate between 10 per cent and 20 per cent. South Asia's EGS II rates are relatively constant around 6–7 per cent and never go negative. For the Caribbean and Latin America the rates decline from 10 per cent in the late 1970s to just below 0 per cent in 1983 from where they have risen again to just over 5 per cent in 1993. More problematic is the region of Sub-Saharan Africa. Its EGS II rate declined from around 5 per cent in the late 1970s to become negative in 1979, slightly positive in 1980 and turned negative again afterwards where it has stayed for the rest of the period, fluctuating around –5 per cent. Still more problematic is the region of North Africa and the Middle East. This region experienced positive rates only in 1972, 1973 and 1986. During the late 1970s and early 1980s it exhibited rates drastically lower than –10 per cent, reaching its climax in 1979 with almost –30 per cent! If persistent EGS II rates are a clear indicator of unsustainability, then Africa and the Middle East appear to be unsustainable.

To analyse what drives EGS II rates to become negative it is best to disaggregate the data still further and look at individual country experiences. I decided, somewhat arbitrarily, to translate 'persistently negative rates' into 'having experienced negative rates for more than 10 years in the period 1970–94' though not necessarily in a row. Twenty-four out of the total of 103 countries were unsustainable thus defined.

For five out of these 24 countries, the EGS II rates are very close to and move very closely with extended net saving (EnetS) rates: Chad, Madagascar, Malawi, Sierra Leone and Uganda. For these countries, therefore, unsustainability can already be explained without having recourse to taking natural capital into account: they are simply unsustainable because they are slowly eating up their stock of man-made capital. Even taking ENetS as an indicator would identify these countries as unsustainable and looking at EGS II instead would not give major new insights. These countries are therefore excluded from the further analysis.

5.1.5.2 Competing methods for computing resource rents

Of particular interest is what drives the EGS II rates below ENetS rates for the other countries. Since ENetS minus rents from natural resource depletion minus (negligible) damage from CO_2 emissions equals EGS II, we have to examine in more detail how the numbers for resource rents are generated.

The Bank values resource rents to be deducted from ENetS as

$$(P - AC) \cdot R \qquad (5.7)$$

where P is the resource price, AC is average cost and R is resource depletion. Note that this formula corresponds roughly to the way resource depletion is treated in the definition of GS in our model of gNNP in equation (5.6), p. 151, except that the more readily available average costs are used instead of marginal costs and a correction term for pollution is missing.[23] No correction term for anticipated price changes is included on either the resource exporter's or importer's side which would be theoretically correct (see the discussion of the open-economy case in Section 5.1.3, p. 152). The reason is presumably that the authors are unsure about the future development of resource prices, so that 'as a default "rule of thumb" for sustainability, simply investing current resource rents is likely to be the prudent course of action' (Atkinson and Hamilton 1996, p. 4) for both importers and exporters.

Resource discoveries do not enter the formula. The Bank values discoveries at average discovery costs in accordance with the definition of GS in equation (5.6), p. 151, except that the more readily available average costs are used as a proxy for marginal costs. Since 'exploration expenditures are treated as investment in standard national accounting' (World Bank 1997a, p. 28) already anyway, there is no correction term for discoveries.

The Bank's method to compute resource rents is just one of at least three. The others I look at here are the so-called El Serafy method (El Serafy 1989, 1991, 1993) and the method of Repetto et al. (Repetto et al. 1989, Repetto and Cruz 1991). There are more methods, but these three are the most popular ones. The formula for the method of Repetto et al. is:

$$(P - AC) \cdot (R - D) \qquad (5.8)$$

where D is resource discoveries. Note that in this method resource discoveries are valued at $P - AC$, that is, at net profits and that the correction term can be positive if $D > R$ in the accounting period. This formula can be derived from another specification of the model of gNNP: if the expenditure function for resource discoveries is modelled as depending positively on the resource stock S instead of depending on the stock of cumulated discoveries X, that is, $g = g(D, S)$, resource discoveries would also be valued at the (modified) Hotelling rent as is resource extraction.[24] Hence, efficient resource pricing according to Hotelling's rule is assumed in the method of Repetto et al. as well. Also note that, strictly speaking, exploration expenditures should be netted out from NNP, if this method is used, in order to avoid partial double counting of resource discoveries.

The formula for the El Serafy method is:

$$(P - AC) \cdot R \cdot \left[\frac{1}{(1+r)^{n+1}} \right] \tag{5.9}$$

where r is the discount rate and n is the number of remaining years of the resource stock if production was the same in the future as in the base year, that is, n is the static reserves to production ratio. If $r > 0$ and $n > 0$, then (5.9) will produce a smaller deduction term for resource depletion than (5.7).

Formula (5.9) is also called the 'user cost' of resource depletion since it indicates the share of resource receipts that should be considered as capital depreciation. Note that no explicit correction term for resource discoveries is needed in this method since discoveries enter the formula via changing n and the formula is computed anew for each year.

The formula for the El Serafy method is derived from the following reasoning: receipts from non-renewable resource extraction should not fully count as 'sustainable income' because resource extraction leads to a lowering of the resource stock and thus brings with it an element of depreciation of the resource capital stock.[25] While the receipts from the resource stock will end at some finite time, 'sustainable income' by definition must last for ever. Hence, 'sustainable income' is that part of resource receipts which if received infinitely would have a present-value just equal to the present-value of the finite stream of resource receipts over the life-time of the resource.

Define resource receipts RC as

$$RC \equiv (P - AC) \cdot R \tag{5.10}$$

The present-value of resource receipts RC at the constant discount rate r over the expected life-time n of the resource stock is equal to:

$$\sum_{i=0}^{n}\frac{RC}{(1+r)^i} = \frac{RC\left[1 - \dfrac{1}{(1+r)^{n+1}}\right]}{1 - \dfrac{1}{1+r}} \tag{5.11}$$

The present-value of an infinite stream of 'sustainable income' SI is

$$\sum_{i=0}^{\infty}\frac{SI}{(1+r)^i} = \frac{SI(1+r)}{r} = \frac{SI}{1 - \dfrac{1}{1+r}} \tag{5.12}$$

Setting (5.11) and (5.12) equal and rearranging expresses SI as a fraction of RC:[26]

$$SI = RC\left[1 - \frac{1}{(1+r)^{n+1}}\right] \tag{5.13}$$

The correction term, representing user cost or the depreciation of the resource stock, would thus be

$$(RC - SI) = RC\left[\frac{1}{(1+r)^{n+1}}\right] = (P - AC)\cdot R\left[\frac{1}{(1+r)^{n+1}}\right] \tag{5.14}$$

which is the formula in (5.9). Note that the El Serafy method computes SI anew for each year, but in computing SI for each year assumes that the receipts from resource exploitation (RC) are constant over time. Because of that, production rates are assumed to be constant in addition to the World Bank's (1997a) assumption of constant net resource prices. Also, an estimate of the life-time of the resource, n, that is, the static reserves to production ratio is required. The El Serafy method does not presume efficient resource pricing — resource rent growing at the rate of interest according to Hotelling's rule — because it is not dependent on an optimisation model. It is an 'ex post approach, capable of accounting for any entrepreneurial decisions regarding extraction' (El Serafy 1997, p. 222). As a consequence future resource receipts have to be discounted and the El Serafy method requires the selection of a discount rate r. If either the life-time of the resource asset, n, or the discount rate r are quite large, the necessary correction term will consequently be rather small (see equation (5.14)). Also note that the correction term can never be positive.

Both the El Serafy method and the method of Repetto et al. have been widely used in practice. Presumably the best-known attempt to measure the value of changes in a nation's resource stock is the World Resources Institute's studies on Indonesia (Repetto et al. 1989) and Costa Rica (Repetto and Cruz 1991) using the method of Repetto et al. Similar studies have been undertaken — using both methods — for Brazil (Serôa da Motta and Young 1995; Serôa da Motta and May 1996); Mexico (Van Tongeren et al. 1993); Papua New Guinea (Bartelmus, Lutz and Schweinfest 1993) and the United Kingdom (Bryant and Cook 1992). More recently, studies have been undertaken by official institutions for the US (US Department of Commerce Bureau of Economic Analysis 1994a, 1994b) and for Canada (Statistics Canada 1995), partly using alternative methods.

Application of the method of Repetto et al. has produced quite large and volatile adjustments to NNP (see Repetto et al. 1989; Repetto and Cruz 1991; Serôa da Motta and May 1996).[27] This volatility was one of the main reasons for El Serafy to develop his method (El Serafy 1993, pp. 249ff.). It produces less volatility because first it values resource discoveries only indirectly in changing the parameter n and, more importantly, it counts only parts of the total net receipts to be subtracted from national product whereas the method of Repetto et al. subtracts the total net receipts of resource depletion from NNP. Only in the limit where the discount rate is set to zero in El Serafy's formula will both methods produce the same numbers for resource depletion. This can easily be verified by setting $r = 0$ in (5.9), p. 165. The reason is that in this limiting case efficient resource pricing is implicitly assumed.

The method of Repetto et al. also produces more volatility than the World Bank's method. This is because Repetto et al. value resource discoveries at full Hotelling rent, instead of valuing at marginal or average discovery cost as suggested in our derivation of gNNP. If resource discoveries were valued at average discovery costs instead the formula would become the same as the one of the World Bank method because exploration expenditures are already included in the traditional natural accounts (World Bank 1997a, p. 28).

Which method to use for resource accounting? This is a question that has been controversially discussed in the literature — see Hamilton et al. (1994), Gomez-Lobo (1993), Hartwick and Hageman (1993), and van Dieren (1995). The United Nations' 'System of Integrated Environmental and Economic Accounting' (United Nations 1993a) proposes using both the El Serafy method and the method of Repetto et al. without indicating a preference for one or the other. In Neumayer (1999f), an article in the journal *Environmental and Resource Economics*, published by Kluwer Academic, it is argued in detail why I regard the El Serafy method as a better method to use than the

World Bank method which is in turn superior to the method of Repetto et al. In short, there are three reasons why the El Serafy method can be argued to be the best method to use: first, it is not dependent on the assumption of efficient resource pricing. None of the data the Bank uses are guaranteed to be the ones that would be generated if a country's economy developed along the optimal path and the Bank does not attempt to estimate any shadow values. Actually, since the Bank excludes future terms-of-trade effects in assuming constant resource prices it even implicitly excludes efficient resource pricing. Hence, to be consistent, it is better to use a method for computing resource rents that does not presume that the underlying data are optimal values either.

Second, in contrast to the World Bank method it counts only part of resource rents as capital depreciation, but the rest as sustainable income which makes more sense. With the World Bank method, a country completely dependent on resource exploitation, the extreme case of Saudi Arabia, could never have positive GS as all resource rents are counted as capital depreciation and could therefore never be sustainable. Hartwick (1994) has shown, however, that a resource-dependent country can ensure WS in investing parts of its resource rent into alternative forms of capital.

Third, application of the World Bank method leads to results that carry little plausibility. Take Saudi Arabia as an example: on average its genuine saving rate as computed by World Bank (1997a) is less than –30 per cent *per annum* (sic!) for the period 1970–93. If we assume for simplicity that Saudi Arabia's capital stock is not that much higher than the average of Middle East countries, then it has a total capital stock of approximately US$150 000 per capita according to World Bank (1997a, p. 11) and a natural capital stock of US$58 000 per capita. With a GNP per capita of around US$7800, Saudi Arabia would have lost a quite dramatic part of its capital, if it really had had an average negative genuine saving rate of about –30 per cent of GNP over a period of 24 years as the World Bank figures indicate. To be fair, it has to be said that the way the World Bank estimates a country's natural capital stock itself is methodologically slightly different from the way it estimates the depreciation of it (see World Bank 1997a, pp. 18f. and 37f.). The natural capital stock is underestimated relative to its depreciation. However, in order for the Bank's depreciation estimates to make sense and in order for the country not to lose almost all its natural capital, Saudi Arabia would have needed a much higher natural capital stock – so high indeed that it would have a natural capital stock that is as high as, if not higher, than the combined man-made and human capital stock of a Western European country.

In what follows below I use the El Serafy method for sensitivity analysis of the World Bank's results in order to show how the Bank's main conclusions are reversed if this method is used. Note that I do not claim that the El Serafy method is perfect — no method is, see Neumayer (1999f). Because the El

Serafy method does not assume optimisation, it is likely to underestimate depreciation of the natural resource stock to some extent. (I am grateful to Kirk Hamilton from the Bank's Environment Department for drawing my attention to this point.) Maybe future research can find a better method for computing resource rents that depends on less strong assumptions.

5.1.5.3 Computing resource rents with the El Serafy method

Which resources to look at for the sensitivity analysis? Table 5.1 shows that for Algeria, Bolivia, Congo, Ecuador, Gabon, Iran, Nigeria, Saudi Arabia, Trinidad and Tobago, and Venezuela the dominating resources are oil and natural gas. Their share is always more than 90 per cent with the exception of Bolivia for which tin is also important. For Papua New Guinea the dominating resources are copper and gold, for Zambia it is copper, for Jamaica it is bauxite, for Mauritania iron ore. For Nepal, Haiti and Ghana, forestry represents a major share of resource rents. For Ghana it is also gold. For the more important countries it is clearly rents from oil and natural gas that dominate.

To compute user costs for resource depletion according to the El Serafy method, one needs to establish four different terms:

- $P - AC$, net resource price
- R, resource depletion (production)
- r, the discount rate
- n, the number of years reserves would last at current production rates.

Appendix 9, p. 236, describes the sources of data used. A discount rate of 4 per cent per annum was applied following the rate which World Bank (1997a) uses for wealth estimations. The sensitivity analysis covers oil, natural gas, bauxite, copper, gold, iron ore and tin. Forestry was excluded due to the many difficulties in getting reliable data. Hence no sensitivity analysis could be undertaken for Nepal and Haiti and for parts of Ghana's resource rents. The sensitivity analysis reveals a number of things:

1. Those countries with huge reserves of resources relative to their production and positive ENetS rates throughout stop having negative EGS II rates (El Serafy) altogether or have only one year with a negative rate. This applies to the following countries: Algeria, Iran, Papua New Guinea, Saudi Arabia, and Venezuela. (As an example, see Figure 5.2 for Iran.) This was to be expected since high reserves to production ratios (a high n in equation (5.9), p. 165) depress the user costs of resource depletion. This is because, for given resource production, a smaller share of the total resource stock is used up.

Table 5.1 Share of single natural resources of total resource rents

Country	1970–74	1975–79	1980–84	1985–89	1990–94
Share of Oil and Natural Gas of Rents in %					
Algeria	96.32	98.85	99.54	99.35	99.35
Bolivia	53.52	64.08	81.33	72.58	68.15
Congo	90.34	97.49	99.49	99.58	100.00
Ecuador	97.94	99.92	99.79	98.01	98.91
Gabon	99.76	99.99	99.99	99.92	99.99
Iran	99.71	99.76	99.74	98.81	99.23
Nigeria	99.77	99.59	99.93	98.27	95.17
Saudi Arabia	100.00	100.00	100.00	100.00	100.00
Trinidad and Tobago	100.00	100.00	100.00	100.00	100.00
Venezuela	94.10	97.81	98.94	97.69	96.94
Share of Copper of Rents in %					
Papua New Guinea	55.18	81.84	61.42	59.09	48.29
Zambia	96.50	91.29	81.15	80.18	81.45
Share of Bauxite of Rents in %					
Jamaica	100.00	100.00	100.00	100.00	100.00
Share of Forestry of Rents in %					
Nepal	98.92	81.48	85.02	99.45	100.00
Haiti	80.09	80.44	92.27	100.00	100.00
Ghana	0.00	9.34	39.72	69.25	75.80
Share of Gold of Rents %					
Ghana	79.64	55.95	48.97	26.91	20.65
Papua New Guinea	43.09	17.38	37.20	40.20	31.16
Share of Iron Ore of Rents in %					
Mauritania	91.93	97.19	100.00	100.00	100.00
Share of Tin of Rents in %					
Bolivia	29.00	27.98	12.81	5.06	8.06

Source: Own computations from World Bank (1997b).

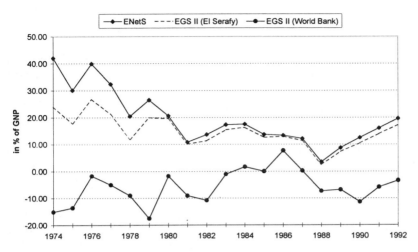

Sources: Own computations from World Bank (1997b) and sources indicated in App. 4, p. 222.

Figure 5.2 Sensitivity analysis for resource rents of Iran

2. The unsustainability of some countries with temporary negative ENetS rates can be explained without taking recourse to EGS II rates. This applies to Bolivia and Jamaica, which for every year of negative EGS II rates (El Serafy) have negative ENetS rates as well. It also applies to Ghana which has only one year (1987) of both a positive ENetS rate and marginally negative EGS II rate (El Serafy). For Zambia EGS II rates (El Serafy) are rather close to and move rather close with ENetS rates as well. Zambia has six years of slightly positive ENetS rates and slightly negative EGS II rates (El Serafy), however.

3. There remain the cases of Congo, Ecuador, Gabon, Nigeria, Mauritania, and Trinidad and Tobago. These countries share a similar experience: although EGS II rates (El Serafy) are considerably higher than EGS II rates (World Bank), in a number of years EGS II rates (El Serafy) are negative while ENetS rates are still positive. For Congo this is true for four years, for Ecuador for seven years, for Gabon for four years, for Nigeria for six years, for Mauritania for three years and for Trinidad and Tobago for seven years. The reasons for this divergence are similar for these countries: they all have relatively low oil reserves to production ratios, with the exception of Mauritania which produces iron ore. Over the period 1970–94, the approximate average oil reserves to production ratios are as follows:

Congo 27 years, Ecuador 21 years, Gabon 17 years, Nigeria 27 years, Trinidad and Tobago 9 years. Mauritania's average iron ore reserves to production ratio is 34 years.

In addition, usually in the 1980s their production increased, while their reserves either remained constant or even declined which further depressed their reserves to production ratio. Because of that the user costs from oil depletion calculated via the El Serafy method are high (although not as high as according to the Bank's method, of course). Interestingly, all these countries with the exception of Gabon exhibit high reserves to production ratios for natural gas over the period 1970–94, that is, their natural gas reserves have not been significantly exploited so far. The average reserves to production ratios are as follows: Congo > 100 years, Ecuador > 100 years, Nigeria > 80 years, Trinidad and Tobago > 70 years.[28] This can provide some hints as to how past mistakes can be avoided in the future as I shall argue in the next section. Before doing so let us ask first, however, whether we can conclude that for these six countries unsustainability can be reliably detected only with EGS II rates (El Serafy), whereas their ENetS rates would misleadingly suggest that these countries are weakly sustainable.

The answer is no, at least not in general. This is because in computing EGS II rates (El Serafy) a rather low rate of discount (4 per cent per annum) was deliberately chosen so as to provide a conservative estimate of the divergence from the EGS II rates (World Bank). Usually, real rates of return, especially in developing countries are much higher than 4 per cent per annum For further analysis I have therefore analysed the effects of choosing a discount rate of 10 per cent per annum which should not be considered absurdly high. Looking back at equation (5.9), p. 165, reveals that a high discount rate (r) depresses user costs. This is because a smaller share of resource receipts has to be invested in an alternative asset in order to provide a sustainable alternative income stream if the rate of return on this investment is higher.

For Congo and Nigeria the EGS II rates (El Serafy) move so close to the ENetS rates if a discount rate of 10 per cent per annum is used that hardly any additional information is revealed by looking at EGS II (El Serafy 10 per cent per annum) rather than ENetS. Gabon stops exhibiting any signs of unsustainability if EGS II (El Serafy) is calculated with the higher discount rate. The same is true for Mauritania except for one year in which its ENetS rate is also negative. For the two remaining countries the picture is less clear-cut. Ecuador has only two years with negative ENetS rates, but still six years of negative EGS II rates (El Serafy 10 per cent per annum) — see Figure 5.3. The gap between EGS II rates (El Serafy 10 per cent per annum) and EGS II rates (World Bank) is quite large (up to about 20 percentage points in 1984), but it is not always enough to bridge the gap between ENetS rates and EGS II rates (El Serafy 10 per cent per annum). The same is basically true for Trinidad and Tobago which has four negative EGS II rates (El Serafy 10 per cent per annum), but only two negative ENetS rates. Especially for these two countries a lesson can be learned from their gap between ENetS and EGS II (El Serafy), whether calculated at 4 per cent per annum or 10 per cent per annum, and it is this the next section focuses on.

5.1.5.4 Policy implications

The divergence between ENetS rates and the EGS II rates (El Serafy), that is detectable even with a discount rate of 10 per cent per annum, can provide some hints for better future resource management. What the divergence suggests is that these countries in the past did not adequately use the opportunities they were given through their oil endowment, or in the case of Mauritania iron ore endowment, to build up and maintain man-made and human capital in exchange for resource depletion. They should learn from their mistake for the future depletion of their as yet hardly exploited natural gas reserves or, in the case of Mauritania, its still considerable iron ore reserves. Unfortunately, their natural gas reserves are smaller in terms of share of world reserves than their oil reserves: Congo has an average share of world natural gas reserves over the period of 1970–94 of about 0.05 per cent as opposed to about 0.1 per cent share of world oil reserves; the analogous figures for Ecuador are 0.12 per

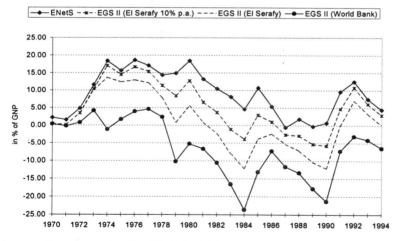

Sources: Own computations from World Bank (1997b) and sources indicated in App. 4, p. 222

Figure 5.3 Sensitivity analysis for resource rents of Ecuador

cent as opposed to 0.3 per cent; 0.07 per cent as opposed to 0.17 per cent for Gabon; 1.87 per cent as opposed to 2.35 per cent for Nigeria. Only Trinidad and Tobago has higher natural gas than oil reserves (0.31 per cent versus 0.11 per cent).

That resource producers with low EGS II rates have a lesson to learn conforms with the World Bank's conclusions: 'The depressed rates of genuine saving ... represent an opportunity not seized. ... [I]t is often the gross saving effort that is insufficient in these countries, which points the finger squarely at broader macroeconomic policies' (World Bank 1997a, p. 35). The fundamental message of this conclusion is not confined to Congo, Ecuador, Gabon, Nigeria, Mauritania, and Trinidad and Tobago, however. Even for countries with very high reserves to production ratios and hence no indication of unsustainability, a large divergence between ENetS rates and EGS II rates (El Serafy) suggests 'that due prudence is not being followed — that some amount of the national [natural resource, E.N.] wealth is simply consumed ...' (ibid., p. 35).

Finally, let us have a look at some aggregate graphs. Figure 5.4 compares EGS II rates (World Bank) for Sub-Saharan Africa and for North Africa and

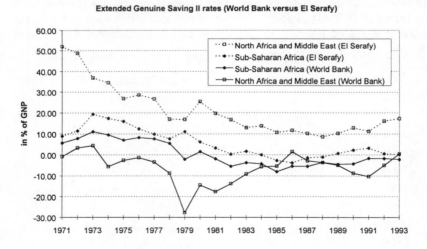

Sources: Own computations from World Bank (1997b) and sources indicated in App. 4, p. 222.

Figure 5.4 Sensitivity analysis for Sub-Saharan Africa, and North Africa and the Middle East

Middle East their EGS II rates (El Serafy) with a discount rate of 4 per cent per annum Whereas Sub-Saharan Africa has 14 years of negative EGS II rates following the World Bank method, there are only four years with slightly negative rates if resource rents are computed with the El Serafy method. The latter paints a picture of much less gloom for the region. Note that the EGS II rate (El Serafy) calculates resource rents according to the El Serafy method only for six out of a total of 30 countries. The rest enters the EGS II rate (El Serafy) with their resource rents still computed according to the World Bank method. If resource rents for the other 24 countries had also been calculated according to the El Serafy method (especially for such important resource producers as Côte d'Ivoire and South Africa) then, no doubt, the EGS II rate (El Serafy) would have been positive throughout the period.

The reversal in conclusion about the sustainability performance of a region is considerably stronger in the case of North Africa and the Middle East. Whereas EGS II rates (World Bank) suggest that this region is clearly unsustainable with only three years of positive rates, the graph of EGS II rates (El Serafy) paints a completely different picture: North Africa and the Middle East never appear to be unsustainable and, better still, exhibit quite strong EGS II rates (El Serafy) that are above 20 per cent in eight years and between 10 per cent and 20 per cent for the rest of the period with the exception of one year!

The policy conclusions from the two methods are completely different: whereas the World Bank method suggests that North African and Middle East countries endanger the welfare of their future populations, the El Serafy method suggests that there is no reason to worry about unsustainability since enough of the resource rents are invested in man-made and human capital to maintain the capacity to provide non-declining future utility. Also, note again that the EGS II rates (El Serafy) compute resource rents according to the El Serafy method only for a subset of the countries in the region: Algeria, Iran and Saudi Arabia. For Bahrain, Egypt, Israel, Jordan, Morocco, Syria and Tunisia resource rents are still computed using the World Bank's method. It follows that EGS II rates (El Serafy) would have been even higher if resource rents of these countries had also been calculated with the El Serafy method.

5.1.5.5 Conclusion
The World Bank (1997a) study claims that many Sub-Saharan and North African and Middle East as well as some countries from other regions are unsustainable. The sensitivity analysis in this section has shown that this conclusion depends crucially on the specific method the World Bank uses to compute resource rents. In calculating resource rents with this method the Bank applies an inconsistent methodology: on the one hand, its method for resource accounting assumes efficient resource pricing as it is derived from a

dynamic optimisation model. On the other hand, the World Bank study implicitly rejects efficient resource pricing in ignoring future terms-of-trade effects according to the Hotelling (1931) rule. Also, the World Bank method counts all resource rents as capital depreciation.

Following the World Bank's results would lead to wrong policy implications for the wrong countries. One policy implication Atkinson and Hamilton (1996, pp. 4ff. and 14) and Atkinson et al. (1997, p. 114) tentatively suggest, is making aid conditional for developing countries who appear to be unsustainable according to the World Bank's method in order to bring them (back) on a sustainable path. It is unclear whether conditionality is supposed to apply to existing development aid or additional aid. Usually, the mentioned authors simply speak of aid in general, but Atkinson et al. (1997, p. 207) propose 'a possible role for *additional* bilateral aid in assisting, where needed, the fulfilment of genuine saving requirements' (my emphasis).

As an alternative to the World Bank's method, the El Serafy method was employed. With a relatively low discount rate of 4 per cent per annum, Sub-Saharan Africa does not exhibit persistent negatives rates of GS any more and the region of North Africa and the Middle East turns out to be a strong genuine saver. This finding holds basically true on a disaggregated level as well for most countries that were detected by World Bank (1997a) as unsustainable: either they do not appear to be unsustainable any more or their unsustainability can be explained with negative ENetS rates alone, that is, without taking recourse to resource depletion. For Congo, Ecuador, Gabon, Nigeria, Mauritania, and Trinidad and Tobago this result held true only after a higher discount rate of 10 per cent per annum was used.

The truth is likely to lie somewhere in between the results that are generated with the two methods. It has been argued here that the El Serafy method is a better method to use, but it is not unproblematic. Its results are radically different from the Bank's results and are arguably more plausible, but it tends to underestimate the extent of natural capital depreciation somewhat.

What are further weaknesses of the World Bank (1997a) study that would need to be improved over time? The coverage of renewable resources and pollutants needs to be extended if enough data of sufficient quality can be established. Forests are an important renewable resource, but not the only one. If possible, resources like water, soil, fish and, more generally, biodiversity should be included. Equally, carbon dioxide emissions are but one pollutant. Again, if possible, pollutants such as sulphur oxides, nitrogen oxides, fecal coliforms and particulate matter should be included. That the more developed countries by and large do not become identified as potentially unsustainable is partly to be explained by their usually quite high net savings rates, but might partly also have to do with the fact that only one pollutant is taken into account so far (compare Atkinson et al. (1997, pp. 85ff.)). Also, it is important to further improve the quality of data used for the computations. Sometimes the World Bank has to employ heroic assumptions to arrive at its numbers (see Kunte et al. 1997). Also, quite often reserve data for natural resources are unavailable. Indeed, it might represent one of the major advantages of such a large-scale study as World Bank (1997a) that it calls upon international and national organisations to collaborate together in order to establish more and better data that would be of wider use if available.

In the concluding section to this chapter more will be said on a proper interpretation and use of practical measures of GS such as the World Bank (1997a) study.

5.1.6 A Critique of the Index of Sustainable Economic Welfare (ISEW)

Over the last decade, a number of scholars have developed the so-called Index of Sustainable Economic Welfare (ISEW). The index is intended to eventually replace a country's gross national product (GNP) or gross domestic product (GDP).[29] ISEWs have been developed out of the concern that GNP is not an adequate indicator for either current welfare or the achievement of sustainability. From this perspective GNP is seen as flawed because, among other things, it does not take into account (a) the value of household labour, (b) the welfare effects of income inequality, (c) the effects of environmental degradation on welfare and sustainability, and (d) considers 'defensive expenditures' wrongly as contributions to welfare.

The ISEW stands in a long tradition of earlier attempts to measure welfare; see, for example, Nordhaus and Tobin (1972), Zolotas (1981) and Eisner (1989). While the first two studies explicitly take account of the environment, the last study is rather silent on resource depletion and environmental degradation. Because of space limitations I cannot examine these older studies here. For an overview, see Eisner (1988).

An important difference between measuring GS and the ISEW is as follows: GS only measures sustainability, that is, whether the capacity to provide non-declining utility is maintained or not. The ISEW, on the other hand, aims to measure the total level of current welfare as well. Thus, with reference to the model in the last section, the ISEW should value the welfare implications of the total *stock* of renewable resources and the total *stock* of pollution (that is, the first two terms of the gNNP function in equation (5.5), p. 147). As we shall see in this section, the existing ISEW studies do not do this but estimate defensive expenditures against pollution as a substitute for valuing the total stock of pollution and do not value environmental amenities from the renewable resource stock at all.

The ISEW includes many more factors determining the total level of current social welfare than are included in the model of gNNP in Section 5.1.2, p. 142, for example, income inequality. It also takes into account many other correction terms for valuing total welfare, for example, the welfare derived from household work or the decrease in welfare due to transportation, health care and other expenditures that allegedly only function as a 'defence' against a decline in welfare. That is, the implicit utility function used in an ISEW study is much more complex than the utility function for a representative consumer introduced in Section 2.1, p. 8. There, a simplistic utility function was deliberately chosen to highlight the major differences between WS and SS and to make the analysis of the book possible.

ISEW studies have been undertaken for, among others, the US (Daly and Cobb 1989; updated in Cobb and Cobb 1994), the United Kingdom (Jackson and Marks 1994; updated in Jackson et al. 1997), Germany (Diefenbacher 1994), Italy (Guenno and Tiezzi 1996, preliminary study only), Sweden (Jackson and Stymne 1996), Austria (Stockhammer et al. 1997) and Chile (Castaneda 1998).[30] What these studies usually demonstrate is that the ISEW of a country has been growing much more slowly since 1945 than its GNP and indeed has fallen since the early 1980s or even late 1970s. This result holds true for virtually every country for which a study of ISEW has been undertaken so far.

Computation of an ISEW usually starts from the value of personal consumption expenditures which is a sub-component of GNP. Consumption expenditures are weighted with an index of 'distributional inequality' of income (usually a modified Gini coefficient). Then, certain welfare-relevant contributions are added and certain welfare-relevant losses are subtracted. As an example, take the US study of Cobb and Cobb (1994): after having weighted personal consumption expenditures by a modified Gini coefficient of pre-tax income distribution data, they add the estimates of the value of the services from household labour, consumer durables and streets and highways. They also add net private investment into man-made capital and changes in the net international investment position of the US. They subtract most expenditures on health and education because these are regarded as mostly defensive expenditures. They also subtract expenditures on consumer durables, estimates of the costs of commuting, car accidents, and the costs of environmental degradation such as water, air and noise pollution, loss of wetlands and farmlands, the depletion of non-renewable resources and long-term environmental damages due to CO_2 emissions. The ISEW is simply the sum of the weighted personal consumption expenditures and all the mentioned corrections.

In this section, I shall first of all give a short overview of existing ISEW studies. I shall then argue that the ISEWs lack a sound theoretical foundation.

I shall show that their conclusions are highly dependent on certain key and rather arbitrary assumptions about the weighting of income distribution, the valuing of the depletion of non-renewable resources and long-term environmental damage and the neglect of technical progress and increases in human capital.

5.1.6.1 A short review of ISEW studies

As mentioned, ISEW studies have been undertaken for a couple of high-income countries and Chile. The detailed methodology varies somewhat from study to study depending on the authors' preferences and the availability of data. The methodology of the Chilean (Castaneda 1998), German (Diefenbacher 1994), Italian (Guenno and Tiezzi 1998), Swedish (Jackson and Stymne 1996), and early UK (Jackson and Marks 1994) studies is basically the same as in Cobb and Cobb (1994), which is a revision and update of the pioneering US study in Daly and Cobb (1989). Cobb and Cobb (1994) in turn is updated in Cobb, Halstrad and Rowe (1995) and Anielski (1999) — in these updates the ISEW is called Genuine Progress Indicator (GPI) and a slightly revised methodology is used. A GPI study also exists for Australia (Hamilton 1999). We shall concentrate on the ISEW studies here which are more popular and better known than the GPI studies.

The update of the UK study (Jackson et al. 1997) and the study for Austria (Stockhammer et al. 1997) have undertaken some changes in methodology, as we will see later on. Importantly, the basic conclusions are the same for all these studies: welfare has risen much more slowly than growth rates of GNP would suggest and, indeed, has fallen from the 1980s onwards. Jackson et al. (1997, p. 2) cite Max-Neef (1995, p. 116) who suggests that the computation of an ISEW for various countries provides evidence for a 'threshold hypothesis' which holds 'that for every country, economic growth (as conventionally measured) brings about an improvement in the quality of life, but only up to a point — the threshold point beyond which more economic growth leads to a decline in the quality of life'.

For the US, for example, covering the period 1950 to 1990, the ISEW is already slightly declining during the 1970s by 0.14 per cent per year — a decline that is accelerating to 1.26 per cent per year in the 1980s according to Cobb and Cobb (1994, p. 76). They suggest resource depletion, long-term environmental damage and a more unequal income distribution as the main factors for the decline in the ISEW.

For Germany, basically the same trend is detected covering the period 1950 to 1987: Diefenbacher (1994, p. 228) finds after 1980 'ongoing growth of the GNP, but a rather sharp decline of the ISEW'. He provides basically the same reasons for this decline in the German ISEW as Cobb and Cobb (1994) do for the US.

Jackson and Marks (1994, p. 28) in a pilot study for the UK found that over the period 1950 to 1990 'there is virtually no overall growth' and the 'per capita ISEW in 1990 is just 3 per cent higher than it was in 1950'. This dismal performance is mainly due to the 1980s for which Jackson and Marks (ibid., p. 29) compute a *decline* in ISEW per capita of 4.7 per cent per annum! They cite rising income inequality and environmental degradation as major reasons for this dramatic decline in the last decade of their period of analysis (p. 32).

In the updated study, Jackson et al. (1997), the period up until 1996 is covered. As mentioned, the methodology for the computation of the revised index has somewhat changed from Jackson and Marks (1994). The two main changes are as follows:

- Income inequality is measured via computing a so-called 'Atkinson income' instead of using a modified Gini coefficient. The Atkinson income indicates 'the proportion of the present total income that would be required to achieve the same level of social welfare as at present if incomes were equally distributed' (Atkinson 1983, p. 57). In varying an explicit parameter for aversion to inequality in income distribution, the valuation of income inequality is undertaken explicitly rather than implicitly as is the case with the Gini coefficient.
- Following the methodology of Cobb and Cobb (1994), Jackson and Marks (1994, p. 24) computed accumulating long-term environmental damage by valuing each tonne of coal equivalent of non-renewable fuels consumed in the UK with a constant, rather arbitrary rate of £3.73 (1985 pounds sterling). The idea behind letting the costs accumulate over time is as follows: Cobb and Cobb (1994, p. 74) 'imagined that a tax or rent of $0.50 per barrel-equivalent had been levied on all non-renewable energy consumed during that period and set aside to accumulate in a non-interest-bearing account .... That account might be thought of as a fund available to compensate future generations for the long-term damage caused by the use of fossil fuels and atomic energy'.

   Jackson et al. (1997) instead use explicit cost estimates for long-term environmental damage from global warming. Starting from an estimate of about £11 marginal costs per tonne of carbon emitted in 1990, they compute the costs per tonne of carbon in retrospect and up to 1996 under the assumption that marginal social costs of carbon emission rise over time according to the cumulative level of emissions from past activities. As Cobb and Cobb (1994) did, Jackson et al. (1997) let the costs from long-term damage *accumulate* over time. This is clearly a methodological mistake since they use *marginal* damage costs for valuing CO_2 emissions. Jackson et al.'s method to compute damage from CO_2 emissions amounts to multiple counting.

In spite of these changes in methodology, Jackson et al. (1997) come to the same basic conclusions as Jackson and Marks (1994). Mayo, MacGillivray and McLaren (1997, p. 1), the short version of Jackson et al. (1997), observe that 'since 1980, according to the ISEW, real well-being has actually fallen by over 20 per cent'. As key reasons for this decline they cite 'environmental degradation (in particular depletion of non-renewable resources and long-term environmental damage) and income inequality' (p. 5). The decline in welfare shown by the updated ISEW is slightly smaller than the one detected by the pilot ISEW of Jackson and Marks (1994). 'The principal reason for this has been the choice of a relatively low aversion to income inequality' (Jackson et al. 1997, p. 34).

For Austria, Stockhammer et al. (1997, p. 32), covering the period 1955 to 1992, come up with similar findings as the other studies. In addition, they cite the substitution of household work with market production as a major reason for the widening gap between GNP and the ISEW: the substitution increases GNP but not the ISEW since Stockhammer et al. (1997, p. 26) value the contribution of household labour to welfare in the ISEW according to market prices. The methodology Stockhammer et al. (1997) use is different in many respects from Cobb and Cobb (1994). The main changes are as follows:

- Instead of weighting the starting point, personal consumption expenditures, by a 'distribution inequality index', it is the final item, the ISEW, that is weighted for changes in income distribution.
- All investment items are multiplied by the productivity of capital in order to convert capital stocks into consumption flows.
- Most defensive expenditures are computed as the expenditures exceeding the level in the base year 1955. The idea is that 1955 represents something close to a sustainable level.
- For air and water pollution *potential* defensive costs are taken into account as well. Stockhammer et al. (1997, p. 23) define potential defensive costs as 'those costs that would have occurred if society had reacted to environmental devaluation in the same way (concerning one "unit of pollution") as it reacts today'.
- Whereas Cobb and Cobb (1994) valued the depletion of non-renewable resources by replacement costs for renewable resources, Stockhammer et al. (1997) value this item as the value added of the Austrian mining

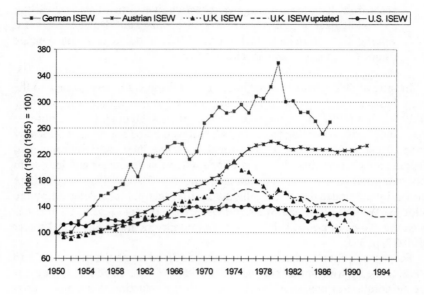

Sources: Cobb and Cobb (1994), Diefenbacher (1994), Jackson and Marks (1994), Jackson et
al. (1997), Stockhammer et al. (1997).

Figure 5.5 ISEW for several countries.

sector. Long-term environmental damage is valued cumulatively similar
to Jackson et al. (1997) and the same criticism that was raised against
this method further above applies to Stockhammer et al. (1997) as well.
One cannot use marginal social cost data and let damage accumulate
over time. Marginal social cost is assumed to be about öS3402.30 in
1987 prices (about 150 pounds sterling) and is not assumed to increase
over time (Hochreiter et al. 1995, p. 447). Note that the figure Hochreiter et al. for marginal social costs per tonne of carbon emitted is at
the upper bound (or even beyond) of available estimates (see Fankhauser 1995, pp. 58–72; IPCC 1996b, p. 215). This stands in marked contrast to Hochreiter et al.'s (1995, p. 450) assertion that their method excludes the possibility of damage overestimation.

To provide a graphical overview, Figure 5.5 shows the development of the
ISEW for the mentioned studies and countries where the base year has been
normalised to 100.

5.1.6.2   ISEWs lack a sound theoretical foundation

One of the most fundamental problems of the ISEW is that it lacks a sound theoretical foundation. The corrections are simply undertaken without giving any theoretically sound justification for doing so. The correction terms, for example, those for the depletion of non-renewable resources and the cost of long-term environmental damage, are not derived from a dynamic optimisation model which, as shown in Section 5.1.2, p. 142, is able to provide a theoretically sound indicator of welfare. The same applies to corrections such as for the decrease in welfare due to traffic costs, health care, pollution abatement and other expenditures that allegedly only function as a 'defence' against a decline in welfare.

The ISEW can also be criticised for being arbitrary in the components it includes or (implicitly) excludes as contributors to welfare. One prominent item, defensive expenditures, provides a case in point. The concept of defensive expenditures is dubious and elusive since it is rather arbitrary what should count as defensive (Jacobs 1991, pp. 228–32). If health expenditures are defensive expenditures against illness, why should food and drinking expenditures not count as defensive expenditures against hunger and thirst? Are holiday and entertainment expenditures to be considered defensive expenditures against boredom? Should they all be subtracted from consumption expenditures?

Daly and Cobb (1989, p. 78) defend their concept of subtracting defensive costs in saying that '"defensive" means a defense against the unwanted side effects of other production, not a defense against normal baseline environmental conditions of cold, rain and so on'. But even accepting Daly and Costanza's definition, one could argue that at least part of food, drink, entertainment and holiday expenditures are caused by the stressful, exhausting and boring modes of modern production that make these expenditures necessary as a defence against their unwanted side effects. As the United Nations' revised system of national accounts rightly retorts: 'Pushed to its logical conclusion, scarcely any consumption improves welfare in this line of argument.' (United Nations 1993b, p. 14). Mäler (1991, p. 10) therefore concludes that subtracting defensive expenditures from GNP 'can hardly be seriously considered'.

Also, it is not necessarily the case that defensive expenditures do not generate real income. In times of widespread unemployment defensive expenditures might use hitherto unused factors of production that do not have to be taken away from alternative uses (Sammarco 1996, p. 38). Defensive expenditures might thus properly count as additions to welfare and should not be subtracted.

The same basic argument holds true for the valuation of leisure time. The ISEWs usually neglect the valuation of leisure time because doing so 'would so totally swamp all other figures in such an index as to make every other aspect of welfare trivial by comparison' (Cobb and Cobb 1994, p. 275) — at least if leisure time is valued by an average wage rate, as is commonly done. Cobb and Cobb (ibid., p. 275) realise, however, that there 'is no particular reason within economic theory' for not including leisure time in a welfare indicator. At least over the very long run, leisure time has increased enormously in most countries so that a valuation of this item would tend to raise the ISEW and increase the index over time quite dramatically. As with many other items, the critical observer gets the impression that the ISEW is constructed in a way that many items that would lower and decrease the index over time are included, whereas items that would raise and increase the index over time are excluded.

That the ISEW lacks a sound theoretical foundation is presumably the reason for committing methodological errors at times. It was mentioned already that Jackson et al. (1997) and Hochreiter et al. (1995) let the costs of long-term environmental damage accumulate over time in spite of using marginal social damage costs for valuation. A simple thought experiment shows that Jackson et al.'s (1997) method *must* be wrong. With a marginal cost of £11 per tonne of carbon and a carbon content of 0.13 tons per barrel of oil (Poterba 1991, p. 75), cumulative damage of CO_2 emissions would amount to about £28 per barrel of oil over a period of only 20 years, if for simplicity discounting is ignored for a moment. If damage from burning a barrel of oil was really so high, then the government should even think about an outright ban for the use of oil! Clearly, multiple counting leads to absurdly high damage costs.

The ISEW also suffers from the fact that there is no objective answer on what are the factors that determine welfare. It is indeed very subjective. If you include a correction term for income inequality, why not include a correction term for the degree of political freedom, a correction term for the extent of crime or a correction term for the degree of equality between the sexes. The difference to GS is that this indicator is derived from a stringent theoretical model that provides its justification, whereas adjustments in the ISEW are largely undertaken *ad hoc*.

Certainly, some of these items just mentioned — the degree of political freedom, the extent of crime or the degree of equality between the sexes — simply cannot be reliably measured in its welfare consequences and therefore would need to be excluded from practical measurement. As with the GS, therefore, the ISEW necessarily provides only a partial indicator. It can only measure what can be measured reliably.

5.1.6.3 Results depend on arbitrary assumptions

To substantiate the critique that the results of the ISEWs depend on arbitrary assumptions, let us have a closer look at the two main determinants of the decline in the ISEWs, namely environmental degradation and 'worsening' income distribution.

Let us start with the latter first: the valuation of the distribution of income in a measure of welfare fails to command general agreement. Mishan (1994, p. 172) is right in noting that 'all efforts to adjust the welfare index to accommodate changes in distribution ... must be regarded with misgivings. They are either arbitrary or politically biased and are, therefore, invariably a focus of attack.' Of course, not undertaking any explicit valuation is tantamount to assuming implicitly that the marginal utility of income is constant and the same for the rich and the poor alike — an assumption, which is admittedly no less arbitrary than the one embraced by the proponents of an ISEW.

The fact that the weighting for income distribution exerts a very substantial influence on the ISEW should caution against adjustments for changes in distribution, however. In Cobb and Cobb (1994) the ISEW for 1990 would be 12 per cent higher without adjustments for income distribution. In Jackson et al. (1997) per capita ISEW between 1973 and 1996 is *declining* by 13.4 per cent if income is weighted by the inequality index, but the ISEW is actually *rising* by 7.8 per cent without adjustment for changes in distribution. It follows that with appropriate weighting widely differing conclusions can be drawn. Further below, therefore, sensitivity analysis for the US and the UK ISEW is undertaken with respect to, among others, the valuation of income distribution.

As concerns long-term environmental damage, the computations are largely dependent on highly disputable *ad hoc* assumptions. Cobb and Cobb (1994, p. 266) value the consumption of a domestically produced barrel of oil or its equivalent in 1988 with US$75, because that is the presumed cost of replacing the barrel with renewable energy from biomass. For other years the replacement costs are computed in retrospect and are forwarded under the assumption that they rise at the constant rate of 3 per cent per annum over time. If you think US$75 is not much, compare it to the costs of importing a barrel of oil from abroad which is about US$20. Or compare it to the cost of providing solar energy in a couple of decades when US non-renewable energy resources are depleted which will certainly be much less than US$75 and is decreasing over time, not increasing, as technical progress makes renewable resource use cheaper.

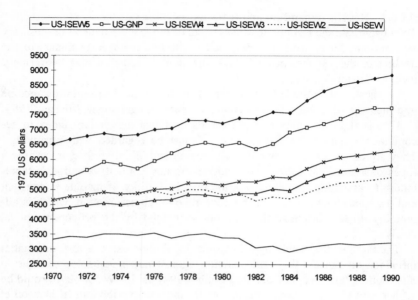

Sources: Cobb and Cobb (1994) and own computations from World Bank (1997b).

Figure 5.6 Sensitivity analysis for US ISEW

Also, Cobb and Cobb (1994, p. 267) arbitrarily assume that the consumption of each barrel of oil or its equivalent causes accumulating environmental damage costs of US$0.50 due to CO_2 emissions and that the production of each kilogram of CFC-11 and CFC-12 causes accumulating damage of US$15 (p. 273). Without the corrections for the depletion of non-renewable resources, long-term environmental damage and ozone depletion the ISEW in 1990 would be 83.5 per cent higher! These items are so large in magnitude that they dominate any other subtraction terms by one or two orders of magnitude.

Figure 5.6 provides a sensitivity analysis for the US ISEW. There are six graphs, all are presented in per capita terms and constant 1972 US$ to relate to Cobb and Cobb (1994). For lack of data, only the period 1970 to 1990 is covered. The lowest graph plots the ISEW as presented in Cobb and Cobb (ibid.).

The dotted line called US-ISEW2 uses a different method for computing the depletion of non-renewable resources and long-term environmental damage than Cobb and Cobb (ibid.). It follows the World Bank's method which

we encountered already in Section 5.1.5, p. 161. There I argued that the El
Serafy method for computing the depletion of non-renewable resources
should be preferred. I use the World Bank's method here nevertheless, because it invariably produces a bigger correction term for resource depletion
than the El Serafy method. This is by intention and to be welcomed since I
want to be rather conservative in changing assumptions from the ISEW computations: if it can be shown that the correction for resource depletion using
the World Bank's method leads to differing conclusions than using Cobb and
Cobb's (1994) method, this result would be substantially strengthened if the
El Serafy method was used instead of the World Bank's method.

The correction term for resource depletion is computed as follows: instead
of arbitrary replacement costs for non-renewable resources, US-ISEW2 subtracts total Hotelling rents from consumption expenditures. Total Hotelling
rents are the product of price minus average cost and resource deple-
tion/harvest:[31] $(P - AC)R$. Data are taken from World Bank (1997b). Note
that US-ISEW2 is covering more non-renewable resources than Cobb and
Cobb (1994) because it takes the depletion of mineral resources into account
as well, not only energy resources. It encompasses Hotelling rents from oil,
natural gas, hard coal, brown coal, bauxite, copper, iron, lead, nickel, zinc,
phosphate, tin, gold, silver and forests.[32]

As concerns long-term environmental damage, US-ISEW2 values annual
CO_2 emissions at US\$20 per metric tonne carbon instead of arbitrarily as-
suming that each barrel of oil equivalent causes accumulating damage of
US\$0.50. The US\$20 is taken from Fankhauser (1995) and is often regarded
as a consensus estimate for the *marginal* cost of CO_2 emissions. Data are
again taken from the World Bank (1997b) data set. Since marginal costs are
used, the damage costs are not accumulated over time (see the discussion
above).

The graph marked by the small triangles called US-ISEW3 is like US-
ISEW2, but with the further change that consumption expenditures are not
weighted with an index of distribution inequality. It is apparent from the
graphs that US-ISEW2 and even more so US-ISEW3 are not only much
higher than US-ISEW, but also follow the shape of US-GNP (per capita GNP,
the graph marked with squares) rather closely. Instead of declining slightly
over time as US-ISEW does, both US-ISEW2 and US-ISEW3 increase over
time.

Hence, changing two sensitive parameters in Cobb and Cobb's (1994)
methodology completely changes the presented picture about the changes in
'sustainable economic welfare'. US-ISEW2 is certainly to be preferred to US-
ISEW on theoretical grounds since its correction terms for resource depletion
and environmental damage are derived from modelling and are not arbitrarily

chosen. Whether US-ISEW3 should be preferred to US-ISEW2 depends on how you value distribution inequality.

Both US-ISEW2 and US-ISEW3 are still below US-GNP. This is because of the 14 items Cobb and Cobb (ibid.) subtract from personal consumption expenditures, I have only changed one (ISEW2) or two (ISEW3), respectively. Yet another criticism is that the ISEWs are constructed in a way that prompts one to suspect that their very aim is to show that welfare is lower than GNP and has risen much more slowly than indicated by GNP or has even fallen — for example, by excluding investment into human capital and technical progress from their measurement (Eisner 1994; Atkinson 1995). Another correction that could be undertaken and would likely raise the ISEW considerably is adjusting for improved quality of consumer goods over time.

As concerns investment into human capital, Cobb and Cobb (1994, p. 53) exclude most expenditures for education because they believe that education 'contributes little to productivity' and should hence not be counted as investment. On the other hand, Cobb and Cobb believe that education should not count as consumption either since

> most schooling appears to be defensive. In other words, people attend school because others are in school and the failure to attend would mean falling behind in the competition for diplomas or degrees that confer higher incomes on their recipients. (ibid., p. 54)

As a consequence, only one-half of post-secondary education is counted as pure consumption (ibid.).

That education contributes little to productivity is at odds with most studies of the determinants of long-run growth (World Bank 1995a, p. 62) which usually hold that 'human capital is the most critical factor of production' (Eisner 1994, p. 99). In the graph with the small crosses called US-ISEW4 in Figure 5.6, education expenditures have therefore been fully added to US-ISEW3.[33] As can be seen in comparison to US-ISEW3, the level of 'sustainble economic welfare' is considerably higher with the inclusion of education expenditures.

As concerns technical progress, Weitzman and Löfgren (1997) have estimated the upward correction to NNP due to expected future technical progress. For the US they estimate that sustainable income in 1987 is about 40 per cent higher than NNP, that is, GNP minus depreciation of man-made capital. The exact magnitude of this estimate is dependent on a series of crucial assumptions about technical progress being exogenous (see ibid.) and should not be given too much credit. More for illustrative purposes therefore, I have simply assumed that the estimate is correct and of the same magnitude for the rest of the period 1970 to 1990. The upper graph in Figure 5.6 with the black

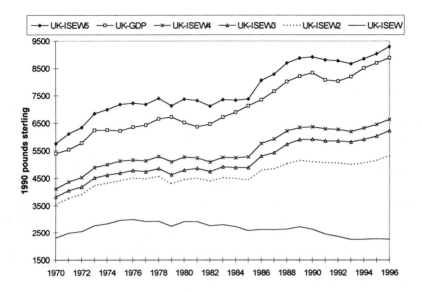

Sources: Jackson et al. (1997) and own computations from World Bank (1997b).

Figure 5.7 Sensitivity analysis for UK ISEW

diamonds called US-ISEW5 plots the graph US-ISEW4 augmented by 40 per cent. For every year, US-ISEW5 lies above US-GNP and would thus signal a higher achievement of 'sustainable economic welfare'.

Figure 5.7 provides an analogous analysis for the UK ISEW. All graphs are again in per capita terms, but constant 1990 pounds sterling. The lowest graph plots the ISEW as presented in Jackson et al. (1997). The graph with the squares represents GDP. All other graphs are computed analogous to the analysis for the US.

That is, UK-ISEW2 is as UK-ISEW, but resource depletion is computed with resource rent data from World Bank (1997b) and annual CO_2 emissions are valued at US$20 per tonne of carbon. UK-ISEW3 is like UK-ISEW2, but without adjustment for income inequalities. UK-ISEW4 is like US-ISEW3, but also taking into account technical progress. For simplicity and lack of different data it is assumed that the upward correction factor for technical progress is also 40 per cent. The conclusions for this sensitivity analysis are quite similar to the analysis for the US analysis: The UK-ISEW2, UK-ISEW3 and UK-ISEW4 graphs move rather close with UK-GDP. There is a growing gap between these modified ISEWs and the original UK-ISEW of Jackson et al. (1997). Again more for illustrative purposes, UK-ISEW5 takes account of the beneficial effects of technical progress which raises UK-ISEW4 by 40 per cent and lies above UK GDP in every year.

5.1.6.4 Conclusion

The ISEW has a number of shortcomings that disqualify it as a serious indicator of sustainable economic welfare. First, it suffers from the lack of a sound theoretical foundation. Second, and connected to the first point, its results depend on a number of assumptions that are arbitrary partly for the reason that they are not based on stringent theoretical modelling. It was shown that the strong conclusion of most ISEW studies that 'sustainable economic welfare' decreased from the early 1980s onwards, if not earlier, was totally reversed if consumption expenditures were not weighted with an index of distribution inequality and a different method for accounting for the depletion of non-renewable resources and for CO_2 emissions was used. With these changes the ISEW for the two countries for which sensitivity analysis was undertaken (the US and the UK) is steadily increasing over time instead of decreasing.

In looking at the methodology for the ISEW the critical examiner gets the impression that they are constructed with the very intention of producing the desired result of decreasing 'sustainable economic welfare'. This can be inferred, for example, from the fact that the ISEW values proxies for environmental disamenities from the stock of pollution, but ignores the counter-value of environmental amenities from the stock of renewable resources. Also, the ISEW largely excludes the beneficial effects of investment into human capital.

Sometimes one gets the impression, however, that the constructors of an ISEW are not bothered very much by the subjectivity of the numbers they produce, as becomes clear in the following quotation taken from Cobb and Cobb (1994, p. 252): 'The point is rather that when the GNP functions politically as a welfare measure, it should not be allowed to masquerade as a measure that is somehow more objective than alternative ways of determining well-being'.

It has to be conceded that Herman Daly, together with John B. Cobb one of the first proponents of an ISEW, seems to be aware of the many criticisms that can be raised against the ISEW. At the same time, however, he claims that it is a much better indicator of 'sustainable economic welfare' than GNP and is thus justified:

Of course we had to make many arbitrary judgements, but in our opinion no more arbitrary than those made in standard GNP accounting — in fact less so. ... We have no illusions that our index is really an accurate measure of sustainable economic welfare ... We did not offer the ISEW as the proper goal of economic policy — it too has flaws. If GNP were a cigarette, then the ISEW would be that cigarette with a charcoal filter. (Daly 1996, pp. 97f.)

Similarly, Daly (ibid., p. 115) acknowledges the difficulties in constructing a measure of welfare, but sees the ISEW justified by preferring 'even the poorest approximation to the correct concept' to 'an accurate approximation to an irrelevant or erroneous concept'. Yet again, at the very same time Daly realises and concedes that 'the mere existence of any numerical index of welfare is a standing invitation to the fallacy of misplaced concreteness' (ibid., p. 98).

In the concluding section to this chapter, some of the implications of the analysis here for a proper use of indicators of WS are examined in more detail. There the somewhat tricky question of what to do against the common and widespread misinterpretation of GNP as an indicator of welfare shall be discussed as well.

5.2 STRONG SUSTAINABILITY: MEASURING THE 'SUSTAINABILITY GAP'

In Section 4.3, p. 103, it was argued that the second interpretation of SS is more reasonable than the first one. If empirical evidence can make a persuasive case for the non-substitutability of certain forms of natural capital, it makes more sense to demand that the physical stocks of these forms of natural capital are preserved, rather than the value of the aggregate of natural capital. There is no presumption that the two measurements will necessarily coincide. In order to measure whether SS is achieved or not it is therefore first of all necessary to determine which forms of natural capital should be preserved and to what extent. As shown in Chapter 4, this is no easy task. Second, one needs environmental information and indicator systems to show whether these standards are fulfilled or if not how big the sustainability gap is. As a third step some authors have proposed to measure monetarily the costs society would have to incur in order to reach the sustainable standards, that is, to close the sustainability gap. Let us examine each of these three different steps now.

5.2.1   Determining the Sustainability Standards

In Chapter 4 it was argued that the distinctive features of natural capital together with risk and uncertainty merely make a case for the qualitative preservation of certain forms of natural capital. It was also argued, however, that
while there are good reasons to defend the non-substitutability of these forms
in toto, it does not necessarily imply that they cannot be substituted for at the
margin. If best available science cannot reliably determine the point after
which a certain form of natural capital loses its basic life-support function but
suggests that it has not been reached yet, then how to decide to what extent
preservation should take place? One option is to balance benefits and costs
for every marginal preservation choice. As was explained with reference to
the precautionary principle and SMS, because of uncertainty and ignorance
the costs of preservation might be allowed to be higher than the benefits by a
certain factor and it is up to society and its political decision-making procedures to decide how big this factor should be. Alternatively, society could
refrain from making any marginal decisions at all, deliberately ignore the
opportunity costs of preservation and decide to preserve the (remaining) total
of 'critical' natural capital stocks. Such a decision might be justified because
first we are uncertain about how much of an environmental resource must be
preserved to keep its life-support function intact and because second natural
capital is regarded as non-substitutable as a direct provider of utility independent of whether basic life-support functions are threatened or not. In
Chapter 4 it was argued that ignoring opportunity costs does not appear to be
in the best interest of either the current or future generations. But surely it is
one possible answer to the problem of uncertainty and ignorance with respect
to the extent of preservation needed for maintaining the life-support functions
of certain forms of natural capital. And it is a defendable position to regard
the existing stock of natural capital as non-substitutable in providing direct
utility to future generations.

Measuring SS would require a clear determination of what forms of natural
capital should be preserved and to what extent and it would have to be done
on a much more detailed and disaggregated basis than was undertaken in
Chapter 4. Indeed, the fact that if one wants to measure SS one has to clearly
define what SS is, is regarded by one of its proponents to be one of the major
advantages of the measuring exercise (Hueting 1991, p. 211). However, if
opportunity costs are allowed to enter the determination of sustainable standards then many valuation studies have to be undertaken and the information
requirements become very high. If, on the other hand, opportunity costs can
be ignored, it is easier to determine the sustainability standards. Hueting and
Reijnders (1998, p. 143), for example, interpret sustainability 'as the use of
vital environmental functions in such a way that they remain available indefi-

nitely'. Similarly, Simon and Ekins (1998, p. 10) set standards for what they call 'environmental sustainability' independent of opportunity costs. The suggested standards are as follows:

- Stable climate.
- Undepleted ozone layer.
- Biodiversity at current levels.
- No loss of function for non-renewable resources.
- Sustainable harvest at desired level for renewable resources.
- Limiting emissions to critical loads in order to protect human health.
- Maintenance of an unspoilt countryside.
- Maintenance of environmental security in restricting environmental risks to low levels.

Simon and Ekins (ibid., p. 10) acknowledge, however, that governments might give priority to other public policy objectives such as economic growth and employment. They would regard such a decision as an indication that a government eschews environmental sustainability only rhetorically.

5.2.2   Measuring the Sustainability Gap in Physical Terms

Once the sustainability standards have been set up, the next step is to monitor whether the standards are achieved. What is generally needed for this task are environmental information and indicator systems. The difference between the two is that information systems bring together a possibly quite enormous extent of largely unconnected data and attempt to give detailed environmental information, whereas indicator systems try to condense specific data into a few meaningful and policy-relevant indicators.

Discussions of indicators and requirements for meaningful and policy relevant indicators can be found in Liverman et al. (1988), Friend and Rapport (1991), and Cansier (1995). As Opschoor and Reijnders (1991) observe, if indicators are to play an important role in political decision making, then their number has to be severely limited. Limiting the number of indicators is no easy task, however, since most often a common base unit is missing. Only sometimes can differently nominated units be converted into a single common unit: greenhouse gases, for example, can be interpreted in global warming potential units, energy resources in tonnes of oil equivalent.

Germany's central statistics office has undertaken major efforts to arrive at a 'total environment–economy analysis' ('Umweltökonomische Gesamtrechnung') in order to describe the state of the environment (stock) and its use (flow) quantitatively. The total analysis consists of resource input–output analyses, statistics of pollution emittents, statistics of environmental expenditures and time trends of environmental indicators (see Radermacher 1992; Bolleyer and Radermacher 1993; Kuhn, Radermacher and Stahmer 1994; Klaus 1994; Beirat Umweltökonomische Gesamtrechnung 1995; Radermacher and Stahmer 1995). Its major objective is to arrive at a few policy-relevant indicators for guiding environmental policy making (Bolleyer and Radermacher 1993, p. 145).

Other countries and institutions have also officially undertaken preliminary efforts for environmental indicator systems, most notably Canada (Statistics Canada 1995), the European Union (Eurostat 1994), the Netherlands (Adriaanse 1993), Norway (Alfsen and Saebo 1993) and the United Kingdom (Department of the Environment 1996; Vaze and Balchin 1996). Also, the OECD (1994, 1998) has proposed a 'pressure–state–response' framework for environmental indicators, featuring indicators of the pressure on the environment, indicators of the state of the environment and indicators of human response to environmental degradation. The GEF has estimated each country's share of the total world's remaining natural areas (Rodenburg, Tustall and van Bolhuis 1995). Desai (1995) has ranked countries according to a few selected environmental indicators in an approach close to the method of UNDP's Human Development Index. For a survey of these undertakings, see Alfsen and Saebo (1993), Klaus (1994), Rennings (1994), Hamilton et al. (1994) and Hammond et al. (1995).

Note that most of the mentioned efforts have not been undertaken with the explicit objective of providing a measure for the achievement of sustainability standards. But they provide the basis on which concrete sustainability indicators would have to be built. And in spite of all the efforts mentioned above, a lot more work needs to be done to provide adequate statistical information on the environment. As the Asian Development Bank has pointed out:

> Statistical information on the environment is scarce, often inaccurate, seldom comparable from country to country, and rarely available in a time series covering a sufficient number of years to indicate trends in a reliable way. Thus, descriptions remain anecdotal and lack the hard edge of quantification which is necessary for analysis and policy formulation. (cited in Carpenter 1994, p. 180)

O'Connor (1994, p. 89) puts emphasis on developing and improving indicators since 'the main problem now seems to be information overload, rather than a lack of basic data'. In many instances, however, it is likely that both basic data and meaningful indicators are still missing, especially in many developing countries. The United Nations' (1993a, p. 22) 'System of Integrated Environmental and Economic Accounting' handbook also emphasises the need to improve basic environmental statistics.

5.2.3 Monetary Valuation of the Sustainability Gap

As a final step one can value the sustainability gap monetarily in estimating the costs that would be necessary to achieve the sustainability standards. First, one needs to establish the necessary measures to achieve the standards. These measures can be either in the form of reducing the output of certain goods and services whose production causes environmental degradation, or in the form of input substitution and pollution abatement in production processes, or finally in the form of direct restoration and preservation. Next, cost curves have to be established for the implementation of each measure. Then all measures are sorted with respect to their marginal cost in order to arrive at an overall cost curve for achieving the sustainability standard. Hypothetically, the measure with the least cost is undertaken first, then the measure with the next highest cost and so on. In so far as there might be practical obstacles for following this sequence of least-cost measures, the estimate for the sustainability gap is too low.

5.2.4 Problems with a Monetary Valuation of the 'Sustainability Gap'

The attempt to measure the 'sustainability gap' monetarily faces a number of problems:

1. In establishing the cost curves for achieving the sustainability standards, a partial analysis is undertaken. The costs for the implementation of each measure are estimated under the *ceteris paribus* assumption. This is the approach taken in, for example, Simon and Ekins (1998). However, if all those measures that are necessary to achieve the sustainability standards were effectively undertaken and not only hypothetically, then the *ceteris paribus* assumption would become fictitious. The relative prices of consumption goods and input factors would change as would the extent and structure of environmental degradation. Economic restructuring, feedbacks and interlinkages would have to be considered in a total equilibrium analysis of the economy. This task can only be achieved with comprehensive modelling. This is the preferred option in Faucheux, O'Connor and van den Hove (1998). *A priori* it is unclear whether the costs for achieving the sustainability standards would be higher or lower in the total analysis relative to a series of partial analyses although some suggest they would be lower (for example, ibid.).

2. It is unclear what the appropriate timeframe is for achieving certain sustainability standards. This holds especially true with respect to stan-

dards for non-renewable resources. Simon and Ekins (1998, p. 10), for example, postulate that the sustainability standard for non-renewable resources should be that their use must not diminish their 'function' which can be achieved via more efficient use, repair, re-use, recycling and substitution with renewable substitutes. However, it is unclear whether the maintenance of functionality must be achieved instantaneously or over a long time period. The latter would be more sensible as there is no immediate danger of a running out of non-renewable resources — see Section 4.3, p. 103. It might be sufficient to calculate the costs for research and development of alternative energy sources then (Cansier and Richter 1995, p. 239). If one opts for the former possibility the cost of achieving the sustainability standard could potentially be very high as a substitute for the loss in function of the non-renewable resource use would have to be provided immediately. Cobb and Cobb (1994) estimate the costs of replacing all domestic energy production in the US instantaneously with renewable substitutes to be in the range of 30 per cent of GNP in 1988! Now, Simon and Ekins (1998) allow for many other measures than substitution with renewable resources to maintain the functionality of the non-renewable resource stock which might be much cheaper. One might also criticise Cobb and Cobb's (1994) replacement cost of US$75 per barrel of oil or its equivalent as too high. But nevertheless costs can be quite high if the complete use value of non-renewable resource depletion has to be compensated for instantaneously rather than over a long time span.

3. For sustainability standards for environmental resources that extend beyond national boundaries, an allocation rule has to be established. This rule must state which country should contribute how much for achieving the standard. For example, if the sustainability standard is a stabilisation of the global climate, then it must not only be established how much overall reduction in greenhouse gas emissions is warranted, but also which country has to reduce emissions by how much. Essentially all the critical points that were highlighted with respect to GS in an open economy in Section 5.1.3, p. 152, apply here as well. For some environmental resources, such as the ozone layer, international treaties exist that allocate responsibilities for reduction among nation-states. But for many resources such a treaty does not exist or still has to be established. Invariably then, international allocation rules for these resources are dependent on the value judgements of the researcher who wants to compute the value of the sustainability gap.

4. It is unclear whether the estimated value for the sustainability gap should be subtracted from NNP or not. Simon and Ekins (1998, p. 19) state that 'it is important to note that the sustainability gap figure thus derived ... is

not commensurable with GDP or the other national accounting product aggregates, and could therefore not be subtracted from, say, NNP, in order to produce a "sustainable income", or "Green GDP" figure'. Hueting and Reijnders (1998, p. 143) on the other hand suggest subtracting the value from national income to arrive at 'sustainable national income' which is defined as 'the level of production and consumption that can be sustained indefinitely with available technology while maintaining the availability of vital functions'. In my view, it would be wrong and misleading, however, to deduct the value of the sustainability gap from NNP. Whereas the NNP as a measure of the value of goods and services minus depreciation of man-made capital is not normative in the sense of achieving certain standards, the value of the sustainability gap is clearly contingent on the normative determination of the sustainability standards. In contrast to gNNP and GS from WS, corrections are not undertaken for actual changes in natural capital, but purely hypothetical measures to reach a pre-specified sustainability standard are valued. Deducting the value for the sustainability gap from NNP would also be misleading as it would suggest that the remaining income can be considered as sustainable income, whereas the very existence of the sustainability gap indicates that sustainability has not been achieved as the sustainability norms have been violated. This is because the achievement of sustainability and therefore the closing of the sustainability gap is purely hypothetical and is not undertaken in reality.

5. However, if one opts for deducting the value for the *hypothetical* measures to reach the sustainability standards from NNP, then one should also deduct the value for the measures that have *actually* been undertaken. In other words, one would need to deduct as well 'defensive environmental expenditures'.[34] This is because hypothetical and actual expenditures are perfect substitutes for each other and should not be treated conceptually different in subtracting from NNP (Cansier and Richter 1995, p. 246). If actual expenditures are lower, hypothetical expenditures must correspondingly be higher and vice versa.

In Section 5.1.2, p. 142, we have seen that defensive expenditures should not be netted out from NNP to arrive at a measure for WS. However, the methodology looked at here for measuring SS is a completely different one. It is not a contradiction to dismiss the subtraction of defensive expenditures in a sustainability measure that attempts to track actual changes in the value of an economy's total capital, but to demand subtraction of defensive expenditures in a sustainability measure that attempts to subtract all necessary expenditures to reach a pre-specified environmental standard (for a similar conclusion, see Brouwer and Leipert (1998)).

Similarly, in Section 5.1.6, p. 177, on the ISEW it was argued that the concept of defensive expenditures is rather elusive since it is arbitrary what should count as defensive expenditures to maintain a given level of welfare and what should count as real contributions to welfare. However, the concept of defensive expenditures looked at here suffers much less from the mentioned problems as it is a rather confined concept that focuses on environmentally defensive expenditures and, more importantly, is not dependent on its relation to welfare. In other words, defensive expenditures are not deducted from NNP because they are regarded as merely maintaining a given level of welfare and should therefore not be counted as real contributors to welfare, but because they are part of the measures needed to maintain a certain pre-specified level of environmental functions. As such, they are not vulnerable to the critique that it is difficult to say which measures contribute to welfare and which do not. On the other hand, it does not mean that existing defensive expenditures are easily separable and reclassified in the traditional system of national accounts (Steurer et al. 1998).

6. The estimated value of the sustainability gap has to be treated with great caution in interpretation. Without a simultaneous knowledge of the physical dimensions of the sustainability gap, wrong interpretations are likely. A high value for the sustainabilty gap can mean either that the actual economy is far from the sustainability norms or that the economy is close to fulfilling the norms, but doing so would be very costly. Similarly, a given value for the sustainability gap does not tell us anything about the relative achievement of sustainability with respect to different norms. It could be that certain norms are drastically violated while others are almost achieved or it could be that the economy is equally far away from achieving all norms. Also, a constant or falling value of the sustainability gap tells us nothing about the state of the environment since this could be *either* the consequence of the economy moving closer to fulfilling the sustainability standards *or* the consequence of a lowering of costs due to, for example, technical progress. Indeed, it is possible to have a decreasing value for the sustainability gap over time, while at the same time the economy moves further and further away from the sustainability standards.

5.3   CONCLUSION

Can sustainability be measured? Theoretical analysis has come quite a long way now in clarifying the correct adjustments to arrive at a theoretically correct indicator of WS, namely genuine saving (GS). In Section 5.1 it was shown how GS can be derived from gNNP and the necessary adjustments for the open-economy case were discussed. In order for GS to be interpreted as an indicator of sustainability one has to assume that the actual economy develops sufficiently close along its optimal path, as GS is derived from a dynamic optimisation model. Several reasons have been put forward that render practical estimations of GS or gNNP and its proper interpretation problematic. A few of these problems have been highlighted in critically assessing the World Bank (1997a) study and several studies of the ISEW.

Whether reliable indicators of WS are possible in practice is a contested matter. Some clearly reject this possibility, for example Hueting (1991), Common (1993), Faucheux, Muir and O'Connor (1997) and Simon and Ekins (1998). Others, among them for obvious reasons the main proponents of a GS measure, clearly do believe that GS provides information that is policy relevant and should guide policy decisions. Pearce, Hamilton and Atkinson (1996, p. 99), for example, state that 'sustainable development can be more than a vague commitment on the part of governments and instead become a measurable concept with wide-ranging policy implications'. As mentioned in Section 5.1.5.4, p. 173, one policy implication Atkinson and Hamilton (1996, pp. 4f. and 14) and Atkinson et al. (1997, p. 114) suggest, is putting conditions on aid to developing countries that appear to be unsustainable in order to ensure that GS rates become positive again.

The analysis in this chapter suggests the conclusion that the GS estimates have to be treated with great care and with much caution in interpretation. First, GS cannot be a positive indicator of sustainability, just a negative indicator of unsustainability. Negative GS rates indicate unsustainability, but positive GS rates do *not* indicate sustainability. In other words, a country that exhibits positive GS rates might well be unsustainable. The claim that 'under most calculations, given the saving rates of all but the lowest-saving countries in the world, most countries now pass this test of sustainability' (IPCC 1996b, p. 140) is misleading as it wrongly suggests that we could measure whether a country is sustainable.

Second, if for practical reasons one has to abandon the assumption of efficient resource pricing, then it is better and more consistent to use a method for resource accounting that does not presume efficient resource pricing either. This was one of the reasons given in Section 5.1.5 for preferring the El Serafy method to the World Bank's method. There it was argued that using the El Serafy method will make GS more reliable as an indicator of WS. In Neumayer (1999b) I use the same method for a constructive proposal on how to link the Human Development Index (HDI) with WS.

Third, practical measures of GS will always be partial in the sense that they can never provide a wholly comprehensive measure for WS. Some forms of capital, for example, cultural and social capital, are at the moment and will presumably always remain basically unmeasurable, as will be changes in these forms of capital. Indeed, as Thage (1989, pp. 319 and 329) observes, even the NNP is hardly used nationally or internationally due to the uncertainty about the estimates of depreciation of man-made capital. For most developing countries no NNP figures were available at all for a long time (van Dieren 1995, p. 217). Similarly, we shall never be able to account for all changes in natural capital. Practical measures of GS have to use readily available data or those that can be established with reasonable reliability. Others have to be left out, although continuing work effort will ensure that more and more variables and better quality data can be used.

There is certainly a clear rationale for natural resource accounting as the stock of marketable resources for many developing countries is a very significant part of their national portfolio and information about which share of the resource receipts should be counted as proper income and which should be counted as capital consumption is extremely important for them. This holds especially true if the government leases the exploitation of its resources to a private firm and wants to compute resource royalties and taxes. As many natural resources are commercially marketed, prices can be established and it is not all that difficult to keep track of changes in their stocks. Without resource accounting, what happens is that the receipts of resource depletion are fully counted as income and no correction is made for the capital loss. This makes little economic sense. A country living off its natural resource endowment might enjoy high 'income' today but will be impoverished as soon as the stock is exhausted. This runs counter to the very idea of sustainability as capital consumption is a 'sure recipe for future economic decline' (El Serafy 1989, p. 10). Some fear already that the sometimes extraordinary economic growth of many a developing country has come at the expense of flogging off its natural resource base (Devarajan and Weiner 1995, p. 1).

The necessarily partial nature of GS is not too problematic if one is always aware of it for the purpose of practical GS measurement. It is worth quoting El Serafy (1993, p. 248) at some length here:

> I submit that we will never be able to make a complete list of the *physical* stock of natural resources existent at any point of time, let alone attach a *money value* to them in order that we might capture the annual changes of such a value in the flow accounts. Any pretense that we shall be able to do so shortly or even, I assert, eventually, should be dismissed as wishful thinking. What is feasible in this area is to identify in individual country situations those aspects of measurable environmental degradation that are of the most importance, and be content with adjusting the conventional accounts, particularly *income*, to reflect such partial degradation.

Fourth, the generated numbers have to be treated with care. The quality of the data is often very poor, the assumptions that give rise to the sustainability interpretation of GS are very strong, some of the practical problems are severe. Consequently, much caution is warranted in deriving policy conclusions. I have no problems with providing aid for developing countries that appear to be unsustainable if the aid is additional to existing levels. Indeed, Neumayer (1999b) calls for additional aid to some developing countries with a very low HDI to help them sustain at least this very low level of human development. In contrast, I do not think that GS is reliable enough that one could justify putting conditions on existing levels of aid to developing countries. In some sense, conditions always punish a country for undesirable behaviour. Even if one accepts the position that an aid donor has in general the right to put conditions on the use of the aid given, GS does not seem to be reliable enough to justify such a severe step now. This is especially true if GS is computed with the World Bank method, but also if it is computed with the El Serafy method.

In Section 5.1.6, the ISEW was largely dismissed as a useful indicator of WS. This was because of the lack of a sound theoretical foundation for the adjustments undertaken. In sensitivity analysis it was shown that the dismal results are reversed with more reasonable assumptions on certain key variables.

Such a position should not be misinterpreted as a defence of GNP in terms of a welfare indicator. GNP as it is currently employed in the national accounts does not and should not measure welfare. I have to admit, however, that I doubt whether one could succeed in preventing policy makers and the general public from misusing GNP as a welfare indicator. Unfortunately, the welfare interpretation of GNP has become absolute folklore and a commonplace.

Instead, GNP fulfils quite well the function it was supposed to accomplish when it was established after the Second World War: to provide an indicator for macroeconomic stabilisation policy of the economic activity in a country (Hamilton et al. 1994, p. 7), that is, an indicator of the total output produced by the economy.[35] The revised system of national accounts states this with unambiguous clarity: 'Neither gross nor net domestic product is a measure of welfare. Domestic product is an indicator of overall production activity' (United Nations 1993b, p. 41). And 'total welfare could fall even though GDP could increase in volume terms' (ibid., p. 14).[36] Carson and Young (1994, p. 112) — one the Director, the other Chief Statistician of the Bureau of Economic Analysis of the US Department of Commerce — are right in arguing that 'the factors determining welfare cannot be reduced and combined into a single measure that would command widespread agreement and acceptance. In this respect, a measure of welfare differs from the GNP'.

The methodology for measuring SS is still in development. Measuring the sustainability gap derives from a different conceptual starting point than GS. It does not attempt to measure monetarily the actual changes in the value of an economy's total capital, but measures the necessary expenditures to reach pre-specified environmental standards that are supposed to ensure SS. Because of this conceptual difference, it was argued that it would be incorrect and misleading to subtract the value of the sustainability gap from NNP to arrive at sustainable income.

The conceptual difference also has implications for whether or not the value of certain items should be computed or not. In Section 5.2.4, p. 195, it was argued that if one opts for subtracting the value of the sustainability gap from NNP, then it is warranted to deduct environmentally defensive expenditures as well. Because measuring the sustainability gap is conceptually different from GS, this does not contradict our earlier finding that defensive expenditures should not be deducted from NNP for a measure of WS.

As with practical measures of GS, the sustainability gap is also a partial indicator. As introduced in Section 5.2, it quite clearly measures only environmental sustainability. However, in principle there is no reason why a similar methodology could not be used for measuring, say, social sustainability or cultural sustainability. In practice, of course, it will presumably be very much more difficult to define these other forms of sustainability and to measure the sustainability gaps, not to speak of providing a monetary valuation for the gaps.

So far, there does not exist a comprehensive empirical study measuring SS. Faucheux and O'Connor (1998) present some model runs with preliminary and exploratory scenario results. Their 'Structural Economy–Environment Simulation Modelling' derives from a similar methodological approach as the one discussed in Section 5.2. But, as yet, no results are offered that could be interpreted as a full measure of SS. Until there exists a comprehensive study trying to measure SS, one cannot say very much on its reliability. Ideally, one would want an empirical study to apply general equilibrium modelling to avoid partial equilibrium estimates of cost curves. However, this makes the study significantly more difficult. Another major difficulty is how to allocate the costs for reaching sustainability standards for international or global environmental resources.

As explained in Section 5.2.4, the value of the sustainability gap has to be treated with great caution. Particularly, it loses much of its explanatory power if the physical measurement of the gap is not taken into account at the same time. This is because the monetary value in itself does not tell as anything about the state of the environment relative to the sustainability standards. 'We will have to continue relying on physical and other special indicators to a large extent in order to judge the performance of the economy with respect to the use of environmental resources'. Mäler (1991, p. 1) made this remark in a different context. He was referring to the practical problems of measuring WS. But his remarks equally carry over to the measurement of SS as well.

NOTES

1 The reader is reminded that the term 'genuine' was introduced by Hamilton (1994) to distinguish it from traditional saving measures which included only changes in man-made capital, but not natural, human and possibly other forms of capital.
2 Shocks are changes in parameters that are exogenous to the model.
3 There is exploration and resource discovering in the model, but all discoveries are anticipated in the sense that their discovery is correctly expected *ex ante*.
4 For simplicity it is assumed that environmental protection takes the form of post-pollution abatement and γ is taken as unchangeably given. This is for convenience only, the results derived later on do not depend on it.
5 For a more complex treatment of human capital, see Aronsson and Löfgren (1996).
6 Labour input is therefore not a control variable of the model.
7 It is disputed whether so-called transversality conditions are necessary for the maximisation over an infinite time horizon (see Chiang 1992, pp. 240ff.). However, all cases that have been discovered so far in which the transversality conditions are unnecessary, involve no time discounting (Barro and Sala-i-Martin 1995, p. 508). In our model there is time discounting, hence the transversality conditions appear to be necessary. I leave them out none the less, however, because they do not illuminate anything of special importance in the model.
8 Note that the equations of motion are just the constraints of the model and are equal to the dynamic changes in the capital stocks as explained further above. The equations of motion together with the dynamic first-order conditions are often called the Euler Equations.
9 Under perfect competition the price for the resource equals its marginal value product.
10 That is, a tax that optimally internalises the environmental externality such that social welfare is maximised. Note that in general in order to maximise welfare it will be optimal to allow for some positive level of pollution.
11 In principle, not in practice, because it is theoretically stringent to add the revenues from an optimal tax, not from an incidentally existing actual tax.
12 The same observation is made by Gomez-Lobo (1993, p. 3).
13 In our model of gNNP this holds true only after some amendments because of resource use and production causing pollution. See Appendix 3, p. 218.
14 This allocation rule is favoured by the United Nations' Statistical Department, see Bartelmus (1998, p. 294).
15 If externalities still existed, they would have to be internalised by optimal Pigouvian taxes. The revenue coming from those taxes would have to be redistributed to consumers by lump-sum subsidies.
16 In the most prominent practical attempt to measure GS (World Bank 1997a), rents from resource depletion and resource harvesting dominate the pollution effect on GS by orders of magnitude for countries with negative rates of GS, see Section 5.1.5, p. 161. Hence, at least for this study, actual changes in GS cannot be trusted to point in the right direction.
17 Strictly speaking, for our model of gNNP this simple rule only holds true with some amendments — for detail and a formal derivation, see Appendix 3, p. 218.
18 To get an impression of its importance note that about 50 per cent of this century's output growth in developed countries is attributed to disembodied technical progress (Burda and Wyplosz 1997, p. 115). Note as well, however, that these estimates usually do not consider

human capital explicitly. Doing so would lower the residual of technical progress that cannot be affiliated with one or the other form of capital.

19 World Bank (1997a) is the follow-up study to World Bank (1995a).

20 Education expenditures are used as a proxy for the increase in human capital valued at marginal investment costs in equation (5.6). Treating all education expenditures as investment is likely to overestimate the savings figures somewhat.

21 In the following, saving rates are always defined as saving divided by GNP.

22 Note that for the savings rates of all income groups and of all regional groups, countries enter the numerator with their savings and the denominator with their GNP, that is, big countries tend to dominate the aggregate figures.

23 It is interesting to compute the overestimation of resource rents due to neglecting pollution. For CO_2 emissions from oil and natural gas consumption the bias can be calculated as follows: each barrel of oil consists of approximately 0.13 tons of carbon (Poterba 1991, p. 75), each thousand cubic feet of natural gas of approximately 0.014 tons of carbon (Carbon Dioxide Information Analysis Center 1998). Taking the World Bank's estimate of US\$20 for marginal social cost per tonne of carbon, $i_A\gamma F_R$ would be about US\$2.6 per barrel of oil and US\$0.32 per thousand cubic feet of natural gas. $(P - AC)$ per barrel of oil usually lies between US\$10 and 20, $(P - AC)$ per thousand cubic feet of natural gas usually lies between US\$2 and 4. Hence the correction terms, although still rather small, are not negligible. If one used higher estimates for marginal social costs of CO_2 emissions, then taking the correction term for pollution into account would become more and more warranted.

24 This is easy to verify for the reader and is therefore not derived here, but simply stated. 'Modified' here means that it is taken into account that resource use causes pollution. Hamilton (1995, p. 64) shows that the modified Hotelling rent $(F_R - f_R - i_A\gamma F_R)$ must be bigger than g_D so that modelling discovery expenditures being dependent on the resource stock leads to higher GS than if expenditures depend on the stock of accumulated discoveries.

25 The same reasoning applies to renewable resource stocks if harvesting exceeds natural regeneration.

26 By assumption, RC accrue at the beginning of the accounting period. If RC accrue at the end of the accounting period, then $n + 1$ in equation (5.13) would be replaced by n.

27 In Indonesia, for example, the corrected income measure rises from 929 bn rupiah in 1973 quite dramatically to 3829 bn rupiah in 1974 from which it fell even more dramatically to 431 bn rupiah in 1975 (Repetto et al. 1989, p. 8).

28 Extremely high reserves to production ratios in years of unusually low production have been excluded in calculating the average in order to provide a conservative estimate.

29 The difference between GNP and GDP is that GDP includes output produced by foreigners within a country and excludes output produced by nationals abroad. The difference for developed countries is usually quite small. Whenever I speak of GNP in the following, strictly speaking it should read GNP/GDP.

30 It is somewhat ironic that Herman Daly is one of the originators of the ISEW which can be interpreted as an indicator of WS as it assumes that natural capital is perfectly substitutable. It is ironic because in all his other writings Herman Daly vehemently tries to defend the non-substitutability of natural capital.

31 Strictly speaking, Hotelling rents are defined in terms of marginal costs. The more readily available average costs are used as a proxy to marginal costs. Note that the value of resource depletion is higher with average than with marginal costs which gives the US-ISEW2 graph a downward bias.

32 For more detail on the data, see World Bank (1997a) and Kunte et al. (1997).

33 Again, the data are taken from World Bank (1997b). Counting all current education expenditures (including teachers' salaries, expenditures on textbooks and so on) as contributions towards increasing the stock of human capital is likely to overestimate this item somewhat. Hence, the US-ISEW4 graph is somewhat biased upwards.

34 The best-known study of defensive expenditures against environmental nuisances and pollution is that of Leipert (1989a, 1989b) for Germany.

35 It has to be conceded, however, that it does so rather imperfectly in developing countries where, often, much of the economic activity in the so-called informal sectors is not taken into account. Also, mainly only marketed economic activity is included since domestic and personal services produced and consumed by members of the same household or provided without payment are omitted. In addition, economic activity in the black market is by its very nature not included in GNP.

36 However, Daly's (1996, p. 112) claim that GNP bears no closer relation to welfare than the stock of gold bullion did in the age of mercantilism is vastly overdrawn. As Beckerman (1995, pp. 108f.) rightly retorts: if this was true, why do people almost always migrate towards the countries with a higher GNP and rarely vice versa? Also, as Dasgupta (1990) and Dasgupta and Weale (1992) show, at least in poor countries GNP is highly correlated with basic indicators of the quality of life such as life expectancy, infant mortality, adult literacy and indices of political and civil rights.

6. Conclusions

The objective of this book was to explore the limits of the two opposing paradigms WS and SS. The analysis was based on the economic methodology since both paradigms are essentially economic. In Chapter 2 development was defined as sustainable if it does not decrease the capacity to provide non-declining per capita utility for infinity. The meaning of this definition was explained and different forms of capital were introduced as the items that together form the capacity to provide utility. The reader is reminded of the fact that sustainability was not defined in direct utility terms, but in terms of maintaining the capacity to provide non-declining utility over time. As a consequence the current generation has already fulfilled its weak sustainability obligation if it maintains for the future the total capital stock or, for the strong sustainability obligation, the natural capital stock in addition. It has no responsibility for the way in which future generations make use of the capital stock they inherit. Indeed, it would be non sensical to put up such an additional responsibility as the current generation has no control over whether the future will use the capital stock it inherits wisely or not. One must not demand more from the current generation than it can possibly achieve.

In Section 2.1 many simplifying assumptions were introduced to make the analysis in this book possible and the insights that arise from the course of examination have to be seen in the light of these assumptions. In other words, the conclusions I arrive at will not necessarily hold if other assumptions or a broader perspective are taken. To give some examples: it was clearly stated that the analysis is confined to *economic* paradigms of sustainability; the definition of SD is anthropocentric and rules out the deep ecology view that non-human entities have value independent of human valuation; population growth was held exogenous to the analysis; finally, for a large part of the book *intra*-generational as opposed to *inter*-generational equity issues were ignored. It would be interesting to see whether and to what extent some conclusions of the book would change if one or the other of the simplifying assumptions were relaxed. I leave this to future research.

Section 2.2 discussed some ethical issues of SD. As the book takes it for granted that the current generation is committed to SD, some justification was provided that makes this commitment plausible as an ethical choice. For similar reasons two misunderstandings about what SD requires were corrected. In Section 2.3 the WS and SS were described. The fundamental divergence between the two paradigms arises from differing assumptions about the substitutability of natural capital. Because SS regards natural capital as non-substitutable it is not sufficient to maintain the total capital stock, but the natural capital stock has to be kept intact as well. It was pointed out that there exist two differing interpretations of SS in the literature: one calls for maintaining natural capital in value terms, the other for preserving the physical stock of (certain forms of) natural capital. The difference matters, as was argued in Section 4.3 — a point to which we shall come back further below.

Section 2.3 stressed the importance of the differing assumptions with respect to the substitutability of natural capital using global warming as a kind of case study. The conflict between those like William Nordhaus who come to the conclusion that only very minor greenhouse gas emission abatement is warranted and those who call for more ambitious abatement is often wrongly portrayed as a dispute about the right rate of discount to be employed. It was argued that the proper conflict must be about whether and to what extent the expected detrimental effect of global warming on natural capital can be compensated with a rise in other forms of capital. Given substitutability of natural capital, there is no need to lower the rate of discount from which more aggressive greenhouse gas emission abatement would follow. Indeed, lowering the discount rate would be inefficient as it would lead to channelling scarce resources into emission abatement which is likely to have a rate of return far inferior to other investment opportunities. As shown in Section 2.3, this conclusion does not become invalid if current and future *intra*-generational inequalities are also taken into account. As long as the substitutability of natural capital is implicitly assumed, large-scale abatement of greenhouse gas emissions to protect the natural capital stock is likely to be inferior to investment in other forms of capital. Demanding aggressive reductions in greenhouse gas emissions can only be warranted if, to some extent at least, natural capital is regarded as non-substitutable. This is an important insight as it helps to frame the discussion on global warming in a way that makes clear where the real conflict lies.

Chapter 3 addressed the question whether science can unambiguously endorse either paradigm given the starkly differing assumptions of WS and SS with regard to the substitutability of natural capital? To answer this question the substitutability of natural capital as an input into the production of consumption goods was analysed first. It was suggested that the resource optimism of WS can be summarised in four propositions that were then critically assessed one after the other. Second came the question of the substitutability of natural capital as a direct provider of utility. It was discussed whether future generations can be compensated for long-term environmental degradation. Finally, the analysis addressed the link between economic growth and environmental degradation. This question had to be addressed because in Section 2.3 the proposition that economic growth will be beneficial to the environment in the long run was considered to be the main proposition of WS, so that the paradigm has to rely less on the assumption that natural capital is substitutable as a direct provider of utility.

Chapter 3 concluded that both paradigms are non-falsifiable and that therefore science cannot unambiguously support either paradigm. The two paradigms fundamentally differ in basic claims about *future* possibilities for substitution and technical progress. While the future is not completely disconnected from the past and the present in that it is contingent on past and present decisions, we are also fundamentally uncertain and ignorant about future developments. This uncertainty and ignorance makes it impossible to falsify either paradigm of sustainability. Take resource optimism as an example: it was argued that there are powerful theoretical arguments as well as strong evidence up to now in favour of natural capital being substitutable as an input into production. But WS holds that natural capital will be substitutable at all points of time in the future as well so that only the total capital stock, not its composition, matters. In making claims about the uncertain future, substitutability really becomes an assumption and stops being a falsifiable conjecture. Science cannot unambiguously endorse this substitutability assumption as there is absolutely no guarantee that substitutability of natural capital, in spite of being logically conceivable and possible in the past, will be possible in practice or likely to occur in the future as well.

The major conclusion from Chapter 3 is an important result because of the almost dogmatic belief of the supporters of WS and SS in the basic assumptions of their paradigm. What is necessary to maintain the capacity to provide non-declining future utility is far less clear than either paradigm would want us to believe. There is reason to be concerned about the substitutability of natural capital as WS cannot be unambiguously endorsed by science. But, on the other hand, any call for the preservation of natural capital can rest on persuasive arguments at best as SS cannot be unambiguously endorsed by science either. This conclusion should remind us of our humility as human beings and should caution us against blindly following either paradigm of sustainability.

In no way should Chapter 3 be misinterpreted as saying that science cannot tell a society that is committed to SD anything about what appears to be necessary to fulfil the sustainability constraint. Chapter 4 therefore took up the discussion where it had stopped in Chapter 3 and the whole first part of Chapter 4 was devoted to elaborating whether and why a persuasive case can be made that certain forms of natural capital are in explicit need of preservation while others are not. To do so, it was necessary to go one step beyond this abstract notion of 'natural capital' and to look at specific forms of natural capital instead. Some of the existing literature all too often does not recognise that a more disaggregated approach towards natural capital is necessary since some forms of natural capital exhibit more features that distinguish them from other forms of capital and are more prone to uncertainty and ignorance.

It has been shown in Chapter 4 that some forms of natural capital that serve basic life-support functions for human beings, such as the global climate, the ozone layer and biodiversity are non-substitutable in their totality, that the accumulation of persistent and highly toxic pollutants should be prevented, and that soil fertility as well as the purity of drinking water reservoirs should be preserved. Conversely, a persuasive case can be made that there is no need for preserving natural resources as an input into the production of consumption goods and, albeit less so, as a food resource. Hence, the substitutability assumption of WS is supported more strongly from the analysis in the first part of Chapter 4 with respect to natural capital as a resource input, whereas the non-substitutability assumption of SS is supported more strongly with respect to natural capital as a provider of pollution absorptive capacity and direct utility. Another consequence is that the second interpretation of SS given in Section 2.3 is more appropriate than the first one: if certain forms of natural capital seem to be non-substitutable, but not others, and if these non-substitutable forms of natural capital are also not substitutable with other forms of *natural* capital, then it makes much more sense to target these forms directly and demand the preservation of their physical stocks than to maintain the value of the aggregate stock of natural capital.

That some forms of natural capital seem non-substitutable in their totality does not imply, however, that they are non-substitutable at the margin. The total value of natural capital is irrelevant, what counts for concrete preservation choices are marginal values. The main focus of Chapter 4 was therefore devoted to the question how these marginal choices can be informed and to what extent and at what cost preservation should take place. It was argued that marginal valuation is likely to be biased against preservation of certain forms of natural capital as the benefits of preservation are often future, uncertain, and difficult to capture because of their intangibility and because they provide positive externalities to others, whereas the costs of preservation are often definite, present and real. In some sense, the precautionary principle and the concept of SMS function as a corrective to this bias. More concretely, SMS in one interpretation deliberately ignores finite preservation costs to prevent potentially near-infinite costs of depletion. In another interpretation SMS allows the costs of preservation to exceed best available estimates of the expected benefits by a certain factor, that is, in this interpretation SMS is subjected to preservation costs not being 'too high'.

It was argued in Chapter 4 that a society that is committed to SD should not follow the first interpretation of SMS. In a world of scarce resources where all choices exclude alternatives it would be unwise to neglect the opportunity costs of preserving certain forms of natural capital. Instead, the objective should be to reduce uncertainty and ignorance and to strengthen the valuation techniques to make marginal choices better informed as well as improving the capture mechanisms so that the preserver can actually receive the benefits of preservation. In this second interpretation, SMS allows the costs of preservation to exceed the benefits of preservation by a certain factor, possibly differentiated for different forms of natural capital. The determination of this factor cannot come from scientists, it was argued, but has to come from society's political decision-making procedures.

Another thing that especially economic science can do is to show ways to achieve preservation at least cost. A society that is committed to SD should first of all abolish subsidies and abate pollution emissions that are both environmentally and economically harmful, should put more emphasis on dynamically efficient market-based instruments and should substitute ecotaxes for taxes on production factors. If these policy measures are targeted for the preservation of those forms of natural capital that are most likely in need of preservation, then a significant step towards achieving SD will have been undertaken.

Chapter 5 was devoted to an examination of whether sustainability can be measured. It was shown how a theoretically correct measure of WS is constructed and which problems practical attempts to measure GS are likely to encounter. Section 5.1.4 highlighted important practical problems that are often neglected in the relevant literature. It is crucial to be aware of these problems as they have implications on the reliability and the interpretation of practical measures of GS. In a critique of the World Bank (1997a) study it was shown how the reliability of the conclusions from this important study can be enhanced if the El Serafy method is used instead of the World Bank's method. Much more effort is still needed to improve the scope and the quality of the database from which GS is computed.

Measuring GS faces serious problems and these problems have to be taken seriously in interpreting practical measuring attempts and should make one cautious in deriving policy implications. Furthermore, one should always be aware that any practical measure is likely to be partial in the sense that it cannot encompass every form of capital. Recently, social capital has come into the focus of concern. However, it is most doubtful whether we can measure changes in social capital with a comparable reliability as we measure changes in man-made capital and natural capital.

It was argued in Section 5.1.6 that the ISEW should be dismissed as a reliable indicator of WS due to its fundamental flaws. It makes an important contribution as a comprehensive critique of the tremendously increasing application of the ISEW methodology in various country studies.

As concerns SS, Section 5.2 described how a measure of the 'sustainability gap' must start from a determination of the sustainability standards, requires good environmental information and indicator systems to measure the gap between the standards and the economy's actual performance and has to estimate the costs of closing the gap to arrive at a monetary valuation. As with WS, a number of problems with practical attempts to measure the sustainability gap were raised. As with WS, these practical problems are sometimes serious and should be taken seriously and should make one cautious in interpreting results from any study attempting to measure the 'sustainability gap'.

So far, there does not exist any such comprehensive study so that no sensitivity analysis analogous to the section on measuring WS could be undertaken. However, two recommendations were given for any attempt to provide such a study. The first one was not to deduct the value of the sustainability gap from NNP to arrive at 'sustainable income' because of the incommensurability between the way the NNP is constructed and the way the 'sustainability gap' is dependent on normative standard setting. The second one was to also deduct environmentally defensive expenditures from NNP, however, if one does not follow the first recommendation and wants to compute a 'sustainable income'. This is because actual and hypothetical measures to reach the sustainability standards should be regarded as perfect substitutes for each other.

Overall the reader might have the impression that many of the conclusions in this book are somewhat pessimistic. The reader should keep in mind, however, that the analysis here was deliberately biased towards exploring the limits of the two opposing paradigms. Exploring the prospects of both paradigms would likely lead to many insights that give rise to more hope with respect to SD. There is still a lot of room for future research and if this book could contribute a small amount to a better understanding of the relevant issues in the debate about SD it has satisfied the aspirations of its author.

Appendix 1 How Present-value Maximisation Can Lead to Extinction

Here is an example that shows how applying present-value maximisation with a constant discount rate as a decision criterion can lead to utmost unsustainability. Imagine that there are two utility paths available. The first one provides an infinite stream of utility at a constant level U_1. The second one provides a stream of utility at a constant level U_2. Assume that U_2 is higher than U_1 ($U_2 > U_1$), but that the second path provides higher utility U_2 only for a finite time T ($T < \infty$) and utility falls to zero for ever after time T. Imagine that there is a social planner who has to choose either of the two paths. The present-value of each utility path, using a constant discount rate r, is:

$$PV_1 = \int_0^\infty U_1 e^{-rt}\, dt, \quad PV_2 = \int_0^T U_2 e^{-rt}\, dt$$

If the social planner applies present-value maximisation as the decision criterion, he or she will prefer path two to path one iff

$$\int_0^T U_2 e^{-rt}\, dt > \int_0^\infty U_1 e^{-rt}\, dt$$

$$\Leftrightarrow \qquad \left[-\frac{U_2}{r} e^{-rt} \right]_0^T > \frac{U_1}{r}$$

$$\Leftrightarrow \qquad -U_2 \left[e^{-rT} - 1 \right] > U_1$$

$$\Leftrightarrow \qquad e^{-rT} < \frac{U_2 - U_1}{U_2}$$

$$\Leftrightarrow$$

$$r > \frac{\ln(U_2) - \ln(U_2 - U_1)}{T}$$

How is this result to be interpreted? Assume U_2 to be 10 per cent higher than U_1 and T to be 50 years.[1] Then r has to be just about 4.8 per cent per annum in order to choose utility path 2, that is, to prefer human extinction in 50 years time for the sake of 10 per cent higher utility over the 50 years to an infinite, albeit lower, utility stream! That is, present-value maximisation can lead to utmost unsustainability. This might appear counter-intuitive to the reader, but is a compelling consequence of the logic of discounting which gives negligible weight to the distant future. Note, however, that this result depends on the discount rate being constant throughout. If the discount rate varies with the welfare level of the future (see the discussion of the Ramsey formula in the next appendix), then present-value maximisation need not lead to unsustainability.

NOTE

1 Because U_2 and U_1 enter the formula only in the form of arguments of an ln–function, we do not have to specify them further. Any numbers that obey our assumption that U_2 is 10 per cent higher than U_1 will give the same results.

Appendix 2   The Hotelling Rule and Ramsey Rule in a Simple General Equilibrium Model

Since we are in a general equilibrium dynamic optimisation context now, we can no longer ask how a representative resource-extracting and resource-harvesting firm would maximise its profits, as we did in Section 3.2.2, p. 51, since this is only the partial equilibrium approach. Instead, here we ask how a 'social planner' would maximise social utility over infinite time.[1]

Let utility be derived from consumption only and let production be dependent on man-made capital and renewable and non-renewable resources only. There is no disembodied technical progress, that is, no technical progress that is not embodied in man-made capital. Labour input is assumed to be constant and is therefore suppressed in the production function. This is the simplest setting possible to derive the two rules.

The problem of the social planner is hence as follows:

$$\text{Max} \int_0^\infty U(C) \cdot e^{-\rho t} dt$$

$$\text{s.t.} \quad \dot{S} = -R$$

$$\dot{Z} = a(Z) - E$$

$$\dot{K} = F(K, R, E) - C - f(R) - h(E)$$

where U is utility, C is consumption, ρ is the society's pure rate of time preference, t is a time index, S is the stock of non-renewable resources, R is resource depletion, Z is the stock of renewable resources, $a(.)$ is the natural growth function of the renewable resource, E is resource harvesting, K is the stock of man-made capital, $F(.)$ is the production function, $f(.)$ is the expenditure function for non-renewable resource extraction, $h(.)$ is the expenditure function for renewable resource harvesting. $\dot{K}$ is investment in man-made capital net of depreciation. It is common to assume that renewable resources follow a logistic growth path, in which the growth rate rises with the stock of the resources initially ($a_Z > 0$ for $Z < Z'$), but falls eventually after the stock has reached a certain size Z' ($a_Z < 0$ for $Z > Z'$). A dot above a variable indicates its derivative with respect to time.

The so-called 'current value Hamiltonian' of this maximisation problem is

$$H = U(C) + \lambda\big[F(K, R, E) - C - f(R) - h(E)\big] - \mu R + \varphi\big[a(Z) - E\big]$$

Its optimal solution is characterised by the following set of 'canonical equations':[2]

i. Static first-order conditions

$$\frac{\partial H}{\partial C} = 0 \quad \Rightarrow \quad U_C = \lambda \tag{A2.i.1}$$

$$\frac{\partial H}{\partial R} = 0 \quad \Rightarrow \quad \lambda\big[F_R - f_R\big] = \mu \tag{A2.i.2}$$

$$\frac{\partial H}{\partial E} = 0 \quad \Rightarrow \quad \lambda\big[F_E - h_E\big] = \varphi \tag{A2.i.3}$$

ii. Dynamic first order conditions

$$\dot{\lambda} = \rho\lambda(t) - \frac{\partial H}{\partial K} \quad \Rightarrow \quad \dot{\lambda} = \rho\lambda - \lambda F_K \tag{A2.ii.1}$$

$$\dot{\mu} = \rho\mu(t) - \frac{\partial H}{\partial S} \quad \Rightarrow \quad \dot{\mu} = \rho\mu \tag{A2.ii.2}$$

$$\dot{\varphi} = \rho\varphi(t) - \frac{\partial H}{\partial Z} \quad \Rightarrow \quad \dot{\varphi} = \rho\varphi - \varphi a_Z \tag{A2.ii.3}$$

Plugging (A2.i.2) into (A2.ii.2) and rearranging gives:

$$\frac{\overline{\dot{\lambda}(F_R - f_R)}}{\lambda(F_R - f_R)} = \rho \quad \text{or} \quad \frac{\dot{\lambda}}{\lambda} + \frac{\overline{(F_R - f_R)}}{(F_R - f_R)} = \rho \tag{A2.1}$$

Similarly, plugging (A2.i.3) into (A2.ii.3) and rearranging gives:

$$\frac{\overline{\dot{\lambda}(F_E - h_E)}}{\lambda(F_E - h_E)} + a_Z = \rho \quad \text{or} \quad \frac{\dot{\lambda}}{\lambda} + \frac{\overline{(F_E - h_E)}}{(F_E - h_E)} + a_Z = \rho \tag{A2.2}$$

Rearranging (A2.ii.1) gives:

$$\frac{\dot{\lambda}}{\lambda} + F_K = \rho \tag{A2.3}$$

Setting (A2.1) and (A2.3) equal and noting that in a general competitive equilibrium F_K is the interest rate and F_R the price of the non-renewable resource we arrive at the desired result that the rate at which the non-renewable resource rent is rising is equal to the interest rate:

$$\frac{\overline{(F_R - f_R)}}{(F_R - f_R)} = F_K \tag{A2.4}$$

(Hotelling rule for non-renewable resources)

Similarly for renewable resources

$$\frac{\overline{(F_E - h_E)}}{(F_E - h_E)} = F_K - a_Z \tag{A2.5}$$

(Hotelling rule for renewable resources)

There is an additional term a_Z to account for the effect resource harvesting has on the stock of renewable resources and thereby on the natural growth rate of the resource (resource-harvesting effect). For $Z < Z'$, $a_Z > 0$, so resource rent is rising at less than the rate of interest. For that case resource harvesting has a negative effect on natural growth via reducing the renewable resource stock. For $Z > Z'$, $a_Z < 0$, so resource rent is rising at more than the rate of interest. For that case resource harvesting has a positive effect on natural growth via reducing the renewable resource stock.

If resource harvesting has a negative stock effect, the resource rent rises at less than the interest rate and therefore starts at a higher initial level. Intuitively, this is because the opportunity cost of current resource harvesting is higher than without the negative effect on the resource stock. Vice versa if resource harvesting exhibits a positive stock effect: the resource rent starts rising from a lower initial level because the opportunity cost of current resource harvesting is lower than without the positive effect on the resource stock.

We shall use this model now to derive another famous rule as well, the so-called Ramsey rule. Plugging (A2.i.1) in (A2.ii.1) and rearranging gives:

$$F_K = \rho - \frac{\dot{U_C}}{U_C} \qquad (A2.6)$$

Noting that $\dot{U_C} = U_{CC} \cdot \dot{C}$ and defining the elasticity of the marginal utility of consumption as

$$\eta(C) \equiv -\frac{U_{CC} \cdot C}{U_C} \qquad (A2.7)$$

equation (A2.6) can be re-expressed as

$$F_K = \rho - \frac{U_{CC} \cdot C}{U_C} \cdot \frac{\dot{C}}{C} = \rho + \eta(C) \cdot \frac{\dot{C}}{C} \quad \text{(Ramsey rule)} \qquad (A2.6')$$

How to interpret this result? If the economy is on a dynamically optimal path then the interest rate (the social discount rate) will be equal to the sum of the pure rate of time preference ρ and the product of the elasticity of the marginal utility of consumption $\eta(C)$ and the growth rate of consumption $\dot{C}/C$.

Setting the pure rate of time preference equal to zero and looking at equation (6') again reveals why discounting, properly undertaken, has some desirable ethical properties as well as was claimed in Section 2.1, p. 8: future streams of consumption should be discounted if future generations enjoy higher consumption ($\dot{C}/C > 0$) which is ethically desirable from a sustainability point of view because if later generations are 'richer' than the present generation anyway then benefits accruing to the distant future should count less than benefits accruing to the present. (Implicitly, diminishing marginal utility ($U_C > 0$, $U_{CC} < 0$) is assumed.)

NOTES

1 The same outcome would be achieved by a decentralised inter-temporal perfect competitive equilibrium (Barro and Sala-i-Martin 1995, pp. 60–71).
2 To keep the exposition as simple as possible all initial and boundary conditions are suppressed as are the equations of motion. All functions are assumed to be well behaved so the first-order conditions are necessary and sufficient for an optimum.

Appendix 3   The Hotelling Rule and the Ramsey Rule for the Model of gNNP

The derivation of GS from gNNP in Section 5.1.2, p. 142, depends on an already quite complicated dynamic optimisation model where both the Hotelling and Ramsey rule are no longer as simple as introduced in Appendix 2. Here it is shown how the rules must be amended and how to interpret the amendments.

The static and dynamic first-order conditions of interest here are

$$\frac{\partial H}{\partial C} = 0 \quad \Rightarrow \quad U_C = \lambda \tag{A3.i.1}$$

$$\frac{\partial H}{\partial R} = 0 \quad \Rightarrow \quad \lambda\left[F_R - f_R\right] + \psi\gamma\, F_R = \mu \tag{A3.i.2}$$

$$\frac{\partial H}{\partial A} = 0 \quad \Rightarrow \quad -\lambda_{iA} = \psi \tag{A3.i.5}$$

$$\dot{\lambda} = \rho\lambda(t) - \frac{\partial H}{\partial K} \quad \Rightarrow \quad \dot{\lambda} = \rho\lambda - \lambda F_K - \psi\gamma\, F_K \tag{A3.ii.1}$$

$$\dot{\mu} = \rho\mu(t) - \frac{\partial H}{\partial S} \quad \Rightarrow \quad \dot{\mu} = \rho\mu + \lambda f_S \tag{A3.ii.2}$$

Plugging (A3.i.2) into (A3.ii.2) and rearranging gives

$$\frac{\overline{\lambda(F_R - f_R - i_A\gamma\, F_R)}}{\lambda(F_R - f_R - i_A\gamma\, F_R)} = \rho + (F_R - f_R - i_A\gamma\, F_R)f_S \tag{A3.1}$$

$$\text{or} \quad \frac{\dot{\lambda}}{\lambda} + \frac{\overline{(F_R - f_R - i_A\gamma\, F_R)}}{(F_R - f_R - i_A\gamma\, F_R)} = \rho + (F_R - f_R - i_A\gamma\, F_R)f_S$$

Plugging (A3.i.5) into (A3.ii.1) and rearranging leads to

$$\frac{\dot{\lambda}}{\lambda} + F_K(1 - i_A\gamma) = \rho \qquad (A3.2)$$

Using (A3.2) and (A3.1) leads to

$$\frac{\overline{(F_R - f_R - i_A\gamma F_R)}}{(F_R - f_R - i_A\gamma F_R)} = F_K(1 - i_A\gamma) + \frac{f_S}{(F_R - f_R - i_A\gamma F_R)} \qquad (A3.3)$$

(modified Hotelling rule)

This is the modified Hotelling rule for non-renewable resources. How to interpret this result? Let us start at the left-hand side of the equation. This represents the rate of change of a modified Hotelling rent in including not only price minus marginal cost but also subtracting the marginal pollution caused by resource extraction valued at marginal abatement cost. This modification is due to resource extraction causing pollution which was not included in the simpler model of Appendix 2. As concerns the right-hand side of the equation, the first term looks familiar to the interest rate. It is corrected by the expression in brackets, however. Since $i_A\gamma$ is positive, the first term on the right-hand side is smaller than the uncorrected interest rate. The interest rate is corrected because it is taken into account that the accumulation of man-made capital to produce output causes pollution which lowers the real rate of return on capital. The second term on the right-hand side is the product of the inverse of the modified Hotelling rent and the decrease in resource-depletion costs due to a marginal increase in S, the stock of non-renewable resource (or equivalently, which might be easier to understand intuitively, the increase in resource-depletion costs due to a marginal decrease in S). This term is negative since f_S is negative. That is, the modified Hotelling rent rises at a rate less than the corrected interest rate. The reason is that resource extraction imposes a negative externality on the costs of resource extraction, that is, raises resource-extraction costs via diminishing the stock of available resources (resource-depletion effect). Because resource extraction has a negative stock effect, resource rent rises at less than the interest rate and therefore starts at a higher initial level. Intuitively, this is because the opportunity cost of current resource extraction is higher than without the negative effect on the resource stock. Re-arranging (A3.3) into (A3.4) allows for yet another interpretation:

$$F_K(1 - i_A\gamma)(F_R - f_R - i_A\gamma F_R) = \overline{(F_R - f_R - i_A\gamma F_R)} - f_S \qquad (A3.4)$$

The left-hand side of (4) can be interpreted as the marginal cost of not extracting an additional unit of the resource: it is the net resource price times the social discount rate (see the derivation of the social discount rate via the modified Ramsey rule, below). Hence it is the utility return forgone of not extracting an additional unit of the resource today, but deferring that extraction to the next period.[1] This is sometimes called the holding cost of the resource stock (Perman, Ma and McGilvray 1996, p. 129). The right-hand side of (A3.4) can be interpreted as the marginal benefit of not extracting an additional unit of the resource: the first term is the appreciation in the price of letting the additional unit of the resource in the ground; the second term is the marginal benefit of postponing an increase in the resource-depletion costs that would have occurred if the additional unit of the resource had been extracted. As was expected, therefore, we have marginal costs equal marginal benefits along the efficient resource extraction path.

Let us derive the modified Ramsey rule now. Plugging (A3.i.1) in (A3.ii.1) we arrive at:

$$F_K(1 - i_A\gamma) = \rho - \frac{\dot{U_C}}{U_C} \tag{A3.5}$$

Noting again that $\dot{U_C} = U_{CC} \cdot \dot{C}$ and defining the elasticity of the marginal utility of consumption as

$$\eta(C) \equiv -\frac{U_{CC} \cdot C}{U_C} \tag{A3.6}$$

equation (A3.5) can be re-expressed as

$$F_K(1 - i_A\gamma) = \rho - \frac{U_{CC} \cdot C}{U_C} \cdot \frac{\dot{C}}{C} = \rho + \eta(C) \cdot \frac{\dot{C}}{C} \tag{A3.5'}$$

(modified Ramsey rule)

which is the modified Ramsey rule. The only difference to the simpler rule in Appendix 2 is the term in brackets on the left-hand side of the equation. Since $i_A\gamma$, expressing the marginal pollution valued at marginal abatement costs, is positive, it says that the modified interest rate (social discount rate), which is lower than the uncorrected version of Appendix 2, should be equal to the sum of the pure rate of time preference and the product of the elasticity of the marginal utility of consumption and the growth rate of consumption. The modified interest rate (social discount rate) is lower since the accumulation of man-made capital to produce output causes pollution which lowers the real rate of return on capital and hence the interest rate. For further interpretation of the Ramsey rule, see Appendix 2.

NOTE

1   The resource owner would have got $\left[F_R - f_R - i_A \gamma F_R\right]$ for the extraction of one resource unit which would accumulate to $\left[1 + F_K(1 - i_A \gamma)\right] \cdot \left[F_R - f_R - i_A \gamma F_R\right]$ in the next period. Since the unit is not extracted, $F_K(1 - i_A \gamma)\left[F_R - f_R - i_A \gamma F_R\right]$ is just the net cost of deferring extraction.

Appendix 4 Proof of Hartwick's Rule for a Model of gNNP

To prevent the presentation from becoming too messy, the stock of non-renewable resources as well as 'human-induced' growth of renewable resources have been left out from the model of gNNP in Section 5.1.2, p. 142, for this proof of Hartwick's rule without loss of generality. The model is described below in compact terms. For more information, see Section 5.1.2.

There are four capital goods: K, man-made capital; Z, the stock of renewable resources; P, the stock of pollution; and M, the stock of human capital. The social planner intends to maximise

$$\int_0^\infty U(C,Z,P) \cdot e^{-\rho t} dt \tag{A4.1}$$

that is, the discounted utility integrated over infinite time, where utility consists of consumption C and Z and P. The dynamics of the economy are as follows:

$$\dot{Z} = a(Z) - E \tag{A4.2}$$

$$\dot{P} = \gamma F(K,E,P,M) - b(P) - A \tag{A4.3}$$

$$\dot{M} = N \tag{A4.4}$$

$$\dot{K} = F(K,E,P,M) - C - h(E,Z) - i(A) - j(N) \tag{A4.5}$$

Equation (A4.2) says that $\dot{Z}$, the change in the stock of renewable resources, is equal to natural growth $a(Z)$ minus resource harvesting E. Equation (A4.3) says that $\dot{P}$, the change in the stock of pollution, is equal to pollution $\gamma F(.)$ minus natural restoration $b(P)$ minus abatement A. Equation (A4.4) says that

M, the change in the stock of human capital, is equal to investment into human capital N. Equation (A4.5) defines K, the change in the stock of man-made capital, as a residual and as equal to output $F(K,E,P,M)$ minus consumption C, minus expenditures $h(E,Z)$ for resource harvesting, minus pollution abatement expenditures $i(A)$, and minus investment expenditures for human capital $j(N)$. Note that K is defined net of depreciation.

The so-called current-value Hamiltonian for this maximisation problem is then given by

$$H = U(C,Z,P) + \lambda[F(.) - C - h(E,Z) - i(A) - j(N)]$$
$$+ \varphi[a(Z) - E] + \psi[\gamma F(.) - b(P) - A] + \xi[N] \qquad \text{(A4.6)}$$

The control variables are C, E, A and N. The dynamics of the model are given by the canonical equations for optimisation:

i. First-order conditions for maximisation:

$$\frac{\partial H}{\partial C} = 0 \quad \Rightarrow \quad U_C = \lambda \qquad \text{(A4.i.1)}$$

$$\frac{\partial H}{\partial E} = 0 \quad \Rightarrow \quad \lambda[F_E - h_E - i_A \gamma F_E] = \varphi \qquad \text{(A4.i.2)}$$

$$\frac{\partial H}{\partial A} = 0 \quad \Rightarrow \quad -\lambda i_A = \psi \qquad \text{(A4.i.3)}$$

$$\frac{\partial H}{\partial N} = 0 \quad \Rightarrow \quad \lambda j_N = \xi \qquad \text{(A4.i.4)}$$

ii. Dynamic first-order conditions

$$\dot{\lambda} = \rho\lambda - \frac{\partial H}{\partial K} \quad \Rightarrow \quad \dot{\lambda} = \rho\lambda - \lambda F_K - \psi\gamma F_K \qquad \text{(A4.ii.1)}$$

$$\dot{\varphi} = \rho\varphi - \frac{\partial H}{\partial Z} \quad \Rightarrow \quad \dot{\varphi} = \rho\varphi + \lambda h_Z - \varphi a_Z - U_Z \qquad \text{(A4.ii.2)}$$

$$\dot{\psi} = \rho\psi - \frac{\partial H}{\partial P} \quad \Rightarrow \quad \dot{\psi} = \rho\psi - \lambda F_P - \psi(\gamma F_P - b_P) - U_P \qquad \text{(A4.ii.3)}$$

$$\dot{\xi} = \rho\xi - \frac{\partial H}{\partial M} \quad \Rightarrow \quad \dot{\xi} = \rho\xi - \lambda F_M - \psi\gamma F_M \qquad \text{(A4.ii.4)}$$

The gNNP function H^*/U_C^* for this model is given by:

$$gNNP = \frac{H^*}{U_C^*} = C^* + \frac{U_Z^*}{U_C^*} \cdot Z^* + \frac{U_P^*}{U_C^*} \cdot P^*$$

$$+ K^* + \left[F_E^* - h_E^* - i_A^* \gamma F_E^*\right] \cdot Z^* - i_A^* P^* - j_N^* M^* \qquad (A4.7)$$

$$\underbrace{}_{Genuine\,Savings}$$

Genuine saving is defined as:

$$GS \equiv K^* + \left[F_E^* - h_Z^* - i_A^* \gamma F_E^*\right] \cdot Z^* - i_A^* P^* - j_N^* M^* \qquad (A4.8)$$

Assertion: For the model described in (A4.1) to (A4.5), $GS \begin{Bmatrix} > \\ = \\ < \end{Bmatrix} 0 \Rightarrow U \begin{Bmatrix} > \\ = \\ < \end{Bmatrix} 0$.

Proof: For ease of exposition, the stars above the variables are suppressed. For simplicity, let ε be a constant such that

$$\dot{K} = -\left[F_E - h_Z - i_A \gamma F_E\right] \cdot Z + i_A P + j_N M + \varepsilon \qquad (A4.9)$$

It follows that $GS \begin{Bmatrix} > \\ = \\ < \end{Bmatrix} 0 \Leftrightarrow \varepsilon \begin{Bmatrix} > \\ = \\ < \end{Bmatrix} 0$.

Rearranging (A4.5) and differentiating with respect to time leads to:

$$\dot{C} = \dot{F} - \dot{h} - \dot{i} - \dot{j} - \ddot{K} = \qquad (A4.10)$$

$$F_K \dot{K} + (F_E - h_E)\dot{E} + F_P \dot{P} + F_M \dot{M} - h_Z \dot{Z} - i_A \dot{A} - j_N \dot{N} - \ddot{K}$$

Differentiating (A4.9) with respect to time leads to:

$$\ddot{K} = -\overline{(F_E - h_E - i_A \gamma F_E)} \dot{Z} - (F_E - h_E - i_A \gamma F_E)\ddot{Z} \qquad (A4.11)$$

$$+ \dot{i}_A \dot{P} + i_A \ddot{P} + \dot{j}_N \dot{M} + j_N \ddot{M}$$

Plugging (A4.11) into (A4.10) and cancelling out terms leads to:

$$C = F_K\,\dot{K} + i_A\gamma\,F_E\,\dot{E} + F_P\,\dot{P} + F_M\,\dot{M} - h_Z\,\dot{Z} + \overline{(F_E - h_E - i_A\gamma\,F_E)}\,\dot{Z}$$

$$- (F_E - h_E - i_A\gamma\,F_E)\,\overline{a(Z)} - i_A\,\dot{P} + i_A\gamma\,\dot{F} + i_A b_P\,\dot{P} + j_N\,\dot{M} \quad (A4.12)$$

Plugging (A4.9) into (A4.12) leads to:

$$\dot{C} = - F_K(F_E - h_E - i_A\gamma\,F_E)\dot{Z} + F_K i_A\,\dot{P} + F_K j_N\,\dot{M} + F_K\,\varepsilon + i_A\gamma\,F_E\,\dot{E}$$

$$+ F_P\,\dot{P} + F_M\,\dot{M} - h_Z\,\dot{Z} + \overline{(F_E - h_E - i_A\gamma\,F_E)}\,\dot{Z}$$

$$- (F_E - h_E - i_A\gamma\,F_E)\,\overline{a(Z)} - i_A\,\dot{P} + i_A\gamma\,\dot{F} + i_A b_P\,\dot{P} + j_N\,\dot{M} \quad (A4.13)$$

Deriving modified Hotelling rules by using (A4.i.2) to (A4.i.4) and (A4.ii.1) to (A4.ii.4) and applying the same steps as laid down in Appendix 2, p. 214, leads to:

$$\overline{(F_E - g_E - i_A\gamma\,F_E)} = (F_K(1 - i_A\gamma) - a_Z)(F_E - g_E - i_A\gamma\,F_E) - \frac{U_Z}{\lambda} \quad (A4.14)$$

$$\dot{i}_A = F_K(1 - i_A\gamma)i_A + \frac{U_P}{\lambda} + F_P - i_A\gamma\,F_P + i_A b_P \quad (A4.15)$$

$$\dot{j}_N = F_K(1 - i_A\gamma)j_N - F_M - i_A\gamma\,F_M \quad (A4.16)$$

Plugging (A4.14), (A4.15) and (A4.16) into (A4.13) and noting that $\overline{a(Z)} = a_Z\,\dot{Z}$ leads to:

$$C = -i_A\gamma\,F_K(F_E - h_E - i_A\gamma\,F_E)\dot{Z} + i_A\gamma\,F_K i_A\,\dot{P} + i_A\gamma\,F_K j_N\,\dot{M} + F_K\,\varepsilon$$

$$- i_A\gamma\,F_K\,\dot{K} - \frac{U_P}{\lambda}\dot{P} - \frac{U_Z}{\lambda}\dot{Z} \quad (A4.17)$$

Plugging (A4.9) into (A4.17) and cancelling out terms leads to:

$$\dot{C} = F_K(1 - i_A\gamma)\varepsilon - \frac{U_P}{\lambda}\dot{P} - \frac{U_Z}{\lambda}\dot{Z} \quad (A4.18)$$

Differentiating (A4.1) with respect to time leads to:

$$\dot{U} = U_C\,\dot{C} + U_Z\,\dot{Z} + U_P\,\dot{P} \quad (A4.19)$$

Plugging (A4.i.1) and (A4.18) into (A4.19) leads to

$$\dot{U} = -\lambda\left[-F_K(1-i_A\gamma)\varepsilon + \frac{U_Z}{\lambda}\dot{Z} + \frac{U_P}{\lambda}\dot{P}\right] + U_Z\dot{Z} + U_P\dot{P} \qquad \text{(A4.20)}$$

of which immediately the desired result follows:

$$\varepsilon\begin{Bmatrix}>\\=\\<\end{Bmatrix}0 \Leftrightarrow GS\begin{Bmatrix}>\\=\\<\end{Bmatrix}0 \Rightarrow \dot{U} = U_C F_K(1-i_A\gamma)\varepsilon\begin{Bmatrix}>\\=\\<\end{Bmatrix}0$$

Appendix 5 The Structure of Data Underlying World Bank (1997a)

In World Bank (1997b), the data set underlying World Bank (1997a), genuine saving is calculated in four steps from Gross Domestic Investment to Genuine Saving II:

- Gross Saving = Gross Domestic Investment – Net Foreign Borrowing + Net Official Transfers [Net Foreign Borrowing + Net Official Transfers = Current Account Balance After Official Transfers]

- Net Saving = Gross Saving – Depreciation

- Genuine Saving I = Net Saving – Resource Rents (Depletion of Natural Resources)

- Genuine Saving II = Genuine Saving I – CO_2 Damage

In the traditional national accounts current educational spending is considered as consumption. In the calculation of Extended Genuine Saving current educational spending is instead considered as an investment in human capital. The difference is relevant, since current expenditures make up more than 90 per cent of all educational expenditures (World Bank 1997a, p. 34). The extended accounting is as follows:

- Extended Domestic Investment = Gross Domestic Investment + Education Spending

- Extended Gross Saving = Extended Domestic Investment – Net Foreign Borrowing + Net Official Transfers [Net Foreign Borrowing + Net Official Transfers = Current Account Balance After Official Transfers]

- Extended Net Saving = Extended Gross Saving – Depreciation

- Extended Genuine Saving I = Extended Net Saving – Resource Rents (Depletion of Natural Resources)

- Extended Genuine Saving II = Extended Genuine Saving I – CO_2 Damage

All values are in current US$. Saving rates are defined as saving divided by GNP which is measured at market prices.

For the computation of natural resource rents the following items have been included: oil, natural gas, hard coal, brown coal, bauxite, copper, iron, lead, nickel, zinc, phosphate, tin, gold, silver and forests. Rents are usually computed as price minus average costs times production/harvest, that is, they are valued at so-called total Hotelling rent where the more readily available average costs are used as a proxy for the theoretically correct marginal costs.

The only pollutant considered so far are CO_2 emissions which are valued at US$20 per metric tonne of carbon. The value is taken from Fankhauser (1995) and is often regarded as a consensus estimate. CO_2 emissions are supposed to function as a proxy for other pollutants.

For more information on the data see World Bank (1997a) and Kunte et al. (1997), for its technical documentation.

Appendix 6 Alphabetical List of Countries in World Bank (1997a)

In brackets are the number of years with negative EGS II rates from 1970–94. Where the data series does not encompass the full 25 years (or rather the full 24 years until 1993 since for many countries the 1994 data were not available), the number of total years is stated as well.

ALGERIA (18)
ANTIGUA AND BARBUDA
              (0 out of 4)
ARGENTINA (1)
AUSTRALIA (0)
AUSTRIA (0)
BAHRAIN (8 out of 14)
BANGLADESH (17)
BARBADOS (0)
BELGIUM (0)
BELIZE (0 out of 15)
BENIN (8)
BOLIVIA (19)
BRAZIL (0)
BURKINA FASO (0)
BURUNDI (13 out of 19)
CAMEROON (6)
CANADA (0)
CENTRAL AFR. REPUBLIC (9)
CHAD (12 out of 21)
CHILE (9)
CHINA (0)
COLOMBIA (0)
CONGO (19)
COSTA RICA (0 out of 23)
COTE D'IVOIRE (10)
DENMARK (0)

DOMINICAN REPUBLIC (0)
ECUADOR (18)
EGYPT (6)
EL SALVADOR (6)
FINLAND (0)
FRANCE (0)
GABON (11)
GAMBIA (8)
GERMANY (0)
GERMANY, FORMER FRG (0)
GHANA (13)
GREECE (2)
GRENADA (0 out of 14)
GUATEMALA (7)
GUINEA (8 out of 9)
GUINEA-BISSAU (2 out of 13)
HAITI (18)
HONG KONG (0 out of 23)
INDIA (0)
INDONESIA (5)
IRAN (15 out of 19)
IRELAND (0)
ISRAEL (0)
ITALY (0)
JAMAICA (16)
JAPAN (0)
JORDAN (2 out of 12)

KENYA (1)
KOREA, REPUBLIC OF (0)
LUXEMBOURG (0)
MADAGASCAR (11)
MALAWI (12)
MALAYSIA (0)
MALI (3)
MAURITANIA (25)
MAURITIUS (2)
MEXICO (6)
MOROCCO (0)
MYANMAR (6)
NAMIBIA (5 out of 15)
NEPAL (14)
NETHERLANDS (0)
NEW ZEALAND (0)
NIGER (8)
NIGERIA (16)
NORWAY (0)
PAKISTAN (2)
PAPUA NEW GUINEA (14 out of 19)
PARAGUAY (1)
PERU (6)
PHILIPPINES (0)
PORTUGAL (0)

RWANDA (8)
SAUDI ARABIA (24)
SENEGAL (7)
SIERRA LEONE (14)
SINGAPORE (0)
SOUTH AFRICA (0)
SPAIN (0)
SRI LANKA (0)
SURINAME (7)
SWEDEN (0)
SWITZERLAND (0)
SYRIAN ARAB REP. (8 out of 22)
TAIWAN, CHINA (0)
THAILAND (0)
TOGO (1)
TRINIDAD AND TOBAGO (22)
TUNISIA (1)
TURKEY (0)
UGANDA (25)
UNITED KINGDOM (0)
UNITED STATES (0)
URUGUAY (1)
VENEZUELA (17)
ZAMBIA (23)
ZIMBABWE (2)

Appendix 7 Grouping of Countries According to World Bank (1997a)

REGIONS

Caribbean
ANTIGUA AND BARBUDA
BARBADOS
DOMINICAN REPUBLIC
GRENADA
HAITI
JAMAICA
TRINIDAD AND TOBAGO

Central America
BELIZE
COSTA RICA
EL SALVADOR
GUATEMALA

East Asia/Pacific
CHINA
HONG KONG
INDONESIA
KOREA, REPUBLIC OF
MALAYSIA
MYANMAR
PAPUA NEW GUINEA
PHILIPPINES
SINGAPORE
TAIWAN, CHINA
THAILAND

INCOME GROUPS

High-income Countries
AUSTRALIA
AUSTRIA
BELGIUM
CANADA
DENMARK
FINLAND
FRANCE
GERMANY, (FRG)
HONG KONG
IRELAND
ISRAEL
ITALY
JAPAN
LUXEMBOURG
NETHERLANDS
NEW ZEALAND
NORWAY
PORTUGAL
SINGAPORE
SPAIN
SWEDEN
SWITZERLAND
TAIWAN, CHINA
UNITED KINGDOM
UNITED STATES

REGIONS	INCOME GROUPS
High OECD	**Low-income Countries**
AUSTRALIA	BANGLADESH
AUSTRIA	BENIN
BELGIUM	BURKINA FASO
CANADA	BURUNDI
DENMARK	CAMEROON
FINLAND	CENTRAL AFR. REPUBLIC
FRANCE	CHAD
GERMANY	CHINA
GERMANY, FORMER FRG	CONGO
IRELAND	COTE D'IVOIRE
ITALY	EGYPT
JAPAN	GAMBIA, THE
LUXEMBOURG	GHANA
NETHERLANDS	GUINEA
NEW ZEALAND	GUINEA-BISSAU
NORWAY	HAITI
PORTUGAL	INDIA
SPAIN	KENYA
SWEDEN	MADAGASCAR
SWITZERLAND	MALAWI
UNITED KINGDOM	MALI
UNITED STATES	MAURITANIA
	MYANMAR
	NEPAL
Middle East	NIGER
BAHRAIN	NIGERIA
IRAN, ISLAMIC REPUBLIC OF	PAKISTAN
ISRAEL	RWANDA
JORDAN	SENEGAL
SAUDI ARABIA	SIERRA LEONE
SYRIAN ARAB REPUBLIC	SRI LANKA
	TOGO
	UGANDA
North Africa	ZAMBIA
ALGERIA	ZIMBABWE
EGYPT	
MOROCCO	
TUNISIA	

REGIONS	INCOME GROUPS

North America
MEXICO

South America
ARGENTINA
BOLIVIA
BRAZIL
CHILE
COLOMBIA
ECUADOR
PARAGUAY
PERU
SURINAME
URUGUAY
VENEZUELA

South Asia
BANGLADESH
INDIA
NEPAL
PAKISTAN
SRI LANKA

Sub-Saharan Africa
BENIN
BURKINA FASO
BURUNDI
CAMEROON
CENTRAL AFRICAN REPUBLIC
CHAD
CONGO
COTE D'IVOIRE
GABON
GAMBIA, THE
GHANA
GUINEA
GUINEA-BISSAU

Lower-middle-income Countries
ALGERIA
BELIZE
BOLIVIA
COLOMBIA
COSTA RICA
DOMINICAN REPUBLIC
ECUADOR
EL SALVADOR
GRENADA
GUATEMALA
INDONESIA
IRAN, ISLAMIC REPUBLIC
JAMAICA
JORDAN
MOROCCO
NAMIBIA
PAPUA NEW GUINEA
PARAGUAY
PERU
PHILIPPINES
SURINAME
SYRIAN ARAB REPUBLIC
THAILAND
TUNISIA
TURKEY
VENEZUELA

Upper-middle-income Countries
ANTIGUA AND BARBUDA
ARGENTINA
BAHRAIN
BARBADOS
BRAZIL
CHILE
GABON
GREECE

REGIONS	**INCOME GROUPS**
KENYA	KOREA, REPUBLIC OF
MADAGASCAR	MALAYSIA
MALAWI	MAURITIUS
MALI	MEXICO
MAURITANIA	SAUDI ARABIA
MAURITIUS	SOUTH AFRICA
NAMIBIA	TRINIDAD AND TOBAGO
NIGER	URUGUAY
NIGERIA	
RWANDA	
SENEGAL	
SIERRA LEONE	
SOUTH AFRICA	
TOGO	
UGANDA	
ZAMBIA	
ZIMBABWE	

Western Europe
GREECE
TURKEY

Appendix 8 Frequency of Negative Extended Genuine Saving II Rates in World Bank (1997a)

Out of 25 possible years, the following countries had negative EGS II rates in World Bank (1997a) for

0 years:	45 countries in total: All high-income countries, plus Antigua and Barbuda, Barbados, Belize, Brazil, Burkina Faso, China, Colombia, Costa Rica, Dominican Republic, Grenada, India, Israel, Malaysia, Morocco, Philippines, South Africa, Sri Lanka, Thailand, Turkey
1–3 years:	13 countries in total: Argentina, Greece, Guinea-Bissau, Jordan, Kenya, Mali, Mauritius, Pakistan, Paraguay, Togo, Tunisia, Uruguay, Zimbabwe
4–6 years:	8 countries in total: Cameroon, Egypt, El Salvador, Indonesia, Mexico, Myanmar, Namibia, Peru
7–10 years:	13 countries in total: Bahrain, Benin, Central African Republic, Chile, Côte d'Ivoire, Gambia, Guatemala, Guinea, Niger, Rwanda, Senegal, Suriname, Syria
> 10 years:	24 countries in total: Algeria, Bangladesh, Bolivia, Burundi, Chad, Congo, Ecuador, Gabon, Ghana, Haiti, Iran, Jamaica, Madagascar, Malawi, Mauritania, Nepal, Nigeria, Papua New Guinea, Saudi Arabia, Sierra Leone, Trinidad and Tobago, Uganda, Venezuela, Zambia

Appendix 9 Sources of Data for Computing User Costs According to the El Serafy Method

To compute user costs for resource depletion according to the El Serafy method, one needs to establish four different terms:

- $P - AC$, net resource price
- R, resource depletion (production)
- r, the discount rate
- n, the number of years reserves would last at current production rates (reserves to production ratio).

$(P - AC)$ was computed by dividing resource rents in World Bank (1997a) through production. If not stated otherwise in the text, the discount rate was assumed to be 4 per cent per annum This is the rate World Bank (1997a) uses for wealth estimations (for a justification, see Kunte et al. 1997, pp. 8f.).

OIL
Production figures covering 1970–94 came from British Petroleum (1980, 1986, 1997) with the exception of Bolivia and Congo. For Congo, production data for 1970–79 came from Petroleum Publishing (various years) and from British Petroleum (1986, 1997) for 1980–94. For Bolivia, production for 1970–94 was taken from Financial Times Oil and Gas (various years).

With the exception of Bolivia, Congo, and Trinidad and Tobago, proven reserves were taken from OPEC (1979) for the years 1970–79 and from OPEC (1997) for 1980–94. For Bolivia, Congo, and Trinidad and Tobago, reserves were taken from Energy Information Administration (1991) for 1970–91 and from Petroleum Publishing (various years) for 1992–94.

NATURAL GAS
Production data covering the period 1970–94 came from OPEC (various years) with the exception of Congo, Ecuador and Gabon. For Ecuador production data for 1991–94, for Gabon production data for 1971–73 and for

Congo production data for the period 1970–94 came from United Nations Yearbook (various years). For 1970–90 production data for Ecuador and for 1974–94 production data for Gabon came from OPEC (various years).

With the exception of Bolivia and Congo proven reserves were taken from OPEC (1980) for 1971–79 and from OPEC (1997) for the years 1980–94. For Bolivia and Congo proven reserves for the period 1970–94 were taken from Petroleum Publishing (various years).

NON-ENERGY RESOURCES
For bauxite, copper, gold and tin production, data for 1981–94 came from World Bureau of Metal Statistics (1991, 1997). For bauxite, copper and tin, data for 1970–80 came from World Bureau of Metal Statistics (1975, 1979, 1984). For gold, data for 1970–80 came from Financial Times Mining (various years). For 1970–94, iron ore production data came from United Nations (1977, 1986, 1996).

Time-series individual country data for proven reserves of non-energy resources are notoriously difficult to get hold of. A couple of short-cut formulas had to be applied therefore where direct data were not available. The bias is likely to be small, however, since according to Bill Kirk from the US Bureau of Mines non-energy reserves tend to be relatively constant over time.

Bauxite reserve data for Jamaica came from US Bureau of Mines (various years) with the help of the Bureau's bauxite specialist Pat Plunkert. Copper reserve data for Zambia came from US Bureau of Mines (various years). For Papua New Guinea individual country reserve data for copper could only be established for 1978–81 and 1990. For 1976–77 reserve data were approximated by world reserves in these years times the 1978 share of the country's reserves of world reserves. The same applies to 1982–86 using the 1981 share and to 1987–89 and 1991–94 using the 1990 share. Individual gold reserve data for Ghana and Papua New Guinea could not be established. For Ghana, gold reserves for 1970–94 were approximated by world reserves in these years times the 1994 share of the country's reserves of world reserves which was provided by George J. Coackley, the US Bureau of Mines' country expert for Ghana. For Papua New Guinea it had to be assumed, somewhat arbitrarily, that its reserve share of world gold reserves for 1976–94 were equal to its production share of world gold production in the corresponding years. Iron ore reserve data for Mauritania are due to personal information from Bill Kirk from the US Bureau of Mines. Tin reserve data for Bolivia for 1978–94 came from US Bureau of Mines (various years). For 1970–77 reserve data were approximated by world reserves in these years times the 1978 share of the country's reserves of world reserves. Where necessary, world reserves were taken from US Bureau of Mines (various years).

Bibliography

Aage, Hans (1984), 'Economic arguments on the sufficiency of natural resources', *Cambridge Journal of Economics*, **8** (1), 105–13.

Aaheim, Asbjorn and Karine Nyborg (1995), 'On the Interpretation and Applicability of a "Green National Product"', *Review of Income and Wealth*, **41** (1), 57–71.

Adelman, M.A. (1990), 'Mineral Depletion, With Special Reference to Petroleum', *Review of Economics and Statistics*, **72** (1), 1–10.

Adelman, M.A. (1995), *The Genie out of the Bottle: World Oil since 1970*, Cambridge (Mass.): MIT Press.

Adriaanse, Albert (1993), *Policy Performance Indicators*, The Hague: Ministry of Housing, Planning and the Environment.

Adriaanse, Albert, Stefan Bringezu, Allen Hammond, Yuichi Moriguchi, Eric Rodenburg, Donald Rogich and Helmut Schütz (1997), *Resource Flows: the Material Basis of Industrial Economies*, Washington DC: World Resources Institute.

Agarwal, Anil and Suita Narain (1991), *Global Warming in an Unequal World*, New Delhi: Centre for Science and Environment.

Albers, Heide J., Anthony C. Fisher and W. Michael Hanemann (1996), 'Valuation and Management of Tropical Forests', *Environmental and Resource Economics*, **8** (1), 39–61.

Alfsen, Knut H. and Hans Viggo Saebo (1993), 'Environmental Quality Indicators: Background, Principles and Examples from Norway', *Environmental and Resource Economics*, **3** (5), 415–35.

Allen, R.G.D. (1938), *Mathematical Analysis for Economists*, London: Macmillan.

Ando, Amy W. (1998), 'Ecosystems, Interest Groups, and the Endangered Species Act', *Resources*, **130**, 7–9.

Anielski, Mark (1999), *The 1998 US Genuine Progress Indicator (GPI)*, San Francisco: Redefining Progress.

Aronsson, Thomas and Karl-Gustaf Löfgren (1993), 'Welfare Measurement of Technological and Environmental Externalities in the Ramsey Growth Model', *Natural Resource Modeling*, **7** (1), 1–13.

Aronsson, Thomas and Karl-Gustaf Löfgren (1995), 'National Product Related Welfare Measures in the Presence of Technological Change: Externalities and Uncertainty', *Environmental and Resource Economics*, **5** (4), 321–32.

Aronsson, Thomas and Karl-Gustaf Löfgren (1996), 'Social Accounting and Welfare Measurement in a Growth Model with Human Capital', *Scandinavian Journal of Economics*, **98** (2), 185–201.

Arrow, Kenneth J., Bert Bolin, Robert Costanza, Partha Dasgupta, Carl Folke, C.S. Holling, Bengt-Owe Jansson, Simon Levin, Karl-Göran Mäler, Charles Perrings and David Pimental (1995), 'Economic Growth, Carrying Capacity, and the Environment', *Science*, **268**, 520–21, also published in *Ecological Economics*, **15** (2), 91–5.

Arrow, Kenneth J. and Anthony C. Fisher (1974), 'Environmental Preservation, Uncertainty, and Irreversibility', *Quarterly Journal of Economics*, **88** (2), 312–19.

Arrow, Kenneth J. and Leonid Hurwicz (1972), 'An Optimality Criterion for Decision-making Under Ignorance', in C.F. Carter and J.L. Ford (eds), *Uncertainty and Expectations in Economics: Essays in Honour of G.L.S. Shackle*, Oxford: Basil Blackwell, pp. 1–11.

Arrow, Kenneth J., R. Solow, P.R. Portney, E.E. Leamer, R. Radner and H. Schuman (1993), 'Report of the National Oceanic and Atmospheric Administration (NOAA) Panel on Contingent Valuation', *Federal Register*, **58**, 4601–14.

Asheim, Geir B. (1986), 'Hartwick's Rule in Open Economies', *Canadian Journal of Economics*, **19** (3), 395–402.

Asheim, Geir B. (1994a), 'Net National Product as an Indicator of Sustainability', *Scandinavian Journal of Economics*, **96** (2), 257–65.

Asheim, Geir B. (1994b), *The Weitzman Foundation of NNP with Nonconstant Interest Rates*, Working Paper No. 75, Munich: Center for Economic Studies, University of Munich, also printed in *Scandinavian Journal of Economics*, **99** (3), 1997, 355–70.

Asheim, Geir B. (1996), 'Capital Gains and Net National Product in Open Economies', *Journal of Public Economics*, **59** (3), 419–34.

Atkinson, A.B. (1983), *The Economics of Inequality*, Oxford: Oxford University Press.

Atkinson, Giles (1995), *Measuring Sustainable Economic Welfare: A Critique of the UK ISEW*, Working Paper GEC 95-08, Norwich and London: Centre for Social and Economic Research on the Global Environment.

Atkinson, Giles, Richard Dubourg, Kirk Hamilton, Mohan Munasinghe, David Pearce and Carlos Young (1997), *Measuring Sustainable Development — Macroeconomics and the Environment*, Cheltenham, UK and Lyme, US: Edward Elgar.

240   *Weak versus Strong Sustainability*

Atkinson, Giles and Kirk Hamilton (1996), 'Sustainable Development and Flows of Assets in International Trade', mimeo, Norwich and London: Centre for Social and Economic Research on the Global Environment.

Ausubel, Jesse H. (1995), 'Technical Progress and Climatic Change', *Energy Policy*, **23** (4/5), 411–16.

Ayres, A. and J. Walter (1991), 'The Greenhouse Effect: Damages, Costs and Abatement', *Environmental and Resource Economics*, **1** (3), 237–70.

Ayres, Robert U. (1997), 'Comments on Georgescu-Roegen', *Ecological Economics*, **22** (3), 285–87.

Ayres, Robert U. and Steven M. Miller (1980), 'The Role of Technological Change', *Journal of Environmental Economics and Management*, **7** (4), 353–71.

Azar, Christian and Thomas Sterner (1996), 'Discounting and Distributional Considerations in the Context of Global Warming', *Ecological Economics*, **19** (2), 169–84.

Baldwin, Richard (1995), 'Does Sustainability Require Growth?', in Ian Goldin and L. Alan Winters (eds), *Economics of Sustainable Growth*, Cambridge: Cambridge University Press, pp. 51–77.

Barbier, Edward B. (1989), *Economics, Natural-resource Scarcity and Development*, London: Earthscan.

Barbier, Edward B. (1994a), 'Natural Capital and the Economics of Environment and Development', in A. Jansson, M. Hammer, C. Folke and R. Costanza (eds), *Investing in Natural Capital: The Ecological Economics Approach to Sustainability*, Washington DC: Island Press, pp. 291–322.

Barbier, Edward B. (1994b), 'Valuing Environmental Functions: Tropical Wetlands', *Land Economics*, **70** (2), 155–73.

Barbier, Edward B., David W. Pearce and Anil Markandya (1990), 'Environmental Sustainability and Cost–Benefit Analysis', *Environment and Planning A*, **22** (9), 1259–66.

Barbier, Edward B., Joanne C. Burgess and Carl Folke (1994), *Paradise Lost? — The Ecological Economics of Biodiversity*, London: Earthscan.

Barde, Jean-Philippe (1996), 'Environmental Taxation: Experience in OECD Countries', in Timothy O'Riordan (ed.), *Ecotaxation*, London: Earthscan, pp. 223–45.

Barnett, Harold J. (1979), 'Scarcity and Growth Revisited', in V. Kerry Smith (ed.), *Scarcity and Growth Reconsidered*, Baltimore: Johns Hopkins University Press, pp. 163–217.

Barnett, Harold J. and Chandler Morse (1963), *Scarcity and Growth: The Economics of Natural Resource Availability*, Baltimore: Johns Hopkins University Press.

Barney, Gerald O. (1980), *The Global 2000 Report to the President of the US — Entering the 21st Century*, A Report Prepared by the Council on Environmental Quality and the Department of State, New York: Pergamon Press.

Barrett, Scott (1992), 'Economic Growth and Environmental Preservation', *Journal of Environmental Economics and Management*, **23** (3), 289–300.

Barrett, Scott and Kathryn Graddy (1997), 'Freedom, Growth, and the Environment', mimeo, London: London Business School.

Barro, Robert J. (1974), 'Are Government Bonds Net Wealth?', *Journal of Political Economy*, **82** (6), 1095–17.

Barro, Robert J. (1996), 'Democracy and Growth', *Journal of Economic Growth*, **1** (1), 1–27.

Barro, Robert J. and Xavier Sala-i-Martin (1995), *Economic Growth*, New York: McGraw-Hill.

Barry, Brian (1991), *Liberty and Justice: Essays in Political Theory 2*, Oxford: Clarendon Press.

Bartelmus, Peter (1998), 'The Value of Nature: Valuation and Evaluation in Environmental Accounting', in K. Uno and P. Bartelmus (eds), *Environmental Accounting in Theory and Practice*, Dordrecht: Kluwer, pp. 263–307.

Bartelmus, Peter, Ernst Lutz and Stefan Schweinfest (1993), 'Integrated Environmental and Economic Accounting: A Case Study of Papua New Guinea', in Ernst Lutz (ed.), *Toward Improved Accounting for the Environment — An UNSTAT–World Bank Symposium*, Washington DC: World Bank, pp. 108–43.

Bartelmus, Peter and Jan van Tongeren (1993), 'Selected Issues in Integrated Environmental-Economic Accounting', in Alfred Franz and Carsten Stahmer (eds), *Approaches to Environmental Accounting: Proceedings of the IARIW Conference on Environmental Accounting 1991*, Heidelberg: Springer, pp. 488–510.

Bateman, Ian, Alistair Munro, Bruce Rhodes, Chris Starmer and Robert Sugden (1997), 'Does Part–Whole Bias Exist? An Experimental Investigation', *Economic Journal*, **107** (441), 322–32.

Baumol, William J. (1986), 'On the Possibility of Continuing Expansion of Finite Resources', *Kyklos*, **39** (2), 167–79.

Becker, Gary S. and George J. Stigler (1977), 'De Gustibus Non Est Disputandum', *American Economic Review*, **67** (1), 76–90.

Becker, Robert A. (1982), 'Intergenerational Equity: The Capital-Environment Trade-Off', *Journal of Environmental Economics and Management*, **9** (2), 165–85.

Beckerman, Wilfred (1972), 'Economists, Scientists, and Environmental Catastrophe', *Oxford Economic Papers*, **24** (3), 327–44.

Beckerman, Wilfred (1974), *In Defence of Economic Growth*, London: Jonathan Cape.

242   *Weak versus Strong Sustainability*

Beckerman, Wilfred (1992a), *Economic Development and the Environment — Conflict or Complementarity?*, Working Paper No. 961, Washington DC: World Bank.

Beckerman, Wilfred (1992b), 'Economic Growth and the Environment: Whose Growth? Whose Environment?', *World Development*, **20** (4), 481–96.

Beckerman, Wilfred (1993), 'The Environmental Limits to Growth: A Fresh Look', in Herbert Giersch (ed.), *Economic Progress and Environmental Concerns*, Berlin et al.: Springer, pp. 3–23.

Beckerman, Wilfred (1994), '"Sustainable Development": Is it a Useful Concept?', *Environmental Values*, **3** (3), 191–209.

Beckerman, Wilfred (1995), *Small is Stupid — Blowing the Whistle on the Greens*, London: Duckworth.

Beckerman, Wilfred and Joanna Pasek (1997), 'Plural Values and Environmental Valuation', *Environmental Values*, **6** (1), 65–86.

Beirat Umweltökonomische Gesamtrechnung (1995), 'Umweltöko-nomische Gesamtrechnung — Zweite Stellungnahme des Beirats 'Umweltökonomische Gesamtrechnung' beim Bundesministerium für Umwelt, Naturschutz und Reaktorsicherheit', *Zeitschrift für angewandte Umweltforschung*, **8** (4), 455–76.

Bell, David E. (1982), 'Regret in Decision Making under Uncertainty', *Operations Research*, **30** (5), 961–81.

Beltratti, Andrea (1995), 'Sustainable Growth: Models and Policy Implications', in Gianna Boero and Aubrey Silberston (eds), *Environmental Economics*, Basingstoke: Macmillan, pp. 296–315.

Beltratti, Andrea, Graciela Chichilnisky and Geoffrey Heal (1998), 'Uncertain Preferences and Conservation', in Graciela Chichilnisky, Geoffrey Heal and Alessandro Vercelli (eds), *Sustainability: Dynamics and Uncertainty*, Dordrecht: Kluwer Academic, pp. 257–76

Berck, Peter (1995), 'Empirical Consequences of the Hotelling Principle', in Daniel W. Bromley (ed.), *Handbook of Environmental Economics*, Cambridge: Cambridge University Press, pp. 202–21.

Berck, Peter and Michael Roberts (1996), 'Natural Resource Prices: Will They Ever Turn Up?', *Journal of Environmental Economics and Management*, **31** (1), 65–78.

Berkes, Firket and Carl Folke (1992), 'A Systems Perspective on the Interrelations between Natural, Human-made and Cultural Capital', *Ecological Economics*, **5** (1), 1–8.

Berkes, Firket and Carl Folke (1994), 'Investing in Cultural Capital for Sustainable Use of Natural Capital', in A. Jansson, M. Hammer, C. Folke and R. Costanza (eds), *Investing in Natural Capital: The Ecological Economics Approach to Sustainability*, Washington DC: Island Press, pp. 128–49.

Berndt, Ernst R. and Barry C. Field (eds) (1981), *Modeling and Measuring Natural Resource Substitution*, Cambridge (Mass.): MIT Press.

Berndt, Ernst R. and David O. Wood (1975), 'Technology, Prices, and the Derived Demand for Energy', *Review of Economics and Statistics*, **57** (3), 259–68.

Berndt, Ernst R. and David O. Wood (1979), 'Engineering and Econometric Interpretations of Energy–Capital Complementarity', *American Economic Review*, **69** (3), 342–54.

Biancardi, C., E. Tiezzi and S. Ulgiati (1993), 'Complete Recycling of Matter in the Frameworks of Physics, Biology and Ecological Economics', *Ecological Economics*, **8** (3), 1–5.

Biancardi, C., E. Tiezzi and S. Ulgiati (1996), 'The "Recycle of Matter" Debate. Physical Principles versus Practical Impossibility', *Ecological Economics*, **19** (3), 195–96.

Binswanger, Mathias (1993), *Gibt es eine Entkopplung des Wirtschaftswachstums von Naturverbrauch und Umweltbelastungen?*, Diskussionsbeitrag No. 12, St. Gallen: Institut für Wirtschaft und Ökologie, Hochschule St. Gallen.

Bishop, Richard C. (1978), 'Endangered Species and Uncertainty: The Economics of a Safe Minimum Standard', *American Journal of Agricultural Economics*, **60** (1), 10–18.

Bishop, Richard C. (1979), 'Endangered Species, Irreversibility, and Uncertainty: A Reply', *American Journal of Agricultural Economics*, **61** (2), 376–79.

Blamey, R.K. and Mick S. Common (1994), 'Sustainability and the Limits to Pseudo Market Valuation', in J.C.J.M. van den Bergh and J. van der Straaten (eds), *Concepts and Methods for Sustainable Development: Critique and New Approaches*, New York: Island Press, pp. 165–205.

Bodansky, Daniel (1991), 'Scientific Uncertainty and the Precautionary Principle', *Environment*, **33** (7), 4–5 and 43–4.

Boehmer-Christiansen, Sonja (1994), 'The Precautionary Principle in Germany — Enabling Government', in Timothy O'Riordan and James Cameron (eds), *Interpreting the Precautionary Principle*, London: Earthscan, pp. 31–60.

Bolleyer, Rita and Walter Radermacher (1993), 'Aufbau der Umweltökonomischen Gesamtrechnung — Ein Bericht aus der Werkstatt', *Wirtschaft und Statistik* (2), 138–52.

Bongaarts, John (1994), 'Can the Growing Human Population Feed Itself? — As Human Numbers Surge Toward 10 Billion, Some Experts Are Alarmed, Others Optimistic. Who Is Right?', *Scientific American*, **270** (3), 18–24.

244   *Weak versus Strong Sustainability*

Boserup, Ester (1990), *Economic and Demographic Relationships in Development*, Baltimore: The Johns Hopkins University Press.

Bovenberg, A. Lans and Lawrence H. Goulder (1995), *Costs of Environmentally Motivated Taxes in the Presence of Other Taxes: General Equilibrium Analyses*, Working Paper No. 5117, Cambridge (Mass.): National Bureau of Economic Research, also printed in *National Tax Journal*, **50** (1), 1997, 59–87.

Bovenberg, A. Lans and Ruud A. de Mooij (1995), 'Do Environmental Taxes Yield a Double-dividend?', in Gianna Boera and Aubrey Silberston (eds), *Environmental Economics: Proceedings of a Conference held by the Confederation of European Economics Association at Oxford 1993*, London: Macmillan, pp. 52–69.

Bovenberg, A. Lans and Sjak Smulders (1995), 'Environmental Quality and Pollution-augmenting Technological Change in a Two-sector Endogenous Growth Model', *Journal of Public Economics*, **57** (3), 369–91.

Bovenberg, A. Lans and Frederick van der Ploeg (1998), 'Consequences of Environmental Tax Reform for Unemployment and Welfare', *Environmental and Resource Economics*, **12** (2), pp. 137–50.

Boyce, James K. (1994), 'Inequality as a Cause of Environmental Degradation', *Ecological Economics*, **11** (3), 169–78.

Boyd, James (1998), *Searching for the Profit in Pollution Prevention: Case Studies in the Corporate Evaluation of Environmental Opportunities*, Discussion Paper 98-30, Washington DC: Resources for the Future

Boyle, Kevin J., William H. Desvouges, F. Reed Johnson, Richard W. Dunford and Sara P. Hudson (1994), 'An Investigation of Part–Whole Biases in Contingent Valuation Studies', *Journal of Environmental Economics and Management*, **27** (1), 64–83.

Boyle, Stewart (1993), 'Toward a Fossil Free Future: The Technical and Economic Feasibility of Phasing Out Global Fossil Fuel Use', in N. Nakicenovic, W.D. Nordhaus, R. Richels and F.L. Toth (eds), *Integrative Assessment of Mitigation, Impacts and Adaptation to Climate Change*, Proceedings of a Workshop held on 13–15 October 1993, Laxenburg: International Institute for Applied Systems Analysis, pp. 353–377.

Brekke, Kjell Arne (1997), 'Hicksian Income from Resource Extraction in an Open Economy', *Land Economics*, **73** (4), 516–27.

Bringezu, Stefan and Helmut Schütz (1996), 'Analyse des Stoffverbrauchs der deutschen Wirtschaft — Status quo, Trends und mögliche Prioritäten für Maßnahmen zur Erhöhug der Ressourcenproduktivität', in Jörg Köhn and Maria Welfens (eds), *Neue Ansätze in der Umweltökonomie*, Marburg: Metropolis-Verlag, pp. 230–51.

British Petroleum (various years), *BP Statistical Review of World Energy*, London: British Petroleum.

Bromley, Daniel W. (1989a), 'Entitlements, Missing Markets, and Environmental Uncertainty', *Journal of Environmental Economics and Management*, **17** (2), 181–94.

Bromley, Daniel W. (1989b), *The Management of Common Property Natural Resources: Some Conceptual and Operational Fallacies*, Discussion Paper 57, Washington DC: World Bank.

Brookes, Len (1990), 'The Greenhouse Effect: The Fallacies in the Energy Efficiency Solution', *Energy Policy*, **18** (2), 199–201.

Brookes, Len (1992), 'Energy Efficiency and Economic Fallacies: A Reply', *Energy Policy*, **20** (5), 390–93.

Broome, John (1992), *Counting the Cost of Global Warming*, Cambridge: Cambridge University Press.

Broome, John (1996), 'The Welfare Economics of Population', *Oxford Economic Papers*, **48** (2), 177–93.

Brouwer, Roy and Christian Leipert (1998), *The Role of Environmental Protection Expenditures in a System of Integrated Economic and Environmental Accounting: Theory, Practice and Future Prospects*, Working Paper GEC 98-01, Norwich and London: Centre for Social and Economic Research on the Global Environment.

Brown, Gardner M. and Barry C. Field (1978), 'Implications of Alternative Measures of Natural Resource Scarcity', *Journal of Political Economy*, **86** (2), 229–43.

Brown, Gardner M. and Barry C. Field (1979), 'The Adequacy of Measures for Signalling the Scarcity of Natural Resources', in V. Kerry Smith (ed.), *Scarcity and Growth Reconsidered*, Baltimore: Johns Hopkins University Press, pp. 218–48.

Brown, Katrina, David W. Pearce, Charles Perrings and Timothy Swanson (1994), *Economics and the Conservation of Global Biological Diversity*, Working Paper No. 2, Washington DC: Global Environment Facility.

Bryant, Chris and Paul Cook (1992), 'Environmental Issues and the National Accounts', *Economic Trends*, **469**, 99–122.

Burda, Michael and Charles Wyplosz (1997), *Macroeconomics — a European Text*, Second Edition, Oxford: Oxford University Press.

Burtraw, D. and M.A. Toman (1997), *The Benefits of Reduced Air Pollutants in the US from Greenhouse Gas Mitigation Policies*, Discussion Paper 98-01, Washington DC: Resources for the Future.

Cameron, James and Will Wade-Gery (1995), 'Addressing Uncertainty: Law, Policy and the Development of the Precautionary Principle', in Bruno Dente (ed.), *Environmental Policy in Search of New Instruments*, Dordrecht: Kluwer, pp. 95–142.

Cansier, Dieter (1995), *Nachhaltige Umweltnutzung als neues Leitbild der Umweltpolitik*, Diskussionsbeitrag No. 41, Tübingen: Wirtschaftswissenschaftliche Fakultät der Eberhard-Karls-Universität Tübingen.

Cansier, Dieter and Wolfgang Richter (1995), 'Erweiterung der Volkswirtschaftlichen Gesamtrechnung um Indikatoren für eine nachhaltige Umweltnutzung', *Zeitschrift für Umweltpolitik und Umweltrecht*, **18** (2), 231–60.

Carbon Dioxide Information Analysis Center (1998): *Frequently Asked Questions*, http://cdiac.esd.ornl.gov/cdiac/home.html, Oak Ridge: Carbon Dioxide Information Analysis Center.

Carpenter, Richard A. (1994), 'Limitations in Measuring Ecosystem Sustainability', in Thaddeus C. Trzyna (ed.), *A Sustainable World: Defining and Measuring Sustainable Development*, London: Earthscan, pp. 175–97.

Carraro, Carlo, Marzio Galeotti and Massimo Gallo (1996), 'Environmental Taxation and Unemployment: Some Evidence on the "Double-dividend Hypothesis" in Europe', *Journal of Public Economics*, **62** (2), 141–81.

Carson, Carol S. and Allan H. Young (1994), 'The ISEW from a National Accounting Perspective', in Clifford W. Cobb and John B. Cobb (eds), *The Green National Product: A Proposed Index of Sustainable Economic Welfare*, Lanham: University Press of America, pp. 111–33.

Carson, Rachel (1962), *The Silent Spring*, New York: Fawcett Crest.

Carson, Richard T. and Robert Cameron Mitchell (1995), 'Sequencing and Nesting in Contingent Valuation Surveys', *Journal of Environmental Economics and Management*, **28** (2), 155–73.

Castaneda, Beatriz E. (1998), *An Index of Sustainable Economic Welfare (ISEW) for Chile*, Solomons: University of Maryland, Institute for Ecological Economics.

Castle, Emery N. (1997), 'A Comment on Georgescu-Roegen, Daly, Solow and Stiglitz', *Ecological Economics*, **22** (3), 305–6.

Castle, Emery N. and Robert P. Berrens (1993), 'Endangered Species, Economic Analysis, and the Safe Minimum Standard', *Northwest Environmental Journal*, **9** (1/2), 108–30.

Cavendish, William and Dennis Anderson (1994), 'Efficiency and Substitution in Pollution Abatement', *Oxford Economic Papers*, **46** (5), 774–99.

Chang, Kuo-Ping (1994), 'Capital-Energy Substitution and the Multi-Level CES Production Funtion', *Energy Economics*, **16** (1), 22–6.

Chapman, D., V. Suri and S.G. Hall (1995), 'Rolling DICE for the Future of the Planet', *Contemporary Economic Policy*, **13** (3), 1–9.

Chiang, Alpha C. (1984), *Fundamental Methods of Mathematical Economics*, New York: McGraw-Hill.

Chiang, Alpha C. (1992), *Elements of Dynamic Optimization*, New York: McGraw-Hill.

Chichilnisky, Graciela (1996), 'An Axiomatic Approach to Sustainable Development', *Social Choice and Welfare*, **13** (2), 231–57.

Chichilnisky, Graciela and Geoffrey Heal (1983): 'Energy–Capital Substitution: A General Equilibrium Analysis', Collaborative Paper, International Institute for Applied Systems Analysis Laxenburg, reprinted in Geoffrey Heal (ed.) (1993), *The Economics of Exhaustible Resources*, Aldershot, UK and Brookfield, US: Edward Elgar, pp. 390–401.

Chichilnisky, Graciela and Geoffrey Heal (1993), 'Global Environmental Risks', *Journal of Economic Perspectives*, **7** (4), 65–86.

Ciriacy-Wantrup, S.V. (1952), *Resource Conservation: Economics and Policies*, Berkeley: University of California Press.

Ciriacy-Wantrup, S.V. (1971), 'Conservation of the California Tule Elk: A Socioeconomic Study of a Survival Problem', *Biological Conservation*, **3** (1), 23–32.

Clark, Colin W. (1995), 'Scale and the Feedback Mechanism in Market Economics', in Timothy M. Swanson (ed.), *The Economics and Ecology of Biodiversity Decline — The Forces Driving Global Change*, Cambridge: Cambridge University Press, pp. 143–8.

Cline, William R. (1991), 'Scientific Basis for the Greenhouse Effect', *Economic Journal*, **101** (407), 904–19.

Cline, William R. (1992), *The Economics of Global Warming*, Washington DC: Institute for International Economics.

Cline, William R. (1996), 'The Impact of Global Warming on Agriculture: Comment', *American Economic Review*, **86** (5), 1309–11.

Cobb, Clifford W. and John B. Cobb (1994), *The Green National Product: A Proposed Index of Sustainable Economic Welfare*, Lanham: University Press of America.

Cobb, Clifford W., Ted Halstrad and Jonathan Rowe (1995), *Redefining Progress — the Genuine Progress Indicator*, San Francisco: Redefining Progress.

Colby, Michael E. (1991), 'Environmental Management in Development: The Evolution of Paradigms', *Ecological Economics*, **3** (3), 193–213.

Cole, H.S.D., Christopher Freeman and Marie Jahoda (eds) (1973), *Thinking About the Future — A Critique of the Limits to Growth*, London: Chatto & Windus.

Common, Mick S. (1989), 'The Choice of Pollution Control Instruments: Why Is So Little Notice Taken of Economists' Recommendations?', *Environment and Planning A*, **21** (10), 1297–314.

Common, Mick S. (1993), *A Cost Effective Environmentally Adjusted Economic Performance Indicator*, Discussion Paper in Environmental Economics and Management 93-07, York: University of York.

Common, Mick S. (1995a), 'Economists Don't Read Science', *Ecological Economics* 15 (2), 101–3.

Common, Mick S. (1995b), *Sustainability and Policy: Limits to Economics*, Cambridge: Cambridge University Press.

Common, Mick S., R.K. Blamey and T.W. Norton (1993), 'Sustainability and Environmental Valuation', *Environmental Values*, 2 (4), 299–334.

Converse, A.O. (1996), 'On Complete Recycling', *Ecological Economics*, 19 (3), 193–94.

Costanza, Robert (1989), 'What is Ecological Economics?', *Ecological Economics*, 1 (1), 1–7.

Costanza, Robert (1994), 'Three General Policies to Achieve Sustainability', in A. Jansson, M. Hammer, C. Folke and R. Costanza (eds), *Investing in Natural Capital: the Ecological Economics Approach to Sustainability*, Washington DC: Island Press, pp. 392–407.

Costanza, Robert and Charles Perrings (1990), 'A Flexible Assurance Bonding System for Improved Environmental Management', *Ecological Economics*, 2 (1), 55–7.

Costanza, Robert and P. Cowell (1992), 'The 4P Approach to Dealing with Scientific Uncertainty', *Environment*, 34 (9), 12–20 and 40.

Costanza, Robert, Ralph d'Arge, Rudolf de Groot, Stephen Farber, Monica Grasso, Bruce Hannon, Karin Limburg, Shahid Naeem, Robert V. O'Neill, José Paruelo, Robert G. Raskin, Paul Suttan and Marjan van den Belt (1997), 'The Value of the World's Ecostystem Services and Natural Capital', *Ecological Economics*, 25 (1), 3–15.

Cropper, Maureen and Charles Griffiths (1994), 'The Interaction of Population Growth and Environmental Quality', *American Economic Review Papers and Proceedings*, 84 (2), 250–54.

Crowards, Tom M. (1996), *Addressing Uncertainty in Project Evaluation: The Costs and Benefits of Safe Minimum Standards*, Working Paper GEC 96-04, Norwich and London: Centre for Social and Economic Research on the Global Environment.

Cummings, R.G. and G.W. Harrison (1995), 'The Measurement and Decomposition of Nonuse Values: A Critical Review', *Environmental and Resource Economics*, 5 (3), 225–47.

d'Arge, Ralph C. (1994), 'Sustenance and Sustainability: How Can We Preserve and Consume Without Major Conflict?', in A. Jansson, M. Hammer, C. Folke and R. Costanza (eds), *Investing in Natural Capital: the Ecological Economics Approach to Sustainability*, Washington DC: Island Press, pp. 113–27.

Daily, Gretchen C., Anne H. Ehrlich and Paul R. Ehrlich (1994), 'Optimum Human Population Size', *Population and Environment* **15** (6), 469–75.

Daly, Herman E. (1988), 'On Sustainable Development and National Accounts', in David Collard, David W. Pearce and David Ulph (eds), *Economics, Growth and Sustainable Environments*, New York: St. Martin's Press, pp. 41–55.

Daly, Herman E. (1991), 'Towards an Environmental Macroeconomics', *Land Economics*, **67** (2), 255–59.

Daly, Herman E. (1992a), *Steady-state Economics — Second edition with new essays*, London: Earthscan, first published in 1977.

Daly, Herman E. (1992b), 'Towards an Environmental Macroeconomics: Reply', *Land Economics*, **68** (2), 244–5.

Daly, Herman E. (1994), 'Operationalizing Sustainable Development by Investing in Natural Capital', in A. Jansson, M. Hammer, C. Folke and R. Costanza (eds), *Investing in Natural Capital: The Ecological Economics Approach to Sustainability*, Washington DC: Island Press, pp. 22–37.

Daly, Herman E. (1995a), 'On Wilfred Beckerman's Critique of Sustainable Development', *Environmental Values*, **4** (1), 49–55.

Daly, Herman E. (1995b), 'On Nicholas Georgescu-Roegen's Contributions to Economics: An Obituary Essay', *Ecological Economics*, **13** (3), 149–54.

Daly, Herman E. (1996), *Beyond Growth*, Boston: Beacon Press.

Daly, Herman E. and John B. Cobb (1989), *For the Common Good*, Boston: Beacon Press.

Daly, Herman E. and Robert Costanza (1992), 'Natural Capital and Sustainable Development', *Conservation Biology*, **6** (1), 37–46.

Daly, Herman E. and Kenneth N. Townsend (1993), 'Introduction', in Herman E. Daly and Kenneth N. Townsend (ed), *Economics, Ecology, Ethics*, Cambridge (Mass.): MIT Press, pp. 1–10.

Daly, Herman E. and Robert Goodland (1994), 'An Ecological-Economic Assessment of Deregulation of International Commerce Under GATT', *Ecological Economics*, **9** (1), 73–92.

Dasgupta, Partha (1990), 'Well-Being and the Extent of its Realisation in Poor Countries', *Economic Journal*, **100** (400), 1–32.

Dasgupta, Partha (1994), 'Optimal versus Sustainable Development', in I. Serageldin and A. Steer (eds), *Valuing the Environment*, Proceedings of the First Annual International Conference on Environmentally Sustainable Development, Washington DC: World Bank, pp. 35–46.

Dasgupta, Partha (1997), *Environmental and Resource Economics in the World of the Poor*, Internet Edition, Washington DC: Resources for the Future. (http:\\www.rff.org).

Dasgupta, Partha (1998), 'Population, Consumption and Resources: Ethical Issues', *Ecological Economics*, **24** (2/3), 139–52.

Dasgupta, Partha and Geoffrey Heal (1974), 'The Optimal Depletion of Exhaustible Resources, *Review of Economic Studies* Symposium, 3–28.

Dasgupta, Partha and Geoffrey Heal (1979), *Economic Theory and Exhaustible Resources*, Cambridge: Cambridge University Press.

Dasgupta, Partha and Martin Weale (1992), 'On Measuring the Quality of Life', *World Development*, **20** (1), 119–31.

Dasgupta, Partha, Scott Barrett and Karl-Göran Mäler (1996), *Intergenerational Equity, Social Discount Rates and Global Warming*, Discussion Paper No. 91, Stockholm: Beijer International Institute of Ecological Economics.

Dasgupta, Swapan and Tapan Mitra (1983), 'Intergenerational Equity and Efficient Allocation of Exhaustible Resources', *International Economic Review*, **24** (1), 133–53.

De Bruyn, S.M. and J.B. Opschoor (1997), 'Developments in the Throughput-Income Relationship: Theoretical and Empirical Observations', *Ecological Economics*, **20** (3), 255–68.

Deacon, Robert T. (1994), 'Deforestation and the Rule of Law in a Cross-Section of Countries', *Land Economics*, **70** (4), 414–30.

Deacon, Robert T. and Paul Murphy (1997), 'The Structure of an Environmental Transaction: The Debt-for-Nature Swaps', *Land Economics*, **73** (1), 1–24.

Deadman, D. and R. Kerry Turner (1988), 'Resource Conservation, Sustainability and Technical Change', in R. Kerry Turner (ed.), *Sustainable Enironmental Management Principles and Practice*, London: Belhaven, pp. 67–101.

Department of the Environment (1996), *Indicators of Sustainable Development for the United Kingdom*, London: Government Statistical Service.

Desai, Meghnad (1995), 'Greening of the HDI?', in Alex McGillivray (ed.), *Accounting for Change*, London: New Economics Foundation, pp. 21–36.

Deshmukh, Sudhakar D. and Stanley R. Pliska (1985), 'A Martingale Characterization of the Price of a Non-renewable Resource with Decisions Involving Uncertainty', *Journal of Economic Theory*, **35** (2), 322–42.

Devarajan, Shantayanan and Robert J. Weiner (1995), *Natural Resource Depletion and National Income Accounting: Is GNP in Kuwait and Norway Really so High?*, Working Paper No. 95-13, Washington DC: School of Business and Public Management, George Washington University.

Diamond, P.A. and J. Hausman (1994), 'Contingent Valuation: Is Some Number Better than No Number?', *Journal of Economic Perspectives*, **8** (4), 45–64.

Diefenbacher, Hans (1994), 'The Index of Sustainable Economic Welfare: A Case Study of the Federal Republic of Germany', in Clifford W. Cobb and John B. Cobb (eds), *The Green National Product: A Proposed Index of Sustainable Economic Welfare*, Lanham: University Press of America, pp. 215–45.

Dijkgraaf, E. and H.R.J. Vollebergh (1998), 'Growth and/or (?) Environment — Is There a Kuznets Curve for Carbon Emissions?', mimeo, Research Center for Economic Policy, Rotterdam: Erasmus University.

Dixit, Avinash, Peter Hammond and Michael Hoel (1980), 'On Hartwick's Rule for Regular Maximin Paths of Capital Accumulation and Resource Depletion', *Review of Economic Studies*, **47** (3), 551–6.

Dobbs, Ian M. (1991), 'A Bayesian Approach to Decision-making under Ambiguity', *Economica*, **58** (232), 417–40.

Downing, Mark and Teofilo Ozuna (1996), 'Testing the Reliability of the Benefit Function Transfer Approach', *Journal of Environmental Economics and Management*, **30** (3), 316–22.

Drèze, Jean and Amartya K. Sen (1989), *Hunger and Public Action*, Oxford: Clarendon Press.

Drèze, Jean, Amartya K. Sen and Athar Hussain (eds) (1995), *The Political Economy of Hunger*, Oxford: Clarendon Press.

Dyson, Tim (1994), 'Population Growth and Food Production: Recent Global and Regional Trends', *Population and Development Review*, **20** (2), 397–411.

Dyson, Tim (1996), *Population and Food — Global Trends and Future Prospects*, London: Routledge.

Ehrenfeld, David (1986), 'Why Put a Value on Biodiversity?', in Edward O. Wilson (ed.), *Biodiversity*, Washington DC: National Academy Press, pp. 212–16.

Ehrlich, Paul R. (1989), 'The Limits to Substitution: Meta-resource Depletion and a New Economic–Ecological Paradigm', *Ecological Economics*, **1** (1), 9–16.

Ehrlich, Paul R. and Anne H. Ehrlich (1992), 'The Value of Biodiversity', *Ambio*, **21** (3), 219–26.

Eismont, Oleg and Heinz Welsch (1996), 'Optimal Greenhouse Gas Emissions under Various Assessments of Climate Change Ambiguity', *Environmental and Resource Economics*, **8** (2), 129–40.

Eisner, Robert (1988), 'Extended Accounts for National Income and Product', *Journal of Economic Literature*, **26** (4), 1611–84.

Eisner, Robert (1989), *The Total Incomes System of Accounts*, Chicago: Chicago University Press.

Eisner, Robert (1994), 'The Index of Sustainable Economic Welfare: Comment', in Clifford W. Cobb and John B. Cobb (eds), *The Green National*

Product: A Proposed Index of Sustainable Economic Welfare, Lanham: University Press of America, pp. 97–110.

Ekins, Paul (1994), 'The Environmental Sustainability of Economic Processes: A Framework for Analysis', in J.C.J.M. van den Bergh and Jan van der Straaten (eds), *Toward Sustainable Development: Concepts, Methods, and Policy*, Washington DC: Island Press, pp. 25–55.

Ekins, Paul (1995), 'Rethinking the Costs Related to Global Warming. A Survey of the Issues', *Environmental and Resource Economics*, **6** (3), 231–77.

Ekins, Paul (1996a), 'The Secondary Benefits of CO_2 Abatement: How much Emission Reduction Do They Justify?', *Ecological Economics*, **16** (1), 13–24.

Ekins, Paul (1996b), 'On the Dividends from Environmental Taxation', in Timothy O'Riordan (ed.), *Ecotaxation*, London: Earthscan, pp. 125–62.

Ekins, Paul (1997), 'The Kuznets Curve for the Environment and Economic Growth: Examining the Evidence', *Environment and Planning A*, **29** (5), 805–30.

Ekins, Paul and Michael Jacobs (1995), 'Environmental Sustainability and the Growth of GDP: Conditions for Compatibility', in V. Bhaskar and Andrew Glyn (eds), *The North, the South and the Environment*, London: Earthscan, pp. 9–46.

El Serafy, Salah (1989), 'The Proper Calculation of Income from Depletable Natural Resources', in Yusuf J. Ahmad, Salah El Serafy and Ernst Lutz (eds), *Environmental Accounting for Sustainable Development: A UNDP–World Bank symposium*, Washington DC: World Bank, pp. 10–18.

El Serafy, Salah (1991), 'The Environment as Capital', in Robert Costanza (ed.), *Ecological Economics: The Science and Management of Sustainability*, New York: Columbia University Press, pp. 168–75.

El Serafy, Salah (1993), 'Depletable Resources: Fixed Capital or Inventories?', in Alfred Franz and Carsten Stahmer (eds), *Approaches to Environmental Accounting: Proceedings of the IARIW Conference on Environmental Accounting 1991*, Heidelberg: Springer, pp. 245–58.

El Serafy, Salah (1997), 'Green Accounting and Economic Policy', *Ecological Economics*, **21** (3), 217–29.

Energy Information Administration (1991), *International Oil and Gas Exploration and Development 1991*, Report DOE/EIA-0577 (91), Washington DC: US Department of Energy.

Eurostat (1994), *European System for the Collection of Economic Information on the Environment (SERIEE)*, Manual 1994, Luxemburg: Eurostat.

Fankhauser, Samuel (1993), *Global Warming Economics: Issues and State of the Art*, Working Paper GEC 93-28, Norwich and London: Centre for Social and Economic Research on the Global Environment.

Fankhauser, Samuel (1994), 'The Economic Costs of Global Warming Damage: A Survey', *Global Environmental Change*, **4** (4), 301–9.

Fankhauser, Samuel (1995), *Valuing Climate Change: The Economics of the Greenhouse*, London: Earthscan.

Fankhauser, Samuel and Richard S.J. Tol (1996), 'Climate Change Costs — Recent Advancements in the Economic Assessment', *Energy Policy*, **24** (7), 665–73.

Farrow, Scott (1985), 'Testing the Efficiency of Extraction from a Stock Resource', *Journal of Political Economy*, **93** (3), 452–87.

Farrow, Scott (1995), 'Extinction and Market Forces: Two Case Studies', *Ecological Economics*, **13** (2), 115–23.

Farzin, Y. Hossein (1995), 'Technological Change and the Dynamics of Resource Scarcity Measures', *Journal of Environmental Economics and Management*, **29** (1), 105–20.

Faucheux, Sylvie and Géraldine Froger (1995), 'Decision-making under Environmental Uncertainty', *Ecological Economics*, **15** (1), 29–42.

Faucheux, Sylvie, Eliot Muir and Martin O'Connor (1997), 'Neoclassical Natural Capital Theory and "Weak" Indicators for Sustainability', *Land Economics*, **73** (4), 528–52.

Faucheux, Sylvie, Martin O'Connor and Sybille van den Hove (1998), 'Towards a Sustainable National Income?', in Sylvie Faucheux and Martin O'Connor (eds), *Valuation for Sustainable Development — Methods and Policy Indicators*, Cheltenham, UK and Lyme, US: Edward Elgar, pp. 261–79.

Faucheux, Sylvie and Martin O'Connor (eds) (1998), *Valuation for Sustainable Development — Methods and Policy Indicators*, Cheltenham, UK and Lyme, US: Edward Elgar.

FAZ (1997), 'UN: Subventionen verursachen Überfischung', *Frankfurter Allgemeine Zeitung*, 10 June 1997, 16.

Ferguson, Dieneke, Christian Haas, Peter Reynard and Simon Zadek (1996), *Dangerous Curves: Does the Environment Improve with Economic Growth?*, Report by the New Economics Foundation for WWF International, Gland: World Wide Fund for Nature.

Feyerabend, Paul (1975), *Against Method*, Third Edition, London: Verso.

Feyerabend, Paul (1988), 'How to Defend Society Against Science', in E.D. Klemke, Robert Hollinger and A. David Kline (eds), *Introductory Readings in the Philosophy of Science*, Buffalo: Prometheus Books, pp. 34–44.

Field, Barry and Charles Grebenstein (1980), 'Capital–Energy Substitution in US Manufacturing', *Review of Economics and Statistics*, **62** (2), 207–12.

Filion, Fern L., James P. Foley and Andre J. Jacquemot (1994), 'The Economics of Global Ecotourism', in Mohan Munasinghe and Jeffrey McNeely (eds), *Protected Area Economics and Policy: Linking Conser-*

vation and Sustainable Development, Washington DC: World Bank, pp. 235–52.

Financial Times Mining (various years), *Mining International Yearbook*, London: Financial Times.

Financial Times Oil and Gas (various years), *Oil and Gas International Yearbook*, London: Financial Times.

Finn, J. (ed.) (1996), *Freedom in the World: Political Rights and Civil Liberties*, New York: Freedom House.

Fisher, Anthony C. (1979), 'Measures of Natural Resource Scarcity', in V. Kerry Smith (ed.), *Scarcity and Growth Reconsidered*, Baltimore: Johns Hopkins University Press, pp. 249–75.

Flores, Nicholas E. and Richard T. Carson (1997), 'The Relationship between the Income Elasticities of Demand and Willingness to Pay', *Journal of Environmental Economics and Management*, **33** (3), 287–95.

Foster, Vivien and Susana Mourato (1997), *Behavioural Consistency, Statistical Specification and Validity in the Contingent Ranking Method: Evidence from a Survey on the Impacts of Pesticide Use in the U.K.*, Working Paper GEC 97-09, Norwich and London: Centre for Social and Economic Research on the Global Environment.

Freeman, Myrick A. (1993), *The Measurement of Environmental and Resource Values*, Washington DC: Resources for the Future.

Friend, Anthony M. and David J. Rapport (1991), 'Evolution of Macro-Information Systems for Sustainable Development', *Ecological Economics*, **3** (1), 59–76.

Georgescu-Roegen, Nicholas (1971), *The Entropy Law and the Economic Process*, Cambridge (Mass.): Harvard University Press.

Georgescu-Roegen, Nicholas (1975), 'Energy and Economic Myths', *Southern Economic Journal*, **41** (3), 347–81.

Georgescu-Roegen, Nicholas (1986), 'The Entropy Law and the Economic Process in Retrospect', *Eastern Economic Journal*, **12** (1), 3–25.

Georgiou, Stavros, Dale Whittington, David W. Pearce and Dominic Moran (1997), *Economic Values and the Environment in the Developing World*, Cheltenham, UK and Lyme, US: Edward Elgar.

Gillies, Donald (1993), *Philosophy of Science in the Twentieth Century: an Introduction*, Oxford: Blackwell.

Goeller, H.E. and A. Zucker (1984), 'Infinite Resources: The Ultimate Strategy', *Science*, **223** (4635), 456–62.

Gomez-Lobo, Andres (1993), 'Sustainable Development, Optimal Growth and Natural Resource Accounting in a Small Open Economy', in Andres Gomez-Lobo, Kirk Hamilton and Carlos Eduardo Young, *Three Essays on Sustainable Development*, Working Paper GEC 93-08, Norwich and London: Centre for Social and Economic Research on the Global Environment, pp. 1–14.

Goodland, Robert (1995), 'The Concept of Environmental Sustainability', *Annual Review of Ecological Systems*, **26** (1), 1–24.

Goodland, Robert and Herman E. Daly (1992), 'Ten Reasons Why Northern Income Growth Is Not the Solution to Southern Poverty', in Robert Goodland, Herman E. Daly and Salah El Serafy (ed.), *Population, Technology, and Lifestyle*, Washington: Island Press, pp. 128–45.

Gordon, Robert B., Tjalling C. Koopmans, William D. Nordhaus and Brian J. Skinner (1987), *Toward a New Iron Age? — Quantitative Modeling of Resource Exhaustion*, Cambridge (Mass.): Harvard University Press.

Gottinger, Hans W. (1995), 'Regulatory Policies under Uncertainty, Value of Information and Greenhouse Gas Emissions', *Energy Policy*, **23** (1), 51–6.

Goulder, Lawrence H. (1994), *Environmental Taxation and the 'Double-dividend': A Reader's Guide*, Working Paper No. 74, Munich: Center for Economic Studies, University of Munich, also printed in *International Tax and Public Finance*, **2** (2), 1995, 157–83.

Gowdy, John M. and Carl N. McDaniel (1995), 'One World, One Experiment: Addressing the Biodiversity–Economics Conflict', *Ecological Economics*, **15** (3), 181–92.

Graham-Tomasi, Theodore, C. Ford Runge and William F. Hyde (1986), 'Foresight and Expectations in Models of Natural Resource Markets', *Land Economics*, **62** (3), 234–49.

Greer, Mark R. (1995), 'Aggressive Greenhouse Gas Policies: How They Could Spur Economic Growth', *Journal of Economic Issues*, **29** (4), 1045–62.

Gren, I.M., C. Folke, R.K. Turner and I. Bateman (1994), 'Primary and Secondary Values of Wetland Ecosystems', *Environmental and Resource Economics*, **4** (1), 55–74.

Griffin, James M. (1981), 'The Energy–Capital Complementarity Controversy: a Progress Report on Reconciliation Attempts', in Ernst R. Berndt and Barry C. Field (eds), *Modeling and Measuring Natural Resource Substitution*, Cambridge (Mass.): MIT Press, pp. 70–80.

Griffin, James M. and Paul R. Gregory (1976), 'An Intercountry Translog Model of Energy Substitution Responses', *American Economic Review*, **66** (5), 845–57.

Gross, L.S. and E.C.H. Veendorp (1990), 'Growth with Exhaustible Resources and a Materials-Balance Production Function', *Natural Resource Modeling*, **4** (1), 77–94.

Grossman, Gene M. (1995), 'Pollution and Growth: What Do We Know?', in I. Goldin and L. Winters (eds), *The Economics of Sustainable Development*, Cambridge: Cambridge University Press, pp. 19–46.

Grossman, Gene M. and Alan B. Krueger (1993), 'Environmental Impacts of a North American Free Trade Agreement', in P. Garber (ed.), *The US–Mexico Free Trade Agreement*, Cambridge (Mass.): MIT Press.

Grossman, Gene M. and Alan B. Krueger (1995), 'Economic Growth and the Environment', *Quarterly Journal of Economics*, **110** (2), 353–77.

Grubb, Michael (1997), 'Technologies, Energy Systems and the Timing of CO_2 Emissions Abatement', *Energy Policy*, **25** (2), 159–72.

Guenno, G. and S. Tiezzi (1998), *An Index of Sustainable Economic Welfare for Italy*, Working Paper 5/98, Milano: Fonazione Eni Enrico Mattei, also on-line under the address www.feem.it/web/feem/workpap/abs98/05-98.pdf.

Guha, Ramachandra (1989), 'Radical American Environmentalism and Wilderness Preservation: A Third World Critique', *Environmental Ethics*, **11** (1), 71–83.

Gutes, Maite Cabeza (1996), 'The Concept of Weak Sustainability', *Ecological Economics*, **17** (2), 147–56.

Hahn, Robert W. (1990), 'The Political Economy of Environmental Regulation: Towards a Unifying Framework', *Public Choice*, **65** (1), 21–47.

Hahn, Robert W. and Robert L. Axtell (1995), 'Reevaluating the Relationship Between Transferable Property Rights and Command-and-control Regulation', *Journal of Regulatory Economics*, **8** (2), 125–48.

Hall, Darwin C. and Jane V. Hall (1984), 'Concepts and Measures of Natural Resource Scarcity with a Summary of Recent Trends', *Journal of Environmental Economics and Management*, **11** (4), 363–79.

Halvorsen, Robert and Tim R. Smith (1991), 'A Test of the Theory of Exhaustible Resources', *Quarterly Journal of Economics*, **106** (1), 123–40.

Hamilton, Clive (1999), 'The Genuine Progress Indicator: Methodological Advances and Results from Australia', *Ecological Economics* (forthcoming).

Hamilton, Kirk (1994), 'Green Adjustments to GDP', *Resources Policy*, **20** (3), 155–68.

Hamilton, Kirk (1995), 'Sustainable Development and Green National Accounts', Ph.D. thesis, London: University College London.

Hamilton, Kirk (1996), 'Pollution and Pollution Abatement in the National Accounts', *Review of Income and Wealth*, **42** (1), 13–33.

Hamilton, Kirk (1997), 'Forest Resources and National Income', World Bank, Environment Department, mimeo, Washington DC: World Bank.

Hamilton, Kirk, David W. Pearce, Giles Atkinson, Andres Gomez-Lobo and Carlos Young (1994), *The Policy Implications of Natural Resource and Environmental Accounting*, Working Paper GEC 94-18, Norwich and London: Centre for Social and Economic Research on the Global Environment.

Hamilton, Kirk and Giles Atkinson (1996), 'Air Pollution and Green Accounts', *Energy Policy* **24** (7), 675–84.

Hamilton, Kirk, Giles Atkinson and David W. Pearce (1997), 'Genuine saving as an Indicator of Sustainability', mimeo, Washington DC, Norwich and London: World Bank and Centre for Social and Economic Research on the Global Environment.

Hammond, Allen, Albert Adriaanse, Eric Rodenburg, Dirk Bryant and Richard Woodward (1995), *Environmental Indicators: A Systematic Approach to Measuring and Reporting on Environmental Policy Performance in the Context of Sustainable Development*, Washington DC: World Resources Institute.

Hammond, P.J. (1988), 'Consequentialist Demographic Norms and Parenting Rights', *Social Choice and Welfare*, **5**, 127–45.

Hanemann, W. Michael (1991), 'Willingness to Pay and Willingness to Accept: How Much Can They Differ?', *American Economic Review*, **81** (3), 635–47.

Hanemann, W. Michael (1994), 'Valuing the Environment Through Contingent Valuation', *Journal of Economic Perspectives*, **8** (4), 19–43.

Hanley, Nick, S. Hallet and I. Moffatt (1990), 'Why is More Notice not Taken of Economists' Prescriptions for the Control of Pollution?', *Environment and Planning* A, **22** (11), 1421–39.

Hanley, Nick and Clive L. Spash (1993), *Cost–benefit Analysis and the Environment*, Aldershot, UK and Brookfield, US: Edward Elgar.

Hanley, Nick, Clive Spash and Lorna Walker (1995), 'Problems in Valuing the Benefits of Biodiversity Protection', *Environmental and Resource Economics*, **5** (3), 249–72.

Hanley, Nick and Jennifer Milne (1996), 'Ethical Beliefs and Behaviour in Contingent Valuation Surveys', *Journal of Environmental Planning and Management*, **39** (2), 255–72.

Hardin, Garrett (1968), 'The Tragedy of the Commons', *Science*, **162** (3859), 1243–48.

Harrison, G.W. (1992), 'Valuing Public Goods with the Contingent Valuation Method: A Critique of Kahneman and Knetsch', *Journal of Environmental Economics and Management*, **23** (3), 248–57.

Hartwick, John M. (1977), 'Intergenerational Equity and the Investing of Rents from Exhaustible Resources', *American Economic Review*, **67** (5), 972–4.

Hartwick, John M. (1978a), 'Substitution Among Exhaustible Resources and Intergenerational Equity', *Review of Economic Studies*, **45** (2), 347–54.

Hartwick, John M. (1978b), 'Investing Returns from Depleting Renewable Resource Stocks and Intergenerational Equity', *Economics Letters*, **1** (1), 85–8.

Hartwick, John M. (1990), 'Natural Resources, National Accounting and Economic Depreciation, *Journal of Public Economics*, **43** (3), 291–304.

Hartwick, John M. (1992), 'Deforestation and National Accounting', *Environmental and Resource Economics*, **2** (5), 513–21.

Hartwick, John M. (1993), 'Notes on Economic Depreciation of Natural Resource Stocks and National Accounting', in Alfred Franz and Carsten Stahmer (eds), *Approaches to Environmental Accounting: Proceedings of the IARIW Conference on Environmental Accounting 1991*, Heidelberg: Springer, pp. 167–98.

Hartwick, John M. (1994), *Sustainability and Constant Consumption Paths in Open Economies with Exhaustible Resources*, Working Paper No. 61, Munich: Center for Economic Studies, University of Munich; published with small amendments in *Review of International Economics*, **3** (3), 275–83.

Hartwick, John M. and Nancy D. Olewiler (1986), *The Economics of Natural Resource Use*, New York: Harper & Row.

Hartwick, John M. and Anja Hageman (1993), 'Economic Depreciation of Mineral Stocks and the Contribution of El Serafy', in Ernst Lutz (ed.), *Toward Improved Accounting for the Environment*, Washington DC: World Bank, pp. 211–35.

Hausman, Daniel M. (1992), *The Inexact and Separate Science of Economics*, Cambridge: Cambridge University Press.

Hausman, J. (ed.) (1993), *Contingent Valuation: A Critical Assessment*, Amsterdam: Elsevier.

Heinen, J.T. (1994), 'Emerging, Diverging and Converging Paradigms on Sustainable Development', *International Journal of Sustainable Development and World Ecology*, **1** (1), 22–33.

Hettige, Hemamala, Robert E.B. Lucas and David Wheeler (1992a), 'The Toxic Intensity of Industrial Production: Global Patterns, Trends, and Trade Policy', *American Economic Review — Papers and Proceedings*, **82** (2), 478–81.

Hettige, Hemamala, Robert E.B. Lucas and David Wheeler (1992b), *Economic Development, Environmental Regulation, and the International Migration of Toxic Industrial Pollution 1960–88*, Working Paper No. 1062, Washington DC: World Bank.

Heyes, Anthony G. and Catherine Liston-Heyes (1995), 'Sustainable Resource Use: The Search for Meaning', *Energy Policy*, **23** (1), 1–3.

Hicks, J.R. (1939), 'The Foundations of Welfare Economics', *Economic Journal*, **49** (196), 696–712.

Hicks, J.R. (1946), *Value and Capital*, Oxford: Oxford University Press.

Hinrichs, Doug (1997), '2500 Economists Agree on Risks to Global Climate Change', *Ecological Economics Bulletin*, **2** (2), 16–18.

Hinterberger, Friedrich and Maria Welfens (1996), 'Warum inputorientierte Umweltpolitik?', in Jörg Köhn and Maria Welfens (eds), *Neue Ansätze in der Umweltökonomie*, Marburg: Metropolis-Verlag, pp. 21–43.

Hinterberger, Friedrich, Fred Luks and Friedrich Schmidt-Bleek (1997), 'Material Flows vs. "Natural Capital" What Makes an Economy Sustainable?', *Ecological Economics*, **23** (1), 1–15.

Hochreiter, Harald, Bernhard Obermayr, Klaus Steiner and Engelbert Stockhammer (1995), *Der Index of Sustainable Economic Welfare (ISEW). Eine empirische Studie zur Entwicklung des Wohlstands in Österreich von 1955 bis 1992*, Wien: Institut für Wirtschaft und Umwelt, Wirtschaftsuniversität Wien.

Hoevenagel, Ruud (1996), 'The Validity of the Contingent Valuation Method: Perfect and Regular Embedding', *Environmental and Resource Economics*, **7** (1), 57–78.

Hohl, Andreas and Clement A. Tisdell (1993), 'How Useful are Environmental Safety Standards in Economics? — The Example of Safe Minimum Standards for Protection of Species', *Biodiversity and Conservation*, **2**, 168–81.

Hohmeyer, Olav (1992), *Adäquate Berücksichtigung der Erschöpfbarkeit nicht erneuerbarer Ressourcen, Fraunhofer-Institut für Systemtechnik und Innovationsforschung*, Bericht im Rahmen des Forschungsvorhabens 'Externe Kosten der Energie' der PROGNOS AG Basel, Karlsruhe: Fraunhofer-Institut.

Holling, C.S. (1995), 'Biodiversity in the Functioning of Ecosystems: an Ecological Synthesis', in Charles Perrings (ed.), *Biodiversity Loss: Economic and Ecological Issues*, Cambridge: Cambridge University Press, pp. 44–83.

Holtz-Eakin, Douglas and Thomas M. Selden (1995), 'Stoking the Fires? CO_2 Emissions and Economic Growth', *Journal of Public Economics*, **57** (1), 85–101.

Hotelling, Harold (1931), 'The Economics of Exhaustible Resources', *Journal of Political Economy*, **39** (2), 137–75.

Howarth, Richard B. (1991), 'Energy Use in US Manufacturing: The Impacts of the Energy Shocks on Sectoral Output, Industry Structure, and Energy Intensity', *Journal of Energy Development*, **14** (2), 175–91.

Howarth, Richard B. (1996), 'Climate Change and Overlapping Generations', *Contemporary Economic Policy*, **14** (4), 100–11.

Howarth, Richard B. (1997), 'Energy Efficiency and Economic Growth', *Contemporary Economic Policy*, **15** (4), 1–9.

Howarth, Richard B. and Richard B. Norgaard (1993), 'Intergenerational Transfers and the Social Discount Rate', *Environmental and Resource Economics*, **3** (4), 337–58.

Hudson, Edward and Dale Jorgenson (1974), 'US Energy Policy and Economic Growth', *Bell Journal of Economics*, **5** (2), 461–514.

Hueting, Roefie (1991), 'Correcting National Income for Environmental Losses: A Practical Solution for a Theoretical Dilemma', in Robert Costanza (ed.), *Ecological Economics: The Science and Management of Sustainability*, New York: Columbia University Press, pp. 194–213.

Hueting, Roefie and Peter Bosch (1990), 'On the Correction of National Income for Environmental Losses', *Statistical Journal of the United Nations ECE*, **7** (2), 75–83.

Hueting, Roefie and Lucas Reijnders (1998), 'Sustainability is an Objective Concept', *Ecological Economics*, **27** (2), 139–47.

Hung, N.M. (1993), 'Natural Resources, National Accounting, and Economic Depreciation: Stock Effects', *Journal of Public Economics*, **51** (3), 379–89.

IEA (1997), *Indicators of Energy Use and Efficiency — Understanding the Link between Energy and Human Activity*, Paris: International Energy Agency

IMF (1997), *World Economic Outlook 1997*, Washington DC: International Monetary Fund.

Ingham, Alan, James Maw and Alistair Ulph (1991), 'Empirical Measures of Carbon Taxes', *Oxford Review of Economic Policy*, **7** (2), 99–122.

Ingham, Alan and Alistair Ulph (1991), 'Market-based Instruments for Reducing CO_2 Emissions', *Energy Policy*, **19** (2), 138–48.

IPCC (1995), *IPCC Second Assessment: Climate Change 1995 — A Report of the Intergovernmental Panel on Climate Change*, place of publication not known.

IPCC (1996a), *Climate Change 1995: The Science of Climate Change — Contribution of Working Group I to the Second Assessment Report of the Intergovernmental Panel on Climate Change*, Cambridge: Cambridge University Press.

IPCC (1996b), *Climate Change 1995 — Economic and Social Dimensions of Climate Change — Contribution of Working Group III to the Second Assessment Report of the Intergovernmental Panel on Climate Change*, Cambridge: Cambridge University Press.

Jackson, Tim (1995), 'Price Elasticity and Market Structure — Overcoming Obstacles to Final Demand Energy Efficiency', in Terry Barker, Paul Ekins and Nick Johnstone (eds), *Global Warming and Energy Elasticities*, London: Routledge, pp. 254–66.

Jackson, Tim and Nick Marks (1994), *Measuring Sustainable Economic Welfare — A Pilot Index: 1950–1990*, Stockholm: Stockholm Environmental Institute.

Jackson, Tim and S. Stymne (1996), *Sustainable Economic Welfare in Sweden: A Pilot Index 1950–1992*, Stockholm: Stockholm Environment Institute.

Jackson, Tim, F. Laing, A. MacGillivray, N. Marks, J. Ralls and S. Stymne (1997), *An Index of Sustainable Economic Welfare for the UK 1950–1996*, Guildford: University of Surrey, Centre for Environmental Strategy.

Jacobs, Michael (1991), *The Green Economy — Environment, Sustainable Development and the Politics of the Future*, London: Pluto Press.

Jacobs, Michael (1995a), 'Environmental Valuation, Deliberative Democracy and Public Decision-making Institutions', mimeo, Lancaster: Centre for the Study of Environmental Change, Lancaster University, reprinted in John Foster (ed.) (1996), *Valuing Nature*, London: Routledge.

Jacobs, Michael (1995b), 'Reflections on the Discourse and Politics of Sustainable Development — Part I: Faultlines of Contestation and the Radical Model', mimeo, Lancaster: Centre for the Study of Environmental Change, Lancaster University.

Jacobs, Michael (1995c), 'Sustainable Development, Capital Substitution and Economic Humility: A Response to Beckerman', *Environmental Values*, **4** (1), 57–68.

Jacobs, Michael (1996), 'Environmental Sustainability and Markets: On the Inadequacy of the Neoclassical Model', mimeo, Lancaster: Centre for the Study of Environmental Change, Lancaster University.

Jaeger, William K. (1995), 'The Welfare Cost of a Global Carbon Tax When Tax Revenues Are Recycled', *Resource and Energy Economics*, **17** (1), 47–67.

Jaffe, Adam B. and Robert N. Stavins (1994), 'The Energy Paradox and the Diffusion of Conservation Technology', *Resource and Energy Economics*, **16** (2), 91–122.

Jaffe, Adam B. and Robert N. Stavins (1995), 'Dynamic Incentives of Environmental Regulations: The Effects of Alternative Policy Instruments on Technology Diffusion', *Journal of Environmental Economics and Management*, **29** (3), S43–S63.

Jaffe, Adam B., Steven R. Peterson and Robert N. Stavins (1995), 'Environmental Regulation and the Competitiveness of US Manufacturing: What Does the Evidence Tell Us?', *Journal of Economic Literature*, **33** (1), 132–63.

Jänicke, Martin, Harald Mönch and Manfred Binder (1992), *Umweltentlastung durch industriellen Strukturwandel? — Eine explorative Studie über 32 Industrieländer (1970 bis 1990)*, Berlin: Sigma.

Jevons, William Stanley (1865), *The Coal Question: An Inquiry Concerning the Prospects of the Nation and the Probable Exhaustion of Our Coal Mines*, London.

Jochem, Eberhard and Edelgard Gruber (1990), 'Obstacles to Rational Electricity Use and Measures to Alleviate Them', *Energy Policy*, **18** (4), 340–50.

Johnson, Manuel H., Frederick W. Bell, and James T. Bennett, (1980), 'Natural Resource Scarcity: Empirical Evidence and Public Policy', *Journal of Environmental Economics and Management*, **7** (3), 256–71.

Kahneman, Daniel and Jack Knetsch (1992), 'Valuing Public Goods: the Purchase of Moral Satisfaction', *Journal of Environmental Economics and Management*, **22** (1), 57–70.

Kaldor, Nicholas (1939), 'Welfare Propositions of Economics and Interpersonal Comparisons of Utility', *Economic Journal*, **49** (195), 549–52.

Kanbur, Ravi (1992), *Heterogeneity, Distribution, and Cooperation in Common Property Resource Management*, Working Paper No. 844, Washington DC: World Bank.

Kant, Immanuel (1785) [1968], *Grundlegung zur Metaphysik der Sitten*, Werke Band XI, Frankfurt: Suhrkamp.

Kaufmann, Robert K. (1992), 'A Biophysical Analysis of the Energy/Real GDP Ratio: Implications for Substitution and Technical Change', *Ecological Economics*, **6** (1), 35–56.

Kelsey, David and John Quiggin (1992), 'Theories of Choice under Ignorance and Uncertainty', *Journal of Economic Surveys* **6** (2), 133–53.

Khalil, E.L. (1994), 'Recycling of Matter. Further Comments', *Ecological Economics*, **9** (3), 193–94.

Khatib, Hisham (1995), 'Energy Intensity: A New Look', *Energy Policy*, **23** (8), 727–9.

Khazzoom, J. Daniel (1987), 'Energy Saving Resulting from the Adoptions of More Efficient Appliances', *The Energy Journal*, **10** (1), 85–89.

Kirchgässner, Gebhard, U. Müller and M. Savioz (1998), *Ecological Tax Reform and Involuntary Unemployment: Simulation Results for Switzerland*, Discussion Paper No. 9806, St. Gallen: University of St. Gallen, Department of Economics.

Klaus, Joachim (1994), *Umweltökonomische Berichterstattung: Ziele, Problemstellungen und praktische Ansätze*, Band 5 der Schriftenreihe Spektrum Bundesstatistik, Stuttgart: Metzler-Poeschel.

Klepper, Gernot and Frank Stähler (1996), *Sustainability in Closed and Open Economies*, Working Paper No. 741, Kiel: Kiel Institute of World Economics.

Knetsch, Jack L. (1990), 'Environmental Policy Implications of Disparities between Willingness to Pay and Compensation Demanded Measures of Values', *Journal of Environmental Economics and Management*, **18** (3), 227–37.

Knight, F. (1921), *Risk, Uncertainty and Profit*, Boston: Houghton Mifflin.

Kolstad, Charles D. (1996), 'Fundamental Irreversibilities in Stock Externalities', *Journal of Public Economics*, **60** (2), 221–33.

Kopp, Raymond J. and Paul R. Portney (1997), *Mock Referenda for Intergenerational Decisionmaking*, Discussion Paper 97-48, Washington DC: Resources for the Future.

Koskela, Erkki, Ronnie Schöb and Hans-Werner Sinn, 'Pollution, Factor Taxation and Unemployment', *International Tax and Public Finance*, **5** (3), 379–96.

Kriström, Bengt and Pere Pere Riera (1996), 'Is the Income Elasticity of Environmental Improvements Less Than One?', *Environmental and Resource Economics*, **7** (1), 45–55.

Krutilla, John V. (1967), 'Conservation Reconsidered', *American Economic Review*, **57** (1), 777–86.

Krutilla, John V. and Anthony C. Fisher (1975), *The Economics of Natural Environments*, Washington DC: Resources for the Future.

Kuhn, Michael, Walter Radermacher and Carsten Stahmer (1994), 'Umweltökonomische Trends 1960 bis 1990', *Wirtschaft und Statistik*, (8), 658–77.

Kuhn, Thomas S. (1962) [1996], *The Structure of Scientific Revolutions*, Third Edition 1996, Chicago: University of Chicago Press.

Kummel, R. (1994), 'Energy, Entropy–Economy, Ecology', *Ecological Economics*, **9** (3), 194–5.

Kunte, Arundhati, Kirk Hamilton, John Dixon and Michael Clemens (1997), 'Estimating National Wealth — Methodology and Results', Washington DC: World Bank, online available at http://www-esd.worldbank.org/eei/wealth/genuinesav.html

Kuznets, S. (1955), 'Economic Growth and Income Inequality', *American Economic Review*, **45** (1), 1–28.

Lakatos, Imre (1978), 'Falsification and the Methodology of Scientific Research Programmes', in John Worrall and Gregory Currie (eds), *The Methodology of Scientific Research Programmes*, Philosophical Papers Vol. 1, Cambridge: Cambridge University Press, pp. 8–101.

Lecomber, R. (1975), *Economic Growth Versus the Environment*, London: Macmillan.

Leggett, Jeremy (ed.) (1990), *Global Warming: The Greenpeace Report*, Oxford: Oxford University Press.

Leipert, Christian (1989a), *Die heimlichen Kosten des Fortschritts — Wie Umweltzerstörung das Wirtschaftswachstum fördert*, Frankfurt am Main: Fischer.

Leipert, Christian (1989b), 'National Income and Economic Growth: The Conceptual Side of Defensive Expenditures', *Journal of Economic Issues*, **23** (3), 843–56.

Lenssen, Nicholas and Christopher Flavin (1996), 'Sustainable Energy for Tomorrow's World — The Case for an Optimistic View of the Future', *Energy Policy*, **24** (9), 769–81.

Leonard, H.J. (1988), *Pollution and the Struggle for the World Product*, Cambridge (Mass.): Cambridge University Press.

Levinson, Arik (1996), 'Environmental Regulations and Industry Location: International and Domestic Evidence', in Jagdish N. Bhagwati and R.E. Hudec (eds), *Fair Trade and Harmonization: Prerequisites for Free Trade?*, Vol. 1, Cambridge (Mass.): MIT Press, pp. 429–57.

Lind, Robert C. (1995), 'Intergenerational Equity, Discounting, and the Role of Cost–Benefit Analysis in Evaluating Global Climate Policy', *Energy Policy*, **23** (4/5), 379–89.

Lipsey, Richard G. and Kelvin J. Lancaster (1956), 'The General Theory of Second-best', *Review of Economic Studies*, **63** (1), 11–32.

Lipton, Michael (1989), *New Seeds and Poor People*, London: Unwin Hyman.

Liverman, Diana M., Mark E. Hanson, Becky J. Brown and Robert W. Merideth, Jr. (1988), 'Global Sustainability: Toward Measurement', *Environmental Management*, **12** (2), 133–43.

Löfgren, Karl-Gustaf (1992), 'Comment on C.R. Hulten, "Accounting for the Wealth of Nations: The Net versus Gross Output Controversy and its Ramifications"', *Scandinavian Journal of Economics*, **94** (0), S25–S28.

Loomes, Graham and Robert Sugden (1982), 'Regret Theory: An Alternative Theory of Rational Choice under Uncertainty', *Economic Journal*, **92** (368), 805–24.

Lopez, Ramon (1992), 'The Environment as a Factor of Production: The Economic Growth and Trade Policy Linkages', in Patrick Low (ed.), *International Trade and the Environment*, Discussion Paper No. 159, Washington DC: World Bank.

Low, Patrick (ed.) (1992a), *International Trade and the Environment*, Discussion Paper No. 159, Washington DC: World Bank.

Low, Patrick (1992b), 'International Trade and the Environment: An Overview', in Patrick Low (ed.), *International Trade and the Environment*, Discussion Paper No. 159, Washington DC: World Bank, pp. 1–14

Lutz, Ernst (1992), 'Agricultural Trade Liberalization, Price Changes, and Environmental Effects', *Environmental and Resource Economics*, **2** (1), 79–89.

Lutz, Ernst (1993), 'Epilogue', in Ernst Lutz (ed.), *Toward Improved Accounting for the Environment — an UNSTAT–World Bank Symposium*, Washington DC: World Bank, pp. 315–18.

Machina, Mark J. (1987), 'Choice under Uncertainty: Problems Solved and Unsolved', *Journal of Economic Perspectives*, **1** (1), 121–54.

Machina, Mark J. (1989), 'Dynamic Consistency and Non-Expected Utility Models of Choice Under Uncertainty', *Journal of Economic Literature*, **27** (4), 1622–68.

Mackellar, F. Landis and Daniel R. Vining, Jr. (1989), 'Measuring Natural Resource Scarcity', *Social Indicators Research*, **21** (5), 517–30.

Magnus, J.A. (1979), 'Substitution between Energy and Non-energy Inputs in the Netherlands 1950–1976', *International Economic Review*, **2** (2), 465–84.

Mäler, Karl-Göran (1991), 'National Accounts and Environmental Resources', *Environmental and Resource Economics*, **1** (1), 1–15.

Malthus, Thomas Robert (1798), *An Essay on the Principle of Population*, London: J. Johnson.

Manne, A.S. and R.G. Richels (1991), 'Buying Greenhouse Insurance', *Energy Policy*, **19** (6), 543–52.

Manne, A.S. and R.G. Richels (1992), *Buying Greenhouse Insurance: The Economic Costs of Carbon Dioxide*, Cambridge (Mass.): MIT Press.

Manne, A.S. and R.G. Richels (1995), 'The Greenhouse Debate: Economic Efficiency, Burden Sharing and Hedging Strategies', *Energy Journal*, **16** (4), 1–37.

Mansson, B.A. (1994), 'Recycling of Matter. A Response', *Ecological Economics*, **9** (3), 191–2.

Markandya, Anil and David W. Pearce (1988), *Environmental Considerations and the Choice of the Discount Rate in Developing Countries*, Environment Department Working Paper No. 3, Washington DC: World Bank.

Markandya, Anil and David W. Pearce (1991), 'Development, the Environment, and the Social Rate of Discount', *World Bank Research Observer*, **6** (2), 137–52.

Markandya, Anil and Charles Perrings (1991), *Resource Accounting for Sustainable Development: A Review of Basic Concepts, Recent Debate and Future Needs*, Discussion Paper DP 91-06, London: London Environmental Economics Centre.

Martinez-Alier, Juan (1995), 'The Environment as a Luxury Good or "Too Poor to be Green"?', *Ecological Economics*, **13** (1), 1–10.

Max-Neef, Manfred (1995), 'Economic Growth and Quality of Life: A Threshold Hypothesis', *Ecological Economics*, **15** (2), 115–18.

Mayo, Ed, Alex MacGillivray and Duncan McLaren (1997), *More Isn't Always Better — A Special Briefing on Growth and Quality of Life in the UK*, London: New Economics Foundation.

McCormick, John (1989), *The Global Environmental Movement*, London: Belhaven.

McCoy, Daniel (1996), 'Reflections on the Double-dividend Debate', in Timothy O'Riordan (ed.), *Ecotaxation*, London: Earthscan, pp. 201–14.

Meadows, Dennis, Donella Meadows, Erich Zahn and Peter Milling (1972), *The Limits to Growth*, New York: Universe Books.

Meadows, Donella, Denis Meadows and Jorgen Randers (1992), *Beyond the Limits: Global Collapse or a Sustainable Future*, London: Earthscan.

Mendelsohn, R. and J. Neumann (eds) (1999), *The Impacts of Climate Change on the US Economy*, Cambridge (Mass.): Cambridge University Press.

Mikesell, Raymond F. (1994), 'Sustainable Development and Mineral Resources', *Resources Policy*, **20** (2), 83–6.

Mikesell, Raymond F. (1995), 'The Limits to Growth — A Reappraisal', *Resources Policy*, **21** (2), 127–31.

Mill, John Stuart (1862), *Principles of Political Economy*, Fifth edition, London: Parker, Son, and Bourn.

Miller, Merton H. and Charles W. Upton (1985), 'A Test of the Hotelling Valuation Principle', *Journal of Political Economy*, **93** (1), 1–25.

Mishan, Ezra J. (1974), 'Growth and Antigrowth: What Are the Issues?', in A. Weintraub, E. Schwartz and J. Richard Aronson (eds), *The Economic Growth Controversy*, London: Macmillan, pp. 3–38.

Mishan, Ezra J. (1994), 'Is A Welfare Index Possible?', in Clifford W. Cobb and John B. Cobb (eds), *The Green National Product: A Proposed Index of Sustainable Economic Welfare*, Lanham: University Press of America, pp. 169–92.

Mitchell, R.C. and R.T. Carson (1989), *Using Surveys to Value Public Goods*, Washington DC: Resources for the Future.

Moazzami, B. and F.J. Anderson (1994), 'Modelling Natural Resource Scarcity Using the "Error-Correction" Approach', *Canadian Journal of Economics*, **27** (4), 801–12.

Mooij, Ruud A. and A. Lans Bovenberg (1998), 'Environmental Taxes, International Capital Mobility and Inefficient Tax Systems: Tax Burden vs. Tax Shifting', *International Tax and Public Finance*, **5** (1), 7–39.

Myers, Norman (1993), 'Biodiversity and the Precautionary Principle', *Ambio*, **23** (1), 74–9.

Neumayer, Eric (1994), 'The World Bank on Key Environmental Issues — A Critical Assessment', MSc thesis in Development Studies, London: London School of Economics and Political Science.

Neumayer, Eric (1998a), 'Is Economic Growth the Environment's Best Friend', *Zeitschrift für Umweltpolitik und Umweltrecht*, **21** (2), pp. 161–76.

Neumayer, Eric (1998b), 'Preserving Natural Capital in a World of Uncertainty and Scarce Financial Resources', *International Journal of Sustainable Development and World Ecology*, **5** (1), 27–42.

Neumayer, Eric (1999a), 'Can Future Generations be Compensated for Long-Term Environmental Degradation', mimeo, London: London School of Economics and Political Science.

Neumayer, Eric (1999b), 'Linking the Human Development with Sustainability: A Constructive Proposal', mimeo, London: London School of Economics and Political Science.

Neumayer, Eric (1999c), 'Global Warming: Discounting is not the Issue, but Substitutability is', *Energy Policy* **27** (1), pp. 33–43.

Neumayer, Eric (1999d), 'The ISEW: Not an Index of Sustainable Economic Welfare', *Social Indicators Research* (forthcoming).

Neumayer, Eric (1999e), 'In Defence of the Principle of Historical Accountability for Greenhouse Gas Emissions', mimeo, London: London School of Economics and Political Science.

Neumayer, Eric (1999f), 'Resource Accounting in Measures of Unsustainability: Challenging World Bank's Conclusions', *Environmental and Resource Economics* (forthcoming).

Neumayer, Eric (1999g), 'Scarce or Abundant? The Economics of Natural Resource Availability', *Journal of Economic Surveys* (forthcoming).

Ng, Yew-Kwang (1983), *Welfare Economics*, London: Macmillan.

Nordhaus, William D. (1973), 'World Dynamics: Measurement without Data', *Economic Journal*, **83** (332), 1156–83.

Nordhaus, William D. (1991a), 'To Slow or not to Slow: The Economics of the Greenhouse Effect', *Economic Journal*, **101** (407), 920–37.

Nordhaus, William D. (1991b), 'Economic Approaches to Greenhouse Warming', in Rüdiger Dornbusch and James M. Poterba (eds), *Global Warming: Economic Policy Responses*, Cambridge (Mass.): MIT Press, pp. 33–66.

Nordhaus, William D. (1992), 'Lethal Model 2: The Limits to Growth Revisited', *Brookings Papers on Economic Activity*, **0** (2), 1–59.

Nordhaus, William D. (1994), *Managing the Global Commons: The Economics of Climate Change*, Cambridge (Mass.): MIT Press.

Nordhaus, William D. and James Tobin (1972), 'Is Growth Obsolete?', in National Bureau of Economic Research, *Economic Growth*, Research General Series No. 96F, New York: Columbia University Press.

Nordhaus, William D. and David Popp (1997), 'What is the Value of Scientific Knowledge? An Application to Global Warming Using the PRICE Model', *Energy Journal*, **18** (1), 1–45.

Norgaard, Richard B. (1986), 'Thermodynamic and Economic Concepts as Related to Resource-Use Policies: Synthesis', *Land Economics*, **62** (3), 325–7.

Norgaard, Richard B. (1990), 'Economic Indicators of Resource Scarcity: A Critical Essay', *Journal of Environmental Economics and Management*, **19** (1), 19–25.

Norgaard, Richard B. (1991), 'Economic Indicators of Resource Scarcity: A More Critical Reply', *Journal of Environmental Economics and Management*, **21** (2), 195–9.

Norton, Bryan G. (1986), 'Commodity, Amenity, and Morality — The Limits of Quantification in Valuing Biodiversity', in Edward O. Wilson (ed.), *Biodiversity*, Washington DC: National Academy Press, pp. 200–205.

Norton, Bryan G. (1995), 'Evaluating Ecosystem States: Two competing Paradigms', *Ecological Economics*, **14** (2), 113–27.

O'Connor, John (1994), 'Toward Environmentally Sustainable Development: Measuring Progress', in Thaddeus C. Trzyna (ed.), *A Sustainable World: Defining and Measuring Sustainable Development*, London: Earthscan, pp. 87–114.

O'Riordan, Timothy (1993), *Interpreting the Precautionary Principle*, Working Paper PA 93-03, Norwich and London: Centre for Social and Economic Research on the Global Environment.

O'Riordan, Timothy and Andrew Jordan (1995), *The Precautionary Principle, Science, Politics and Ethics*, Working Paper PA 95-02, Norwich and London: Centre for Social and Economic Research on the Global Environment.

Oates, Wallace E., Karen Palmer and Paul R. Portney (1993), *Environmental Regulation and International Competitiveness: Thinking about the Porter Hypothesis*, Working Paper No. 93-11, Washington DC: Resources for the Future.

OECD (1994), *Environmental Indicators: OECD Core Set*, Paris: OECD.

OECD (1997), *Environmental Taxes and Green Tax Reform*, Paris: OECD.

OECD (1998), *Towards Sustainable Development — Environmental Indicators*, Paris: OECD.

Olson, Mancur (1993), 'Dictatorship, Democracy, and Development', *American Political Science Review*, **87** (3), 567–76.

OPEC (1997), *Annual Statistical Bulletin on Disk*, Vienna: Organisation of Petroleum Exporting Countries.

OPEC (various years), *Annual Statistical Bulletin*, Vienna: Organisation of Petroleum Exporting Countries.

Opschoor, Hans (1991), 'GNP and Sustainable Income Measures: Some Problems and a Way Out', in Onno Kuik and Harmen Verbruggen (eds), *In Search of Indicators of Sustainable Development*, Dordrecht: Kluwer, pp. 39–44.

Opschoor, Hans and Lucas Reijnders (1991), 'Towards Sustainable Development Indicators', in Onno Kuik and Harmen Verbruggen (eds), *In*

Search of Indicators of Sustainable Development, Dordrecht: Kluwer, pp. 7–27.

Özatalay, Savas, Stephen Grubaugh and Thomas Veach Long II (1979), 'Energy Substitution and National Energy Policy', *American Economic Review*, **69** (2), 369–71.

Page, Talbot (1983), 'Intergenerational Justice as Opportunity'; in Douglas MacLean and Peter Brown (eds), *Energy and the Future*, New Jersey: Rowman & Littlefield, pp. 38–57.

Page, Talbot (1997), 'On the Problem of Achieving Efficiency and Equity, Intergenerationally', *Land Economics*, **73** (4), 580–96.

Page, Talbot and Douglas MacLean (1983), 'Risk Conservatism and the Circumstances of Utility Theory', *American Journal of Agricultural Economics*, **65** (5), 1021–26.

Palmer, Karen L. and David R. Simpson (1993), 'Environmental Policy as Industrial Policy', *Resources*, **112**, 17–21.

Palmer, Karen, Wallace E. Oates and Paul R. Portney (1995), 'Tightening Environmental Standards: The Benefit–Cost or the No-cost Paradigm?', *Journal of Economic Perspectives*, **9** (4), 119–32.

Panayotou, Theodore (1993), *Empirical Tests and Policy Analysis of Environmental Degradation at Different Stages of Economic Development*, World Employment Programme Research Working Paper, Geneva: International Labour Office.

Panayotou, Theodore (1994), 'Conservation of Biodiversity and Economic Development: The Concept of Transferable Development Rights', *Environmental and Resource Economics*, **9** (1), 91–110.

Panayotou, Theodore (1997), 'Reducing Biodiversity Expenditure Needs: Reforming Perverse Incentives', in OECD: *Investing in Biological Diversity — The Cairns Conference*, Paris: OECD, pp. 217–33.

Parfit, Derek (1983), 'Energy Policy and the Further Future: The Identity Problem', in Douglas MacLean and Peter Brown (eds), *Energy and the Future*, New Jersey: Rowman & Littlefield, pp. 166–79.

Parry, Ian W.H. (1998), *Pollution Regulation and the Efficiency Gains from Technologial Innovation*, Discussion Paper 98-04, Washington DC: Resources for the Future.

Parry, Ian W.H., Roberton C. Williams III and Lawrence H. Goulder (1997), *When Can Carbon Abatement Policies Increase Welfare? The Fundamental Role of Distorted Factor Markets*, Working Paper 5967, Cambridge (Mass.): National Bureau of Economic Research; also published in *Journal of Environmental Economics and Management*, **37** (1), 1999, 52–84.

Patterson, Murray G. (1996), 'What is Energy Efficiency?', *Energy Policy*, **24** (5), 377–90.

Pearce, David W. (1991), 'The Role of Carbon Taxes in Adjusting to Global Warming', *Economic Journal*, **101** (407), 938–48.

Pearce, David W. (1993a), *Economic Values and the Natural World*, London: Earthscan.

Pearce, David W. (1993b), 'Sustainable Development and Developing Country Economics', in R. Kerry Turner (ed.), *Sustainable Environmental Economics and Management: Principles and Practice*, London: Pinter, Belhaven Press, pp. 70–105.

Pearce, David W. (1994a), *Joint Implementation: A General Overview*, Working Paper GEC 94-19, Norwich and London: Center for Social and Economic Research on the Global Environment.

Pearce, David W. (1994b), 'The Precautionary Principle and Economic Analysis', in Timothy O'Riordan and James Cameron (eds), *Interpreting the Precautionary Principle*, London: Earthscan, pp. 132–51.

Pearce, David W. (1995), *Blueprint 4: Capturing Global Environmental Value*, London: Earthscan.

Pearce, David W. (1997a), *An Economic Overview of Wildlife and Alternative Land Uses*, Working Paper GEC 97-05, London and Norwich: Centre for Social and Economic Research on the Global Environment.

Pearce, David W. (1997b), *Economic Valuation and Ecological Economics*, Working Paper PA 97-01, London and Norwich: Centre for Social and Economic Research on the Global Environment.

Pearce, David W. (1997c), 'Substitution and Sustainability: Some Reflections on Georgescu-Roegen', *Ecological Economics*, **22** (3), 295–97.

Pearce, David W. (1997d), *Can Non-market Values Save the Tropical Forests?*, Working Paper GEC 97-13, London and Norwich: Centre for Social and Economic Research on the Global Environment

Pearce, David W., Anil Markandya and Edward Barbier (1989), *Blueprint for a Green Economy*, London: Earthscan.

Pearce, David W. and R. Kerry Turner (1990), *Economics of Natural Resources and the Environment*, New York: Harvester Wheatsheaf.

Pearce, David W., Edward B. Barbier and Anil Markandya (1990), *Sustainable Development: Economics and Environment in the Third World*, Aldershot, UK and Brookfield, US: Edward Elgar.

Pearce, David W. and Giles Atkinson (1993), 'Capital Theory and the Measurement of Sustainable Development: An Indicator of 'Weak' Sustainability', *Ecological Economics*, **8** (2), 103–8.

Pearce, David W. and David Ulph (1995), *A Social Discount Rate for the United Kingdom*, Working Paper GEC 95-01, Norwich and London: Centre for Social and Economic Research on the Global Environment.

Pearce, David W., Kirk Hamilton and Giles Atkinson (1996), 'Measuring Sustainable Development: Progress on Indicators', *Environment and Development Economics*, **1** (1), 85–101.

Pearson, Mark (1995), 'The Political Economy of Implementing Environmental Taxes', *International Tax and Public Finance*, **2** (2), 357–73.

Pemberton, Malcolm and David Ulph (1998), 'Measuring Income and Measuring Sustainability', mimeo, Department of Economics, London: University College London.

Perman, Roger, Yue Ma and James McGilvray (1996), *Natural Resource and Environmental Economics*, Harlow: Addison Wesley Longman.

Perrings, Charles (1989), 'Environmental Bonds and Environmental Research in Innovative Activities', *Ecological Economics*, **1** (1), 95–110.

Perrings, Charles (1994), 'Biotic Diversity, Sustainable Development, and Natural Capital', in A. Jansson, M. Hammer, C. Folke and R. Costanza (eds), *Investing in Natural Capital: The Ecological Economics Approach to Sustainability*, Washington DC: Island Press, pp. 92–112.

Perrings, Charles, Carl Folke, and Karl-Göran Mäler (1992), 'The Ecology and Economics of Biodiversity Loss: The Research Agenda', *Ambio*, **21** (3), 201–11.

Perrings, Charles and Hans Opschoor (1994), 'The Loss of Biological Diversity: Some Policy Implications', *Environmental and Resource Economics*, **4** (1), 1–11.

Perrings, Charles and David W. Pearce (1994), 'Threshold Effects and Incentives for the Conservation of Biodiversity', *Environmental and Resource Economics*, **4** (1), 13–28.

Pethig, Rüdiger (ed.) (1994), *Valuing the Environment: Methodological and Measurement Issues*, Dordrecht: Kluwer Academic.

Petroleum Publishing (various years), *Oil and Gas Journal*, Tulsa: Petroleum Publishing.

Pezzey, John (1992a), 'Sustainability: An Interdisciplinary Guide', *Environmental Values*, **1** (4), 321–62.

Pezzey, John (1992b), *Sustainable Development Concepts: An Economic Analysis*, World Bank Environment Paper No. 2, Washington DC: World Bank.

Pezzey, John (1995), *Sustainable Development, Intergenerational Equity and Environmental Policy*, Department of Economics Discussion Paper No. 95-01, London: University College London.

Pezzey, John and Cees Withagen (1995), *Single-peakedness and Initial Sustainability in Capital-resource Economies*, Department of Economics Discussion Paper No. 95-09, London: University College London.

Pigou, A.C. (1932), *The Economics of Welfare*, London: Macmillan.

Pindyck, Robert S. (1978), 'The Optimal Exploration and Production of Non-renewable Resources', *Journal of Political Economy*, **86** (5), 841–61.

Pindyck, Robert S. (1979), 'Interfuel Substitution and the Industrial Demand for Energy: An International Comparison', *Review of Economics and Statistics*, **61** (2), 169–79.

Porter, Michael E. and Claas van der Linde (1995), 'Toward a New Conception of the Environment–Competitiveness Relationship', *Journal of Economic Perspectives*, **9** (4), 97–118.

Poterba, James M. (1991), 'Tax Policy to Combat Global Warming: On Designing a Carbon Tax', in Rüdiger Dornbusch and James M. Poterba (eds), *Global Warming: Economic Policy Responses*, Cambridge (Mass.): MIT Press, pp. 33–98.

Prell, Mark A. (1996), 'Backstop Technology and Growth: Doomsday or Steady State?', *Journal of Environmental Economics and Management*, **30** (2), 254–64.

Preston, Samuel H. (1996), 'The Effect of Population Growth on Environmental Quality', *Population Research and Policy Review*, **15** (2), 95–108.

Price, Colin (1995), 'Emissions, Concentrations and Disappearing CO_2', *Resource and Energy Economics*, **17** (1), 87–97.

Proops, John L.R. and Giles Atkinson (1994), *A Practical Sustainability Criterion When There is International Trade*, Working Paper GEC 94-05, Norwich and London: Centre for Social and Economic Research on the Global Environment.

Prywes, Menahem (1986), 'A Nested CES Approach to Capital-Energy Substitution', *Energy Economics*, **8** (1), 22–8.

Putnam, Robert D. (1993), *Making Democracy Work — Civic Traditions in Modern Italy*, Princeton: Princeton University Press.

Rabl, Ari (1996), 'Discounting of Long-term Costs: What would Future Generations Prefer us to Do?', *Ecological Economics*, **17** (3), 137–45.

Radermacher, Walter (1992), 'Konzept für eine Umweltökonomische Gesamtrechnung des Statistischen Bundesamtes', *Wirtschaft und Statistik*, (7), 411–17.

Radermacher, Walter and Carsten Stahmer (1995), 'Vom Umwelt-Satellitensystem zur Umweltökonomischen Gesamtrechnung: Umweltbezogene Gesamtrechnungen in Deutschland — Zweiter Teil', *Zeitschrift für angewandte Umweltforschung*, **8** (1), 99–109.

Ramsamy, M. Sen (1994), 'Sustainable Tourism', in Wolfgang Lutz (ed.), *Population, Development, Environment*, New York: Springer, pp. 175–90.

Ramsey, F.P. (1928), 'A Mathematical Theory of Saving', *Economic Journal*, **38** (152), 543–59.

Randall, Alan (1991), 'The Value of Biodiversity', *Ambio*, **20** (2), 64–8.

Ravaioli, Carla (1995), *Economists and the Environment: What the Top Economists Say about the Environment*, London: Zed Books.

Rawls, John (1972), *A Theory of Justice*, Oxford: Oxford University Press.

Ray, George F. (1983), 'Industrial Materials: Past, Present and Future', in S.F. Frowen (ed.), *Controlling Industrial Economies*, London: Macmillan, pp. 61–82.

Ray, George F. (1984), 'Mineral Reserves: Projected Lifetimes and Security of Supply', *Resources Policy*, **10** (2), 75–80.

Ready, Richard C. and Richard C. Bishop (1991), 'Endangered Species and the Safe Minimum Standard', *American Journal of Agricultural Economics*, **73** (2), 309–12.

Rees, William E. and Mathis Wackernagel (1994), 'Ecological Footprints and Appropriated Carrying Capacity: Measuring the Natural Capital Requirements of the Human Ecology', in A. Jansson, M. Hammer, C. Folke and R. Costanza (eds), *Investing in Natural Capital*, Washington DC: Island Press, pp. 362–90.

Reich, Utz-Peter (1994), 'Der falsche Glanz am Ökosozialprodukt', *Zeitschrift für Umweltpolitik und Umweltrecht*, **17** (1), 25–41.

Rennings, Klaus (1994), *Indikatoren für eine dauerhaft-umweltgerechte Entwicklung*, Stuttgart.

Repetto, Robert, W. Magrath, M. Wells, C. Beer and F. Rossini (1989), *Wasting Assets: Natural Resources in the National Income Accounts*, Washington DC: World Resources Institute.

Repetto, Robert and Wilfrido Cruz (1991), *Accounts Overdue: Natural Resource Depreciation in Costa Rica*, Washington DC: World Resources Institute.

Repetto, Robert, Dale Rothman, Paul Faeth and Duncan Austin (1997), 'Has Environmental Protection Really Reduced Productivity Growth?', *Challenge*, **40** (1), 46–57.

Ricardo, David (1817), *Principles of Political Economy and Taxation*, London: John Murray.

Richter, Wolfgang (1994), *Monetäre Makroindikatoren für eine nachhaltige Umweltnutzung: eine Diskussion theoretischer und praktischer Aspekte des Ökosozialproduktkonzeptes*, Marburg: Metropolis.

Robinson, Warren C. (1998), 'Global Population Trends — The Prospects for Stabilization', *Resources*, **131**, 6–9.

Rodenburg, Eric, Dan Tustall and Frederik van Bolhuis (1995), *Environmental Indicators for Global Cooperation*, Working Paper No. 11, Washington DC: Global Environment Facility.

Roodman, David Malin (1996), *Paying the Piper: Subsidies, Politics, and the Environment*, Worldwatch Paper No. 133, Washington DC: Worldwatch Institute.

Royal Society (1992), *Risk: Analysis, Perception, Management*, London: The Royal Society.

Rueschemeyer, Dietrich, Evelyne Huber Stephens and John D. Stephens (1991), *Capitalist Development and Democracy*, Cambridge: Cambridge University Press.

Ruttan, Vernon W. (1991), 'Constraints on Sustainable Growth in Agricultural Production: Into the 21st Century', *Canadian Journal of Agricultural Economics*, **39** (4), 567–80.

Sachs, Jeffrey D. and Andrew M. Warner (1995), *Natural Resource Abundance and Economic Growth*, Working Paper No. 5398, Cambridge (Mass.): National Bureau of Economic Research.

Sammarco, Giuseppe (1996), 'Environmental Accounting: Problems and Proposals', in Ignazio Musu and Domenico Siniscalco (eds), *National Accounts and the Environment*, Dordrecht: Kluwer, pp. 33–47.

Schelling, Thomas C. (1991), 'Economic Responses to Global Warming: Prospects for Cooperative Approaches', in Rüdiger Dornbusch and James M. Poterba (eds), *Global Warming: Economic Policy Responses*, Cambridge (Mass.): MIT Press, pp. 197–221.

Schelling, Thomas C. (1995), 'Intergenerational Discounting', *Energy Policy*, **23** (4/5), 395–401.

Schneider, Kerstin (1997), 'Involuntary Unemployment and Environmental Policy: the Double Dividend Hypothesis', *Scandinavian Journal of Economics*, **99** (1), 45–59.

Schuh, Hans (1995), 'Viele Arten, wenig Wissen', *Die Zeit* 24 November, 25.

Scott, Anthony and Peter Pearse (1992), 'Natural Resources in a High-tech Economy — Scarcity Versus Resourcefulness', *Resources Policy*, **18** (3), 154–66.

Sefton, J.A. and M.R. Weale (1996), 'The Net National Product and Exhaustible Resources: The Effects of Foreign Trade', *Journal of Public Economics*, **61** (1), 21–47.

Selden, Thomas M. and Daqing Song (1994), 'Environmental Quality and Development: Is There a Kuznets Curve for Air Pollution Emissions?', *Journal of Environmental Economics and Management*, **27** (2), 147–62.

Selden, Thomas M., Anne S. Forrest and James E. Lockhart (1996), *Analyzing the Reductions in US Air Pollution Emissions: 1970 to 1990*, Environmental Law Institute Discussion Paper, September, Washington DC: Environmental Law Institute.

Sen, Amartya K. (1967): 'Isolation, Assurance and the Social Rate of Discount', *Quarterly Journal of Economics*, **81** (322), 112–24.

Sen, Amartya K. (1982), 'The Choice of Discount Rates for Social Benefit-Cost Analysis', in R.C. Lind (ed.), *Discounting for Time and Risk in Energy Policy*, Washington DC: Resources for the Future, pp. 325–52.

Sen, Amartya K. (1987), *On Ethics and Economics*, Oxford: Blackwell.

Serageldin, Ismail (1996), *Sustainability and the Wealth of Nations: First Steps in An Ongoing Journey*, Washington DC: World Bank.

Serôa da Motta, Ronaldo and Peter H. May (1996), 'Measuring Sustainable Income: The Case of Mineral and Forest Depletion in Brazil', in Peter H. May and Ronaldo Serôa da Motta (eds), *Pricing the Planet — Economic Analysis for Sustainable Development*, New York: Columbia University Press, pp. 197–208.

Serôa da Motta, Ronaldo and Carlos Young (1995), 'Measuring Sustainable Income from Mineral Extraction in Brazil', *Resources Policy*, **21** (2), 113–25.

Shafik, Nemat (1994), 'Economic Development and Environmental Quality: An Econometric Analysis', *Oxford Economic Papers*, **46** (5), 757–73.

Shafik, Nemat and Sushenjit Bandyopadhyay (1992), *Economic Growth and Environmental Quality — Time-series and Cross-country Evidence*, Working Paper No. 904, Washington DC: World Bank.

Shavell, Steven (1993), 'Contingent Valuation of the Nonuse Value of Natural Resources: Implications for Public Policy and the Liability System', in Jerry A. Hausman (ed.), *Contingent Valuation: A Critical Assessment*, Amsterdam: Elsevier, pp. 371–88.

Sheng, Fulai (1995), *Real Value for Nature: An Overview of Global Efforts to Achieve True Measures of Economic Progress*, Gland: World Wide Fund for Nature.

Shogren, Jason F., Joseph A. Herriges and Ramu Govindasamy (1993), 'Limits to Environmental Bonds', *Ecological Economics*, **8** (2), 109–33.

Simon, H.A. (1982), *Models of Bounded Rationality*, 2 vols, Cambridge (Mass.): MIT Press.

Simon, Julian L. (1990), *Population Matters: People, Resources, Environment, and Immigration*, New Brunswick: Transactions Press.

Simon, Julian L. (1996), *The Ultimate Resource*, Second Edition, Princeton: Princeton University Press.

Simon, Sandrine (1998), 'Making Sustainability Operational: Critical Natural Capital and the Implications of a Strong Sustainability Criterion (CRTIINC)', *European Society for Ecological Economics Newsletter*, **5**, May, p. 7.

Simon, Sandrine and Paul Ekins (1998): 'Achieving Environmental Sustainability — Theoretical Framework and Policy Implications', paper prepared for the Fifth Biennial Meeting of the International Society or Ecological Economics, Santiago, Chile, 15–19 November, Keele University: Department of Environmental Social Sciences.

Slade, Margaret E. (1982), 'Trends in Natural-resource Commodity Prices: An Analysis of the Time Domain', *Journal of Environmental Economics and Management*, **9** (2), 122–37.

Slade, Margaret E. (1987), 'Natural Resources, Population Growth, and Economic Well-being', in D. Gale Johnson and Ronald D. Lee (eds), *Population Growth and Economic Development: Issues and Evidence*, Wisconsin: University of Wisconsin Press, pp. 331–69.

Slade, Margaret E. (1988), 'Grade Selection Under Uncertainty: Least Cost Last and Other Anomalies', *Journal of Environmental Economics and Management*, **15** (2), 189–205.

Slade, Margaret E. (1992), *Do Markets Underprice Natural-resource Commodities?*, Working Paper No. 962, Washington DC: World Bank.

Smil, Vaclav (1994), 'How Many People Can the Earth Feed?', *Population and Development Review*, **20** (2), 255–92.

Smith, V. Kerry and John V. Krutilla (1979), 'Endangered Species, Irreversibilities, and Uncertainty: A Comment', *American Journal of Agricultural Economics*, **58** (2), 371–5.

Smith, V. Kerry and Carol Mansfied (1998), 'Buying Time: Real and Hypothetical Offers', *Journal of Environmental Economics and Management* **36** (3), 209–24.

Smulders, Sjak (1995), 'Environmental Policy and Sustainable Economic Growth', *De Economist*, **143** (2), 163–95.

Söllner, Fritz (1997), 'A Reexamination of the Role of Thermodynamics for Environmental Economics', *Ecological Economics*, **22** (3), 175–201.

Solow, John L. (1987), 'The Capital–Energy Complementarity Debate Revisited', *American Economic Review*, **77** (4), 605–14.

Solow, Robert M. (1974a), 'Intergenerational Equity and Exhaustible Resources', *Review of Economic Studies*, Symposium, 29–46.

Solow, Robert M. (1974b), 'Is the End of the World at Hand?', in A. Weintraub, E. Schwartz and J. Richard Aronson (eds), *The Economic Growth Controversy*, London: Macmillan, pp. 39–61.

Solow, Robert M. (1974c), 'The Economics of Resources or the Resources of Economics', *American Economic Review*, **64** (2), 1–14.

Solow, Robert M. (1986), 'On the Intergenerational Allocation of Natural Resources', *Scandinavian Journal of Economics*, **88** (1), 141–9.

Solow, Robert M. (1993a), 'An Almost Practical Step Toward Sustainability', *Resources Policy*, **19** (3), 162–72.

Solow, Robert M. (1993b), 'Sustainability: An Economist's Perspective', in R. Dorfman and N. Dorfman (eds), *Selected Readings in Environmental Economics*, New York: Norton, pp. 179–87.

Solow, Robert M. (1997), 'Georgescu-Roegen versus Solow/Stiglitz', *Ecological Economics*, **22** (3), 267–8.

Spash, Clive L. (1993), 'Economics, Ethics, and Long-term Environmental Damages', *Environmental Ethics*, **10** (1), 117–32.

Spash, Clive L. (1994), 'Double CO_2 and Beyond: Benefits, Costs and Compensation', *Ecological Economics*, **10** (1), 27–36.

Spash, Clive and Nick Hanley (1995), 'Preferences, Information and Biodiersity Preservation', *Ecological Economics*, **12** (3), 191–208.

Stahmer, Carsten (1995), 'Utz-Peter Reichs Kritik am Ökosozialprodukt: Eine Erwiderung', *Zeitschrift für Umweltpolitik und Umweltrecht*, **18** (1), 101–10.

Statistics Canada (1995), *Environmental Perspectives 2*, Ontario: National Accounts and Environment Division Statistics Canada.

Stavins, Robert N. (1995), 'Transaction Costs and Tradeable Permits', *Journal of Environmental Economics and Management*, **29** (3), 133–48.

Stavins, Robert N. (1996), 'Correlated Uncertainty and Policy Instrument Choice', *Journal of Environmental Economics and Management*, **30** (2), 218–32.

Stavins, Robert N. (1998), *Market-based Environmental Policies*, Discussion Paper 98-26, Washington DC: Resources for the Future.

Stern, David I., Michael S. Common and Edward B. Barbier (1996), 'Economic Growth and Environmental Degradation: The Environmental Kuznets Curve and Sustainable Development', *World Development*, **24** (7), 1151–60.

Steurer, A., G. Gie, C. Leipert, C. Pasurka and D. Schäfer (1998), 'Environmental Protection Expenditure and its Representation in National Accounts', in K. Uno and P. Bartelmus (eds), *Environmental Accounting in Theory and Practice*, Dordrecht: Kluwer, pp. 309–19.

Stevens, Thomas H., Jaime Echeverria, Ronald J. Glass, Tim Hager and Thomas A. More (1991), 'Measuring the Existence Value of Wildlife: What Do CVM Estimates Really Show?', *Land Economics*, **67** (4), 390–400.

Stiglitz, Joseph (1974), 'Growth with Exhaustible Natural Resources: Efficient and Optimal Growth Paths', *Review of Economic Studies*, Symposium, 123–37.

Stockhammer, Engelbert, Harald Hochreiter, Bernhard Obermayr and Klaus Steiner (1997), 'The Index of Sustainable Economic Welfare (ISEW) as an Alternative to GDP in Measuring Economic Welfare. The Results of the Austrian (Revised) ISEW Calculation 1955–1992', *Ecological Economics*, **21** (1), 19–34.

Summers, R. and A. Heston (1991), 'The Penn-World Table (Mark 5): An Expanded Set of International Comparisons, 1950–1988', *Quarterly Journal of Economics*, **106** (2), 327–68.

Suri, Vivek and Duane Chapman (1998), 'Economic Growth, Trade and Energy: Implications for the Environmental Kuznets Curve', *Ecological Economics* **25** (3), 195–208.

Swanson, Timothy M. (1994), 'The Economics of Extinction Revisited and Revised: A Generalised Framework for the Analysis of the Problems of Endangered Species and Biodiversity Loss', *Oxford Economic Papers*, **46** (5), 800–821.

Swanson, Timothy M. (1996), 'The Reliance of Northern Economies on Southern Biodiversity: Biodiversity as Information', *Ecological Economics*, **17** (1), 1–8.

Swanson, Timothy M. (1997), *Global Action for Biodiversity*, London: Earthscan.

Swierzbinski, Joseph and Robert Mendelsohn (1989), 'Information and Exhaustible Resources: A Bayesian Analysis', *Journal of Environmental Economics and Management*, **16** (3), 193–208.

Tahvonen, Olli and Jari Kuuluvainen (1993), 'Economic Growth, Pollution, and Renewable Resources', *Journal of Environmental Economics and Management*, **24** (2), 101–18.

Thage, Bent (1989), 'The National Accounts and the Environment', in Yusuf J. Ahmad, Salah El Serafy and Ernst Lutz (eds), *Environmental Accounting for Sustainable Development: A UNDP–World Bank Symposium*, Washington DC: World Bank, pp. 314–36.

Thompson, M., M. Warburton and T. Hatley (1986), *Uncertainty on a Himalayan Scale*, London: Milton Ash Editions.

Tilton, John E. (1977), *The Future of Nonfuel Minerals*, Washington DC: The Brookings Institution.

Tilton, John E. (1996), 'Exhaustible Resources and Sustainable Development', *Resources Policy*, **22** (1/2), 91–7.

Tindale, Stephen and Gerald Holtham (1996), *Green Tax Reform — Pollution Payments and Labour Tax Cuts*, London: Institute for Public Policy Research.

Tobey, James A. (1990), 'The Effects of Domestic Environmental Policies on Patterns of World Trade: An Empirical Test', *Kyklos*, **43** (2), 191–209.

Tol, Richard S.J. (1994), 'Communication — The Damage Costs of Climate Change: A Note on Tangibles and Intangibles, Applied to DICE', *Energy Policy*, **22** (5), 436–8.

Toman, Michael A. (1985), 'Optimal Control with an Unbounded Horizon', *Journal of Economic Dynamics and Control*, **9** (3), 291–316.

Toman, Michael A., John Pezzey and Jeffrey Krautkraemer (1995), 'Neoclassical Economic Growth Theory and 'Sustainability'', in Daniel W. Bromley (ed.), *Handbook of Environmental Economics*, Cambridge: Cambridge University Press, pp. 139–65.

Torras, Mariano and James K. Boyce (1997), 'Income, Inequality, and Pollution: A Reassessment of the Environmental Kuznets Curve', mimeo, Amherst: University of Massachusetts at Amherst, also printed in *Ecological Economics*, **25** (2), 147–60.

Torsello, Loredana and Allessandro Vercelli (1998), 'Environmental Bonds: A Critical Assessment', in Graciela Chichilnisky, Geoffrey Heal and Alessandro Vercelli (eds), *Sustainability: Dynamics and Uncertainty*, Dordrecht: Kluwer, pp. 243–55.

Toth, Ferenc L. (1995), 'Discounting in Integrated Assessments of Climate Change', *Energy Policy*, **23** (4/5), 403–9.

Trainer, F.E. (1995), 'Can Renewable Energy Sources Sustain Affluent Society?', *Energy Policy*, **23** (12), 1009–26.

Turner, R. Kerry (1995), *Sustainable Development and Climate Change*, Working Paper PA 95-01, Norwich and London: Centre for Social and Economic Research on the Global Environment.

Turner, R. Kerry and David W. Pearce (1992), *Sustainable Development: Ethics and Economics*, Working Paper PA 92-09, Norwich and London: Centre for Social and Economic Research on the Global Environment.

Turnovsky, Michelle, Michael Folie and Alistair Ulph (1982), 'Factor Substitutability in Australian Manufacturing with Emphasis on Energy Inputs', *Economic Record*, **58** (160), 61–72.

Ulph, Alistair and David Ulph (1997), 'Global Warming, Irreversibility and Learning', *Economic Journal*, **107** (442), 636–50.

UNCED (1992), Agenda 21, on-line on the Internet under the address gopher://gopher.un.org/11/conf/unced.

United Nations (1977), *Yearbook of Industrial Statistics 1975*, New York: United Nations.

United Nations (1986), *Yearbook of Industrial Statistics 1984*, New York: United Nations.

United Nations (1993a), *Integrated Environmental and Economic Accounting — Interim Version. Studies in Methods, Handbook of National Accounting*, Series F, No. 61, New York: United Nations.

United Nations (1993b), *System of National Accounts 1993*, New York: United Nations.

United Nations (1996), *Yearbook of Industrial Statistics 1994*, New York: United Nations.

United Nations (1997), *World Population Prospects*, New York: United Nations Department for Economic and Social Information and Policy Analysis, Population Division.

United Nations Yearbook (various years), *Energy Statistics Yearbook*, New York: United Nations.

Uri, N.D. and R. Boyd (1995), 'Scarcity and Growth Revisited', *Environment and Planning A*, **27** (11), 1815–32.

US Bureau of Mines (various years), *Mineral Commodity Summaries*, Washington DC: US Department of the Interior.

US Congress (1978), *Endangered Species Act Amendments of 1978*, Report No. 95-1625 on the Endangerd Species Act of 1973 (Public Law 93-205) as amended by the 95th Congres, Washington DC: US Congress.

US Department of Commerce Bureau of Economic Analysis (1994a), 'Integrated Economic and Environmental Satellite Accounts', *Survey of Current Business*, **74** (4), 33–49.

US Department of Commerce Bureau of Economic Analysis (1994b), 'Accounting for Mineral Resources: Issues and BEA's Initial Estimates', *Survey of Current Business*, **74** (4), 50–72.

Usher, Dan (1994), 'Income and the Hamiltonian', *Review of Income and Wealth*, **40** (2), 123–41.

Vadnjal, Dan and Martin O'Connor (1994), 'What is the Value of Rangitoto Island?', *Environmental Values*, **3** (4), 369–80.

Van Dieren, Wouter (ed.) (1995), *Mit der Natur rechnen: Der neue Club-of-Rome-Bericht: vom Bruttosozialprodukt zum Ökosozialprodukt*, Basel: Birkhäuser, also printed in English: Wouter van Dieren (ed.), *Taking Nature into Account: A Report to the Club of Rome: Toward a Sustainable National Income*, New York: Copernicus.

Van Tongeren, Jan, Stefan Schweinfest, Ernst Lutz, Maria Gomez Luna and Guillen Martin (1993), 'Integrated Economic and Environmental Accounting: A Case Study for Mexico', in E. Lutz (ed.), *Toward Improved Accounting for the Environment — An UNSTAT–World Bank symposium*, Washington DC: World Bank, pp. 85–107.

Varian, Hal R. (1992), *Microeconomic Analysis*, New York: Norton.

Vatn, A. and D.W. Bromley (1994), 'Choices without Prices without Apologies', *Journal of Environmental Economics and Management*, **26** (2), 129–48.

Vaze, Prashant and Stephen Balchin (1996), 'The Pilot United Kingdom Environmental Accounts', *Economic Trends*, **514**, 41–71.

Vercelli, Alessandro (1998), 'Sustainable Development and the Freedom of Future Generations', in Graciela Chichilnisky, Geoffrey Heal and Alessandro Vercelli (eds), *Sustainability: Dynamics and Uncertainty*, Dordrecht: Kluwer, pp. 171–87.

Victor, Peter A. (1991), 'Indicators of Sustainable Development: Some Lessons from Capital Theory', *Ecological Economics*, **4** (3), 191–213.

Victor, Peter A., J.E. Hanna and A. Kubursi (1995), 'How Strong is Weak Sustainability', *Economie Appliquée*, **48** (2), 75–94.

Vincent, Jeffrey R., Theodore Panayotou and John M. Hartwick (1997), 'Resource Depletion and Sustainability in Small Open Economies', *Journal of Environmental Economics and Management*, **33** (3), 274–86.

Vitousek, Peter M., Paul R. Ehrlich, Anne H. Ehrlich and Pamela A. Mason (1986), 'Human Appropriation of the Products of Photosynthesis', *BioScience*, **36** (6), 368–73.

Volokh, Alexander (1996), *Punitive Damages and Environmental Law: Rethinking the Issues*, Policy Study No. 213, Reason Foundation.

Waggoner, Paul E. (1994), *How Much Land Can Ten Billion People Spare for Nature?*, Task Force Report No. 121, Ames: Council for Agricultural Science and Technology .

Weber, Max (1922), *Gesammelte Aufsätze zur Wissenschaftslehre*, edited by Marianne Weber, Tübingen: J.C.B. Mohr.

Weisbrod, Burton A. (1964), 'Collective Consumption Services of Individual Consumption Goods', *Quarterly Journal of Economics*, **77** (3), 71–7.

Weitzman, Martin L. and Karl-Gustaf Löfgren (1997), 'On the Welfare Significance of Green Accounting as Taught by Parable', *Journal of Environmental Economics and Management* **32** (2), 139–53.

Welsch, Heinz (1995), 'Greenhouse Gas Abatement under Ambiguity', *Energy Economics*, **17** (2), 91–100.

Wheeler, D. and P. Martin (1992), 'Prices, Policies and the International Diffusion of Clean Technology: The Case of Wood Pulp Production', in Patrick Low (ed.), *International Trade and the Environment*, Discussion Paper No. 159, Washington DC: World Bank, pp. 197–224.

Willis, Ken and Guy Garrod (1995), 'Transferability of Benefit Estimates', in Ken Willis and J. Corkindale (eds), *Environmental Valuation — New Perspectives*, Oxon: CAB International, pp. 191–212.

Wilson, E.O. (1988), *Biodiversity*, Washington DC: National Academy Press.

Withagen, Cees (1996), 'Sustainability and Investment Rules', *Economics Letters*, **53** (1), 1–6.

Woodward, Richard T. and Richard C. Bishop (1995), 'Efficiency, Sustainability and Global Warming', *Ecological Economics*, **14** (2), 101–11.

Woodward, Richard T. and Richard C. Bishop (1997), 'How to Decide When Experts Disagree: Uncertainty-based Choice-rules in Environmental Policy', *Land Economics*, **73** (4), 492–507.

World Bank (1991), *World Tables 1991*, Washington DC: World Bank.

World Bank (1992), *World Development Report 1992 — Development and the Environment*, New York: Oxford University Press.

World Bank (1995a), *Monitoring Environmental Progress: A Report on Work in Progress*, Washington DC: World Bank.

World Bank (1995b), *World Tables 1995*, Washington DC: World Bank.

World Bank (1997a), *Expanding the Measure of Wealth: Indicators of Environmentally Sustainable Development*, Washington DC: World Bank, on-line available at http://www-esd.worldbank.org/eei/wealth/genuinesav.html

World Bank (1997b), *Excel 5.0-file with Data Underlying World Bank (1997a)*, Washington DC: World Bank, online available at http://www-esd.worldbank.org/eei/wealth/genuinesav.html

World Bureau of Metal Statistics (1975, 1979, 1984), *World Metal Statistics Monthly Bulletin*, Ware: World Bureau of Metal Statistics.

World Bureau of Metal Statistics (1991, 1997), *World Metal Statistics Year Book*, Ware: World Bureau of Metal Statistics.

World Commission on Environment and Development (1987), *Our Common Future*, Oxford: Oxford University Press.

World Scientists (1997), *World Scientists' Call for Action at the Kyoto Climate Summit*, available on-line on the Internet under the address http://dieoff.org/page123.htm.

WRI (various years), *World Resources* — a joint publication from the World Resources Institute, United Nations' Environment Programme, United Nations' Development Programme and World Bank, Washington DC.

Young, Jeffrey T. (1991), 'Is the Entropy Law Relevant to the Economics of Natural Resource Scarcity?', *Journal of Environmental Economics and Management*, **21** (2), 169–79.

Zeckhauser, Richard J. and W. Kip Viscusi (1995), 'Risk Within Reason', in Julian L. Simon (ed.), *The State of Humanity*, Cambridge (Mass.): Blackwell, pp. 628–36.

Zimmermann, Horst (1995), 'Das Ökosozialprodukt — kein neues Gesamtmaß', *Zeitschrift für Umweltpolitik und Umweltrecht*, **18** (2), 261–68.

Zolotas, Xenophon (1981), *Economic Growth and Declining Social Welfare*, New York: New York University Press.

Index